Stalin, Mao, Communism, and their 21st-Century Aftermath in Russia and China

Stalin, Mao, Communism, and their 21st-Century Aftermath in Russia and China

By

Miguel A. Faria, Jr.

Cambridge Scholars Publishing

Stalin, Mao, Communism, and their 21st-Century Aftermath in Russia and China

By Miguel A. Faria, Jr.

This book first published 2024

Cambridge Scholars Publishing

Lady Stephenson Library, Newcastle upon Tyne, NE6 2PA, UK

British Library Cataloguing in Publication Data
A catalogue record for this book is available from the British Library

Copyright © 2024 by Miguel A. Faria, Jr.

All rights for this book reserved. No part of this book may be reproduced, stored in a retrieval system, or transmitted, in any form or by any means, electronic, mechanical, photocopying, recording or otherwise, without the prior permission of the copyright owner.

ISBN (10): 1-5275-6437-1
ISBN (13): 978-1-5275-6437-4

Contents

List of Color Plates viii

Acknowledgments ix

Introduction x

Part I: Joseph Stalin and the Years of Terror

Chapter 1 2
Young Stalin—The Georgia Bandit

Chapter 2 11
A Literary Overview of Stalin's Meat Grinder

Chapter 3 22
Stalin's Meat Grinder—A Panoramic View of the Human Devastation

Chapter 4 40
The Executioners—Nikolai Yezhov and Lavrenti Beria

Chapter 5 58
Stalin and Notable Events in the Spanish Civil War (1936–1939)

Chapter 6 71
Stalin's Secret Agents in the FDR Administration

Part II: Stalin and World War II (1939–1945)

Chapter 7 88
Operation Barbarossa, Deception, Espionage, and Total War

Chapter 8 108
The Horrific War Unfolds in the East

Part III: Stalin in the Post-War World (1945–1953)

Chapter 9 120
The Plot Against the Jewish Doctors (1948–1953)

Chapter 10 133
A Tribute to Aleksandr Solzhenitsyn

Part IV: Mao Tse-tung, the Mythic Long March (1934–1935), and China After Mao

Chapter 11 150
Mao Tse-tung—The Chairman Who Led China into a Communist Inferno

Chapter 12 167
The Mythic Long March of the Chinese Red Army

Chapter 13 181
China-United States Relations Since the 1990s

Chapter 14 195
Chinese Espionage Against the U.S. and the West

Part V: Espionage—The KGB and CIA Battles During the Cold War

Chapter 15 218
Four Seminal Books Chronicling KGB Activities in the Cold War

Chapter 16 229
Espionage—The Wilderness of Mirrors During the Cold War

Chapter 17 242
Cataloging the Spies of the Cold War

Chapter 18 255
The Story of FAREWELL—The Patriot Who Gave His Life for Russia's Freedom

Chapter 19 266
Two Major Intelligence Operations: One Helped Prevent and the Other Almost Caused World War III

Part VI: The New Russia After the Fall of Communism

Chapter 20 276
An Introduction to the New Russia

Chapter 21 291
Russian Geopolitics

Epilogue... 309
The 2022 Russian Invasion of Ukraine and Its Aftermath

Appendix A 321
Cuba's Adventurism as Soviet Proxy in Africa (1961–1991)

Appendix B.. 325
An Abbreviated History of the CIA to the 2011 Death of Osama bin Laden

Appendix C.. 334
Is America a Staunch Friend and Ally or a Nation that Forgets Friends When They Are No Longer Useful?

Appendix D 338
A CIA Agent in the Iranian Revolutionary Guards

Appendix E.. 342
Turkey—Russia's Neighbor to the South (2016)

Appendix F 345
List of Figure Credits

Notes.. 358

Selected Bibliography 414

Index.. 419

LIST OF COLOR PLATES

1 The "Big Three" (seated, left to right): British Prime Minister Clement Attlee, U.S. President Harry S. Truman, and Soviet Premier Joseph Stalin pose with their principal advisors at Potsdam, Germany, 1945. *Courtesy: National Archives and Records Administration*
2 Lavrenti Beria, branded "enemy of the people," on the July 20, 1953, cover of Time magazine. *Courtesy: Time, Inc.*
3 Italian translation of The Gulag Archipelago by Aleksandr Solzhenitsyn published in Milan in 1974. *Courtesy: Archivi Mondadori*
4 U.S. President Ronald Reagan says goodbye to Soviet General Secretary Mikhail Gorbachev after the last meeting at Hofdi House, Reykjavik, Iceland, October 12, 1986. *Courtesy: White House Photographic Collection*
5 View of the Berlin Wall in 1986 from the West showing graffiti art on the Wall. The "death strip" lies on the East side of the Wall. *Courtesy: Thierry Noir*
6 President Ronald Reagan at Brandenburg Gate West Berlin on June 12, 1987, urging General Secretary Gorbachev to "tear down this wall." *Courtesy: White House Photographic Collection*
7 President Ronald Reagan's July 21, 1987, meeting with MI6 asset, Oleg Gordievsky. *Courtesy: Mary Anne Fackelman, Ronald Reagan Presidential Library*
8 President Ronald Reagan's November 16, 1988, meeting with British Prime Minister Margaret Thatcher in the White House Oval Office. *Courtesy: National Archives and Records Administration*
9 A contingent from the Communist Party of Great Britain (Marxist-Leninist) carrying a banner of Joseph Stalin at a May Day march through London, 2008. *Courtesy: Wikimedia Commons*
10 March in Hong Kong on July 15, 2017, in memory of Liu Xiaobo, Nobel Peace Prize laureate, who called for the end of communist one-party rule in China. *Courtesy: Voice of America*

ACKNOWLEDGMENTS

First, I wish to thank my wife Helen Faria for assiduously helping me research, edit, and type the material contained in this book. Her advice and assistance were valuable and greatly appreciated. Nevertheless, any errors remain my own.

Second, I extend my appreciation to Ms. Helen Edwards, Commissioning Editor at Cambridge Scholars Publishing (CSP) for inviting me to write the book as she did in the past with my two previous books published by CSP, *Controversies in Medicine and Neuroscience: Through the Prism of History, Neurobiology, and Bioethics* (2023) and *Cuba's Eternal Revolution through the Prism of Insurgency, Socialism, and Espionage* (2023).

Third, I want to thank Amanda Millar, Typesetting Manager at CSP for her professionalism, promptness in communication, and amazing efficiency in typesetting manuscripts. She helped me in my previous two books published by CSP and it has been a pleasure to work with her again.

Fourth, I want to acknowledge my friend, Adam R. Bogart, PhD., for the motivating conversations we have had over the years about Stalin, the horrific Soviet Gulag, and the interesting Bolshevik women in Lenin and Stalin's circle. Those conversations proved inspiring.

Finally, I want to thank Mhairi Nicol, Book Cover Designer at CSP for her assistance and ability to comply with the artwork that I drafted and submitted for this and my previous two books. She made it happen, just as I had hoped and envisioned.

INTRODUCTION

In modern political theory, there is a distinction made between socialism and communism, and thereby the relative positions they occupy on schematic diagrams of the political spectrum.

In communism, the state, incarnated in one political party, owns all means of production, distribution, and even consumption, ostensibly under an egalitarian and "on need" basis. In practice, communist party officials, as political elites, are "more equal than others," and reserve to themselves their "fair share" at the expense of the masses. Moreover, communism comes about by the "class struggle" and imposition by force and violent revolution, for the establishment of the "dictatorship of the proletariat."

To paraphrase Mao Tse-tung, communism is the attainment of political power by the barrel of a gun and complete control of all services and the methods of production, distribution, and consumption of goods by the omnipotent state. There are minimal or no private property rights. The repressive machinery of the secret police and the military maintain the social, economic, and political power structure in the nation.

My definition of modern socialism is the assumption and maintenance of power via incremental evolution—that is, seduction of the population by political elites who promise something for nothing but in reality, take from some to give to others; the use of envy to incite class strife and the dark side of human nature in order to justify wealth redistribution schemes carried out by legalized plunder. The redistribution of wealth and management of power is orchestrated by the political elites who are above the rest of the common people, and ostensibly to protect the common people for their own good. This unnatural "equality" is maintained by the state controlling through regulation or taxation the means of production, such as manufacturing, the distribution of products via transportation or communication, and the consumption of goods or services (for example, food, health care, housing, education indoctrination, et cetera).

Therefore, communism and socialism are derived from Marxist dogma—a fact that is frequently forgotten. Both communism and socialism are collectivist forms of regimes of the left in the political spectrum, as predicated by the tenets of excessive, oppressive, or brutally authoritarian governments. These "isms" are considered "working class movements" by the ones espousing them. The seemingly benign connotation of socialism today as democratic and altruistic would be a source of laughter to the innovators, namely, Karl Marx (1818–1883) and Friedrich Engels (1820–1895), and to the actual applicators like Vladimir I. Lenin (1870–1924), Joseph Stalin (1879–1953), Mao Tse-tung (1893–1976) or Fidel Castro (1926–2016). If one visited the Communist Party USA (CPUSA) website, or read the *Collected Works of Lenin*, or listened to the speeches of Fidel Castro, one would quickly realize that all communist demigods use the terms socialism and communism interchangeably.

In the Preface to *The Communist Manifesto*, Friedrich Engels explained why he and Marx chose to call their manifesto "communist" rather than "socialist." Marx and Engels wanted to differentiate their political theory from other brands of socialism and not be confused with the British or European movements then in vogue, which referred to themselves as "socialists." Thus, their incendiary document was named *The Communist Manifesto* instead of "The Socialist Manifesto."[1]

Vladimir Lenin wrote that in the relentless march of history (positivism) and the class struggle (dialectical materialism or dialectics), the ultimate goal of socialism was communism and the establishment of the dictatorship of the proletariat. Lenin called American and European liberals of his day "useful idiots" and "fellow travelers" because they wanted to believe in the "workers' paradise" instead of the harsh reality of Soviet socialism. It was Lenin, and not Joseph Stalin, who heralded the era of the concentration camps in Soviet Russia and ordered the formation of the Cheka, the infamous secret police under the direction of Felix Dzerzhinsky. Lenin also began the extermination of the Kadets (Constitutional Democrats) to his right and Socialist Revolutionary (LSR) opponents to his left in the political struggle. Stalin intensified the process and not only exterminated the purported "enemies of the people" but also wiped out almost the entire ranks of Lenin's old Bolshevik comrades, including Lev Kamenev, Gregory Zinoviev, Nikolai Bukharin, Karl Radek, Vladimir Antonov-Ovseenko (leader of the Bolshevik Military Organization that stormed the Winter Palace during the 1917 October Revolution), Gleb I. Bokii, Y.A. Ganetsky (Polish communist who was Lenin's liaison with the Germans during World War I and the sealed train affair), and Leon Trotsky, et cetera. No one killed more communists than the communist-in-chief himself, Joseph Stalin.[2]

So, class warfare, the inception of the labor camps, the Gulag, the Red Terror, the extermination of class enemies and political opponents all began with Vladimir Lenin soon after the October Revolution of 1917 and, as we shall learn in the following chapters, intensified to a fevered pitch under Joseph Stalin. That is why Aleksandr Solzhenitsyn's *The Gulag Archipelago* contains *1918–1956* in the title.[3] Those years include the Lenin, Stalin, and early years of the collective Soviet leadership, ostensibly led by Georgy Malenkov.

Soviet repression moderated under Nikita Khrushchev. But even Khrushchev crushed the Hungarian Revolution in 1956, the same year he denounced Stalin at the 20th Congress of the Communist Party of the Soviet Union. He also ordered the construction of the Berlin Wall in 1961 and brought the world to the brink of nuclear war in the Cuban Missile Crisis in 1962. Leonid Brezhnev, who engaged United States President Richard Nixon and the West in détente, ordered the crushing of the Prague Spring in 1968 and the fatal invasion of Afghanistan in 1979. Thus, Soviet repression did not end, in fact, until the collapse of the Berlin Wall and the disintegration of the USSR and its satellites (1989–1991). Nevertheless, authoritarianism seems to be an inherent part of the Russian character and persists to this day under Russian "democracy" and Vladimir Putin.[4]

And as much as the proponents of social democracy (SD) would like to forget, social democracy is also derived from Marxist ideology and grounded in the social revolutionary faith.[5] At the turn of the century, Rosa Luxemburg (1871–1919) and Karl Liebknecht (1871–1919) were the patron saints of Marxism and social democracy in Germany. Later, they participated in the Spartacus League and founded the Communist Party of Germany. Their counterpart in Russia was Georgi Plekhanov (1856–1918), the father of the Social Democratic Party of Russia to which both Vladimir Lenin and Joseph Stalin initially belonged before the SD split into the more moderate, democratic Mensheviks and the conspiratorial, communist Bolsheviks.

After Alexander Kerensky's Provisional Government was overthrown in the October Revolution, it was Vladimir Lenin and the Bolsheviks that came to power. Many of the Mensheviks went into exile, and those who stayed in Russia were hunted down by Lenin's Cheka or exterminated by Stalin's security apparatus or in the destructive gulag labor camps. Furthermore, the derivation of social democracy from Marxism is not denied or contended by the European social democratic parties today.

Despite the fall of the Berlin Wall, socialism in the Western democracies, including in the United States, has continued to grow either surreptitiously or openly and incrementally by the seduction of the masses rather than by a violent class struggle or radical revolution. In the United States, socialism is expanding in the form of increased dependence on government and the welfare state.

Governments that fully embrace socialism soon find their economies weakened or near collapse from debt and overindulgence. When they try to dump Karl Marx's socialism, riots ensue as we have seen repeatedly in many nations of Western Europe. It is difficult for people who have become dependent on government to move away from it and regain personal autonomy. It is a vicious cycle of dependency that is very difficult to break once instituted.

Socialism is the theoretical and historic precursor to communism. The nations of Central and Eastern Europe that experienced the full brunt of socialism and communism in the past no longer brag about Marxism and are trying to move as far away as they can from collectivism.

It is time we heed the warnings and learn from the brutal lessons of totalitarian history.

Finally, this book is not a comprehensive or a chronological history of the Soviet Union, China, or Russia in the 20th and 21st centuries. It is a literary investigation annotating the salient events in the history of the Soviet Union under Stalin and, very briefly, of some of his successors. We only take a glimpse of Mao Tse-tung and China, and "democratic" Russia under Vladimir Putin.[6] The events that piqued my interest are the ones described in this tome.

Miguel A. Faria, Jr., M.D.
Milledgeville, Georgia
September 6, 2023

Part I

Joseph Stalin and the Years of Terror

CHAPTER 1

YOUNG STALIN—
THE GEORGIA BANDIT

Joseph Vissarionovich Djugashvili (1879–1953), later known as Stalin, began his revolutionary career as a communist subversive or, more accurately, a bandit in his native country of Georgia, part of the Tsarist Russian Empire. The story is enthrallingly recounted in *Young Stalin*, the absorbing and authoritative biography of Stalin's early years, written by Simon Sebag Montefiore. There is a lot more that we learn from Montefiore that was not commonly known or written about in the previous biographies of Stalin, especially during his early years before he became the Red Tsar.

In the tantalizing Prologue, Montefiore related the details of the audacious robbery and bloody bombing at the festive Yerevan Square in the center of the town of Tiflis (now Tbilisi, the capital of the Republic of Georgia). The heist, which was carried out on June 13, 1907, by the 29-year-old Soso (Stalin's nickname) and his band of Georgian gangsters, was orchestrated to help finance Vladimir Lenin's communist revolution.[1]

The terrorists made off with an incredible sum of money, approximately 300,000 rubles or over $34 million U.S. dollars. Dozens of innocent bystanders as well as Tsarist Cossack guards were killed or wounded in the attack when the terrorists detonated a number of powerful bombs that shook the center of the town. Nevertheless, it was the perfect crime in that afterwards no one talked (even then Stalin ran a tight ship with hermetically sealed security) and no one got arrested.[1]

Most of the stolen money was funneled clandestinely to Lenin, who had authorized the young Stalin to carry out the sanguinary deed. However, the blood money caused financial bickering among the revolutionaries, and the carnage marred the image of the more radical faction in the Russian Social-Democrats that was led by Stalin in Georgia and by Lenin, the supreme leader or "the eagle of the mountain," in Russia.

By 1912, the Russian Social-Democratic Workers' Party (SDP) had irrevocably split between the factions of Lenin's Bolsheviks, the purported "majority," and the more moderate Mensheviks, the followers of Jewish revolutionist Yuli Martov and Georgi Plekhanov, the father of the

SDP. Generally, the Bolsheviks wanted a small, tightly controlled, conspiratorial, intellectual group to rule in the name and place of the workers in order to establish a "dictatorship of the proletariat." For the Bolsheviks, the end always justified the means so violence, assassinations, and bank robberies were considered necessary, and suspected traitors were promptly annihilated to "protect" the revolution. Young Stalin became an "immediate" Bolshevik.

Figure 1: Police photograph of Stalin ("Soso") when he was 23 years old in 1902. Batum Gendarme Administration

On the other hand, the Mensheviks tended to be somewhat more democratic, and were prepared to allow both workers and peasants to participate in the ruling oligarchy. The Mensheviks were also less violent and by in large condemned terrorism, murder, and bank robbery. So a split between the two rival factions of the SDP was bound to occur. Soso and his Georgian bandits helped to accelerate that split and make it irrevocable. Decades later and when firmly in power, Stalin would hunt down former members of the Menshevik Party in one of his early purges, the 1931 Menshevik Trial.[2]

Stalin had a "saintly" mother, Ekaterina "Keke" Geladze, who sacrificed everything in order to educate her poor but gifted son in a seminary in an attempt to convert and have him embrace the Orthodox Church. But he also had a drunkard for a father, a cobbler named Vissarion "Beso" Djugashvili, who frequently beat young Soso and Keke.

The reader is also introduced to the three powerful men who protected Soso and Keke from Beso as the young Stalin grew up. All three men at various times were suspected of being Stalin's real father. Stalin would not have survived childhood without them.[3]

Figure 2: Ekaterina Djugashvili ("Keke" Geladze), mother of Joseph Stalin in 1892. Gori photographer

Montefiore describes the evolving attitude and explains the psychological profile of the studious child and rebellious youth who grows up to be a ruthless, sanguinary, unforgiving young adult with an imperturbable and treacherous disposition. In rapid strides the child becomes a man, a man who becomes a monster, a monster that reigns as communist dictator over the vast Russian Empire (1924–1953)—the same empire over which the ineffectual Romanov Tsar, Nicholas II, was forced to abdicate following the February Revolution of 1917.

Montefiore used archival material that laid forgotten in dusty storage for years, interviewed eyewitnesses or their descendants, and perhaps most importantly, uncovered and published material made available for the first time from a number of previously unpublished memoirs. This included material from Stalin's former girlfriends, terrorist comrades, and revolutionary rivals who knew him well; many of them later turned against him and perished.

Lazar Kaganovich, a Bolshevik and a Stalin stalwart, once said there were several versions of Stalin's persona. Indeed, we learn about young Stalin's various developing personalities: The hard working and gifted student; the talented Georgian poet; the seminary choirboy and later tenor singer; the "consummate actor"; and the revolutionary bandit and terrorist enforcer. It is easy to follow the progression then from Bolshevik leader to communist tyrant, and ultimately to totalitarian monster.

Figure 3: Lazar Moiseevich Kaganovich in the 1930s, Deputy Premier of the Soviet Union and Stalin's henchman in his inner circle. Eleazar Langman

Additionally, we are reassured by Montefiore that what we learned from authors like exiled and literary figures Fyodor Dostoevsky and Aleksandr Solzhenitsyn about the Tsarist prison and exile system, where many revolutionary figures spent considerable time prior to the October Revolution of 1917, was indeed correct.[4]

In fact, Montefiore expounded on the Tsarist judicial system as it related to revolutionaries:

> *The Tsarist authorities recognized, due to the special challenges of evidence and secrecy, that terrorists and revolutionaries could not be tried by jury or judge: the local Gendarme officer recommended a sentence to the local Governor-General who forwarded it on to the Special Commission—five Justice and Interior officials who passed sentence. The Interior Minister confirmed it; the Emperor signed off. Stalin was habitually sentenced this way. Between 1881 and 1904, only 11,879 were sentenced like this, while during Stalin's reign of the same approximate time span, he presided over the deportation of an astonishing 28 million, several million of whom never returned. As for capital punishment under the Tsars, Catholic Poles and Jews in the western provinces were much more likely to be hanged than Orthodox Russians or Georgians.[5]*

The Tsarist prison-exile penal system was very lenient, particularly for well-placed revolutionaries like Vladimir Lenin. Even Montefiore—who wrote at times with subtle admiration for the idealist, young revolutionaries and almost always with clear distaste for the old Tsarist regime—was forced to admit:

> *Siberian exile was regarded as one of the most terrible abuses of the Tsarist tyranny. It was certainly boring and depressing, but once settled in some god-forsaken village, the exiles, intellectuals who were frequently hereditary noblemen, were usually well treated. Such paternalistic sojourns more resembled dull reading holidays than the living hell of Stalin's murderous Gulag. The exiles even received pocket money from the Tsar—12 roubles for a nobleman such as Lenin, 11 roubles for a school graduate such as Molotov, and 8 for a peasant such as Stalin—with which to pay for clothes, food and rent. If they received too much money from home, they lost their allowance.[6]*

In support of Alexander Ostrovsky, who denied the much-disputed assertion that Stalin had been a part-time agent of the Tsar's secret police, the Okhrana, in pre-revolutionary days, Montefiore agreed that it would have been easy for Stalin to obtain the money for the false papers he needed to escape at various times because escape was not difficult from the lenient Tsarist exile:

Between 1906 and 1909, over 18,000 obscure exiles out of a total of 32,000 raised the 100 roubles needed 'to buy their boots'—the false papers needed to escape.[7]

Even in exile Stalin preferred to associate with the criminal elements rather than with his political intellectual confreres. And from these associations, he learned valuable lessons that he would continue to apply criminally and politically after he became dictator—for example, to manipulate the criminal elements to do his bidding as informants, enforcers, and later as dreaded members of his security apparatus.

The similarities in the upbringing and modus operandi of Joseph Stalin and Fidel Castro in their youth are so striking that I cannot pass up the opportunity to point them out. Although the two men came from different socioeconomic backgrounds, as youngsters both thought they were special, different from and better than other children, despite the fact they grew up in the shadow and stigma of possible illegitimacy. Both children went to religious schools, where they excelled and strove to be the best at everything, but they were also bullies and had to be the leaders. As they became older, these men became more ruthless and unforgiving, and did not hesitate to eliminate opponents; they were troublemakers and trouble followed them wherever they went (for example, Stalin in Batumi and burning Baku, and Castro in Santiago de Cuba and Havana student days and in Colombia's "Bogotazo").[8]

Both men became criminal gangsters and carried guns (Stalin was a "Mauserist," Castro, a "pistolero"), but they learned to delegate the dirty work of killing to others (enforcers). They were master conspirators, who controlled the underground (Stalin was the supreme instigator of *konspiratsia*); and both were actors and orators (at this, Castro was the better of the two). Both men came to believe that because of their sense of revolutionary mission and leadership, they were owed everything that their comrades, and anyone who came in contact with them, could provide (for example, shelter, food, money and women). When in prison, both Stalin and Castro were treated very leniently, at times almost like celebrities, and so frequently they made successful demands upon their jailers, such as the use of books, and permission to teach their militant catechism to fellow prisoners—all of which would be unthinkable for prisoners of communist regimes.

Both Stalin and Fidel Castro used women as lovers and were frequently supported by them, but these women comrades were discarded when they were of no further use to the two leaders. Both men vehemently condemned the "crimes" of their predecessors (namely, Tsar Nicolas II and Fulgencio Batista), only to vastly surpass them in cruelty and barbarity once they attained power. And when Stalin and Castro reached supreme power, they knew how to wield it and hold onto it, so that even the members of their inner circle and security apparatus feared them.

Figure 4: Joseph Stalin in 1920 (left) and Fidel Castro in the 1950s (right). Stalin Digital Archive/Mondadori Publishers

Yet, both men could be pragmatic when they had to be, such as Stalin opening churches during World War II to inspire patriotism and temporarily closing the Comintern to charm the allies, and Fidel Castro allowing tourism and travel to Cuba for much needed hard cash and supporting the Soviets during the crushing of the Prague Spring in 1968.

Both men reinterpreted Marxism-Leninism to serve their needs in wielding absolute power and to feed their cults of personality. In short, one cannot avoid drawing the conclusion that the two men differ only in quantity, not in kind. Fidel Castro ruled over a circumscribed and captive island; Stalin ruled over a vast empire with influence over the entire globe. As Lord Acton's aphorism observed, "Power tends to corrupt; absolute power corrupts absolutely.[9]

I would also be remiss if I did not state that I agree with Montefiore in one of his underlying themes, namely that Stalin played a much larger role in the Russian revolution than we have heretofore been led to believe by some historians and documentary filmmakers. Following Leon Trotsky's judgment of Stalin as "an outstanding mediocrity of our Party" (a fatal error on his part) and his insistence that Stalin's role in the revolutionary struggle was minimal, many historians took note. Trotsky, for example, wrote that Stalin spent the Revolution of 1905 (what Trotsky famously called the "dress rehearsal") "in an unpretentious office writing dull comments on brilliant events."[10] Unquestionably, historians have followed the historical line of Trotsky, who was a prolific writer and lived in Mexico until his assassination at Stalin's direct order in 1940.

Figure 5: Stalin (right) confers with an ailing Lenin at Gorki in September 1922. Maria Ulyanova

In 1956, Nikita Khrushchev began to dismantle Stalin's cult of personality and rewrite the story of the Russian revolution that had been previously revised by Stalin and Lavrenti Beria to give Stalin the central role next to Lenin. In the subsequent revision processes, the early part Stalin played in Georgia, and later in Russia, was ignored and forgotten. Montefiore's *Young Stalin* brings that forgotten history to the fore, accurately readjusting the chronicles to document Stalin's proper role up to the time of the Revolution of 1917. Suffice to say, Stalin had a major and bloody role to play as a Georgian bandit, conspiratorial enforcer, ruthless terrorist, efficient organizer, even orator and Bolshevik. While Lenin tarried in Zurich, bickering with other exiles and the German Social Democrats or at times remaining disconsolate, doubting that revolution would ever come to Russia[11]; Stalin was active, robbing banks and eliminating enemies, yet imperturbable, even in prison or in exile in Siberia, certain that "blood would run in torrents" and that the Bolsheviks would topple the Tsar and gain power.

Young Stalin is a well-organized tome of over 400 pages and includes Stalin's family tree, maps, quaint and rare illustrations and photographs, lists of characters, et cetera. The text, source notes, selected bibliography and index are 397 pages. Montefiore's research is exemplary. He has written a fascinating book for those interested in Stalin and Soviet history as well as political science, terrorism, revolutions, the psychology and incarnation of evil, and ultimately the ascent to power of arguably the worst tyrant and the greatest mass murderer in history, except perhaps Mao Tse-tung. The book adds significantly to those areas and becomes absolutely the authoritative biography of Stalin in his early years. One caveat, despite Montefiore's view to the contrary, some readers may still not be convinced that Stalin did not at times cooperate with the Okhrana as a double agent.[12]

Although Montefiore carried out superb scholarship and was very diligent in condemning Stalin's crimes, I must warn the readers that he evinced an almost subliminal admiration for Stalin the revolutionary that may be disconcerting for some readers who have experienced the evils of communism first hand. Indeed in his Acknowledgments, Montefiore humorously wrote that his wife found the "blood soaked presence of Stalin in our marriage a trial of endurance," but after publication of the work, "we finally enter our own period of deStalinization."[13] I expect his deStalinization to be complete now, and I congratulate him on this magnificent tour de force.

CHAPTER 2

A LITERARY OVERVIEW OF STALIN'S MEAT GRINDER

Several Russian and non-Russian authors have written excellent biographies of Joseph Stalin from the time of Mikhail Gorbachev's glasnost and perestroika to the democratic Russia of Boris Yeltsin. Let us now briefly mention several of those biographies in this chapter for those seeking material on this subject for further research.

Stalin in "Triumph and Tragedy" (1988)

As head of the Institute of Military History of the USSR and General of the Soviet Army, Dmitri Volkogonov had access to secret Soviet documents that were not available to other historians up to the time of Mikhail Gorbachev's glasnost and perestroika.

Volkogonov's *Stalin: Triumph and Tragedy* is authoritative, engaging, and an instructive biography of the Joseph Stalin, the Red Tsar of Soviet communism. It was published in Russia in 1988 but was not translated into English and published in the West until 1991—the pivotal year when the Russian bear stumbled, bringing about the total collapse of Soviet communism.[1]

The fact that Volkogonov's biography of Stalin was completed and published during the years of glasnost and perestroika is crucial in understanding his work. One gets the impression that he had ambivalent feelings about the ideals, utility, and worthiness of Soviet communism, which he usually referred to as socialism. His ambivalence may have been the result of political doubts and anxiety from his dual life in the communist Soviet Union and then in a democratic Russia in transition.

Even by 1988, the general had not quite shed the skin of his "socialist" background. To all outward appearances, Volkogonov was a hardline military man, a general, and deputy chief of the main political section of the Soviet army and navy. Secretly, he was a historian, researching and writing about the life of crime of the Red Tsar, Joseph

Stalin. One is left to wonder if Volkogonov would have concluded his assessment differently had the Russian edition been finished in 1992 or 1993, rather than 1988.

At times, Volkogonov seemed to imply that if Stalin had not usurped the reins of power and Vladimir Lenin's course had been followed then Soviet communism in the USSR—as originally traced by Lenin and theoretically enforced after his death by a collective leadership—might have ended in a more democratic socialism, a true Russian socialistic, but always elusive, "workers' paradise."

At other times, Volkogonov seemed to admit that even with the collective leadership, the course of Russian history might not have made a difference because Lenin, just like Stalin, had called for the pragmatic use of force and terror.

In a footnote, Volkogonov recalled that after the February Revolution, the Provisional Government convened a Constituent Assembly that would have established a constitution for the Russian people to "determine the nature of the state." But lawful, constitutional rule never happened. After Lenin seized power, elections were held, but when the Bolsheviks received less than a quarter of the votes, they quickly dispersed the Assembly by force on January 18, 1918—thereby ending the one and only "democratic" session.[2]

Neither Lenin nor Stalin wanted democracy or constitutional rule; they wanted to eliminate the opposition at any cost and establish a "dictatorship of the proletariat"—not in the image of the workers or peasants as they proclaimed, but in their own conspiratorial and dictatorial image. And yet, Volkogonov was at times reluctant to cast Lenin and Stalin in the same collectivist, autocratic, totalitarian mold. The general insisted that events could have taken a different turn if only they had paid heed to Lenin's less strident course.

Volkogonov asserted that possibility, despite the fact that he himself provided evidence that, except for Nikolai Bukharin in the 1920s and 1930s, all of the Bolsheviks followed the lead of Lenin and Stalin—not only Stalin's minions, such as Vyacheslav Molotov, Kliment Voroshilov, and Lazar Kaganovich, but also Leon Trotsky, Lev Kamenev, and Gregory Zinoviev. All of the Bolsheviks sanctioned the use of violence, the use of coercive state power, and the use of terror in peacetime or wartime to consolidate Soviet power and subdue the Russian masses in whose name they supposedly ruled.[3]

Volkogonov documented that Kamenev and Zinoviev, leading Politburo members, ironically orchestrated Stalin's election to the office of General Secretary of the USSR. They erred in the belief that they could manipulate Stalin against Trotsky and that they could then exercise more power through the influential Politburo. Simply, they feared Trotsky more than they feared Stalin. They would later pay with their lives for that misjudgment and become two of Stalin's most celebrated Bolshevik victims.[4]

Figure 6: Nikolai Bukharin in 1930, Marxist philosopher and former Editor-in-Chief of *Pravda*, shot by Stalin's NKVD in 1936 during the Terror

Stalin's craftiness and will power were vastly underestimated by his Bolshevik comrades. During the Party Congresses, verbal duels over Trotsky's call for "world revolution" versus Stalin's state policy of "socialism in one country" erupted. Trotsky thought of Stalin as an "outstanding mediocrity," another misjudgment that later proved fatal to Trotsky.[5]

Volkogonov's engaging narrative takes us through the political purges, the meat grinding of Russian society, and the elimination of Stalin's real or imagined opponents: The "Right deviationists," such as Alexei Rykov, Mikhail Tomsky, and of course, their leader, Bukharin (who Lenin called "the favorite of the whole Party") and the military exemplified by Marshal Mikhail Tukhachevsky; the Left internationalists like Trotsky and his followers; and the vacillators, including the Bolshevik duo, Kamenev and Zinoviev.[6]

Figure 7: Leon Trotsky in January 1924 on the cover of the magazine *Prozhektor*

Even those who once served in Stalin's secret police, the NKVD, were not immune from scrutiny, and a number of them who had killed other comrades in his name, such as Genrikh Yagoda and Nikolai Yezhov, were executed as the meat grinder continued. Other NKVD security personalities survived Stalin, such as Viktor Abakumov, but feared by the collective leadership that followed, was finally executed in 1954 under the regime of Georgy Malenkov and Nikita Khrushchev.[7]

One cannot help but note the similarities to events that took place in France a little more than a century earlier. In the French Revolution, Maximilien Robespierre destroyed his royalist enemies first; next, the courageous Girondins led by Madame Roland, Jacques Pierre Brissot, Pierre Vergniaud and their followers on the right; followed by the vicious troublemakers of the left, including the cowardly "enrages," René Hébert (founder and editor of *Le Pere Duchesne,* the extreme radical newspaper) and the Paris Commune leader Pierre Gaspard Chaumette; and finally, the moderate "indulgents," who eventually included Camille Desmoulins and Georges Danton, the "Titan of the French Revolution."

Figure 8: Andrey Vyshinsky in 1940, Procurator General of the Soviet Union ("hanging judge"), Soviet diplomat. Grigory Mikhailovich Vayl/RIA Novosti

Even Stalin's sanguinary state prosecutor, the odious Andrey Vyshinsky, who tormented and harangued "enemies of the people" during the secret or kangaroo trials of the Great Purge of 1937 elicits in the reader images of Antoine Fouquier-Tinville, the sinister, bloodthirsty Prosecutor for the Revolutionary Tribunals during the French Revolution. Acting under orders from Robespierre, just as Vyshinsky acted under orders from Stalin, Fouquier-Tinville administered grotesque impersonations of justice, preordained convictions, summary executions, and the perpetuation of terror. But unlike the reign of terror of Robespierre, which lasted less than two years, Stalin's reign of terror lasted decades, fluctuating in intensity as he saw fit during the entire period of his emerging dictatorship from approximately 1924 until the day of his death, March 5, 1953. And Stalin's legacy of totalitarian communism lived on until 1991.

Therefore, it was with good reason that the French Girondin Deputy and orator, Vergniaud, exclaimed, "The revolution, like Saturn, devours its own children."[8] And so it did in Russia too. Toward the end, only Stalin and his inner circle of loyal henchmen (dissimulating or not) survived; that circle included, Beria, Malenkov, Molotov, Kaganovich, Anastas Mikoyan, Nikolai Bulganin, and Khrushchev.

While General Volkogonov described the brutality and the crimes of the Stalin years in graphic detail—reconstructed from interviews as well as secret documents from the archives of the Communist Party of the USSR, military records, Comintern papers, and letters—one must keep in mind that intelligence (NKVD) records were not available to him.

Ironically, for secret foreign intelligence and Stalin's use of espionage and the KGB against the United States and Western Europe, one must still turn to materials mostly collected and published in the West—for example, books on the decrypted Venona documents, the Mitrokhin Archive, and the excellent work of the British historian Christopher Andrew—which will be cited in later chapters.

Stalin as "Breaker of Nations" (1991)

Stalin: Breaker of Nations by the British-American historian, Robert Conquest, covers the life of Joseph Stalin, from his childhood in Gori in the Republic of Georgia, to his death at his Nearer dacha in Kuntsevo, a former town near Moscow, on March 5, 1953.[9]

Conquest began by informing the reader:

In the early summer of 1918, the Bolsheviks moved into a 'socialist phase,' with nationalization, food requisitioning and all the other dictatorial measures later described as 'War Communism'—though at the time clearly presented as the fulfillment of the party's long term aims.[10]

Only popular opposition and peasant rebellions forced Lenin to temporarily change course with the New Economic Policy. Without exception, all of the Bolsheviks—that is, Lenin, Trotsky, Kamenev, Zinoviev, Bukharin, Yakov Sverdlov, Sergo Ordzhonikidze, et cetera—condoned violence and terror against the enemies of the Revolution, real or imagined. What separated Stalin from the rest was that Stalin would use terror indiscriminately as a matter of course, not only against the civilian population but also most ominously and unflinchingly against his former comrades, and without sparing the families of his political opponents (including his own).[11]

Through the sequential Congresses of the Party, one follows Stalin's career as he ascended the levels of power with words and deeds, until he reached the zenith of despotic, autocratic, and absolute power.

After the 17th Party Congress of 1934, "the Congress of Victors," Stalin's triumph was complete. Then, the Congress ceased convening. He now ruled with his inner circle, his minions, who flattered and cajoled him but also feared him.

Figure 9: Stalin speaking at the 17th Party Congress of 1934, "the Congress of Victors"

Shortly thereafter, Stalin used the assassination of Sergei Kirov in Leningrad as an excuse to launch the Great Terror of 1936–1938 despite the fact his power was unchallenged.[12] Millions of Russian citizens perished, either starved to death in government-planned famines, executed after show trials, or worked to death in the Gulag labor camps.[13]

Although Conquest's book was fatefully published as the Soviet Empire crumbled to dust with the collapse of communism in Russia and her satellites in 1991, the tome contains a set of photographs that put faces with the names of Stalin's victims and adds tangible personification to the almost surreal sense of totalitarian horror, namely, socialist terror incarnate.

The meat grinder in action is exemplified with the seven Bolsheviks who were elected to the Politburo in 1924 after Lenin's death: For six of them, their deaths were directly or indirectly orchestrated by the only remaining one, the most cunning and dangerous of all, Stalin. Kamenev, Zinoviev, Bukharin, and Rykov were executed following conviction at show trials. Tomsky committed suicide instead of facing arrest by the NKVD for trumped up charges during the First Moscow Trial of Zinoviev and Kamenev. And finally, acting under direct orders from Joseph Stalin, Spanish communist and NKVD agent, Ramón Mercader, assassinated Trotsky with an ice axe in Mexico City in 1940.

Regarding the nature of revolutions, Joseph Conrad, the Polish-British novelist, observed:

The last thing I want to tell you is this: in a real revolution—not a simple dynastic change or a mere reform of institutions—in a real revolution the best characters do not come to the front. A violent revolution falls into the hands of narrow-minded fanatics and of tyrannical hypocrites at first. Afterwards comes the turn of all the pretentious intellectual failures of the time. Such are the chiefs and the leaders…The scrupulous and the just, the noble, humane, and devoted natures; the unselfish and the intelligent may begin a movement—but it passes away from them. They are not the leaders of a revolution. They are its victims: the victims of disgust, of disenchantment—often of remorse. Hopes grotesquely betrayed, ideals caricatured—that is the definition of revolutionary success. There have been in every revolution hearts broken by such successes. But enough of that. My meaning is that I don't want you to be a victim.[14]

To Conrad's wise observation one can only add that Stalinism was worse, much worse in cruelty and the human toll than could be imagined from a literary passage. And yet, there are other examples of socialist and communist horrors—namely, Red China under Mao Tse-tung, Cambodia under Pol Pot, and Cuba under Fidel Castro. All of the totalitarian communist revolutions of the 20th century magnify Conrad's observation in brutality and evil.

And the "hopes grotesquely betrayed, ideals caricatured" worsen: Desolation, cruelty, and death follow in the path of "building socialism," a path that began, not with Stalin but with Lenin, and was asserted at various points of the revolution by Trotsky (who crushed the Kronstadt rebellion without mercy in 1921) and the other Bolsheviks, including "the favorite of the whole Party," Nikolai Bukharin.[15]

Conquest also reminded the reader that a very critical stage for Stalin's career, even his political survival, took place in the years 1922 to 1924, when Lenin was very ill and partially incapacitated. Lenin recognized Stalin's boundless cruelty and unquenchable thirst for personal, political power. Stalin had even insulted Lenin's devoted wife, Nadezhda Krupskaya, but it was too late. After Lenin's stroke of March 7, 1923, until his death on January 21, 1924, Stalin's career hung in the balance, but his political opponents, like Lenin, had underestimated him.[16]

Before closing this subheading, it should be noted that following the 12th Party Congress of 1923 and despite the implied suggestion of what Bukharin called "the theory of sweet revenge," Stalin admitted to Felix Dzerzhinsky, the Director of the Cheka, and Lev Kamenev, a Politburo member:

To choose one's victims, to prepare one's plans minutely, to slake an implacable vengeance, and then go to bed…there is nothing sweeter in the world.[17]

Stalin was able to do that repeatedly and with tremendous precision through his anti-Semitic campaign against alleged "cosmopolitanism" and the Doctors' Plot affair two decades later and up to the eve of his death in 1953.[18]

Stalin as Revealed by Investigative Journalist Edvard Radzinsky (1996)

Stalin: The First In-depth Biography Based on Explosive New Documents from Russia's Secret Archives by Edvard Radzinsky is another brilliant and edifying biography of the Red Tsar of the Soviet Union, Joseph Stalin. The book was published in Russia in 1996 and immediately translated and published in an English edition that same year—only five years after the Russian bear had stumbled with fatal results for the USSR and its communist satellites. Without Stalin's legacy of coercion, persecution, and force, the communist world could not survive on its own merit or against the free choice of the people over whom it ruled.[19]

Figure 10: Edvard Radzinsky, journalist and historian, in 2013. Dmitry Rozhkov

There is factual objectivity in this biography, and yet there are not moral penumbras over right and wrong and the evil nature of Soviet communism. The suspenseful facts speak for themselves, and Radzinsky has ended up writing a cliffhanger biography and history that will not be surpassed for years to come.

Radzinsky's in-depth biography of Stalin proved to be a journalistic labor of love after years of painstaking research in Russia's secret archives in the early years of democratic Russia under Boris Yeltsin. The tome is written in electrifying prose and fluent narration. One is also indebted to the late H. T. Willetts, for his marvelous literary English translation.

In the poignant Preface, setting the tone for his book, Radzinsky wrote:

> *[Following the death of Stalin in March 1953... I see myself in the crowd of mourners. How lonely I felt among all those grief-crazed people. Because I myself hated him.[20]*

Radzinsky's father, also a journalist of Jewish descent, initially supported but rapidly became disenchanted with the Bolshevik Revolution and Stalinism. He told his son, "perhaps one day you will write about him."[20]

Unlike Volkogonov's book, there is no ambivalence about the perversity of Stalinism; there is no confusion about what it might have been in Radzinsky's book. Stalin was a monster, and communism was an evil and a disastrous philosophy for Russia, whether it was in the hands of Lenin, Stalin, or "the collective leadership" that followed. It was only a matter of degrees. So Radzinsky squarely agrees with Boris Yeltsin, who said in 1991:

> *Our country has not been lucky.... It was decided to carry out this Marxist experiment on us.... It has simply pushed us off the path the world's civilized countries have taken.... In the end, we proved that there is no place for this idea.[21]*

The final chapters on Stalin's death and his plans for the future— that is, political and military plans that he was not able to carry out because of his timely, mysterious demise[22]—are chapters that set Radzinsky's book apart from the others and make this book an outstanding biography.[23]

I would be remiss if I did not at least mention in passing, *Stalin: The Court of the Red Tsar* by Simon Sebag Montefiore. This is an eloquently enticing and seductively enthralling biography of Joseph Stalin and the minions in his inner circle.

With stunning attention to detail, personal information that was not available in previous biographies, Montefiore provides us with a galvanizing portrait of Stalin "as human and complicated as he is brutal" and chronicles the lives of those notorious henchmen who entered the court of the Red Tsar.[24]

CHAPTER 3

STALIN'S MEAT GRINDER—
A PANORAMIC VIEW OF THE HUMAN DEVASTATION

Various scholars estimated that 20 million and perhaps up to 40 million people were killed between 1924 and 1953 during the communist dictatorship of Joseph Stalin. His victims included Russians, Tatars, Poles, Czechs, Cossacks, Chechens, and Turks as well as every other nationality that came within the grasp of the Red Soviet Empire.[1]

Citizens died from privations, neglect, and mistreatment; of starvation from government-orchestrated famines; diseases due to malnutrition; and mass executions or a simple shot to the back of the head. They died in prisons, in their homes, during mass deportations, and from overwork or exposure while slaving away in the Gulag system of destructive labor camps.

Stalin not only exterminated purported "enemies of the people" but also came close to liquidating the entire slate of communist Bolshevik leaders, including those who had been his or Lenin's comrades during the 1917 Russian revolution. In fact, Stalin probably killed more communists from every nationality than his fascist and Western democratic enemies combined during peacetime.[1]

The following vignettes are not intended to provide a comprehensive list of common victims caught in Stalin's meat grinder, but rather a sampling of high-ranking "communists devouring communists" during the 29-year performance of the Soviet *danse macabre* ("dance of death") conducted by Joseph Vissarionovich Djugashvili, better known as Stalin, "the man of steel."

Old Bolshevik Cadres

We will destroy every enemy, even if he is an Old Bolshevik, we will destroy his kin, his family. Anyone who by his actions or thoughts

Stalin's Meat Grinder—A Panoramic View of the Human Devastation   23

encroaches on the unity of the socialist state, we shall destroy relentlessly.
—Joseph Stalin, November 1937.[2]

Sovietologists remind us that after the kangaroo trials, Stalin began a purge and had Bolshevik leaders like Lev Kamenev, Gregory Zinoviev, and Ivan Smirnov accused of being "leftist Trotskyites," arrested, psychologically tortured, and then shot in 1936 by his dreaded secret police, the NKVD, a precursor to the KGB.

Later in 1936, the "right-wing" communists, Bukharin and his followers, Rykov, Nikolay Krestinsky, and Christian Rakovsky, came next. They were arrested and executed as members of the "rightist Trotskyite Bloc."[3]

Figure 11: April 1925 photo of Old Bolshevik cadres (left to right): Joseph Stalin, General Secretary of the Communist Party; Alexei Rykov, Chairman of the Council of People's Commissars (Prime Minister); Lev Kamenev, Deputy Chairman of the Council of People's Commissars (Deputy Prime Minister); and Gregory Zinoviev, Chairman of the Comintern's Executive Committee. Nikolai Petrov

Vladimir Antonov-Ovseenko, the military leader of the Bolshevik organization that "stormed" the Winter Palace during the October Revolution and brutally suppressed the Tambov Rebellion (1920–1921), was purged in 1938 and executed.[4]

Mariya Spiridonova was one of the leaders of the Left Socialist-Revolutionaries Party (Left SR). This radical revolutionary faction represented the peasants, and when their concerns were not addressed, they felt betrayed by the Bolsheviks.

On July 4, 1918, at the Fifth All-Russian Soviet Congress dominated by the Bolsheviks, Mariya Spiridonova, a 32-year-old woman with dark hair and wearing pince-nez, rose to the podium and attacked the Bolsheviks with words of fire:

> *I accuse you of betraying the peasants, of making use of them for your own ends. In Lenin's philosophy, you are only dung—only manure. When the peasants, the Bolshevik peasants, the Left SR peasants, and the non-party peasants are alike humiliated, oppressed and crushed—crushed as peasants—in my hand you will find the same pistol....[5]*

The British secret agents, Bruce Lockhart and Sidney Reilly, were at the Bolshoi Theater in Moscow where the Congress had convened but was vacated by the events of the day.

Figure 12: Maria A. Spiridonova before 1906, a Left Socialist-Revolutionary persecuted for years, imprisoned in the Gulag, and executed in 1941

When the expected Left SR uprising against the Bolsheviks failed, Spiridonova awaited her fate calmly and with composed resolve. She was arrested and jailed in the summer of 1918. Twenty Left SR hostages were shot. Spiridonova was sent to the Gulag. The rest of her Left SR comrades—like the Kadets and Mensheviks—were hunted down and virtually exterminated by Lenin and Stalin.

Spiridonova was persecuted for years, arrested, harshly interrogated, released, re-arrested, sentenced and resentenced repeatedly, sent to various labor camps and settlements in the Gulag and in exile. Finally, she was executed in 1941, three months after the German invasion of the USSR in the Medvedevsky Forest massacre by order of Stalin.[5]

One might also remember from history or from reading *Special Tasks* written by NKVD General Pavel Sudoplatov how he was personally tasked by Stalin to arrange the assassination of Leon Trotsky in Mexico City. At the time, Sudoplatov was not only a Soviet spymaster but also the chief of "Special Tasks" or "wet affairs" (that is, assassinations) for the NKVD, and the details surrounding the dramatic event are vividly recounted in his remarkable book.[6]

Figure 13: Leonid Eitingon, Pavel Sudoplatov's trusted lieutenant in "wet affair" operations, in 1957

Aware of the lethality and "wet affair skills" of a trusted lieutenant, Leonid Eitingon, Sudoplatov decided to tap him for the assignment.

Eitingon had served "with distinction" in Spain during the Spanish Civil War (1936–1939). Nevertheless, Stalin had been purging the NKVD leaders serving abroad and Eitingon had not only been arrested but also come close to being executed. Sudoplatov was able to fish him out of prison for the "special task" of arranging Trotsky's assassination.

Eitingon successfully accomplished the deed with the help of his Spanish-communist mistress, Caridad Mercader and her son, Ramón. In 1940, after stalking Trotsky for some time and finally befriending him, the Spanish communist and NKVD agent, Ramón Mercader, assassinated Trotsky with an ice axe in Mexico City.[6]

The Great Illegals and the Foreign Intelligence Services

"Illegal" agents were Soviet spies working under deep cover in Western countries with no diplomatic cover or immunity. Some of them became legends in Soviet hagiographic history for their masterful espionage activities against the West, particularly when it involved the recruitment and running of five notorious British traitors, collectively referred to as the Cambridge Five (dubbed the Magnificent Five by the KGB), namely, Kim Philby, Donald Maclean, Guy Burgess, Anthony Blunt, and John Cairncross.[7,8]

Arnold Deutsch was a Jewish-Austrian intellectual and an illegal deep cover Soviet agent. He was the recruiter and controller of the infamous British traitors, the Cambridge Five. Deutsch was recalled to Moscow and although he survived, his ultimate fate remains uncertain to this day.[7,9]

Theodore Maly was the head of the illegal London (Soviet) residency in 1936. Maly completed the recruitment, training, and running of the Cambridge Five spy ring. He was also recalled, denounced as an enemy of the people, and shot.[7,10]

Moisei Akselrod was another deep cover Soviet agent operating in Italy. He was denounced as a traitor to the motherland, recalled to Russia, and executed during the Great Terror of 1936–1938.[11]

Not only were the Soviet illegal agents hunted down but also the Soviet foreign spymasters were targeted. Abram Slutsky, head of the INO (*Inostranny Otdel*)—the foreign intelligence service that was then part of the NKVD, the successor agency to the Cheka—was found dead of a "heart attack" (most likely cyanide poisoning) in his office in 1938. His department was being purged of enemies of the people in the Great Terror.[12]

Figure 14: Abram Slutsky (left), Soviet intelligence officer and head of the INO; and General Jan Berzin (right), official NKVD photo after his arrest in 1937

Slutsky's immediate successors, Zelman Passov and Sergey Shpigelglas, soon followed him and were likewise executed as enemies of the people.[12] Their counterparts in the internal security police, the NKVD, Genrikh Yagoda and Nikolai Yezhov, as we shall see in subsequent chapters, would be purged and executed too.[13]

General Jan Berzin (1889–1938) was a Latvian Bolshevik and Chekist, and the creator of Soviet military intelligence (GRU). He served with KGB general Alexander Orlov as head of Red Army Intelligence in Spain (1936–1937). He was purged by Stalin and shot in 1938.[7,14]

The Red Army

Scholars of Russian military history are familiar with events surrounding the purge, trial, and execution in 1937 of the most capable and distinguished general in the Red Army, Mikhail Tukhachevsky, Marshal of the Soviet Union.

According to Stalin and the NKVD, Tukhachevsky was a member of the Trostkyite-Bukharinite-Fascist counterrevolutionary conspiracy and, therefore, a traitor to the motherland. Along with Tukhachevsky, 40,000 Red Army personnel were eliminated during the Terror of 1937–1938.[15]

Almost the entire Defense Council of the Red Army, including Generals Pavel Dybenko, Alexander Yegorov, and Ian Zhigur, would all be shot within six months after the trial and execution of Tukhachevsky. Only one general did not break under interrogation, General Vasily Blyukher, who died in prison after being repeatedly tortured.[15]

Figure 15: The first five Marshals of the Soviet Union, clockwise from top left: Budyonny, Blyukher, Yegorov, Voroshilov and Tukhachevsky in November 1935. Only Voroshilov and Budyonny would survive Stalin's Great Purge

According to the Russian historian, General Dmitri Volkogonov, Stalin's security police eliminated 45 percent of the army and navy command as well as political staff from the positions of Brigade commander through the officer ranks. When World War II came two years later and the German Panzers rolled over the western expanse of the USSR, the Red Army was not ready. It had been decapitated.[15]

NKVD and Security Services

Stalin also routinely purged the security services (that is, the secret police). Genrikh Yagoda, head of the NKVD, was purged and executed in 1936 for not being efficient enough in persecuting and prosecuting purported enemies of the state, namely the Old Bolsheviks, including his failure to promptly falsify evidence to convict the "right-wing" Bolshevik leader, Nikolai Bukharin.[13] Yagoda's successor was the blood-drenched, dwarfish Nikolai Yezhov.[13]

Figure 16: Genrikh Yagoda (middle) inspecting the construction of the Moscow-Volga Canal in 1935. Behind Yagoda's right shoulder is young Nikita Khrushchev

As previously stated, the "right-wing" communists were arrested in 1936 by Yagoda, and Bukharin, Rykov, Krestinsky, and Rakovsky were executed for being members of the "rightist Trotskyite Bloc." Their final persecutor was Nikolai Yezhov, who presided over the Great Terror and Purges of 1937–1938, a period that is sometimes referred to as the Yezhovshchina, as if Yezhov, and not Stalin, was chiefly responsible. Yezhov would also be arrested, purged by Stalin, and executed a couple of years later in 1940.[13]

Yakov Blyumkin was the assassin of the German Ambassador to the USSR during the Brest-Litovsk negotiations in 1918. Although pardoned for that crime in 1919, he was later accused of being a Trotskyite and executed on order of Joseph Stalin in 1929.[16]

Martyn Latsis was a Bolshevik and an assistant to Felix Dzerzhinsky, "Iron Felix," the founder and director of the Cheka, the first Soviet secret police authorized by Lenin to spread terror and eliminate enemies of the people without bourgeoise moral prejudices.

During Lenin's Red Terror of 1918, Comrade Latsis ordered the extermination of White Russian suspects and prisoners in the Crimea. He exhorted:

> *We are not carrying out war against individuals. We are exterminating the bourgeoisie as a class. We aren't looking for evidence or witnesses to reveal deeds or words against the Soviet power. The first question that we ask is—to what class does he belong, what are his origins, upbringing, education, or profession. These questions define the fate of the accused. This is the essence of Red Terror.[17]*

But for Latsis, the chickens came home to roost. During Stalin's Great Terror, Latsis was purged and executed in 1938.[17]

Gleb Bokii was a deputy head of the Cheka under Felix Dzerzhinsky but was purged in 1937 and died in the Gulag in 1941.[18]

Viktor Abakumov was the former SMERSH ("Death to Spies") commander during World War II and then NKVD Chief. He was arrested during the Doctors' Plot affair; purged, imprisoned, and tortured. He was executed in 1954 during Khrushchev's reign.[19,20]

Internationalist Communists

Yakov Ganetsky was a Polish communist and Lenin's liaison with the German High Command during the Great War. He was purged and shot in 1937.[21]

Fritz Platten was a Swiss Social Democrat and guarantor of the sealed train affair that brought Lenin and his Bolsheviks through Germany to Russia in 1917. Even though Platten saved Lenin's life during an assassination attempt, he was purged by Stalin and died in a labor camp in the Gulag.[22]

Eino Rahja was a Finnish communist and Lenin's friend and bodyguard in the early years of the Revolution. He was purged and died on the eve of the Great Terror in 1936.[23]

Karl Radek was a Russian communist who began his career in Polish and German Social-Democratic Party politics. Later he became a Bolshevik, and served as an Internationalist in the Comintern. He was purged in 1937 and sent to the Gulag where he was killed. Russian sources vary on the circumstances surrounding Radek's demise. One source claimed that Radek was killed in a fight; another that he was killed on orders of an NKVD operative in 1939.[21,24]

Figure 17: Karl Radek, a Social-Democratic Party operative and an associate of Lenin's in Switzerland, in 1919

Solomon Mikhoels, chairman of the Jewish Anti-Fascist Committee, was assassinated in Minsk in 1948 during Stalin's anti-cosmopolitan campaign and on his direct order.[25]

Intelligentsia

Vladimir Mayakovsky was a modernist poet and early supporter of the Bolsheviks. He became discontented with the cultural censorship and socialist realism dictated by the Soviet state. Although some authors claim that he died because of tumultuous love affairs gone awry, it is more likely that he committed suicide in 1930 in protest of Stalin's dictatorship and disillusionment with the totalitarian direction of Soviet Russia [26]

Figure 18: Poet Vladimir Mayakovsky at his 20 Years of Work exhibition in 1930

Maxim Gorky was a poet, novelist, proletarian writer, early supporter of the Bolsheviks, and later critic of Lenin's communist repressive tactics. He was exiled in 1921, but was enticed to return to Russia by Stalin in 1932. He was then utilized as a captive, useful propaganda tool in Stalin's Russia. He and his son died under mysterious circumstances. During the Moscow Trials, it was charged that Yagoda's NKVD agents killed Gorky. For his part, Stalin later claimed that Gorky and his son were both killed in the Doctors' Plot in which the Kremlin doctors "conducted terrorist activity by means of prescribing to the patients such treatment that ruined their health, complicated the illness, and led to their demise."[27]

Dr. Yakov G. Etinger was a Jewish intellectual and renowned physician. He was arrested, tortured, and died in the custody of the secret police in 1951 before fully confessing in Stalin's Doctors' Plot.[28]

Hundreds of artists and members of the intelligentsia—including writers, poets, painters, musicians, composers, actors, economists and engineers—who did not compote to Stalin's ideals of socialist realism in art form that dictated cultural development should serve the purposes of socialism and communism, were condemned to the Gulag. Many were purged; some survived and were released after Stalin's death. Others were consumed by the destructive labor camps and died of privation and despair or were unceremoniously shot.

Figure 19: 1946 postage stamp from the USSR, "10 years since the death of M. Gorky." Ivan Dubasov

The Soviet writer, Yevgeniya Ginzberg, spent 18 years in prison camps. The painter, Mikhail Sokolov, was arrested in 1938 and sentenced to seven years in the Taiga. Vladimir I. Nevsky, the Soviet historiam, was arrested in 1935 and his fate is unknown. Georgi I. Lomov-Oppokov, the Soviet economist, died in prison in 1938. Pyotr A. Palchinsky, economist and mining engineer, was shot in 1929. Dmitri D. Pletnev, a Soviet physician, was sentenced to 25 years after his short trial in 1938. He died in the Gulag in 1953. Varlam T. Shalamov, the Soviet writer, spent 17 years in the Kolyma camps and lived to write about his experiences. Yuri M. Steklov, a Soviet historian and editor of *Izvestiya*, was purged and died in 1954. The Soviet poet, Pavel N. Vasilyev, wrote about the countryside and was accused of idealizing kulaks. He died in 1937 at the age of 27. Nikolai I. Vavilov, a prominent Soviet geneticist and botanist, was arrested in 1940 and died in prison under harsh conditions. Maksimilian A. Voloshin, poet and watercolorist, who opposed the Bolsheviks, was banned and became a "non-person" in the Soviet Union. He was fortunate to die in 1932 before becoming another victim of the Great Terror.

Figure 20: Associated Press photo of Polina Zhemchuzhina Molotova in 1936, Soviet politician and wife of Foreign Minister Vyacheslav Molotov. She was imprisoned in the Gulag under false charges and released after Stalin's death

Polina Molotova, the wife of Vyacheslav Molotov, was arrested for treason in 1948 and sentenced to five years in a labor camp. She did not believe that Stalin knew about her imprisonment. She was released by Beria a few days after Stalin's death, and she fainted when she learned of Stalin's death.[26] The fact remains that we do not know the names of most of the minor artists and members of the intelligentsia who died in the Gulag.

Kulaks and the Proletariat

One must never forget that during the Great Terror of 1936–1938, also known as the Great Purge, when Stalin eliminated the Old Bolsheviks and Communist Party functionaries, the Soviet state continued to grind down upon the very citizens the revolution had sworn to liberate and protect. Beginning with Lenin at the inception of the Revolution of October 1917 through Stalin's intensified repression and up to the end of the Soviet era, the common Russians suffered the most.

Millions of kulaks and poorer Russian peasants were killed during the forced establishment of collective farms. Peasants fought requisition and collectivization by slaughtering farm animals, hoarding, or burning crops.

Stalin's Meat Grinder—A Panoramic View of the Human Devastation   35

Stalin's militia and secret police fought back by drowning, shooting, and starving some peasants, while others were sent to the Gulag to be used as slave labor in the construction of the White Sea and Volga Canals or in timber and lumber projects in the tundra and taiga. The average lifespan of the peasant or worker (the proletariat in chains) was barely three months in the labor camps.[29]

Figure 21: Front page of Chicago American newspaper depicting the starvation and death of six million Ukrainians by Soviet collectivization policies in 1933

     Likewise, millions of workers (the sanctified proletariat) denounced each other in the suspicious, paranoid atmosphere of Stalinist Russia. Many of them heard the dreaded knock on the door in the middle of the night and were quickly whisked away in the "Black Marias" of the feared NKVD secret police, or were directly removed from the assembly or workplace, taken to the Gulag, and summarily shot as "wreckers," spies, saboteurs, and enemies of the people.[1,29]

Nikolai Krylenko served as Prosecutor General of the USSR from 1929 to 1931, and the People's Commissar of Justice from July 1936 to September 1937.[30]

Figure 22: Nikolai Krylenko, People's Commissar for Justice in the USSR, in 1918, who succumbed to "socialist legality" and was executed during the Great Purge

Krylenko was an exponent of "socialist legality"—that is, political consideration rather than guilt or innocence determines culpability and punishment. Under that sham legal theory, he sent thousands of individuals, including members of the intelligentsia, the Party as well as common Russians, kulaks and proletarians, to their deaths; but Krylenko received his just deserts. He was arrested during the Great Purge, interrogated, tortured, and confessed to "wrecking" and "anti-Soviet agitation." Ironically, he was tried in accordance with the dictates of his "socialist legality" theory and executed in 1938.[30]

Krylenko was succeeded by another sanguinary prosecutor, Andrey Vyshinsky, who would survive Stalin.

Commissars of Death

Yakov Sverdlov was a hard-working Bolshevik, confidante, and closest advisor to Lenin. After Lenin himself, Sverdlov was probably the one person most responsible for authorizing the execution of the Russian

Imperial family—namely, Tsar Nicolas II; the Tsarina Alexandra; the Grand Duchesses, Olga, Tatiana, Mariya, and Anastasia; the Tsarevitch Alexei; and four of their servants—at the Ipatiev House in the Ural city of Yekaterinburg, which subsequently was renamed after him, Sverdlovsk.[31]

Although Sverdlov died a natural death in 1919, consider the fate of the actual murderers of the Imperial family in what can only be conceptualized as an "eye for an eye" justice.

Figure 23: Yakov Sverdlov in 1919, Chairman of the Secretariat of the Russian Communist Party (Bolsheviks). After Lenin, Sverdlov was the one person most responsible for the execution of the Russian Imperial family

Other than Sverdlov and Lenin himself, no other persons were more directly responsible for the murder of the Imperial family, by either insisting on their execution or carrying it out, other than the following bloodthirsty trio:

Yakov Yurovsky was the Ural Cheka chief; he actually took his Chekists to the Ipatiev House, armed them and led the shooting of the captive family. Yurovsky was arrested in the summer of 1930 in a roundup of intellectuals that included imminent technologists and economists, such as M. Ramzin, director of the Moscow Thermal-Technical Institute, and Nikolai Kondratiev, a noted economist. They were accused of "wrecking" as a "clandestine Industrial Party" that had been plotting to seize power.

Kondratiev was shot in 1938, and Yurovsky was either shot or died of a peptic ulcer that same year, depending on the Russian source of information.[32]

Aleksandr Beloborodov was the Ural Soviet District chief, who kept urging Moscow to authorize the execution of the Tsar and his family; he was purged and executed under orders of Stalin in 1938.[33]

Filipp Goloshchekin was a Commissar of the Urals. Like Comrade Beloborodov, Goloshchekin urged for the execution of the Tsar, and like his counterpart, the Ural Soviet District chief, he was also purged. He died in a concentration camp in 1941.[34]

One of the Three "Greatest Russians"

Under the entry for Joseph Vissarionovich Stalin in *The Encyclopedia of Revolutions and Revolutionaries,* editor Martin van Creveld summarized:

Stalin, as general secretary, convened the 17th Communist Party Congress, dubbing it 'the Congress of Victors.' In the 10-member Politburo chosen at the end of the Congress, only Stalin remained of those who had been included in the first post-Lenin Politburo a decade earlier... The wave of arrests and executions that followed was bolstered by draconian emergency laws proposed by Stalin. The blood purges lasted until Stalin's death, interrupted only by World War II, and in the end struck virtually every pre-existing institution in the Soviet Union: the Communist Party (98 of 135 central committee members were shot and 1,108 of the 1,966 delegates to the 17th Congress of the Communist Party were arrested and tried); the Red Army (3 of 5 marshals were executed, as were almost all the commanders of armies, and about one-third of the officer corps was arrested); the political police (two of its heads were purged); the governmental apparatus and cultural organizations.[35]

In 2008 a widely conducted poll in Russia found that third place for "the Greatest Russian" went to the greatest mass murderer not only of Russians but also of his communist comrades, Joseph Stalin.[36] First and second place went to the legendary Alexander Nevsky and, surprisingly, the assassinated Prime Minister, Pyotr Stolypin (1911), who served under Nicholas II, the last Tsar of Russia, respectively.[36]

Yet between 20 to 40 million sons and daughters of Russia were killed on orders from Stalin or lost their lives as a result of Soviet communism.

Russia needs to come to terms with its Stalinist and communist past, reject the lies, and face the stern and sobering reality of past repression, mass terror, and mass extermination of citizens for the principles of false equality, the deceptive brotherhood of workers, and other lies of communism.

Figure 24: Pyotr Stolypin, 3rd Prime Minister of the Russian Empire (1906–1911). He was assassinated while attending a performance of Rimsky-Korsakov's *The Tale of Tsar Saltan* at the Kiev Opera House. George Grantham Bain, Library of Congress

CHAPTER 4

THE EXECUTIONERS—
NIKOLAI YEZHOV AND LAVRENTI BERIA

Throughout the years of his dictatorship, Joseph Stalin had several loyal executioners in the secret police that not only carried out the dirty deeds of eliminating his real or imagined opposition but also stoked the fire of terror to various levels of intensity, depending on Stalin's caprice or arbitrariness at the moment.

After disposing of Genrikh Yagoda in 1936 for his delay in eliminating Nikolai Bukharin, who Lenin had once called "the favorite of the whole Party," Stalin chose Nikolai Yezhov to head the People's Commissariat of Internal Affairs, namely the NKVD, from 1936 to 1938.

But in Stalin's Russia, even the position of head of the NKVD was not beyond scrutiny and fraught with imminent risk of ruin and more likely death. All who held that position were eventually charged with disloyalty and eliminated. All, that is, except Lavrenti Beria, who survived Stalin.

Nikolai Yezhov (People's Commissar of Internal Affairs, NKVD; 1936–1938)

Stalin's Loyal Executioner: People's Commissar Nikolai Ezhov, 1895–1940 by Marc Jansen and Nikita Petrov provides numerous revealing insights into the life of Nikolai Yezhov and the nature of Soviet communism. By contrasting details about the life of Yezhov with the political times, the moral degeneracy of the Soviet leadership, the Communist Party and the secret police, the Soviet state is shown rotting from its evil communist ideology and moral perversion. This book will remain the authoritative source on the life of Nikolai Yezhov until the Russian archives are once again fully opened to scholars.[1]

The Great Terror of 1936–1938 was an unprecedented period in the chronicles of the USSR because of the sheer number of victims—the vast majority of which were communists and even Stalinists, who allegedly had not been sufficiently vigilant in rooting out "enemies of the people" in their midst. In other words, they had not been vigilant communists, and had not informed on or identified sufficient victims, purportedly potential opponents to Stalin's supreme authority.

Moreover, Stalin had decided to get rid of the Old Bolsheviks and Chekists that he no longer "trusted" or who stood in the way of his revisionist history of Soviet communism—a history where only Comrade Stalin would be allowed to stand shoulder to shoulder with the esteemed Lenin.

One must remember that the creation of the police state, political assassinations, arrests in the middle of the night, and the use of systematic torture and generalized terror began with the father of the October Revolution, Vladimir I. Lenin; and that "permanent revolution" was the invention of Leon Trotsky. The use of concentration or labor camps, the implementation of "revolutionary terror," the extermination of "class enemies," and the founding of the Cheka, the ruthless political police, were all instituted by the totalitarian state created by Lenin. Consequently, the Red Terror of 1918–1922, in which thousands perished, was primarily the work of "Iron Felix" Dzerzhinsky, the head of the Cheka; Red Army Commissar Leon Trotsky; and most of all the Starik (*старик*; old man) of Russian communism, namely Lenin.[2]

Figure 25: "Iron Felix" Dzerzhinsky (1877–1926), Chairman of the Cheka, the first Soviet secret police organization. RIA Novosti Archive

Thus, a precedent for the use of terror by the Soviet state was established early in its history. By 1936, Stalin needed an NKVD chief who not only would be personally loyal to him but also would not hesitate to exterminate what remained of the notable Old Bolsheviks, such as the "leftist" Trotskyites, Kamenev and Zinoviev; the "party swamp," Radek, Pyatakov, and "their followers"; and the "rightist bloc," Bukharin, Rykov, et cetera—who in Stalin's mind still posed a threat to his authority. The younger, ambitious, and amoral communist comrade, Nikolai Yezhov, was just the man Stalin needed to accomplish that horrendous task.[3]

According to Stalin, Genrikh Yagoda, who was the sanguinary NKVD chief from 1934 to 1936, had not acted fast enough during the Great Purge to expose and exterminate the contrived Trotskyite-Zinovievite-Bukharinite conspiracy following the assassination of Leningrad Party chief, Sergei Kirov, in December 1934. Yezhov assisted Yagoda in the investigations, interrogations, and the gathering of evidence. Using torture and threats, Yezhov extracted the needed confessions from the Bolsheviks, and pleased Stalin with his methods and results.

Figure 26: 1938 photo of Nikolai Ivanovich Yezhov, head of the NKVD (1936–1938). Yezhov was executed in 1940

The ambitious Yezhov soon displaced Yagoda as chief of the NKVD and served in that capacity from 1936 to 1938.[4] Yezhov performed his bloody symphony of terror satisfactorily and completely as required by Stalin, the great conductor. Later in the 1950s, this period would be labeled the Yezhovshchina, so as to make Yezhov responsible for the atrocities and "excesses" of the Great Purge.[5]

After the Great Purge was completed, which took about 18 months, Stalin knew enough about expediency to get rid of the now completely alcoholic, sexually perverted, and morally degenerate Yezhov.[6] Stalin conveniently maneuvered to "put the burden of guilt for the terror of 1937–1938 on the executors."[7] Besides, he knew there were always other "careerists" waiting in the wings; and in this case, willing to assume the mantle of NKVD chief. Lavrenti Beria, the next NKVD chief, followed Yezhov, just as Yezhov had followed in the footsteps of Yagoda. Beria rounded up, purged, and exterminated Yezhov's appointees, installed his "Georgia Gang" in the state security organ, and maintained his status in the Soviet communist hierarchy through his intelligence and cunning, virtually until Stalin's death in 1953.

Yagoda and Yezhov, and much later Beria, even with the assumption of power by the collective leadership in 1953, ended up with a bullet to the back of the head, the standard treatment for Soviet scapegoats as well as "traitors."

Yezhov fell from power because he was no longer needed; in fact, he had done an excellent job fulfilling and exceeding the quotas of victims set by Stalin to eliminate the "enemies of the people" throughout Russia from the top of the Soviet hierarchy in the Communist Party, the state security organs, the military, and the regional and district nomenklatura to the lower echelons of Soviet society. The paranoid and vengeful arm of Stalin was indeed long in time and geography because the episodes of purges and terror included captive nationalities in the 1930s to captive nations, such as Poland, Czechoslovakia, and Hungary, in the 1940s up to Stalin's death in 1953.[8]

Jansen and Petrov related that:

During the Great Terror of 1937–1938...approximately 1.5 million people were arrested; almost half of them were executed. The main executor of this gigantic operation was Stalin's state security chief of those years, Nikolai Yezhov.[9]

At the height of the terror, Yezhov made two, very telling, pronouncements, which spoke volumes about his character:

If during this operation an extra thousand people will be shot, that is not such a big deal, and better too far than not far enough.[9]

Therefore, the reader should not be surprised to learn that the Central Executive Committee voted to award Yezhov the Order of Lenin.[10] With the approval of the Politburo, the Order of Lenin was ceremoniously bestowed upon him on July 17, 1937, citing:

For his outstanding success in leading the NKVD organs in their fulfillment of government assignments.[10]

Stalin's Loyal Executioner is a portrait of evil that encompasses many faces. It is important to remember that Nikolai Yezhov was not created in a vacuum; he was a product of the evil philosophy of communism in the USSR, just like the "Gang of Four" was a product of communism in China under the Cultural Revolution of Mao Tse-tung and the mass extermination of the population was a product of communism in Cambodia under Pol Pot.

And as the reader will learn, the evil philosophy of communism, repression, and terror in the USSR continued under Yezhov's successor.

Lavrenti Beria (People's Commissar of Internal Affairs, NKVD; 1938–1946)

As Lavrenti Beria stood over Joseph Stalin's deathbed in early March 1953, witnesses observed that he could barely contain his pleasure in watching the leader edge toward his final moments of life.[11]

Amy Knight, a Senior Research Analyst at the Library of Congress, possesses a unique gift for elegant writing and turning revealing phrases, and demonstrates a keen understanding of the psychopathology of Soviet leaders, particularly Joseph Stalin, Nikita Khrushchev, and Lavrenti Beria, the subject of her exemplary biography, *Beria: Stalin's First Lieutenant*.

Joseph Stalin surrounded himself with malleable bureaucrats and communist minions to whom he effectively applied a "divide and conquer" strategy in an atmosphere of constant suspicion that not only threatened their existence with physical annihilation but also deterred disloyalty on the part of his lieutenants.

However, Lavrenti Beria was not the typical unimaginative follower. As an astute operative and as a fellow Georgian, Beria was steeped in the Georgian ideals of loyalty, betrayal, and fear of death and quickly divined his compatriot's psychopathology. Beria nurtured Stalin's fears, paranoia, and unquenchable need for praise, and used his abilities to accumulate power and ensure his personal survival.

Figure 27: Lavrenti Pavlovich Beria (1899–1953), People's Commissar of Internal Affairs (NKVD) of the Soviet Union between 1938 and 1946

Although Stalin and Beria were both from Georgia, they came from different regions of the Caucasus. Beria was 20-years Stalin's junior. A member of the next generation of Soviet leaders, Beria had no qualms about helping to exterminate the few remaining Old Bolsheviks, who could challenge Stalin's power or correct the version of revolutionary history the "Great Leader" (Vozhd) had set out to re-write to fit with his unfolding cult of personality.

Beria could use extreme measures of repression against his fellow countrymen, but unlike Stalin, he maintained close connections to Georgia. He protected his private fiefdom in the Transcaucasia as much as possible, which included Armenia, Azerbaijan and Georgia. Stalin overtly left Georgia behind, and became a Russian, embarking on his harsh Russification policy at the expense of the various nationalities, including Georgians.

Unlike Beria, Nikita Khrushchev ran his fiefdom in the Ukraine without concern for the Ukrainians or his fellow Russian countrymen, and did nothing to protect the region from the Bolshevik and Soviet onslaught.

During the 1920s and 1930s, Beria served as a police chief in the NKVD and Communist Party leader in Georgia and Transcaucasia. He won Stalin's confidence by enforcing the great leader's repressive measures, including the rapid industrialization of urban areas, the compulsory requisitioning of crops and foodstuffs from the peasantry, and the forced collectivization of the peasants' farms (*kolkhozes*).[11]

Beria managed to survive the Yezhovshchina, the Great Terror of 1937 to 1938, even though he narrowly escaped becoming one of its victims. In July 1938, Nikolai Yezhov, the NKVD chief in Moscow, signed an order to arrest Beria, who was party chief in Georgia. However, Sergei Goglidze, the Georgian NKVD chief and a trusted protégé (later one of the "Georgia Gang"), warned Beria.[12]

Beria bid his family goodbye at the Tbilisi airport, expecting to be arrested upon arrival in Moscow and executed. But instead of accepting that fate, he went directly to Stalin and convinced him to spare his life. Beria reminded the great leader how useful, exacting, and loyal he had been in efficiently carrying out party orders in Georgia and Transcaucasia. Shortly thereafter, instead of Beria, it was Yezhov who was purged; and Beria became the new NKVD chief.[13]

Beria quickly insinuated himself into Stalin's inner circle. He also promoted and furthered Stalin's personality cult to dizzying heights. Beria was the most powerful security chief in Kremlin history, until his fall from power in 1953.

As chief of the NKVD, Beria was nearly omniscient and omnipotent in the Soviet communist pantheon just below Stalin. He not only bore responsibility for internal repression, foreign intelligence, and counterintelligence but also oversaw the functioning of the concentration or slave labor camps of the Soviet Gulag system, which were so well described in Aleksandr Solzhenitsyn's masterpiece, *The Gulag Archipelago*.[2]

With the advent of World War II, Beria assumed the titanic task of evacuating the Russian defense and armament industries and moving them eastward as the German Wehrmacht advanced.[14]

In 1945, at the end of World War II, Stalin placed Beria in command of the Soviet atomic bomb project, including responsibility for atomic espionage, liaison with the Russian scientists that were assigned to the ultra-secret project, such as Igor Kurchatov, Petr Kapitsa, and Andrei Sakharov, who would later be known as the "father of the Soviet hydrogen bomb."[15]

Beria was also in charge of the special NKVD research centers for various projects (that is, the *sharashka*), where prisoner scientists were forced to work under the auspices of the NKVD.[15] For example, Aleksandr Solzhenitsyn, who was a trained mathematician and physicist, was forced to work in one of the *sharashka* while in captivity in the Gulag. Solzhenitsyn's experience was described in fictionalized form in his masterpiece, *The First Circle*.[16]

Figure 28: September 1931 photo of Lavrenti Beria holding Stalin's daughter Svetlana on his lap with Joseph Stalin in the background

Nevertheless, the testing and production of a Soviet atomic bomb remained Beria's first priority between 1945 and 1949. He completed the task with incredible success on August 29, 1949, leaving the West astounded by the rapid Soviet achievement that was years ahead of the time frame American intelligence estimates had forecast—namely, mid-1950 to mid-1953.[15] Beria also achieved full Politburo membership in 1946 and was awarded the Order of Lenin for his success in 1949.[15]

During the entire period, Beria also saw to it that Georgia and his native region of Mingrelia were protected as much as possible from the economic turbulence of the time, and made sure that his political allies governed in all of Transcaucasia.

In the first eight chapters of the book, Knight expounded on the rise of the man who became Stalin's first lieutenant in maintaining communist orthodoxy. In the remaining chapters, she described how Beria maneuvered through the maze of Kremlin politics after the Great Patriotic War and how, after Stalin's death, Beria attempted to initiate reforms and liberalize the Soviet Union, which proved to be his downfall.

After the war against Hitler was over, Joseph Stalin was ready once again to stoke the system of repression and re-implement terror on a grand scale, this time designed to include the repression of Russian Jews and the purging of not only the Soviet security apparatus but also members of his inner circle. Toward that end, Stalin concocted a series of conspiracies; some of which were interrelated. But only Stalin, the master conspirator and the great conductor of terror, knew where each conspiracy led and the ultimate objective. The concocted plots included the "Leningrad Affair"; the anti-Semitic, anti-cosmopolitan campaign; and the "Doctors' Plot" that enmeshed Jewish intellectuals, Communist Party members, state security organs, Kremlin doctors, and even the loyal, long-time chief of Stalin's personal bodyguards, General Nikolai S. Vlasik.[17]

Toward the end, Stalin began to mistrust Beria, and he concocted the so-called "Mingrelian conspiracy," which in Stalin's paranoid mind involved corruption of political leaders in Georgia, who were allies and protégés of Beria, and a treasonous separatist "bourgeois nationalist" movement with ties to Turkey.[17]

By 1950, of his inner circle only Georgy Malenkov and two newer members, Nikita Khrushchev and Nikolai Bulganin, still enjoyed Stalin's "confidence," but that trust hung capriciously over their heads like a sword of Damocles. Suspicion had already fallen on former comrades like Molotov, Voroshilov, Kaganovich, Mikoyan, and Beria. It seemed that the turmoil of the Jewish Doctors' Plot and the Mingrelian affair were the final strokes for Beria, who, perhaps with the connivance of Malenkov and Khrushchev, decided to act to protect themselves.[17]

Immediately after Stalin's death on March 5, 1953, Beria moved rapidly to seize power. And almost as suddenly, he became a liberal political reformer. He defended the rights of non-Russian nationalities, such as the Ukrainians and Georgians, vis-à-vis the former Russification policy of Stalin. He admitted that both the Jewish Doctors' Plot and the Mingrelian affair were concocted by Stalin's underlings and had those involved arrested.[18]

Beria then began to decentralize and dismantle the secret police and the Gulag system as part of his broader program of liberalization. He granted amnesty to a large category of Gulag political prisoners. With the repudiation of the Doctors' Plot, the doctors were released from prison, and the campaign of anti-Semitism was ended. Under Beria, de-Stalinization began at a faster pace than would be reestablished later under Khrushchev.[17,18]

But a crisis in East Germany provided Nikita Khrushchev with the needed pretext to challenge Beria's power in the Kremlin. Malenkov, who had been Beria's ally, was won over by Khrushchev's intrigues, as were some important segments of the Russian military, which had come to resent the prominence of Beria and his secret police.[19]

In the face of economic problems in East Germany in May 1953, Beria had recommended a radical liberalization policy to the communist East German leaders of the German Democratic Republic (GDR). Beria drafted and signed the "Measures to Improve the Political Situation in the GDR," which included the following six recommendations:

(1) Abandon the policy of forced construction of socialism; (2) Work for the creation of a united, democratic, peace-loving and independent Germany; (3) Stop forcing the creation of agricultural cooperatives, which have met with great resistance from the peasants; (4) End the policy of eliminating private capital, which is premature, and draw private capital into different areas of the economy, including agriculture; (5) Introduce broad steps to improve the financial system; and (6) Take broad measures to ensure individual citizens' rights and put an end to unjust and cruel judicial treatment; review cases of those already in prison.[19]

Additionally, Beria replaced the Russian military commander in East Germany with a civilian commissioner.[19]

But Beria had made a mistake. He had moved too fast in the liberalization of East Germany. The iron-fisted East German Chancellor Walter Ulbricht opposed the recommended reforms, and the contradictory statements confused the political situation, creating instability and fueling public discontent. Influenced by Beria's intended reforms, East German protestors, whose objectives now included not only economic liberalization but also the removal of the hardliner, communist Chancellor Ulbricht, took to the streets. By June 17, 1953, Soviet tanks rolled into East Germany to crush the rebellion.[19]

Malenkov, who now supported Khrushchev, along with Bulganin and Molotov, blamed Beria for the crisis in East Germany. Knight correctly asserted that "the East German crisis provided Khrushchev with the pretext for rallying opposition against Beria," and that Khrushchev and Molotov would later denounce Beria's program at the July 1953 Central Committee Plenum, "accusing him of turning against socialism and playing into the hands of the West by trying to create a united, neutral bourgeois Germany."[20]

Perhaps the most intriguing portion of Knight's book was the plot that Khrushchev successfully instigated against Beria and how he carried it out. Stalin's first Lieutenant had greatly underestimated Khrushchev, the former operative leader in the Ukraine, who had been brought to Moscow by Stalin only recently and as the current head of the Secretariat was now Beria's chief opponent in the Kremlin power struggle.

Figure 29: Georgy Malenkov in 1954, Premier of the Soviet Union (1953–1955). Dutch National Archives, The Hague

Khrushchev persuaded Malenkov, Molotov, and Bulganin to take an active role in the coup, while Kaganovich, Voroshilov, and Mikoyan assumed more passive roles, believing it to be more politically expedient not to interfere until the coup had been carried out.[21]

Beria was arrested by military men at a hastily convened meeting of the Presidium on June 26, 1953, only nine days after the East German insurrection was squelched by Russian troops. Khrushchev had been moving feverishly within the Politburo and the military to undermine and gather forces against Beria, who was uncharacteristically caught off guard and entered the Presidium without suspecting the plot and the coup that awaited him. Once inside the Presidium, MVD guards (security apparatus successor to the NKVD) posted outside were dismissed by Defense Minister Bulganin and replaced with military troops loyal to General K.S. Moskalenko and Soviet Marshal Georgy Zhukov, who had been brought into the plot. Beria's fate was sealed.[20,21]

Beria was arrested by the generals as former comrades lambasted him. Bulganin even gave his pistol to Leonid Brezhnev, who had been summoned and made aware of the plot, and who, in 1964, would replace Khrushchev as General Secretary of the Communist Party.[20] Most members of the Politburo were not privy to the plot, but quickly fell in line.

Figure 30: Lavrenti Beria, after his fall from power in June 1953 and branded "enemy of the people," on the July 20, 1953, cover of *Time* magazine. Time, Inc.

Following Beria's arrest, Khrushchev moved swiftly. He began arresting Beria's closest associates and purging the upper echelons of the MVD. Most of the top MVD officers remained loyal to Beria and were later executed. The only high ranking MVD officers to desert Beria immediately after his arrest were Sergei Kruglov and Ivan Serov, who were not considered part of the "Georgia Gang." For their acquiescence in the affair, Khrushchev later promoted them.[22]

The secret proceedings of the Central Committee dated July 2–7, 1953, remained locked in the Russian archives until 1991. Knight wrote:

It provides a fascinating and revealing picture of the events surrounding Beria's arrest, making it clear that Beria's opponents were still on very shaky ground at this point and were thus 'pulling out all the stops' to contrive a criminal case against Beria and persuade Central Committee members that they had done the right thing.[23]

The trials of Beria and his lieutenants were conducted *in camera* from December 18–23, 1953. To this day, controversy exists about whether Beria participated in the proceedings or had been executed along with his comrades by the time the trials took place six months after their arrest.[24]

Among the many charges levied against them, they were accused of attempting "to seize power and liquidate the Soviet worker-peasant system for the purpose of restoring capitalism and the domination of the bourgeoisie."[25]

Although Khrushchev adopted many of Beria's policies, including de-Stalinization, despite opposition from the Soviet nomenklatura, Knight shrewdly observed:

> *Khrushchev was incapable of making substantial reforms because he was too deeply cast in the Stalinist mold. Although he no longer relied on police terror, he quickly adopted the highly personalized, capricious, and autocratic style of the Soviet leadership that had characterized the Stalin period and never focused on the deeply rooted institutional problems.[26]*

Figure 31: Nikita Khrushchev in East Berlin in June 1963 while watching East German leader Walter Ulbricht at his 70th birthday. German Federal Archives

Khrushchev willingly carried out the collectivization and general repressive measures included in the bloody purges in 1937–1938. Like Stalin's other lieutenants, his hands were drenched with Ukrainian and Russian blood. In contrast to Stalin's other sycophantic lieutenants, Knight accurately summarized Beria's life in this manner:

If Beria was an exception, it was not because he was amoral, sadistic, and cruel. Rather, it was because he was intelligent, astute, and devoted to achieving power. He was also adept at the kind of court politics that prevailed in the Kremlin and below. His deviousness and two-faced behavior was an asset in this environment, particularly in dealing with Stalin. Beria never ceased to maintain his flattering tone—'As usual, you have hit the nail on the head, Joseph Vissarionovich' though by the end he was heaping scorn on Stalin behind his back.[27]

Beria: Stalin's First Lieutenant is a welcomed addition to Soviet history. Appropriately, Knight sagaciously ends her book with this concluding thought:

The habit of blaming everything on specific individuals rather than looking for the deeper causes of a corrupt and dysfunctional system dies hard in the former Soviet Union. Indeed the official portrayal of the August 1991 coup attempt reflects this tendency. The plotters, who included the head of the KGB, were declared traitors for "attempting to seize power"—the same charges leveled at Beria—though they were simply resorting to the well-established methods of settling power struggles that their predecessors used. The failure of the coup was hailed as a victory for democracy, which to some extent of course it was. But, as the case of Beria reminds us, it takes more than simply getting rid of a few "villains" at the top to change a political system. The long history of rule by dictatorial methods in the former Soviet Union has left an enduring legacy, which, despite the continued progress toward democracy, could affect its political evolution for years to come.[27]

A Victim of the Great Terror—A Literary Composite

Darkness at Noon by Arthur Koestler is a historic, psychological thriller that once again reminds us of Jacques Mallet du Pan's famous adage, "Like Saturn, the Revolution devours its children."[28] The novel is a political and psychoanalytic dissection of an old Bolshevik who is imprisoned and awaiting execution. In a larger context, Koestler wrote a vivid and brilliant condemnation of authoritarian socialism and communism— that is, nuances of the same evil political philosophy of collectivism—a spectral ideology that refuses to die, despite the crumbling of the Berlin Wall, the collapse of Soviet communism, and the disintegration of the USSR.

The book is both a literary masterpiece and a tour de force in intellectual historical drama. It is eloquently written, given the subject matter; and more intense than Aleksandr Solzhenitsyn's *One Day in the Life of Ivan Denisovich*[29]—although both dramas are fast moving and intensely emotive. Solzhenitsyn's little epic dealt with matters of injustice, imprisonment, useless labor, and hopelessness. Koestler's *Darkness at Noon* delves into themes such as the hypocrisy inherent in communist ideology; the individual versus the collective; and morality and political responsibility.

Figure 32: Arthur Koestler in 1969. Eric Koch for Anefo, Dutch National Archives, The Hague

The personal significance and historical context of this masterpiece was inextricably entwined with the life and career of the author. Arthur Koestler (1905–1983) was a Hungarian ethnic Jew, a journalist, and a former member of the German Communist Party.[30] Koestler became disillusioned when many of his communist friends and comrades, some of them Jews, were executed as enemies of the state during Stalin's purges in the 1930s. Koestler knew the men were loyal Party members and devoted communists, not traitors, even though they were made to confess imaginary political crimes. Many communists rationalized Stalin's crimes in the interest of the Party and ideology.

Koestler also participated in the Spanish Civil War, and was arrested by General Franco's forces in 1937. He was condemned to death, but unlike his comrades who had been recalled to Moscow and executed, Koestler was imprisoned for four months. During the months of confinement, he underwent a process of introspection and rejected communism. After his release, he broke from the Communist Party in 1938, and over the next two years, wrote the timeless classic, *Darkness at Noon.*

Koestler escaped from Occupied France in 1940 and reached England where he continued to write articles and books denouncing totalitarianism and communism. He gained fame as a great writer, and traveled widely espousing anti-communist political causes. In 1972, he was made a Commander of the Order of the British Empire.[31]

Koestler succinctly summarized his odyssey when he wrote:

I went to Communism as one goes to a spring of fresh water, and I left Communism as one clambers out of a poisoned river strewn with the wreckage of flooded cities and the corpses of the drowned.[32]

Koestler's historic novel revolves around the arrest, incarceration, and serial interrogations of a fictional character Nicholas Salmanovitch Rubashov, an old Bolshevik and apparatchik whose hands were not completely clean, and who had participated in bringing about the state of persecution and terror that recently ensnared him. Rubashov was sentenced to death by the Party. Flashbacks, reminiscences, introspection, and mental self-recriminations go around in his mind as he is interrogated while awaiting his fate. Florid phrases adorn the narrative like when Rubashov, during underground activities in Belgium, recalls "the smell of the harbour, a mixture of rotting seaweed and petrol,"[33] and remembers Lenin as "the old man with the slanting Tartar eyes."[34]

Rubashov also reminisces about the work he performed for the Party and "the Person of No. 1," (namely, Joseph Stalin). He faithfully served the Party and carried out the distasteful pragmatic decisions, but not all had gone well with Stalin. Rubashov had traveled to Germany to support the Communist Party there, had been arrested, and recalled to Moscow. In Belgium and elsewhere, he had enforced Party discipline on other "diversionist" members; he had sent hundreds to their deaths for failure to obey Party instructions; he had even obeyed orders to send supplies to enemies of communism, fascist Italy and Germany, by orders of the Party "because it was expedient to the Cause."[30] He had obeyed and informed on those who disagreed with the Party, even though he had thought those policies were wrong and harmful. In short, Rubashov had sacrificed his morality for the pragmatism and expediency of the Party.

The character of Rubashov was a composite of several executed Bolsheviks. In fact, Koestler wrote:

The characters in this book are fictitious. The historical circumstances which determined their actions are real. The life of the man N.S. Rubashov is a synthesis of the lives of a number of men who were victims of the so-called Moscow Trials. Several of them were personally known to the author. This book is dedicated to their memory. —Paris, October 1938-April, 1940.[35]

In the historical context, Lev Kamenev (1883–1936) and Gregory Zinoviev (1883–1936) immediately come to mind with superimposed echoes of Leon Trotsky. Perhaps it was Nikolai Bukharin that Koestler had in mind in the composite character.[36]

All in all the fictional character Rubashov behaved with more composure and courage than most of the Old Bolsheviks behaved when confronted by Stalin, his secret police, and the show trials. On the other hand, Koestler's own arrest and incarceration, inner rebellion, and rejection of communism in many ways parallels the mental odyssey and anguish of the prisoner Rubashov.

Darkness at Noon was credited with helping to turn the political tide against collectivism in Europe after its initial publication in 1940 as well as exposing the evil realities of Soviet communism to the world. I believe it did. Despite the fall of communism and the evil Soviet empire, Koestler's masterpiece remains timeless not only because of the emotive elements and the intense psychological drama but also because of the historic parallels.

Postscript

Given the barrage of media propaganda and Marxist ideology propounded by liberal academicians, many young people in the West today are embracing socialism and rejecting capitalism, mistakenly believing that it is more moral than free enterprise and a more compassionate philosophy than capitalism. Koestler's novel needs to be read. The fact that it is a fictionalized story might do for the present generation what George Orwell's *1984* has done for previous generations and continues to do—and that is, to warn about the evil seduction of collectivism and authoritarianism in any form.

Finally, one may not be surprised to learn that after Koestler's death the progressive academicians found ways to throw various slanderous accusations against him like they did with Whittaker Chambers and other disillusioned liberals. Koestler shattered their messianic dreams of a coming socialist utopia. Academe and the liberal press very seldom make distasteful imputations against progressive icons. Instead, they have a penchant to publish luminous obituaries full of fluff listing the various progressive causes espoused by their favored notable during his frequently vacuous existence. To his credit, Arthur Koestler does not fall into that category.

CHAPTER 5

STALIN AND NOTABLE EVENTS IN THE SPANISH CIVIL WAR (1936–1939)

Despite the cautious attitude of the Western democracies regarding involvement in the volatile situation in Spain in 1936, more than 35,000 volunteers from 52 countries flocked to Spain to fight in a war that they mistakenly believed would be the epic battle between fascism and freedom.[1] In *Deadly Illusions: The KGB Orlov Dossier Reveals Stalin's Master Spy,* John Costello and Oleg Tsarev described the inception of the International Brigades of the Spanish Civil War and related:

> *An indifferent Britain and nervous France sought to avoid clashing openly with Germany and Italy. All the help the so-called Loyalists received from the democratic countries was unofficial. The International Brigades, a rag-tag army of international volunteers whose socialist and Marxist convictions led many to their deaths among the Spanish olive groves, came from England and other European countries, besides including a large contingent from the United States calling itself the Abraham Lincoln Battalion.[2]*

The majority of the 35,000 foreigners that comprised the International Brigades were socialists and communists, as were most members of the Spanish Loyalist forces. In fact, the Brigades were organized by the Communist International, although their allegiance was ostensibly to the Second Spanish Republic and fought for the "Republican" cause. Journalist Dave Roos added, "More than 2,800 Americans, many who were members of the American Communist Party, crossed the Atlantic to volunteer as part of the Abraham Lincoln Brigade."[1] Additionally, the Loyalist (or Republican) forces contained a large contingent of anarchists from the city of Barcelona and the region of Catalonia in Spain. As we shall see, a young Englishman named George Orwell was one of the socialist volunteers who believed the romanticized version of the struggle but discovered that this could not be further from the truth.

Stalin and Notable Events in the Spanish Civil War (1936-1939)   59

Figure 33: Women anarchist militia (*milicianas*) from the region of Catalonia in Spain during the festive atmosphere that prevailed in July 1936

Costello and Tsarev succinctly explained why Joseph Stalin decided to risk involvement in the Spanish Civil War as well as why an NKVD General-Major named Alexander Orlov was dispatched to the Iberian Peninsula. They wrote:

> Stalin had answered the appeals from Madrid that summer, not out of conscience, but to further Soviet ambitions. He grudgingly dispatched arms and military advisors — including Alexander Orlov, now a General-Major—to assist the Spanish government with counterintelligence and guerrilla warfare operations.[2]

Years later, the same Alexander Orlov defected to the West and ostensibly switched allegiance from the USSR to the United States, denouncing Stalin and the crimes committed in the Soviet Union during the 1930s under the auspices of his former boss. Nevertheless, after his defection Orlov remained an elusive figure. His whereabouts were unknown for more than a decade, and despite this obscurity, Orlov was protected by the United States. Whether Orlov was a bona fide defector, a double agent, or an asylum-seeker has been debated in at least two major books.[2,3]

In Spain, Alexander Orlov headed and conducted numerous missions for Joseph Stalin and the Soviet Union. Two missions are particularly significant and will be discussed in some detail in this chapter.

The first mission involved the extermination of Soviet allies—namely, the anarchists and "leftist" Trotskyites—even though the factions were fighting against a common enemy, the Nationalists under General Francisco Franco.[4-6] Communist brigades of NKVD units working under Stalin's orders carried out the eliminations. The units were sent to Spain to wipe out former Soviet allies because Stalin no longer trusted them. Moreover, Stalin considered Trotsky and Trotsky's followers to be his number one enemy and therefore no quarter should be given to them. In fact, the exterminations of former friends and allies by the Soviet NKVD commandos was carried out with more avidity than when they fought the "fascist" forces of Generalissimo Franco.[4-6]

Figure 34: Portrait of Generalissimo Francisco Franco, "Caudillo." Biblioteca Virtual de Defensa, Madrid

Pavel Sudoplatov, the Soviet spymaster who held high positions in the state security apparatus, recalled:

From 1936 to 1939 there were two life-and-death struggles in Spain, Both of them civil wars. One pitted nationalist forces, led by Francisco Franco, aided by Hitler, against the Spanish Republicans, aided by communists. The other was a separate war among communists themselves. Stalin in the Soviet Union and Trotsky in exile each hoped to be the savior and the sponsor of the Republicans and thereby became the vanguard for the world communist revolution. We sent our young inexperienced Intelligence operatives as well as our experienced instructors. Spain proved to be a kindergarten for our future intelligence operations. Our subsequent intelligence initiative all stemmed from contacts that we made and lessons that we learned in Spain. The Spanish Republicans lost, but Stalin's men and women won. When the Spanish Civil War ended, there was no room left in the world for Trotsky.[4]

The other mission was carried out towards the end of the Spanish Civil War just before the defeat of the communists and prior to Orlov's defection. The NKVD general assisted Stalin in virtually robbing Spain of its gold reserves—that is, gold that had accumulated over centuries of Spanish history.

The Astounding Case of Soviet Defection Deception

In *Alexander Orlov: The FBI's KGB General*, former FBI agent Edward Gazur tried to prove the impossible—namely that Alexander Orlov was a true defector, a man who switched allegiances from the Soviet Union to America and repudiated international communism.[3]

Gazur ardently believed that Orlov, who became his friend and who Gazur came to view as a father figure, had genuinely cooperated with the FBI and the CIA. Gazur's own book, unfortunately, proved quite the opposite.

Moreover, Costello and Tsarev revealed that Orlov had a tacit agreement with Stalin—that is, Orlov would not reveal any intelligence secrets to the West and in turn Stalin's agents would not hunt him down or harm his family.[7] They wrote:

What Orlov did was to issue a blackmail threat to Stalin: [Orlov] sent a letter to Stalin and to the chief of the NKVD, Yezhov, warning Stalin that if they took revenge on his family or if they succeeded in murdering him, then Orlov had directed his lawyer to publish all the data known to him about Stalin's crimes, which he enumerated in the two 'thirty-seven-page' blackmail letters.[7]

According to Orlov's KGB dossier, the original letter Alexander Orlov sent to Yezhov in Moscow had survived. Costello and Tsarev further related:

In carefully penned Cyrillic characters, the letter was addressed to 'Strictly Personal To Nikolai Ivanovich Yezhov. Not To Be Opened By Anyone Else,' and initialed 'from SCHWED' (Orlov's operational code name.)[7]

However, the authors noted that interestingly the letter contained in the KGB dossier was now "eleven, not thirty-seven pages long with only a two-page attachment. No trace of the copy Orlov claimed to have sent to Stalin has been found….but the surviving letter made clear the substance of the threat that Orlov delivered."[7]

Years later in testimony before the U.S. Senate on September 28, 1955, Alexander Orlov denounced Stalin, who had annihilated many of his compatriots in the various purges.[8] But that testimony does not make him a genuine defector. Orlov never fully cooperated with U.S. authorities.

Sudoplatov explained:

His disappearance was of concern to us because Orlov was also aware of our NKVD network in France and Germany. He even knew of Philby, Maclean, Burgess, and Blunt and the state of their cooperation with us. His defection raised serious doubt whether Philby and his friends had been compromised. Yet in November 1938, Beria summoned me and among other instructions ordered me to stop any efforts to locate Orlov....The order from Beria was that the Central Committee had decided to leave him alone.[9]

Orlov never divulged to U.S. authorities any significant or timely intelligence information that would have been detrimental to the Soviet Union. His knowledge of the Cambridge Five as well as NKVD networks operating in France and Germany would have been disclosures of immense importance to the United States and the world at the time.

Costello and Tsarev concur:

If Orlov had broken faith with Lenin's Revolution and had given the secret list of underground Soviet agents to the FBI instead of withholding the information, he might single-handedly have changed the course of history. Had he blown the 'illegal' networks in 1938 he would have deprived Stalin of vital information from such agents as [Kim] Philby and the Rote Kapelle [Red Orchestra], which played a part in World War II. If he had exposed these Soviet underground networks, Stalin's agents might never have stolen the secrets of the atomic bomb.[10]

According to one CIA official, Alexander Orlov always remained the consummate professional. "Orlov never fully unburdened all his secrets...He only revealed what he wanted to reveal."[10]

Curiously, Gazur wrote his tome *after* an FBI colleague brought to his attention the book *Deadly Illusions*, which was based on KGB files opened to scholars at the time. *Deadly Illusions* presented Orlov in a very different light. Gazur was astonished and claimed, "What I read about Orlov and the man I knew personally and called a close friend seemed to be two entirely different people."[11] Indeed.

As previously stated, what Gazur wrote in his book, by commission or omission, actually indicted the KGB officer and revealed that Orlov had perpetrated one of the most astounding cases of defection deception in U.S. history. Nevertheless, Gazur's *apologia* for the elusive career of the KGB general should not be completely discounted by history researchers and scholars of communist historiography of the 20th century. One learns how the Soviet general survived in the United States, eluded the FBI and the CIA for 15 years while remaining virtually in hiding, and then managed to provide the FBI, CIA, and the Immigration and Naturalization Service (INS) with enough tidbits of information and circumlocution to enable him to remain in the United States.

Orlov passed on historical information and personal anecdotes, skillfully navigating himself among the Congressional committees and half-hearted debriefing sessions by American security agents, but he never revealed specific and timely details that would have been helpful to the U.S. or the West during the Cold War.

Orlov never once betrayed the USSR or any of the Soviet agents who had operated or were still operating against the U.S. and the West. More apropos, Orlov did not expose the British traitor Kim Philby or any others in the Cambridge spy ring, the Cambridge Five, who did so much harm to America and the West. Neither did Orlov expose specific Soviet operations undermining the security of the United States. Orlov did not even reveal to Gazur that he had traveled to England on a false American passport and had been the head of the London *rezidentura* from summer 1934 to fall 1935—not to mention that he had headed for a time the recruitment of the notorious spy ring and handled the British agents himself.[12]

Figure 35: NKVD General Alexander M. Orlov in an early 1930s photo for a fraudulent passport and *Rezident* in the Second Spanish Republic

Alexander Orlov served Stalin for more than a decade before he allegedly defected. He not only exterminated the Trotskyites and anarchists in Spain but also masterfully plundered the Spanish treasury towards the end of the war. Three-fourths of Spain's gold reserves were moved to the USSR on Stalin's order and with the consent of the Spanish communist leaders in the Republican (Loyalist) government, which wanted the Soviets to "safeguard" the Spanish gold since Franco's Nationalist army was rapidly advancing towards Madrid.[13]

Approximately 7,900 boxes, each containing 145 pounds of gold cast ingots and gold coins, a fabulous national wealth accumulated through the centuries and extending all the way back to Spain's *Siglo de Oro*, were "transferred" by the communist leaders of "Republican" Spain to the USSR for "safe keeping."[14]

Needless to say, the Soviet Union (and now Russia) never returned the gold. As Stalin told Nikolai Yezhov, "They will never see their gold again, just as they do not see their own ears."[15] To their everlasting shame and for their unforgivable betrayal of their country—not to mention incredible stupidity—the Spanish communist leaders in the Republican (Loyalist) government had made a tragic blunder of gargantuan proportions.

Stalin's "Horrible Secret"

Costello and Tsarev also contend that Joseph Stalin harbored a "horrible secret," namely that as a young revolutionary the Red dictator had been an informant for the Tsarist secret police, the Okhrana. There is some evidence to support the claim that Stalin might have collaborated and informed on fellow revolutionaries prior to the October 1917 Russian revolution but as previously discussed in chapter 1, that contention remains sketchy and not totally convincing.

Figure 36: Marshal Mikhail N. Tukhachevsky in 1936, a Hero of the Soviet Union, executed by Stalin in 1937

Suffice to say that as a result of this "secret" becoming known to several top communist Politburo and Soviet military leaders, Marshal Mikhail N. Tukhachevsky, a Hero of the Soviet Union, and seven Red Army generals became involved in a plot to overthrow Stalin.[10] In the minds of the conspirators, Stalin's secret could have provided the needed justification for involvement in a coup d'état.

However, the conspirators were betrayed, and the ill-fated plot was nipped in the bud before it could come to fruition. On June 11, 1937, Moscovites were stunned to learn that Marshal Tukhachevsky and seven other generals had been arrested. Later that same day, a special military tribunal was convened that quickly convicted the "traitors." On June 12, they were summarily executed for plotting a coup to rid Russia of one of the worst mass murderers in history, Joseph Stalin.[16,17]

Yet, this episode contains another twist. Although Stalin's henchmen in the NKVD were credited with unraveling the plot, behind the scenes they may have received assistance or disinformation, depending on one's point of view, from the Nazi secret service.

Figure 37: Walter Schellenberg (left) in September 1943, head of foreign intelligence for Nazi Germany; and SS Chief Reinhard Heydrich (right), circa 1940-1941. Kurt Alber and Heinrich Hoffmann, German Federal Archives

Walter Schellenberg, head of the German Secret Service, revealed in his memoirs that SS Chief Reinhard Heydrich learned about Tukhachevsky's plot to overthrow Stalin. Schellenberg wrote, "Heydrich at once grasped the tremendous importance of this piece of intelligence. If used correctly, a blow could be stuck at the leadership of the Red Army from which it would not recover for many years."[18] Schellenberg continued:

> To unmask Tukhachevsky might be helping Stalin to strengthen his forces or might equally well push him into destroying a large part of his general staff. Hitler finally decided against Tukhachevsky and intervened in the affairs of the Soviet Union on Stalin's side.[18]

Schellenberg noted that the decision to expose the plot to Stalin was a major turning point in German-Soviet relations until Operation Barbarossa in 1941: "It eventually brought Germany into a temporary alliance with the Soviet Union and encouraged Hitler to attack the West before turning against Russia. Once Hitler made that decision, Heydrich of course supported him."[18]

For Heydrich, the goal of the destruction of the Soviet military leadership was accomplished. As we will see in subsequent chapters, Heydrich's gamble paid handsome dividends when Hitler launched Operation Barbarossa, at least initially.

In *Stalin: The Court of the Red Tsar*, Montefiore summarized the episode:

> The army had been the last force capable of stopping Stalin, reason enough for the destruction of its High Command. It is possible that the generals knew about Stalin's record as an Okhrana double agent and had considered action. The usual explanation is that German disinformation persuaded Stalin that they were plotting a coup. Hitler's spymaster, Heydrich, had concocted such evidence that was passed to Stalin by the well-meaning Czech President Beneš. But no German evidence was used at Tukhachevsky's trial—nor was it necessary.[17]

Stalin needed no evidence. He turned the NKVD loose on the Red Army and the purges escalated. As we will see in subsequent chapters, Stalin will pay a price for decapitating the leadership of the Soviet Red Army.

Orwell and *Homage To Catalonia*

Homage To Catalonia is George Orwell's memoir about his involvement in the Spanish Civil War as an English member of the 29th Division of the Party of Marxist Unification (POUM; *Partido Obrero de Unificación Marxista*)—a radical socialist, internationalist organization. Later, POUM was denounced by the Stalinist communists as being a

"Trotskyite organization and Franco's Fifth Column" because it contained a few internationalist Jewish members that followed Trotsky rather than Stalin in Marxist orthodoxy and world revolution.[19] Orwell noted that "the charge was repeated over and over in the Communist Press, especially from the beginning of 1937 onwards. It was part of the world-wide drive of the official Communist Party against 'Trotskyism,' of which POUM was supposed to be representative in Spain," adding that "anyone who criticizes Communist policy from a Left-wing standpoint is liable to be denounced as a Troskyist."[20]

Orwell wrote about the six-month period from late December 1936 to June 1937. During that time, he fought against Franco's rebellious "fascist" army in the Aragon Front of Catalonia. *Homage to Catalonia* does not include the beginning or the end of the Spanish Civil War.

Orwell was seriously wounded by a shot fired from a sniper and described the incident: "Roughly speaking it was the sensation of being *at the centre* of an explosion. There seemed to be a loud bang and a blinding light all round me, and I felt a tremendous shock—no pain, only a violent shock, such as you get from an electric terminal…"[21] The bullet entered and exited his neck causing considerable damage, and it took many weeks for him to recover. He was taken from the front to one facility and then transferred to another for medical care. After recuperating in various military hospitals, he returned to Barcelona.[21]

In Barcelona, Orwell received his medical discharge papers, but also discovered a very troubling fact. Barcelona was now a changed city. Formerly, when the anarchists had been in power, there had been a jubilant, more relaxed, egalitarian, and revolutionary comradeship among people, army, workers, police, et cetera. Now, the situation had changed for the worse. Orwell stated:

In Barcelona, during all those last weeks I spent there, there was a peculiar evil feeling in the air—an atmosphere of suspicion, fear, uncertainty, and veiled hatred…a perpetual vague sense of danger, a consciousness of some evil thing that was impending.[22]

The communists had definitely come into power and had created a reign of terror. No one was safe. The Caballero Spanish "Republican" government had fallen, giving way to the new regime of Juan Negrín López that was controlled by Stalin and his long arm of the Soviet secret police, the NKVD. The Negrín government was simply subservient to Stalin, who was providing them with military support and arms.

Former revolutionaries and militia members were being persecuted, accused of being Trotskyites, arrested, and many were being shot by the

Soviet NKVD or the subservient Spanish communist secret police, which were actively operating in "Republican" areas of Spain, prior to Franco's victory. One of the chiefs of the secret NKVD "flying squads" of professional assassins was none other than Alexander Orlov.[23]

Moreover, some socialist and even diversionary communist leaders were disappearing in dungeons or being executed. "On June 16, 1937, Andreu Nin Pérez and 40 other POUM leaders were arrested, their militia battalions were disbanded and their headquarters at the Hotel Falcon in Barcelona closed…POUM was promptly declared illegal."[23]

All POUM members were now being rounded up. Orwell was being sought merely for fighting with the socialist POUM battalion. Please note: Orwell was not having to escape from the fascists, but from his former communist comrades, who were eliminating their previous allies, the socialists and anarchists. Orwell related that, "The notion of 'liquidating' or 'eliminating' everyone who happens to disagree with you does not yet seem natural. It seemed only too natural in Barcelona. The 'Stalinists' were in the saddle, and therefore it was a matter of course."[24]

After a terrible ordeal of being pursued by his former leftist allies, George Orwell successfully escaped to France, and eventually made his way back to England.

Despite the trials and tribulations Orwell experienced during his brief six months in Spain, he made several observations that deserve mention before closing the chapter. Orwell wrote:

> *I record this, trivial though it may sound, because it is somehow typical of Spain—of the flashes of magnanimity that you get from Spaniards in the worst of circumstances. I have the most evil memories of Spain, but I have very few bad memories of Spaniards….They have, there is no doubt, a generosity, a species of nobility, that do not really belong to the twentieth century…Few Spaniards possess the damnable efficiency and consistency that a modern totalitarian state needs.[25]*

Additionally, Orwell noted how easily situations could lead to conflicting thoughts, noting that although the arrests, raids, and searchers "were continuing without pause" and the police were even "boarding the French ships that periodically took off refugees and seizing suspected 'Trotskyists' "; yet, as an Englishman, he maintained the "ineradicable English belief that 'they' cannot arrest you unless you have broken the law." However, Orwell concluded that, "It is a most dangerous belief to have during a political pogrom."[25]

In summary, the first priority of the Soviet communists controlling the Spanish government was not fighting Franco's army but the extermination of anarchists and Trotskyites (mostly internationalist, Jewish socialist revolutionaries). The anarchists were considered enemies because their political philosophy was diametrically opposed to that of the communists, and they refused to give up their weapons.

Figure 38: George Orwell, introducing a literary program on the BBC, circa 1940

It is extremely fortuitous for the ones living in freedom that George Orwell, the author and the participant, survived the conflict with his eyes opened to the realities of socialism and communism. Orwell would go on to write *Animal Farm* and *1984*, denouncing collectivism, totalitarianism, and communism.[26,27] It was a mistake for the Stalinists to incorrectly label Orwell a Trotskyite merely because he had been assigned to an international socialist POUM battalion—but their mistake was a gain for liberty in general and literature in particular.

After safely returning to England—that is, southern England and the tranquil environs of his childhood—George Orwell prophetically expressed concerns for coming world events: "Sometimes I fear that we shall never wake till we are jerked out of it by the roar of bombs."[28]

CHAPTER 6

STALIN'S SECRET AGENTS IN THE FDR ADMINISTRATION

Stalin's Secret Agents: The Subversion of Roosevelt's Government was written by two recognized authorities on the Cold War, M. Stanton Evans and Herbert Romerstein. Evans was a veteran journalist, broadcaster, and the author of eight books, including *Blacklisted by History* (2009), a biography of Senator Joseph McCarthy. Romerstein was the former head of the Office to Counter Soviet Disinformation at the U.S. Information Agency and a congressional staffer on the U.S. House Intelligence Committee. Their collaboration produced a shocking exposé that not only corrects and augments the incomplete and distorted historic record but also reveals the true moral character of a number of Americans who betrayed the nation for a venal ideology based on lies—namely, communism.[1]

Stalin's Secret Agents documents the degree of penetration in the U.S. government by American traitors and Soviet spies, and the extent of subversion high up in the Franklin Delano Roosevelt (FDR) administration by "agents of influence," who were subservient to Stalin and the USSR. It is an inimical tale of repeated betrayal that the authors recount in an enthralling narrative using crisp and succinct prose.

Evans and Romerstein record how the agents of influence were able to do so much damage by covertly or overtly influencing policy decisions at the highest levels in the U.S. government. In fact, Whittaker Chambers, an American journalist, and former member of the Communist Party who spied for the Soviets, but in 1938 "defected" from the Soviet underground, noted in his 1952 memoir *Witness*:

> *That power to influence policy has always been the ultimate purpose of the Communist Party's infiltration. It was much more dangerous, and, as events have proved, much more difficult to detect, than espionage, which beside it is trivial, though the two go hand in hand.*[2]

Although some naive individuals in the West may consider agents of influence to be merely unwitting, innocent idealists, the KGB does not.

They recognize that these individuals are willing to betray their country based on ideology and, therefore, can serve as valuable Soviet agents. They nurture these individuals and tend to their distorted psychological needs.

Figure 39: Portrait of Franklin Delano Roosevelt in the early 1930s. Vincenzo Laviosa, Getty Center

In the case of the Roosevelt administration, the agents of influence operated under the aegis of the President of the United States. Indeed, FDR surrounded himself and suffused the Executive Branch with communists, Soviet agents, and "fellow travelers," who did untold damage to America and the free world.[2]

According to the Mitrokhin Archive:

On September 2, 1939, the day after the outbreak of war in Europe, Whittaker Chambers had told much of what he knew about Soviet espionage in the United States to Adolf Berle, Assistant Secretary of State and President Roosevelt's adviser on internal security. Immediately afterwards, Berle drew up a memorandum for the president, which listed Alger Hiss, Harry Dexter White, and other leading Soviet agents for whom Chambers had acted as courier. One of those on the list was a leading presidential aid, Lauchlin Currie. Roosevelt, however, was not interested. He seems to have dismissed the whole idea of espionage rings within his administration as absurd.[2]

Taking a cue from the president, Berle did not even send a copy of his memorandum to the Federal Bureau of Investigation (FBI) until it was requested by the agency in 1943.[2]

Foremost among the Soviet agents was presidential aide and FDR's closest wartime adviser, Harry Hopkins. During World War II, much of America's foreign policy toward the United Kingdom and the USSR was virtually dictated by Hopkins, who also lived in the White House from 1941 to 1943.

Figure 40: Photograph of President Franklin D. Roosevelt and Harry Hopkins in the back seat of an automobile in Rochester, Minnesota, in September 1938. Associated Press, Library of Congress

As Roosevelt's closest confidant, Hopkins attended the major conferences held by the Allied powers, including the Casablanca Conference in January 1943; the November 1943 Cairo Conference and the back-to-back Tehran Conference from November 28 to December 1, 1943; and the Yalta Conference in February 1945.

At the Quebec Conference in August 1943 between FDR and British Prime Minister Winston Churchill, an American policy paper written by Hopkins was carried into the meeting. Among other things, the document stated:

Russia's post-war position in Europe will be a dominant one. With Germany crushed, there is no power in Europe to oppose her tremendous military forces. The conclusions from the foregoing are obvious. Since Russia is the decisive factor in the war, she must be given every assistance and every effort must be made to obtain her friendship.[3,4]

Evans and Romerstein summed up what the U.S. position meant:

In official U.S precincts, the impending dominance of Soviet power in Europe was not something to be combated, deplored, or counterbalanced, but rather an outcome to be accommodated and assisted.[3,4]

That policy was seconded by FDR, who stated to William Bullitt, his first envoy to Moscow:

I think that if I give him [Stalin] everything I possibly can and ask for nothing from him in return, noblesse oblige, he won't try to annex anything and will work for world democracy and peace.[5]

Apparently, British Prime Minister Winston Churchill, a veteran geostrategist, was the only Allied leader concerned about the growth of burgeoning Soviet power and to recognize its potential danger to post-war Europe.[6] Churchill presaged the great tragedy of World War II when he wrote:

After all the exertions and sacrifices of millions of people, and of victories of the Righteous cause, we will not have found peace and security and that we lie in the grip of even worse perils than we have surmounted.[7]

Unfortunately, by the time of the Tehran and Yalta conferences, FDR had begun to distance himself from Churchill, to make common cause with Joseph Stalin, and "adopted an increasingly hostile attitude toward London in his effort to placate Moscow."[8] As history revealed, the fates of millions of people worldwide were adversely affected by that serious misjudgment.

The enormity of Harry Hopkins' influence and power within the Roosevelt administration cannot be overstated. William Rusher, a distinguished fellow at the Claremont Institute for the Study of Statesmanship and Political Philosophy, accurately wrote in rebuttal to those defending Hopkins in the mainstream American media and academia:

But there are still many people alive who can remember when the chief confidant of President Franklin Roosevelt was a man named Harry Hopkins. And they will be understandably astonished to learn that in a message dated May 29, 1943, Iskhak Akhmerov, the chief Soviet 'illegal' agent in the United States at the time, referred to an Agent 19 who had reported on discussions between Roosevelt and Winston Churchill in Washington at which the agent had been present. Only Harry Hopkins meets the requirements for this agent's identity. Small wonder that Akhmerov, in a lecture in Moscow in the early 1960s, identified Hopkins by name as 'the most important of all Soviet wartime agents in the United States.'[9]

Unaware that Hopkins was considered a Soviet agent by the KGB[9], he has nevertheless been described as an agent of influence and sometimes reluctantly labeled an "unconscious agent" of Soviet influence or even a patriot by some historians.[10,11] Ideological and moral excuses were concocted to shield Hopkins so that the image of FDR as a four term, popular American president would not be tarnished. After all, Roosevelt had presided over America's recovery from the Great Depression, and he was the U.S. president through most of World War II. Describing Harry Hopkins as a full-fledged communist agent would constitute a major blow to the confidence the free world had placed in America's determination to contain communism and preserve freedom.

In addition to Hopkins, Evans, Romerstein, and Breindel catalog the treasonous activities of other Soviet spies and agents of influence in the FDR administration, such as Assistant Secretary of the Treasury, Harry Dexter White; Administrative Assistant to the President, Lauchlin Currie; influential member of the Institute for Pacific Relations (IPR), Owen Lattimore; Treasury official, Solomon Adler; State Department official, Alger Hiss; and Duncan Lee, a Soviet spy in the Office of Strategic Services (OSS; the precursor to the CIA during the World War II). Those agents were willing to do the bidding on behalf of Stalin and the Kremlin at the expense of their own country.[12,13]

And for the most part, the agents of influence were not publicly exposed or punished for their betrayal—some fled the country while others remained at their posts for years.[13] The mounting evidence of their treason has not been properly archived or published in the history textbooks, resulting in an incomplete and distorted historical record.[12,13]

The shocking revelations documented by Evans and Romerstein are consistent with the intelligence provided by previous Soviet defectors, such as Oleg Gordievsky, Stanislav Levchenko, and Victor Kravchenko[14]; disclosed in the Vassiliev papers[15] and the Mitrokhin Archive[16];

substantiated by the decrypted Venona transcripts[17]; and corroborated by citations in congressional committee reports.[18]

Figure 41: Economist Lauchlin Currie in 1939, Administrative Assistant to President FDR, Assistant Director of the Federal Reserve Board's Division of Research and Statistics, agent of influence and Soviet asset, who helped betray China to the communists. Harris & Ewing Photographs, Library of Congress

There are other disturbing disclosures contained in *Stalin's Secret Agents*. Let us consider the following three examples:

First, how "war hawks" in the FDR administration, including Harry Dexter White, not only deliberately blocked Japan from access to oil imports and other raw materials crucial for its economy but also froze Japanese holdings in the U.S. banking channels.[19] In 1941, deprived of oil and vital resources Japan was forced to go to war as the "only alternative to economic strangulation and political revolution."[19] Japan was then manipulated into attacking the U.S. instead of turning its forces toward Russia thereby preventing the USSR from being invaded from the East and crushed between two fronts.[19]

To understand how this came about one must return briefly to the eve of World War II and a little-known conflict called the Nomonhan Incident by the Japanese or the Battle of Khalkhin Gol by the Russians.[20]

Figure 42: Harry Dexter White working for the U.S. Treasury in 1939 while spying for the Soviet Union. Harris & Ewing Photographs, Library of Congress

The Battle of Khalkhin Gol and Operation Snow

From May 11 to September 16, 1939, an undeclared war between Japan and the Soviet Union raged close to the Manchurian-Mongolian frontier. However, the Battle of Khalkhin Gol was more than a mere border skirmish and had far-reaching military consequences. Troops from the Imperial Empire of Japan and the Soviet Union clashed in the vicinity of the village of Nomonhan and fought to a climax on August 20-31, 1939. Over 100,000 soldiers were involved in the fighting. The Japanese army was decisively defeated by the elite Siberian Soviet army units led by Marshal Georgy Zhukov, who was awarded the Hero of the Soviet Union medal, his first of four.[20,21]

The drubbing the Japanese had suffered at Khalkhin Gol two years earlier in 1939 was probably still foremost in their minds in 1941 and convinced them to proceed with the southern strategy for the conquest of the Far East and the Pacific, rather than the invasion of Siberia, where the Soviets still kept their best troops.[21]

After the defeat in Mongolia and other concerns—among them, the vast supplies of oil and raw materials available in Southeast Asia that Japan desperately needed—the reasons why the Japanese navy's arguments for a southern naval strategy prevailed over the army's Northern Siberian military strategy becomes obvious and explains why the Japanese chose to invade Southeast Asia, instead of attacking Siberia and the USSR, as Hitler and the German High Command had wanted. If the Japanese armies had turned toward Russia, the Soviet Union could have been crushed between two fronts in 1941—that is, the Germans invading from the West and the Japanese invading from the East.

Figure 43: Japanese soldiers creeping in front of wrecked Soviet armored cars in the Battle of Khalkhin Gol, July 1939. Dōmei Tsushin, Empire of Japan

Moreover, the Japanese attack on Pearl Harbor and the entrance of the U.S. into World War II would have been delayed or, possibly, if the attack had not taken place at all, the U.S could have stayed out of the war longer, increasing the chances of an Axis victory.

Nevertheless, the Imperial Empire of Japan marched its army southward into Southeast Asia and turned its air force against the U.S. at Pearl Harbor, sparing the Soviet Union and propelling America into war against the Axis powers.[19] And, as we have seen, there were other factors at work inside the FDR administration, namely the Soviet spy and agent of influence, Assistant Secretary of the Treasury Harry Dexter White, who helped to pushed the Japanese into a corner by deliberately blocking access to oil and other vital resources.[19] Thus, Operation Snow, the deep Soviet plot that sought to "divert the Japanese into fighting the Americans rather than the Russians" manipulated the island nation into attacking the United States and prevented the USSR from being attacked and crushed between two fronts.[19]

Figure 44: U.S. President Franklin D. Roosevelt signing the declaration of war against Japan, December 8, 1941. Abbie Rowe, National Archives and Records Administration

The Betrayal of Eastern Europe and Nationalist China

We have discussed in detail the provocation of Japan to attack the United States. Let us now consider other disturbing disclosures contained in *Stalin's Secret Agents* and other sources already cited about imperiling the security of the West in general and the United States in particular by the betrayal of other nations to the communist powers.

Second, agents of influence inside the White House and the U.S. State and Treasury departments, such as Harry Hopkins, Alger Hiss, Harry Dexter White, and others, militated to successfully allow Stalin to seize and enslave parts of Central Europe and all of Eastern Europe, including Czechoslovakia and Poland—the same countries that Nazi Germany's invasions had triggered France and England's declaration of war and started World War II. For extra measure, the Soviet agents of influence inside FDR's administration doomed efforts by the anti-communist underground forces in Poland and in Yugoslavia, where anti-communist leader Draza Mihailovich was betrayed to the communist forces headed by Marshal Tito and was subsequently shamefully executed by Tito in 1946.[22]

Figure 45: Alger Hiss, accused Soviet spy, testifying in 1948 and convicted of perjury in 1950. New York World-Telegram & Sun Collection, Library of Congress

Third, we should not fail to mention how Nationalist leader Chiang Kai-shek was deliberately calumniated, abandoned, and betrayed; and how China was turned over to the communists and Mao Tse-tung by the agents of influence, particularly Owen Lattimore, Solomon Adler, Harry Dexter White, and the diplomat and "fellow traveler," John Stewart Service. Those men spread disinformation about alleged venal conditions in the Nationalist government, calumniated Chiang Kai-shek, and praised Mao Tse-tung.[23] Information from defectors and the Venona files verify what Evans and Romerstein document, namely that a concerted campaign of disinformation was created and propagated by the agents of influence to tilt American opinion away from Chiang and the American government away from rendering the needed assistance to the Nationalists, while helping Mao seize control of China.[23]

Stalin and the Atomic Bomb

Robert B. Farquhar, an anti-nuclear activist, wrote a book on nuclear weapon proliferation titled *Duck and Cover: A Pictorial History of Nuclear Weapons*. In the book Farquhar asserted that, "In 1946, the U.S. had about 7 atomic bombs, none completely assembled; by 1956, 5,000, all assembled; Russia had about 150."[24]

However, based on intelligence provided by the atomic bomb spies, including physicists Klaus Fuchs and Theodore Hall, Stalin and Beria estimated that the number of atomic bombs possessed by the United States at that time was much lower.

Figure 46: Los Alamos badge photo of Klaus Fuchs, convicted Soviet spy. Los Alamos National Laboratory, U.S. Department of Energy

Pavel Sudoplatov, deputy director of Soviet Foreign Intelligence and director of the Administration Special Tasks ("wet affairs") from 1939 to 1942; head of the Intelligence Bureau of the Special Committee of the USSR on Atomic Problems (1942–1946); and a protégé of Lavrenti Beria from 1939 to 1953, offered the following glimpse into Stalin's reasoning and geopolitical strategy at the time:

> *Atomic espionage was almost as valuable to us in the political and diplomatic spheres as it was in the military. When [Klaus] Fuchs reported the unpublished design of the bomb, he also provided key data on the production of uranium 235. Fuchs revealed that American production was one hundred kilograms of U-235 a month and twenty kilos of plutonium per month. This was of the highest importance, because from this information we could calculate the number of atomic bombs possessed by the Americans. Thus, we were able to determine that the United States was not prepared for a nuclear war with us at the end of the 1940s or even in the early 1950s.[25]*

Additionally, Sudoplatov stated:

> *Stalin pursued a tough policy of confrontation against the United States when the Cold War started; he knew he did not have to be afraid of the American nuclear threat, at least until the end of the 1940s. Only by 1955 did we estimate the stockpile of American and British nuclear weapons to be sufficient to destroy the Soviet Union.*
>
> *That information helped to assure a Communist victory in China's civil war in 1947–1948. We were aware that President Harry Truman was seriously considering the use of nuclear weapons to prevent a Chinese Communist victory. Then Stalin initiated the Berlin crisis, blockading the Western-controlled sectors of the city in 1948. Western press reports indicated that Truman and Clement Attlee, the British prime minister, were prepared to use nuclear weapons to prevent Berlin's fall to communism, but we knew that the Americans did not have enough nuclear weapons to deal with both Berlin and China. The American government overestimated our threat in Berlin and lost the opportunity to use the nuclear threat to support the Chinese Nationalists.*
>
> *Stalin provoked the Berlin crisis deliberately to divert attention from the crucial struggle for power in China...He was preoccupied with the idea of a Sino-Soviet axis against the Western world.[25]*

Therefore, the Soviets believed that America's seven atomic bombs either could not be assembled rapidly enough to make a difference or the United States did not have enough uranium and plutonium for two or three simultaneous theaters of operation; and the information emboldened Stalin and Beria to be more belligerent.[25]

As noted, the nuclear stockpile misinformation helped to assure a communist victory in China in the civil war of 1947–1948, and Mao Tse-tung, with Soviet assistance, prevailed over the Nationalist leader Chiang Kai-shek. The Soviets believed the United States did not possess enough atomic bombs or fission material to confront them simultaneously in Eastern and Central Europe, Berlin, and China, but that assessment was incorrect. Although, the Russians had seriously underestimated U.S. nuclear capabilities in the late 1940s and early 1950s, despite their well-placed spies, the reality was that, after the atomic explosions at Hiroshima and Nagasaki in 1945, the U.S. was no longer willing to use nuclear weapons to roll back or even contain communism, except in the case of overwhelming Soviet aggression against either the United States itself or its allies in Europe.

The U.S. could have used the atomic bomb in China during the civil war or years later during the Korean War, but American leaders were not like the Soviet leaders. President Harry Truman sanctioned the use of the atomic bombs only after experts estimated that avoiding an Allied invasion of the Japanese mainland would save at least one million lives. Debate over that analysis continues to this day.

Figure 47: Pavel A. Sudoplatov, NKGB/MGB lieutenant general and Soviet master spy. Ministry of Defence of the Russian Federation, Mil.ru

Shortly before his death in 1953, Stalin was close to unleashing another holocaust in Russia with his concocted plot against the Jewish doctors.[26] But one must also consider that after the successful detonation of the Soviet atomic bomb in 1949, the frightening possibility existed that Joseph Stalin could also unleash another global conflict—namely, World War III where a Sino-Soviet axis might wage war against the Western world.[25]

Aftermath

Because the Soviets believed that the U.S. would not hesitate to use atomic weapons at any serious provocation from the Soviet or Chinese communist powers, the fact remained that America's nuclear arsenal posed a deterrent to Stalin in 1946–1953, as it did during the Khrushchev (1954–1964) and Brezhnev years (1964–1982) as well as their successors. America's nuclear deterrent prevented the powerful Red Army from overrunning Europe and protected the free world until the Berlin Wall came tumbling down and the evil empire disintegrated from within.

However, the U.S. did not learn about the nuclear weapons gap in America's favor until Soviet Colonel Oleg Penkovsky revealed the secrets of Soviet ordnance and rocketry (1961), and the methodology of nuclear construction by which, for example, the Central Intelligence Agency deciphered the meaning of the U-2 photos during the Cuban Missile Crisis in October 1962.[27]

Figure 48: Photograph of GRU Colonel Oleg Penkovsky, code name: HERO. Central Intelligence Agency

Soviet Premier Nikita Khrushchev knew that the U.S. had the upper hand in nuclear weapons, a gap that Leonid Brezhnev, despite détente, later tried to correct with bankrupting consequences for the USSR. With Penkovsky's revelations, Khrushchev was also aware that the U.S. knew the gap was in America's favor. The Missile Crisis was defused when Khrushchev agreed to remove the missiles from Cuba. It was at the very least a political and public relations defeat for Khrushchev and the Soviet

Union, although in reality the U.S. also agreed to remove rockets from Turkey and President Kennedy pledged that the U.S. would not invade Cuba, virtually assuring that communism would remain entrenched in the impoverished and hapless island.[27]

Part II

Stalin and World War II (1939–1945)

CHAPTER 7

OPERATION BARBAROSSA, DECEPTION, ESPIONAGE, AND TOTAL WAR

Just before dawn on June 22, 1941, Adolf Hitler's Wehrmacht launched a massive invasion of the Soviet Union. Operation Barbarossa, the mightiest battle in history, began. The blitzkrieg invasion force consisted of 3.6 million German and other Axis troops, 2,700 aircraft, 17 Panzer divisions with 3,400 tanks, and 600,000 motorized and armored vehicles. The Germans quickly overran the Russian expanse in a front that stretched nearly 1,800 miles toward the Baltic and the Black Seas.[1-3]

Hitler's Declaration of War on the Soviet Union, June 22, 1941:

GERMAN PEOPLE!

NATIONAL SOCIALISTS

Weighted down with heavy cares, condemned to months-long silence, the hour has now come when at last I can speak frankly...

German people! At this moment a march is taking place that, as regards extent, compares with the greatest the world hitherto has seen. United with their Finnish comrades, the fighters of the victory of Narvik are standing in the Northern Arctic. German divisions commanded by the conqueror of Norway, in cooperation with the heroes of Finnish freedom, under their marshal, are protecting Finnish soil.

Formations of the German Eastern Front extend from East Prussia to the Carpathians. German and Rumanian soldiers are united under Chief of State Antonescu from the banks of the Pruth along the lower reaches of the Danube to the shores of the Black Sea. The task of this front, therefore, no longer is the protection of single countries, but the safeguarding of Europe and thereby the salvation of all.

I therefore decided today again to lay the fate and future of the German Reich and our people in the hands of our soldiers...[4]

The German Strategic Plan

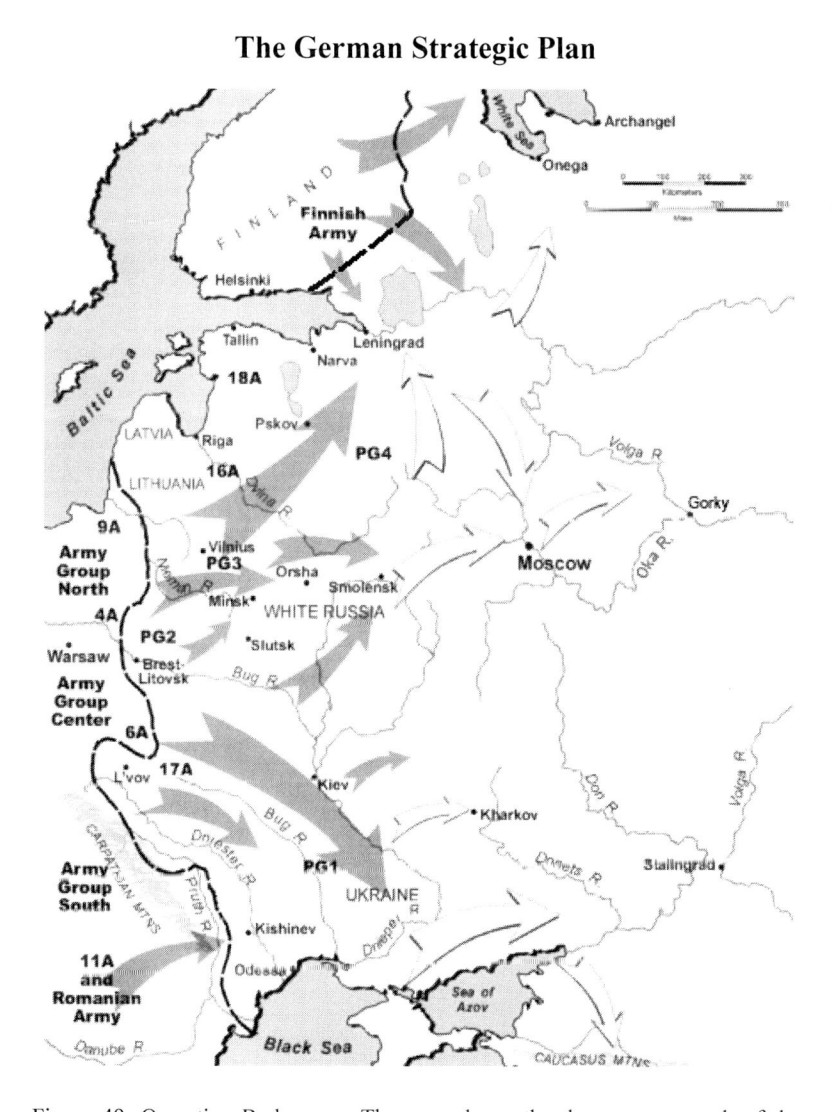

Figure 49: Operation Barbarossa: The map shows the three-prong attack of the German army on the Soviet Union. The arrows show the movements of Army Group North, Army Group Center and Army Group South. The Germans were supported by the Finnish army in the north and the Romanian army in the south. U.S. Army

The Wehrmacht's order of battle in Operation Barbarossa was:

German Army Group North, commanded by Field Marshal Wilhelm Ritter von Leeb, was to "spread through the Baltic states, recently subjugated by Stalin, capture the sea ports and cut off Leningrad, securing the Baltic Sea for shipment of iron ore to Germany from Scandinavia."[3]

German Army Group Center was aimed like a dagger toward Moscow. Commanded by Field Marshal Fedor von Bock and with Panzer Group 2 led by General Heinz Guderian, their objective was to attack toward the Soviet nerve center itself, Moscow.[3,5]

German Army Group South, commanded by Field Marshal Gerd von Rundstedt, was to overrun the Ukraine, capture Kiev, and conquer the Caucasus region.[5]

The Soviet forces that initially met the invading German armies suffered heavily. Several divisions of the Red Army were completely annihilated, and some 1,200 Soviet aircraft were destroyed, "two-thirds while parked on the ground."[1] Hundreds of Soviet tanks were destroyed. Byelorussia was overrun. In four days, the Wehrmacht had thrust nearly 200 miles into Soviet territory.[5]

Figure 50: German soldiers during the invasion of the Soviet Union in Operation Barbarossa, 1941. National Archives and Records Administration

Germany's invasion of the USSR was one of history's turning points. Hitler had several strategic objectives but the two most immediate goals for the Wehrmacht were in the southern and northern flanks.

Hitler wanted the Panzers in the south to capture the Ukraine, the breadbasket of the USSR, and protect Germany's access to the vital Romanian oil fields. Victory in the Ukraine would also clear the way to the Soviet oil fields of Baku in the Caucasus, Grozny in Chechnya, and the Caspian Sea.[5]

Figure 51: Hitler during a meeting at the headquarters of Army Group South. The three generals standing to the left of Hitler are Friedrich Paulus, Eberhard von Mackensen, and Field Marshal Fedor von Bock. German Federal Archives

In the north, Hitler wanted the German army to protect the Baltic Sea route through which Scandinavian iron ore, a vital product for Germany's armament industry, was transported. Leningrad had to be captured to protect that northern sea route and block Soviet usage.

Hitler's generals were also adamant that Moscow needed to be captured for strategic and psychological reasons. However, Hitler ordered the Center campaign to yield so as to accomplish his immediate objectives in the north and south. By July 30, since victory on all fronts was not achievable, Hitler directed Army Group Center to slow down and become a tactical reserve for Army Groups North and South.[5] And on August 18, Hitler issued Führer Directive 34, making the Wehrmacht's primary objective the southern mission.[5] Despite the objections of Field Marshal Walter von Brauchitsch, the Army Chief of Staff, the southern army, reinforced by Panzer Group 2 and led by General Heinz Guderian, rolled south.[5] The thrust was successful, and Kiev, the capital of the Ukraine, capitulated to Generals Guderian and Rundstedt. Hitler turned down Stalin's peace feelers.[1]

Figure 52: General Heinz Guderian (second from left) inspecting a Panzer regiment during Operation Barbarossa, August 1941. German Federal Archives

Hitler became more confident, and he went along with his generals' wishes for Army Group Center to begin its drive toward Moscow. On September 6, Hitler directed the army to capture Moscow. By October 16, 1941, not quite four months after the launch of Operation Barbarossa, the Soviet Union had lost 3 million men, more than the entire Red Army possessed at the beginning of the war.[5]

The German High Command now mistakenly believed that the USSR had no further reserves, and that Moscow could be conquered before the winter set in. They were wrong on both counts.

The Russians kept coming. By now, Stalin had ordered fresh Siberian troops to move west. The Siberian reinforcements were the seasoned troops that had defeated the Japanese in Mongolia at Khalkhin Gol at the prelude of World War II, and this army was led by the best of the Russian generals, Field Marshal Georgy Zhukov.

The Battle for Moscow was stalled. On December 5, 1941, Stalin gave permission for the reinforced Red Army under Zhukov to begin the Soviet counteroffensive. Wehrmacht soldiers and the German war machine were stunned. For the first time, the "Germans were forced into a retreat."[5] Moreover, they were not prepared for the harsh Russian winter that had already begun in the east and the minus 40-degree Fahrenheit temperatures.[1]

The Molotov-Ribbentrop Non-Aggression Pact

The Soviet Union was unprepared for war with Germany in June 1941. In fact, Stalin had been completely blindsided by the German invasion. The number of Soviet casualties at the outset was not only a catastrophic loss for the Soviet Union but also humiliating for Stalin. The Soviet Union had been caught off guard. How had that happened?

In August 1939, Soviet Russia and Nazi Germany had entered into an unholy alliance as signatories of the Molotov-Ribbentrop Non-Aggression Pact; and the two partners in that sordid alliance shamefully dismembered Poland and the Baltic states. One must remember that both political philosophies—that is, communism for the Soviets and National Socialism for the Nazis—are of the totalitarian and collectivist variety with only superficial differences.

Stalin thought that the Molotov-Ribbentrop Non-Aggression Pact that he signed with the Führer would give him more time to prepare for the coming war and to rearm the Soviet Union. And as we shall see, he had hoped Hitler would remain embroiled in the West with his conquest and subjugation of Europe.

Operation Barbarossa taught Stalin the same bitter lesson the rest of the world had previously learned—namely, that signing an agreement or pact with Adolf Hitler offered no guarantee it would be honored.

For example, in 1938, Czechoslovakia, the mother country of the Czech Republic, had been sacrificed by its allies, Great Britain and France. At the Munich negotiations, British Prime Minister Neville Chamberlain was deceived by Hitler and returned to England with a piece of paper claiming he brought "peace in our time." The Sudetenland was yielded to Hitler to avoid war, and promptly seized by the Nazis. Not content with only that part of the territory, Hitler subsequently went further and took all of Czechoslovakia. Following the outbreak of war, Czechoslovakia became a giant armament factory and fortress for the Nazis run by SS General Reinhard Heydrich, governor of the Protectorate of Bohemia and Moravia, until his assassination in 1942.

Figure 53: Neville Chamberlain (Great Britain), Édouard Daladier (France), Adolf Hitler (Germany), Benito Mussolini (Italy), and Galeazzo Ciano (Italy) just before signing the Munich Agreement, September 29, 1938. German Federal Archives

Realizing that war with the West would be inevitable not only because of the violation of the Munich Agreement but also because of his plans for Poland, Hitler had concocted the Non-Aggression Pact with Stalin to temporarily protect Germany's eastern flank and secure the supply routes of oil and other raw materials coming from the East that were vital to the German war effort.[1]

Once in cahoots with the Soviet dictator, Hitler felt safe to act, and Poland was wiped off the face of the European map by the German *blitzkrieg* of September 1939. Poland was invaded from the west by the German Army and from the east by the Soviet Red Army. Caught between the well-equipped, modern, and gigantic Nazi and Soviet armies, the sovereign nation of Poland was crushed and dismantled by her behemothic neighbors; and the Baltic nations, such as Latvia and Estonia, Bessarabia, and even parts of Finland, were secretly yielded to quench Stalin's insatiable thirst for territory bordering Russia.[1]

After World War II, the "liberating" Russian communists, who occupied by force much of Central and all of Eastern Europe using the Soviet army working in tandem with the KGB, became the new masters in the region, and the subjugated people were impoverished, disarmed, and enslaved.

Stalin had foreseen that a war would be inevitable too. But for him, it was more of a matter of when the Soviet Union would enter the war and on which side. In a speech before the Politburo on August 19, 1939, Stalin justified the Non-Aggression Pact with Germany and explained his rationale and objective by stating:

> On the other hand, if we accept Germany's proposal...and conclude a non-aggression pact with her, she will certainly invade Poland, and the intervention of France and England is then unavoidable. Western Europe would be subjected to serious upheavals and disorder. In this case we will have a great opportunity to stay out of the conflict, and we could plan the opportune time for us to enter the war.
>
> ...Comrades, I have presented my considerations to you. I repeat that it is in the interest of the USSR, the workers' homeland, that a war breaks out between the Reich and the capitalist Anglo-French bloc. Everything should be done so that it drags out as long as possible with the goal of weakening both sides. For this reason, it is imperative that we agree to conclude the pact proposed by Germany, and then work in such a way that this war, once it is declared, will be prolonged maximally. We must strengthen our propaganda work in the belligerent countries in order to be prepared when the war ends.[1]

Stalin reasoned that by doing everything to drag out the war "as long as possible with the goal of weakening both sides," all of his enemies as well as his allies would then be exhausted, and Russia would be ready for the communist conquest of the globe. After all, that had been the dream of Lenin, Trotsky, and himself—namely, world communist revolution under Soviet domination.

The history of the entire world might have turned out very differently if Adolf Hitler had originally marched east against Russia to satisfy his need for *lebensraum* (living space) for the German people rather than following his fixation and moving against the West.[6] Although Hitler subdued most of Western Europe and Scandinavia, after launching Operation Barbarossa, he created a two-front war, which pitted Germany against England and eventually the United States in the west and the Soviet Union in the east.

Of course, the German grand strategy had been to crush the USSR by a two-front attack: The German Panzers were to roll into the USSR from the west, which actually took place on June 22, 1941, and the Japanese Imperial Army would attack Siberia from the east, which never took place. The Germans had pleaded with the Japanese to invade Siberia and catch the Russians in the crossfire between the two powerful, invading armies.[7]

One must remember that before the onset of World War II, the Japanese Imperial Army in Mongolia had been decisively defeated in a border conflict by elite Siberian Soviet army units at Khalkhin Gol in September 1939. Some of Stalin's best troops remained stationed in eastern and southern Siberia in case of any renewed hostilities with Japan. The troops included heavily armored and motorized divisions, well stocked, and outfitted in suitable winter clothing—heavy, white snow fur coats designed to not only protect from the severe cold but also to blend in with the Siberian terrain. Therefore, the troops were well equipped and provisioned to wait for the Japanese, who never came.

Figure 54: Joseph Stalin (left) and German Foreign Minister Joachim von Ribbentrop (right) shake hands after the signing of the Molotov-Ribbentrop Pact, August 23, 1939. German Federal Archives

As stated in chapter 6, the drubbing the Japanese had suffered at Khalkhin Gol two years earlier in 1939 was probably still foremost in their minds in 1941. After the defeat in Mongolia and for other geopolitical concerns, specifically oil and other vital raw materials, the Japanese high command decided they wanted a different prize—that is, the Pacific region. So, the Japanese navy's arguments for a southern naval strategy with its conquest of the Far East and the Pacific prevailed over the army's Northern Siberian military strategy and its invasion of Siberia, where the Soviets still kept their best troops.[7,8] Nevertheless, Stalin would keep a nervous eye peeled toward Siberia.

The Japanese "Surprise" Attack on Pearl Harbor

On September 22, 1940, the Empire of the Rising Sun had formally entered World War II when it invaded French Indochina. Five days later, Japan officially formed an alliance with Nazi Germany.[9]

Three months later, on December 18, 1940, Adolf Hitler signed Führer Directive Number 21, authorizing Operation Barbarossa.[10] Within days of Hitler's signature, the Soviet master spy, Richard Sorge, sent a copy of Directive 21 to NKVD headquarters in Moscow. On May 12, 1941, Sorge warned Moscow that, "150 German divisions were massed along the frontier." And three days later, Sorge confirmed June 21 as the date set for the German invasion of the Soviet Union.[10]

At the time, Stalin ignored the warnings. Instead, he believed Hitler would not break their Non-Aggression Pact and that this "disinformation" was just part of another "anti-Soviet plot hatched by British Prime Minister Winston Churchill" to start a war between the Soviet Union and Germany.[11] As we shall see, Stalin would not repeat the mistake of ignoring Sorge's messages in the future.

By the summer of 1941, Japan was in desperate need of vital raw materials and oil, resources crucial to its economy and survival. As discussed in chapter 6, the administration of U.S. President Franklin D. Roosevelt (FDR) had been infiltrated with American traitors, Soviet spies and agents of influence, subservient to Stalin and the USSR.[12] Led by the Soviet spy, Harry Dexter White, the Assistant Secretary of the Treasury, the "war hawks" inside FDR's administration deliberately blocked Japan from access to oil imports and other raw materials, and FDR froze Japanese holdings in the U.S. banking channels.[12]

So, when Richard Sorge radioed Moscow on October 9, 1941, and reassured Stalin that there would not be a Japanese invasion of Siberia[13], Stalin paid attention. According to Sorge's information, "Japan was preparing for war in the Pacific and would not attack the Soviet Far East as the Russians feared."[10,14] After receiving that assurance, Stalin transferred additional Siberian divisions west to reinforce Soviet troops fighting in the Battle for Moscow.[15]

On December 7, 1941, "a day that will live in infamy," the Japanese navy and air force attacked Pearl Harbor. The American Pacific fleet was devastated but the vital U.S. aircraft carriers had "fortuitously" gone out to sea and were spared. A year later, the Roberts Commission placed much of the blame for America's lack of preparedness unfairly on Rear Admiral Husband E. Kimmel and Lt. General Walter C. Short, the Navy and Army commanders.[16] We know where the blame laid, and the "buck" should have stopped with U.S. President Franklin D. Roosevelt.

Figure 55: Richard Sorge in 1940, German journalist and Soviet spy who warned Stalin about the impending German invasion of the Soviet Union. He later reassured Stalin that Japan would not be invading Siberia. German Federal Archives

Stalin's Spy in Hitler's Inner Sanctum

In *Hitler's Traitor: Martin Bormann and the Defeat of the Reich*, Pulitzer-Prize winning journalist Louis C. Kilzer provides compelling arguments that Martin Bormann was the spy "Werther," who spied for the Soviets from deep inside the Third Reich. Bormann was the only person who was able either to attend all the Wehrmacht conferences or have his informants and official stenographers record in minute detail the German High Command's top secret transactions and military plans.[17] Thus, from his lofty position next to Adolf Hitler and the German High Command, Werther was able to relay information to the Russians, and sometimes before the German generals were able to review and put the plans into action. Not even Ultra—Winston Churchill's secret weapon at Bletchley Park and the name given for the breaking of the German Enigma codes—was able to provide such detailed information and feedback.[18]

Figure 56. Portrait of Martin Bormann, head of the Nazi Party Chancellery (1941–1945) and Hitler's private secretary (1943–1945). German Federal Archives

Werther radioed the secret German military plans to Moscow Center via the Lucy spy ring in Switzerland immediately after the Wehrmacht conferences were over. His messages were detailed and included the names of those who had attended the conference and what each of the conferees had stated during the discussions. Werther was also able to answer specific questions posed by the Moscow Center's controller in Switzerland, Maria Poliakova (codenamed GISELA), the young, attractive, secretive, Russian-Jewish spymaster. Kilzer showed that only one man was in the key position to know all the information, and that man could only have been Martin Bormann, the Führer's trusted secretary.[18]

Hitler was ruthless but, unlike Stalin, he was not a paranoid individual. And surprisingly, he allowed treasonous activity to thrive within the military that included Generals Ludwig Beck and Georg Thomas; police officials, like Heinrich Müller, head of the Gestapo and creator of the *funkspiel*, the radio playback messages to Moscow; and even German military intelligence, such as officials Hans Bernd Gisevius, General Hans Oster, and Admiral Wilhelm Canaris, the head of the Abwehr. Canaris was a double agent and the West's top man in Hitler's circle. This group of aristocratic, high-ranking military and intelligence officers spying for the West were referred by the Gestapo as the "Black Orchestra" (*Schwarze Kapelle*). Hitler's foreign intelligence chief, Walter Schellenberg, who worked under SS General Reinhard Heydrich, remained loyal almost to the end. When he realized all was lost, Schellenberg tried to contact the West with a peace offering to avoid more bloodshed, especially for the Jews and other prisoners who were still in Nazi hands in Germany and in Scandinavia.[17,18]

Figure 57: Wilhelm Canaris, German Admiral and chief of the Abwehr, Germany's military intelligence service (1935–1944). German Federal Archives

It was not until the assassination attempt by Colonel Claus von Stauffenberg at the Wolf's Lair on July 10, 1944, that Hitler struck back with a vengeance against the conspirators. Only then, as the Third Reich rapidly crumbled, did Hitler become sadistically vindictive and unforgiving to the suspected opponents within the German military. And yet, Hitler never distrusted Martin Bormann, his faithful secretary, who could get things done. On April 29, 1945, as he prepared for death, Hitler appointed Bormann the executor of his will and praised him as his "most faithful Party comrade."[18]
But Admiral Canaris, an honorary member of the Black Orchestra that spied for the West, suspected Bormann, the "Brown Bolshevik."[18] One of Bormann's mistresses was a communist operative in the German resistance, but that incriminating fact was not known at the time, and so Bormann was not suspected. Toward the end of World War II, some of the top surviving Nazis had come to suspect Bormann's betrayal to the Russians. The full extent of his betrayal only became evident and was confirmed as revelations came to light during the Nuremberg war crime trials where they were being prosecuted. On the stand, when the prosecutor asked Hermann Göring if he believed Bormann was dead, the Reichsmarschall replied, "…I hope he is frying in hell. But I don't know."[18]

What information did the spy Werther provide to Moscow Center that was so vital to the Soviets? No less than very detailed and specific military intelligence that led to the defeat of the Wehrmacht at the pivotal Battle of Stalingrad from the fall of 1942 to the winter of 1943 and the decisive Battle of Kursk during the summer of 1943. The Battle of Stalingrad was the deadliest battle of World War II, and the Battle of Kursk was the largest tank battle in history. After those two losses, the Third Reich never recovered the initiative on the Eastern Front.[18]

However, one question remains. Why then did Bormann not seek a timely escape route to communist Russia before the final collapse of the Third Reich? Bormann might have been guarding his identity even from the Soviets. To escape, he attempted; but to surrender, he probably thought would be futile. He had interpreted and carried out the Führer's order of genocide of the Jews during the Holocaust and the elimination of the Ukrainians during the Wehrmacht's drive to the east. All that can be said is that Bormann's betrayal was ideological; other motives will never be known.

Before closing this subsection, a few other notable spies, who infiltrated the nerve center of Nazi military intelligence and spied for the West, deserve to be mentioned. Fritz Kolbe, German diplomatic courier, passed documents to his Office of Strategic Services (OSS) handler, Allen Dulles, in Switzerland. Dulles gave Kolbe the code name "George Wood."[19] Gero von Schulze-Gaevernitz, a German economist, also assisted Allen Dulles in Europe.[20] Hans Gisevius, the high-ranking Abwehr intelligence officer, served as a liaison in Zürich between Allen Dulles and the German resistance.[21]

Figure 58: Hans Bernd Gisevius, German diplomat and intelligence officer, at the Nuremberg Trials in 1946. U.S. Army Signal Corps

Interestingly, after the war on September 20, 1945, the United States Office of Strategic Services was dissolved. Two years later on September 18, 1947, U.S. President Harry Truman signed the National Security Act of 1947 that created a new independent, civilian intelligence agency in the Executive Branch of the U.S. government, namely the Central Intelligence Agency (CIA). In 1952, Allen Dulles became the 5th Director of the CIA.[22]

And as stated previously, the Allies had a very secret espionage weapon against the Axis. Anglo-American intelligence could read the German Enigma traffic because the British had broken the German codes at Bletchley Park via Ultra. Likewise, the Japanese secret messages were being read by American intelligence because American cryptologists had broken them. Some years later, American code breakers, led by Meredith Gardner, would also break and decipher the Soviet codes in the Venona transcripts.[23]

Winston Churchill's Deception

In a second book, *Churchill's Deception: The Dark Secret That Destroyed Nazi Germany*, Louis Kilzer also shed light on how British Prime Minister Winston Churchill, with the assistance of the British Secret Intelligence Service (SIS), conceived of a deception strategy to encourage Hitler to turn his war machine on Soviet Russia in order to save England from the German onslaught. Churchill was prepared to do what was necessary to save the British Empire and its citizens.[24]

Churchill had read and studied *Mein Kampf*, and knew to some degree how the mind of the Führer worked. Hitler was obsessed with the preservation of the British Empire and Nordic solidarity between England and Germany. Churchill knew that and also understood that Hitler's main objective was to invade and conquer the east and establish hegemony over Central and Eastern Europe. Hitler wanted *lebensraum* (living space) for the German Volk in the east, including Poland, the Ukraine, White Russia, et cetera. Moreover, Hitler detested Stalin and Bolshevism.

Following the Anschluss with Austria and Hitler's seizure of the Sudetenland and shortly thereafter the rest of Czechoslovakia in 1938 as well as the *blitzkrieg* and partition of Poland in 1939, France and England distrusted Hitler and were committed to war to stop Germany's western expansion. The Phony War was a period of overt inactivity, except for covert negotiations and peace feelers that led nowhere.[25]

Figure 59: Winston Churchill, "The Roaring Lion," by photographer Yousuf Karsh, December 30, 1941. Library and Archives Canada

After Germany's western conquests—namely, Denmark, Belgium, Norway, the Netherlands, and France—Hitler wanted to make peace with England so he could turn his attention to the conquest of the East, particularly the Ukraine and the Caucasus, where he needed the Soviet oil fields to fuel his Panzers. But Churchill refused to make peace openly. Instead, Churchill created a sham, unofficial, and secretive "Peace Party," which included the Duke of Windsor and the Duke of Hamilton, and with the connivance of the SIS, the specious agents lured Rudolf Hess, Hitler's trusted Deputy Führer, to Scotland under a pretext to negotiate an Anglo-German peace.[26]

Hess' secretive solo flight was to end with his landing at the Duke of Hamilton's estate at Dungavel House. Kilzer makes the point that this was a planned mission authorized secretly by Adolf Hitler and manipulated by the SIS.[27] I'm not convinced that Hitler authorized or even knew about this secret operation, and I lean to the proposition that Hess carried out the mission on his own, thinking that if the mission was successful it would benefit Nazi Germany and please Hitler. But the mission was not successful because from the start it was conceived by Churchill to deceive Germany.

The purpose of the mission from the standpoint of the British was for Churchill to hedge his bets and encourage Hitler and the Wehrmacht to turn eastward and abandon the Battle of Britain.[28] In fact, the day that

Hess parachuted into Scotland, May 10, 1941, was also the deadliest day for England. Reichsmarshall Hermann Göring had unleashed his Luftwaffe with a vengeance in an attempt to force England to reach an understanding with Hess while he was in Scotland and before Germany launched Operation Barbarossa against the Russians in the east, an invasion that began like thunder barely six weeks later.[29]

Figure 60: Rudolf Hess in 1935, Deputy Führer of the Nazi Party (1933–1941). German Federal Archives

Kilzer also intimated that later, while England waited for the outcome of Operation Barbarossa, Hitler became convinced that his western flank was protected and that an understanding had been reached between his captive Deputy Führer Hess and the British "Peace Party," the illusory front organization that had been orchestrated by Churchill.[30]

According to Kilzer, when Joseph Stalin found out about the Hess Affair "deception" a year and a half later in October 1942, it marked the beginning of the Cold War.[30] That assumption is debatable. Given all that is known about Joseph Stalin's personality and his desire for world domination—not to mention, the protracted reign of terror, the mass murders, the revelations contained in books like Aleksandr Solzhenitsyn's *Gulag Archipelago*, the government-contrived famines, purges, repression, and hatred for the West—one can agree that the Cold War began before World War II was over, *but regardless of the Hess Affair*. We know this from the nest of spies that Stalin was already employing against his Western "allies" prior to the Hess Affair.[31]

One might also disagree with Kilzer's other assumption that had Churchill made peace with Hitler, the 50 million lives of World War II, including six million Jews, could have been saved.[32] If an Anglo-German alliance had been reached in 1941, perhaps all of the conquered territories of Western Europe may have regained their freedom—for a time at least. Hitler was prepared to do that if only England would sign a peace treaty and allow him a free hand in the east. With this understanding, England and Western Europe would have remained at peace, while Hitler and Stalin would have fought the war over to its horrific conclusion. Hitler would have proceeded with Operation Barbarossa and the conquest of the East, as he had planned, and the extermination of the Jews would have proceeded with even more confidence, as he had pledged to do in *Mein Kampf.*[32]

The Katyn Forest Massacre and the NKVD Executioner, Vasily Blokhin

In *Stalin: The Court of the Red Tsar*, Simon Sebag Montefiore provided a galvanizing portrait of Joseph Stalin "as human and complicated as he is brutal" and chronicled the lives of the notorious henchmen who entered the Court of the Red Tsar.

Among the many atrocious incidents cited in the book, there was one that stood out above the others, namely, the Katyn Forest massacre— the atrocious killing of Polish military officers, police officials, and Polish intelligentsia in a series of mass executions carried out by the Russian NKVD. The Polish officers had been captured and the officials arrested after the Soviet seizure of eastern Poland in September 1939, and "held in three camps, one of which was close to Katyn Forest."[33] The fate of 26,000 Polish officers was finally decided on March 5, 1940, at the Politburo, and the atrocity was covered up for over 50 years.[33]

Stalin perpetrated the atrocity efficiently and secretly with his sanguinary NKVD (the People's Commissariat for Internal Affairs), the Soviet secret police, to incriminate and blame the Germans. In one stroke, he succeeded in wiping out the future intellectual elite of the Polish nation; and by eliminating the active and reserve officers, who in their civilian functions were mostly professionals—the elite members of Polish society— the Soviets decapitated the leaders of the anti-communist Poles, making the remaining Poles easier to subdue.

Montefiore wrote that "this massacre was a chunk of 'black work' [*Vishka*] for the NKVD who were accustomed to a few victims at a time, but there was a man for the task," Vasily Mikhailovich Blokhin, the 41-

year-old Checkist and "one of the most prolific executioners of the century."[33-35]

Figure 61: Polish POWs captured by the Red Army during the Soviet invasion of Poland in 1939. TASS

Describing how the executions were performed, Montefiore wrote:

Blokhin travelled down to the Ostachkov Camp in 1940 where he and two other Chekists outfitted a hut with padded, soundproof walls and decided on a Stakhanovite quota of 250 shootings a night. He brought a butcher's leather apron and cap which he put on when he began one of the most prolific acts of mass murder by one individual, killing 7,000 in precisely twenty-eight nights, using a German Walther pistol to prevent future exposure. The bodies were buried in various places—but the 4,500 in the Kozelsk camp were interred in Katyn Forest.[33]

The Germans discovered the remains of the Polish officers during their invasion of Eastern Poland and Russia.[36] In 1943, the German government went public with the atrocity and blamed the Russians. But Nazi Germany was not believed. Some high-level American government officials, including FDR, should have suspected the truth, but kept silent so as not to offend the Soviet allies.[33-35]

Operation Barbarossa, Deception, Espionage, and Total War 107

Figure 62: Vasily M. Blokhin, Chief Executioner and Commander, NKVD

Figure 63: Photo from 1943 exhumation of mass grave of Polish officers killed by NKVD in Katyn Forest in 1940. Germans showing their findings to an international commission made up from POW officers from Great Britain, Canada, and the United States.

In the next chapter, we will continue with the retrenchment of the German war machine, the dénouement of the war, and recount some little-known incidents of World War II.

CHAPTER 8

THE HORRIFIC WAR UNFOLDS IN THE EAST

Joseph Stalin mistakenly placed his trust in Adolf Hitler and the Molotov-Ribbentrop Non-Aggression Pact of 1939, whereby Poland was carved up between the two totalitarian leaders. As discussed in chapter 7, Stalin had been forced by circumstances to trust Hitler, but Hitler despised the Bolsheviks and communism. So, while the two totalitarian dictators talked cooperation, Stalin hedged for the time needed to rebuild the Red Army after his decimating purges, and Hitler planned Operation Barbarossa to secure oil fields for the German war effort and obtain *lebensraum* (living space) for the German people, the Volk. As soon as the Battle of Britain on the Western Front stalemated, Hitler turned his forces east and launched Operation Barbarossa—the mammoth invasion of Russia that overran the Russian expanse in a front that stretched nearly 1,800 miles toward the Baltic and the Black Seas.[1-3]

Soviet spies in the "Red Orchestra" (*Rote Kapelle*), and most notably, Richard Sorge, had uncovered the exact date of June 22, 1941, for the German invasion of Russia, and had tried to forewarn Stalin.[4] But Stalin refused to believe the warning. Simon Sebag Montefiore explained:

> *In the contest that Molotov called 'the great game,' Stalin thought Russia might manage to stay out of the war until 1942. 'Only by 1943 could we meet the Germans on an equal footing,' he told Molotov. As ever, Stalin was trying to read himself out of the problem, carefully studying a history of the German-French War of 1870, and repeatedly quoting Bismarck's sensible dictum that Germany should never face war on two fronts: Britain remained undefeated hence Hitler would not attack. 'Hitler's not such a fool,' Stalin said.[5]*

Stalin, who was also naturally suspicious of others' motives, including those of British Prime Minister Winston Churchill, refused to believe warnings from Churchill as well. Montefiore related:

> *When Stafford Cripps, the British Ambassador, delivered a letter from Winston Churchill warning of the invasion, it backfired, convincing Stalin that Britain was trying to entrap Russia. 'We're being threatened with the*

Germans, and the Germans with the Soviet Union,' Stalin told Zhukov, 'They're playing us off against each other.' [5]

Initially, the German forces were extremely successful. They conquered a large expanse of Soviet territory, including the Russian breadbasket region of the Ukraine and the most populated regions in western European Russia.[1]

But the Germans needed oil and refineries badly for the war effort, and the situation became more acute and demanding when they failed to knock Russia out on the first blow before the winter of 1941–1942 set in.

Figure 64: Soviet Foreign Minister Vyacheslav Molotov signs the Molotov-Ribbentrop Pact in Moscow on September 28, 1939, surrounded by German and Soviet officials, including Stalin. National Archives and Records Administration

One must remember that the Molotov-Ribbentrop Pact of 1939 between Russia and Germany was a negotiated trade agreement with an additional side agreement, the "Secret Protocol," that partitioned Poland and allowed the Soviets to take over and occupy Baltic territories.[6] As alluded to in chapter 7, Hitler needed to secure supplies of oil and other precious raw material for the German war effort. The terms of the Nazi-Soviet pact required Russia to supply Germany with tons of raw material, such as natural rubber, iron ore, scrap metal, and pig iron, and the Germans supplied industrial equipment and machines to the Soviet Union.[7] By mid-1940, the Trans-Siberian railroad that ran across the vast territory of the USSR was being used to transport materials from the Far East and the Pacific port of Vladivostok through Siberia and all the way to Germany. The German historian Heinrich Schwendemann noted that, "By the summer of 1940, the Soviet Union had become the most important supplier of raw materials to the Third Reich."[8] Russian deliveries of oil to Germany up to June 1941 amounted to at least 900,000 tons.[7] Schwendemann further commented, "Apart from the liquidation of the Soviet consignment of raw materials up to the last few hours before the German attack was the spectacular ending of Stalin's misguided German policy, which led the Soviet Union to the verge of a catastrophe."[8]

A Napoleonic Mistake

The Germans though did not run out of oil during the initial stages of Operation Barbarossa. However, they did begin to run out of oil when they lost their offensive capabilities.

What halted the Germans was the combination of the severe Soviet winter and lack of proper winter clothing; the immensely unending and vast expanse of the Russian territory; and the reinforcement of the Russian Western Front by fresh Soviet divisions.[2]

Additionally, Hitler unwittingly made the same mistake as Napoleon of fighting on two fronts, something he had sworn not to do. Japan had made its error as we noted in chapter 6, and Germany had now made its mistake. Stalin finally listened to his master spy, Richard Sorge, and sent the 700,000 reserve troops from the Far Eastern Army that had been guarding against Japan to the Russian Western Front to stop the German juggernaut.[9,10] Simon Sebag Montefiore explained:

Richard Sorge reported that Japan would not attack. On October 12, Stalin discussed this with his Far Eastern satraps who then confirmed Tokyo's lack of hostile intentions from local intelligence. Kaganovich arranged non-stop trains that, within days and hours, rushed 400,000 fresh troops, 1,000 tanks and 1,000 planes across the Eurasian wastes, in one of the most decisive logistical miracles of the war. The last train left on the 17th and these secret legions began to mass behind Moscow.[10]

Let us indulge in a brief segment of speculative history. As previously stated, if the Japanese had attacked Russia in the Siberian east, instead of attacking the U.S. at Pearl Harbor, the Russians would almost certainly have been defeated, crushed between two Axis fronts. And although FDR and the "war hawks" in his administration were hankering to enter the war, without suffering the direct attack on the United States like at Pearl Harbor, the U.S. would not have entered the war until much later, and possibly too late to change the outcome.

Without the United States as an active participant in the war, Great Britain would have been forced to accommodate Hitler and make peace with Germany or risk certain defeat by a reinvigorated German naval force and war machine. If Churchill and the British Parliament insisted on war to the death with the Nazis, Britain would have become exhausted, and forced to surrender. At that point in time, it would have been impossible to convince the American people that the U.S. needed to enter a war to attempt to restore an already conquered Europe or end Japan's hegemony in the east.

However, it is reasonable to assume that eventually the victorious Nazis and their Japanese allies would have attacked the United States, and then possibly each other. Remember, Germany was ahead in rocketry at this time.[11] In the end, with a total Axis victory, it is probable that German would have emerged as the lingua franca and not English, as is almost universally the case today. It is difficult to see it any other way. So, at this point, let us return to historic events.

As mentioned in chapter 7, German Army Group North was commanded by Field Marshal Wilhelm Ritter von Leeb and its objective was to capture the Baltic sea ports and converge in Leningrad as well as to protect the iron ore shipments from Sweden. Army Group North made it to Leningrad, and with the assistance of German-allied Finnish troops formed a ring around the city and set up a military blockade. The fierce battle and subsequent siege of Leningrad began on September 8, 1941, and lasted until January 27, 1944, when Soviet forces were finally able to break the prolonged blockade. While the German Army Group North suffered 580,000 casualties; the Russians suffered over 4 million casualties, including military killed in the Red Army's Northern Front as well as civilians who were killed or died of starvation during the 900-day siege.[12]

German Army Group Center was aimed toward Moscow. This army group was commanded by Field Marshal Fedor von Bock with the objective of capturing the Soviet nerve center itself, Moscow. First, Army Group Center and two elite Panzer units led by German Panzer General Heinz Guderian were ordered to defeat the Soviet army at Belarus and move quickly and occupy Smolensk. Strong resistance in Smolensk delayed the advance, and Hitler ordered a postponement of the drive toward Moscow and to quicken the advance on the Ukraine. The German forces encountered fierce resistance from Red Army units and partisans. The drive to Moscow was halted as the strategic aim again changed and became the capture of the oil fields in the south and other army units were diverted to support Army Group South.

Figure 65: Erich von Manstein in 1938, Field Marshal of the Wehrmacht. German Federal Archives

Army Group South, which was originally headed by Field Marshal Gerd von Rundstedt, was to overrun the Ukraine, capture Kiev, conquer the Caucasus region, and capture the Soviet oil fields. Army Group South formed the bulk of the German forces once the strategic aim became the capture the oil fields for the war effort. This army was constituted and reconstituted at various times, and subsequently led by Field Marshals Walter von Reichenau, Fedor von Bock, Maximilian von Weichs, and Erich von Manstein between 1941 and 1944.

The German Sixth Army, led by Field Marshal Friedrich Paulus, rolled into Stalingrad in September 1942 and encountered heavy resistance. After five months of intense fighting that went building by building and house by house through the city, the Sixth Army was encircled, and Field Marshal Paulus surrendered his forces on February 2, 1943. German losses totaled more than 200,000 killed, wounded, or captured; and an estimated 750,000 Soviets died defending the city in the deadliest battle of World War II. Before Stalingrad, the Sixth Army had been one of the most decorated units. Field Marshal Paulus and 24 other German generals were captured. Only 5,000 soldiers in this field army unit ever returned to Germany.[13]

Despite Stalingrad, fierce fighting would continue in southern Russia and the Ukraine. And a few months later in the summer of 1943, the largest tank battle in World War II would follow.

The Pivotal Battle of Kursk

The year, 1943, had not started off well for the German army. After the defeat at Stalingrad, Hitler needed a victory to regain Germany's dominance and control of the Eastern Front. And a dramatic clash between the Wehrmacht and the Soviet Red Army was being prepared on both sides. An article in *ARMOR* offered the following explanation of the importance of Kursk:

> *Germany and Russia had reached an impasse by the winter of 1943 from Leningrad to the Black Sea. And at the center of the disputed area, a year's worth of fighting had created a massive salient (an outward-protruding bulge of land on a battle line) approximately 150 miles from north to south and 100 miles from east to west. At the center of the salient lay the Russian city of Kursk. The salient became known as the Kursk Bulge and was a strategic location for Germany. Hitler also wanted the tactical advantage of controlling Kursk's railways and roads.[14,15]*

The German commander of Army Group South at the Battle of Kursk was Field Marshal Erich von Manstein. His counterpart in the Red Army was Marshal Georgy Zhukov, who had been handpicked by Stalin, the Vozhd (the "Great Leader").

Figures of men and equipment were rounded up from several sources, but by the beginning of the battle, the Germans had amassed 800,000 men under arms; the Russians, over 2 million troops. The Germans had 3,000 tanks and big guns. The Russians threw more than 10,000 tanks and big guns into the battle. The battle unfolded as follows:

> *In early July, Germany and the USSR concentrated their forces near the city of Kursk in western Russia, site of a 150-mile-wide Soviet pocket that jutted 100 miles into the German lines. The German attack began on July 5, and 38 divisions, nearly half of which were armored, began moving from the south and the north. However, the Soviets had better tanks and air support than in previous battles, and in bitter fighting Soviet antitank artillery destroyed as much as 40 percent of the German armor, which included their new Mark VI Tiger tanks. After six days of warfare concentrated near Prokhorovka, south of Kursk, the German Field Marshal Gunther von Kluge called off the offensive, and by July 24 the Soviets had forced the Germans back to their original positions.[15,16]*

Figure 66: Soviet Field Marshals Georgy Zhukov (center) and Ivan Konev (right) during the Battle of Kursk, 1943. Ministry of Defence of the Russian Federation, Mil.ru

In the end, the Germans suffered slightly over 200,000 casualties; the Russians lost almost one million men. The Germans had 720 tanks and assault guns destroyed; the Russians, had 6,000 tanks and assault guns destroyed.[16] Nevertheless, the Russians technically won the battle.

The German loss at the Battle of Kursk ended Hitler's dream of conquering Russia. The Russian victory at both Stalingrad and Kursk meant the beginning of the end for Nazi Germany and turned the tide of war to the Allied powers. From this point on, Germany would be fighting on multiple fronts, including pulling troops from Russia back to Sicily to defend Italy and stop the Allied invasion.

But there was more to the Battle of Kursk than meets the eye, and one factor specifically gave the Soviets a decisive advantage. Stalin's secret agents in the Nazi hierarchy and the German High Command, along with the playback *funkspiel* operations, played a pivotal role in disclosing the German order of battle and the secret plans of the Wehrmacht to the Russians. Unbeknownst to the Germans, Stalin and Marshal Zhukov were notified in advance of Nazi military tactics and every move the German Panzers were ordered to make.

Figure 67: Battle of Kursk: Soviet troops of the Voronezh Front counterattacking behind T-34 tanks at Prokhorovka, July 12, 1943. Ministry of Defence of the Russian Federation, Mil.ru

Highly placed spies, such as "Werther" and "the Red Orchestra" learned of the German plans. For example, 700 German tanks were lost due to land mines that had been strategically placed. The information about Panzer movements and routes was gleaned from human intelligence provided by highly placed spies in the German High Command. It is information like that, which can make all the difference in the outcome of a battle.

The British may have also helped the Soviets by sending disguised decoded Enigma codes as well.[17] The fact remains that with U.S. supplies and assistance, the Russians could afford to lose 6,000 tanks, but the Germans could not afford to lose seven hundred. The Russians won a technical and decisive military victory. Thus, the Battle of Kursk ended on August 23, 1943, with the German offensive repulsed by the Soviets at a heavy cost.[17]

World War II on American Soil

During World War II, there were a number of enemy attacks on U.S. soil, other than Pearl Harbor. The Japanese sent thousands of "fire balloons" but only approximately 350 balloons ever reached the North

American Pacific coast. Miraculously, five children and one woman were the only known casualties.[18]

On June 3, 1942, the Japanese Air Force bombed Dutch Harbor in the Aleutian Islands, killing more than 100 Americans. The bombing was followed up shortly thereafter with the Japanese invasion of the Aleutian Islands, Attu and Kiska, territories of the United States. The Japanese occupied the islands for nearly a year. Aleut islanders were taken prisoner and held in Japanese concentration camps for the duration of the war.[19]

The Japanese also launched a submarine attack on an American military base on June 21, 1942. The submarine, which penetrated U.S. territorial waters, surfaced in the estuary of the Columbia River in Oregon and fired missiles at Fort Stevens. No serious damage or casualties were sustained, and the submarine escaped.[18] Another Japanese submarine raid on the west coast during World War II included a raid on an oil field, which led to an "invasion scare" in California.[18] Additionally, there were several successful torpedo attacks of ships on the west coast.[18,20] There was even one aerial attack, the only aerial bombing of continental U.S. soil by a foreign enemy, when the Japanese unsuccessfully attempted to start a forest fire in California.[20]

Figure 68: Buildings burning after the first Japanese attack on Dutch Harbor in the Aleutian Islands, Alaska, USA, June 3, 1942. U.S. Army

German activity was heavy on the east coast of America and inflicted heavy losses in U.S. shipping. There were infiltration attempts and spy rings, but no German invasion of the United States mainland. There were several German landings in Canada and Newfoundland, which were of no consequence in the vicissitudes of the war.[20]

In the next post-war chapter, we deal with Stalin after the war and his final years.

Part III

Stalin in the Post-War World (1945–1953)

CHAPTER 9

THE PLOT AGAINST THE JEWISH DOCTORS (1948–1953)

After the "Great Patriotic War," the major dilemma for a person living in Stalin's Russia remained essentially the same as before the war—that is, survival. The moral conundrum in the Kafkaesque drama of life in the Soviet Union was how to survive; and if arrested, how to survive without denouncing innocent people. Yet the perception existed that survival in most cases—or at least the delaying as long as possible of the loss of life or limb by the avoidance of physical torture—was dependent upon denouncing others and thereby placing their lives in jeopardy. But what was one to confess to without divining what Stalin was formulating in his monstrous mind?

Thankfully for some, there was the critical issue of timing. The clock was ticking rapidly, and time was running out. Some victims would beat the clock and survive; others would not and would perish.

So, even though the times had changed, the repressive Soviet system had not, and neither had Joseph Stalin. Stalin had realized long ago that he could utilize a purge not only to destroy enemies but also, and more importantly *to create them*.[1] A purge did not produce stability but rather helped to destabilize the country. Only under crisis conditions could supreme power be maintained.

Additionally, all of Stalin's previous plots had possessed one common thread. They had all focused on a collective group of people. In the 1920s, it had been the kulaks and the bourgeoisie. In the 1930s, it had been the Trotskyites. Now in the post-World War II world, Stalin had selected his next group—namely, the Jews and Jewish nationalism.[1]

In *Stalin's Last Crime*, Brent and Naumov added that, "By providing the plot with a Jewish character, Stalin could broaden the conspiracy outside the boundaries of the Kremlin to the international scene in which America and the newly formed state of Israel posed significant, if still potential, threats to Soviet power and prestige."[1]

The Anti-Cosmopolitan Campaign

From 1945 to 1947, overt anti-Semitism was suppressed in the USSR for three reasons.

First, immediately after the war Stalin was considered a savior to the Jews, the man who defeated Hitler and liberated several Eastern European concentration camps from the Nazis, including Auschwitz, Birkenau, and Monowitz.[1,2] Moreover, during the early post-war years Stalin needed the Jews for propaganda purposes.

Second, many of the Old Bolsheviks were Jewish, including Leon Trotsky, Lev Kamenev, Gregory Zinoviev, Lazar Kaganovich, Maxim Litvinov, Yakov Sverdlov, and Polina Zhemchuzhina Molotova, the wife of Vyacheslav Molotov. Jewish communists, such as the legendary founder of the Cheka, Felix Dzerzhinsky, and his successors, Abram Slutsky, Sergey Shpigelglas, and Genrikh Yagoda, had led the intelligence and security organs of the Bolsheviks and subsequently the Soviet state. And there were still many Jewish cadres in the cultural organs, the Party, the intelligence services, and the security apparatus.[1]

Third, Stalin had initially supported the creation of the Jewish state of Israel.[3]

However, in the fall of 1948, Golda Meir visited the Soviet Union. Russian Jews had been too festive, too enthusiastic, and had shown too much admiration for the Israeli Prime Minister. The United States had recognized Israel as an independent state on May 14, 1948; and America and Israel were now forging closer ties of friendship and cooperation. Many Jews in Russia had family or acquaintances in the U.S. and the West.

There was also the matter of the Jewish Anti-Fascist Committee (JAC). Since many of the "cosmopolitan" members had traveled extensively outside the USSR, the Vozhd (the "Great Leader") had become suspicious of them as well.[3]

Stalin was convinced that Israel and Jewish internationalists, including Russian Jews, were a threat to the Soviet state. He cautiously began his anti-cosmopolitan campaign that soon developed a life of its own in Mother Russia, the land of pogroms and anti-Semitism.

Suddenly, all Jews were potential traitors and enemies of the Soviet state, or spies in the service of the American or British intelligence services. On Stalin's direct order, Solomon Mikhoels, the leader of the Jewish Anti-Fascist Committee (JAC), was assassinated in Minsk in January 1948, and by August 12, 1952, virtually all of the members of JAC had been arrested and shot.[3]

Brent and Naumov noted:

Stalin changed his 'truths' continually in relation to political and social circumstances. In 1943 the Jews were useful to him, and he sent Mikhoels and others to America to raise money and goodwill for the Soviet war effort; in 1947, he supported the establishment of the state of Israel and allowed, if unwillingly, his daughter to marry Grigory Morozov, a Jew. By 1951 the Jews had become a nation of spies, and by 1952 those he had sent to America in 1943 were either assassinated or faced the firing squad.[3]

Figure 69: German physicist Albert Einstein (center) speaking with the Yiddish poet Itsik Fefer (left) and the Russian actor Solomon Mikhoels (right) in the United States in 1943. Mondadori Publishers

The French Foreign Minister Charles Maurice de Talleyrand once stated, "Treason is only a matter of dates." And so it was in Stalin's Russia. The year 1948 had been pivotal not only for the formulation of the Soviet Jewish question in Stalin's mind but also for his belief that the old guard in the MGB (that is, the feared Soviet repressive security organ and precursor to the KGB) and its current Minister, Viktor S. Abakumov, could no longer be trusted.

The Soviet Security Organs—"Waiters in White Gloves, Ordinary Nincompoops"

Viktor Abakumov, the former head of SMERSH—the Russian acronym for "Death to Spies," the counterintelligence, death-squad units formed during World War II—knew too much. He was, like his predecessors Genrikh Yagoda and Nikolai Yezhov, simply expendable now. He was arrested and charged with being a sympathizer and protector of the nonexistent, criminal Jewish underground—even though Abakumov had "presided over the post-war anti-Semitic campaign, the murder of Mikhoels, and the arrest of the members of the Jewish Anti-Fascist Committee."[4]

The once feared Abakumov was thrown unceremoniously in the pot, linked to the Jewish Doctors' Plot, and likewise accused of working for the American and British intelligence services.[4]

Figure 70: Viktor Abakumov, former head of SMERSH and later Minister of State Security (MGB), photo taken between 1943 and 1951. Ministry of Defence of the Russian Federation, Mil.ru

For good measure, the names of former communist officials previously involved in the Leningrad Affair were added to the developing plan and linked to the Jewish Doctors' Plot as well. Those party officials were arrested in 1949 and executed in 1950 because they had the temerity of staging an "All-Russia" trade fair in Leningrad without Stalin's permission.[5]

Stalin believed that there was a malaise in Russia. The citizens of the USSR were becoming stagnant. The Russian people had been overcome with "thoughtlessness," losing sight of "wreckers" and failing to "unmask the enemies of the people" living in their midst. Even the members of the Politburo, his close inner circle—namely Vyacheslav Molotov, Lavrenti

Beria, Georgy Malenkov, Nikita Khrushchev, and Anastas Mikoyan—had been dressed down at one time or another.[6] In his memoirs, Nikita Khrushchev wrote:

> *In those days, anything could have happened to any one of us. Everything depended on what Stalin happened to be thinking when he glanced in your direction.*[5]

Stalin also told the Central Committee: "Here, look at you—blind men, kittens, you don't see the enemy, what will you do without me—the country will perish because you are not able to recognize the enemy."[7]

And according to Stalin, even the MGB security officers were filled with Chekists who could "see nothing beyond their own noses," agents who "are degenerating into ordinary nincompoops and…don't want to fulfill the directives of the Central Committee,"[7] Essentially, the MGB had become merely "waiters in white gloves." And when the interrogations seemed to be going too slow, Stalin harangued Semyon Ignatiev, the MGB Minister who had succeeded Abakumov, "If you want to be Chekists, take off your gloves." Stalin demanded and insisted that torture be used to obtain the necessary confessions. He sensed the clock was ticking, and he needed results quickly.[8]

"Criminal (Jewish) Doctors…Wreckers," and "Medical Saboteurs"

The trigger for the inception of the master plan against the Jewish physicians was the death on August 31, 1948, of Andrei A. Zhdanov from a heart attack.[9] Zhdanov, a leading member of the Politburo and Minister of Culture and the Arts, had been sacked and secretly disgraced. He had fallen from grace because his son, Yuri Zhdanov, a young scientist, had openly criticized the Soviet geneticist, Trofim D. Lysenko, who was then in high favor with Stalin. The Vozhd was still hoping that the charlatan Lysenko would deliver on his promise to produce a large harvest of a genetically engineered "potato-tomato" crop that would revolutionize Soviet agriculture.[10]

Unhappily for Zhdanov's doctors, Dr. Lidia Timashuk, an MGB operative and EKG specialist in the *Lechsanupra*—a complex of medical units called the Kremlin Hospital—wrote letters of denunciation to Stalin, alleging that Zhdanov's medical treatment was criminal. The Kremlin doctors led by Professor P. Yegorov were implicated in the letter. As it turned out, the physicians were not Jewish but Russians, part of the Soviet nomenklatura, which even included Stalin's personal physician, Professor Vladimir N. Vinogradov.[11]

But fortune did not smile on the venerable physician. Recently, Professor Vinogradov had recommended to Stalin that he step down as head of the Soviet government because of his failing health and high blood pressure—a grave mistake.[12]

Figure 71: Andrei A. Zhdanov in 1944, Second Secretary of the Communist Party and head of the Propaganda and Agitation Department of the Central Committee

As the accusations mounted and the nightmare unfolded, imaginary plots were uncovered (under torture, of course) and members of the Soviet intelligentsia were arrested. Gradually, the denunciations came to include the necessary Jewish physicians. Prestigious doctors, such as Sophia Karpai and Yakov G. Etinger, who was the most eminent physician in Russia at the time, were arrested.[13] Etinger, an outspoken Jewish physician, became the obvious and necessary link in the plan. But unfortunately for Stalin, Dr. Etinger died a few weeks later during interrogation and torture. His confession was incomplete and not credible.[14]

Another Jewish physician had to be found. Dr. Sophia Karpai, a young cardiologist, became the next link in the plan, but the seemingly delicate, EKG specialist turned out to be a hard nut to crack. Dr. Karpai was the only doctor in this horrible nightmare who did not crack under intense and prolonged, physical torture. (The other notable exception had been Viktor Abakumov, who knew firsthand that his confession would not help him.[4]) Dr. Karpai's failure to admit complicity in the nonexistent plot gave many doctors the time they needed to survive the ordeal.[13]

Nevertheless, as Stalin's diabolical plan evolved from July 1951 through December 1952, more and more people were caught in the net of denunciations in the Jewish Doctors' Plot. And Stalin was careful to unwrap his master plan circumspectly, fostering the illusion of a slow, piece-by-piece collection of evidence being uncovered by the MGB security police.

A "Pygmy" Terrorist at the Helm

Stalin appeared to have conceptualized the full dimensions of his plan after the arrest of the prominent Jewish physician in 1951, which conveniently connected Dr. Etinger back in time, however tenuously, to both the 1948 Zhdanov case and the 1945 Shchervakov case.[14]

A. S. Shchervakov was a party member who died of a heart attack during the World War II Soviet Victory celebration in 1945. Nevertheless, his case provided another necessary link to the plot of the "medical saboteurs."[15]

Past and closed cases proved to be no obstacle; and the physicians who ministered to Maxim Gorky and his son were again denounced for having poisoned them in the 1930s. Stalin was trying to tell the people "there was a pattern to this deviltry," going back in time and extending into the future.[16]

The torture and death of Dr. Etinger coincided with Abakumov's removal from office and arrest on July 12, 1951. The secret letter of the Central Committee (*zakrytoe pismo*) in acceptance of Stalin's Doctors' Plot was a direct result of the MGB operative Mikhail D. Ryumin's letter of July 2 denouncing his boss Viktor Abakumov and the rest of the Jewish leadership in the MGB.[4,13,14]

Mikhail D. Ryumin was a short, balding man with a paunch, who did not mind getting his hands dirty or bloody during interrogations. He preserved his job in the MGB (where he was about to be fired for corruption and incompetence) by denouncing Viktor Abakumov. With that denunciation, Ryumin provided Stalin with the evidence the Vozhd needed to proceed with his master conspiracy plan.[17]

Following Abakumov's arrest, Ryumin was quickly promoted to Deputy Minister of the MGB and head of the Investigative Unit. But Stalin was no fool and recognized Ryumin for what he really was, calling him "pygmy" (*shibadik*). Nevertheless, MGB Deputy Minister Ryumin would be uncovering plots and extracting the necessary confessions until he was replaced by Sergo A. Goglidze near the end of the conspiracy, and both men were eventually executed.[17,18]

Figure 72: Mikhail D. Ryumin, Deputy Minister of the Soviet MGB (Ministry of State Security), who avidly pursued the "Doctors' Plot" affair (1952-1953), photographed in the mid-1940s

A Multi-Dimensional Conspiracy Conceived in Stalin's Mind

One could begin to fathom the inner workings of Joseph Stalin's mind by considering the following anecdote. Shortly after the death of Georgi Dimitrov, the communist leader of Bulgaria, Stalin was vacationing at Sochi, his favorite resort on the Black Sea. It was the winter of 1949, and he had a conversation with his friend, the Minister of Health Security, Yefim Smirnov. Stalin was in an unusually jovial mood, showing Smirnov the citrus trees, when suddenly he turned and said, "Isn't it strange, the same doctors treated Zhdanov and Dimitrov, and they both died?" Smirnov was shaken and tried to defend the doctors.[19] Not long after the incident, Minister Smirnov was sacked and arrested, enmeshed in the plot.[20]

But the instructive point of the exchange was that Stalin was pondering the question of "medical sabotage" and "medical wrecking" two years ahead of the complete conceptualization. He needed time, though, to build his case, while remaining in the background, just as he had done in the 1930s during the kangaroo trials. The working of his hands could not be seen until the very end.

The plot was not only multi-dimensional in time but also in space. Vertically it now extended up the chain of command to implicate the head of the MGB, Viktor Abakumov, his deputies, and a slate of Jewish MGB officers as well as the head of the Directorate of Kremlin Guards, Lieutenant General Nicolai S. Vlasik, who had been Stalin's loyal, longtime bodyguard.[21]

Figure 73: Nikolai Vlasik, State security (NKVD-NKGB-MGB) officer and head of Stalin's bodyguards, in his office in the late 1930s

The plot extended back in time to encompass the already executed members of the Leningrad Affair and A.A. Kuznetsov and N.A. Voznesensky, who were shot in 1950.[22] Horizontally, the plot expanded to include the imaginary Jewish underground, Jewish bourgeois nationalists, and the medical wreckers—all controlled by the proverbial American and British intelligence services. And the plot was still expanding.

Ryumin's torture was yielding results. Dr. Yegorov, the Kremlin doctor and head of the *Lechsanupra*, was said to have sold out to Kuznetsov for a mess of pottage.[23] Jews were said to have "wormed themselves into the MGB," and Stalin told Ryumin's new boss, MGB Minister Semyon D. Ignatiev, that he "no longer trusted the old guard in the MGB." In other words, more arrests were needed, and the security organs needed to be further purged.[24]

Figure 74: Semyon D. Ignatiev was the last head of the MGB appointed by Stalin. He survived the Vozhd and died Moscow in 1983. FSB of the Russian Federation

Suffice to say, Stalin had several conspiratorial threads and objectives going on simultaneously in his own mind. Only he was privy to how and when they would become interconnected in his master plan. These threads were separated in time and space, but they were meant to converge when the time to act was right. And then heads would begin to roll, and a new holocaust would engulf Russia and the world.

The Plot to Blow Up the Kremlin

The plot soon began moving from the strange to the bizarre with the "uncovering" of the "Plan of the Internal Blow," an enemy plot confessed to by a newly arrived prisoner named Ivan Ivanovich Varfolomeyev. The prisoner was a White Russian arrested in China as a spy and brought to Moscow for interrogation at Lefortovo prison, the same prison where many of the doctors and MGB personnel were held.[25]

Varfolomeyev claimed to be part of a plot hatched by American intelligence to blow up the Kremlin and the Soviet leadership. "According to the scenario Varfolomeyev related, the 'Plan of the Internal Blow' consisted of a plot to fire five nuclear devices using new 'noiseless' ejectors at the Kremlin from the windows of the American embassy in Moscow."[25]

MGB interrogators did not believe Varfolomeyev—dates, names of people, and places did not add up. The MGB concluded that Varfolomeyev's side plot and "confession" were implausible and contrived.

However, Stalin thought otherwise; it could be a useful addition to the Jewish conspiracy. He sternly told the MGB interrogators that, "it was the job of the MGB to make it believable," and that the enemy plot needed to be woven into the tapestry of the Doctors' Plot.[25] Ryumin promptly ordered MGB staff to contact Soviet military intelligence and have them "fill in the gaps" in Varfolomeyev's confession.[25]

Stalin needed to connect the dots before he could reveal the plot to the Russian people. The MGB still had to do more of his bidding. Months of denunciations and confessions followed. Brent and Naumov noted:

> *By November 1952, three distinct foci had been established for the Doctors' Plot: an alleged political-military attack on Kremlin leadership from the MGB, the physical murder of Kremlin leaders by Jewish doctors, and the pervasive, international threat to the USSR from America.[23]*

By December 1952, Stalin was ready to act, and he ordered the arrest of the remaining doctors, mostly Jewish physicians, only tenuously connected to the alleged plot. Stalin called them "criminals in white coats." The Vozhd ordered the MGB to "beat them with death blows," until they confessed to being part of his invented, world Jewish conspiracy.[26]

Members of the Politburo were not privy to all of Stalin's intentions. He had told an assistant, "If this matter is successful, I myself will tell them." And so, the alleged Jewish Doctors' Plot (*dyelo vrachey*) that had not been revealed to the Politburo until November 1952, was finally revealed to the Russian people and the rest of the world in January 1953 when it was announced in *Pravda*.[27]

Kangaroo Court Trials That Failed to Materialize

The trials of Viktor Abakumov and the MGB "nincompoops" (most of them were Jewish, but not all of them) were to take place in closed sessions. The doctors' trials were to be used as show trials in open sessions to make the "thoughtless" nation aware of the vast conspiracy that had been threatening Mother Russia. The trials were planned for late March 1953.[26]

The groundwork had been carefully laid. Stalin had concocted the vast conspiracy, and the enemies had been invented by the state. By painstakingly describing the interconnecting details of the plot, Brent and Naumov uncovered the diabolical enigma wrapped in the dark recesses of Stalin's multi-dimensional mind. The Jewish Doctors' Plot was not only directed against the Jewish physicians but also against the Russian nation— for Stalin's ulterior and political motives. It was not just anti-Semitism and paranoia. Stalin had wanted to unleash a new reign of terror in Russia and, perhaps, even commence World War III before his health failed him.

According to Dmitri Volkogonov, the night before Stalin became ill, he had asked Lavrenti Beria about the status of the case against the doctors and specifically about the interrogation of Professor Vinogradov. Beria told him that, "apart from his other unfavorable qualities, the professor has a long tongue. He has told one of the doctors in his clinic that Comrade Stalin has already had several dangerous hypertonic episodes."[28]

"Right," Stalin said, "what do you propose to do now? Have the doctors confessed? Tell Ignatiev [Minister of the MGB security organs] that if he doesn't get full confessions out of them, we'll reduce his height by a head."

Beria reassured Stalin, "They'll confess. With the help of Timashuk and other patriots, we'll complete the investigation and come to you for permission to arrange a public trial."

"Arrange it," Stalin ordered.[28]

And so, to the last moments of his conscious life, Joseph Stalin was still scheming to complete his sinister master plan. Only his death averted the unfolding catastrophe.

Why Unleash a Soviet Jewish Holocaust in 1953?

Stalin wanted to not only eliminate political opponents but also, and more grandiosely, to replicate the times of the great purges and the Red Terror, the terrible days of the 1930s. He needed to arouse a stagnant Soviet nation to action through surveillance and terror, and unmask wreckers, spies, and saboteurs, while exercising absolute power. Stalin abided by the old revolutionary precept of Nikolai Chernyshevsky, which Vladimir Lenin also subscribed to:

The worse the conditions of the people, the better. Illegitimate power can only be preserved in a climate of such fear and terror, in an atmosphere of perpetual crisis in which an autocrat must exert his iron hand of order and eliminate the real or imagined 'enemies of the people.'[29]

Stalin was a master at creating terrible conditions for the exertion, potentiation, and perpetuation of power. Fortunately for some of the doctors, the world, and the Russian people—it was the Vozhd who ran out of time. After all, he was mortal. Stalin's death on March 5, 1953, saved the doctors, the Jews, and the world from an impending holocaust—possibly even a third World War.[30]

Figure 75: Nikolai G. Chernyshevsky (1828–1889), Socialist philosopher and Russian nihilist, circa 1880. Russian Information Bureau, New York, 1918

After Stalin's death, Lavrenti Beria quickly but briefly took over the reins of Soviet power. He released the imprisoned doctors and the MGB officers, who were being prepared for trials that never took place. The doctors were fully exonerated.

As previously discussed in chapter 4, Beria was embarking on a liberalization program, when on June 26, 1953, he was suddenly arrested along with his close security personnel and subsequently executed on December 23, 1953.[31] Beria could not be trusted by the collective leadership. Eventually, Nikita Khrushchev emerged as the leader, and in 1956 after the 20th Communist Party Congress secret speech, he began his de-Stalinization program and admitted that the Doctors' Plot had been wholly and fully contrived by Joseph Stalin.[31]

CHAPTER 10

A TRIBUTE TO ALEKSANDR SOLZHENITSYN

At this point in the narrative, it would be a significant historical, moral, and literary dereliction not to include a tribute to Aleksandr Solzhenitsyn in this book. Although unknown to Joseph Stalin, Solzhenitsyn was perhaps the greatest opponent of the immoral Soviet system created by Stalin and the other Bolsheviks. And along with U.S. President Ronald Reagan, British Prime Minister Margaret Thatcher, and St. Pope John Paul II, Aleksandr Solzhenitsyn completed the group of four who were most responsible for the fall of the Berlin Wall in 1989 and the eventual collapse and disintegration of the USSR in 1991.

One can easily agree with the tenets of the life and philosophy of Aleksandr Solzhenitsyn contained in Daniel J. Mahoney's *The Other Solzhenitsyn*.[1] The book provides an insightful intellectual profile of Solzhenitsyn as recounted by Mahoney, who was a political scientist at Assumption University at the time of the book's publication. In fact, the book is a masterful semi-biographical and inspirational tome on Solzhenitsyn, the literary genius, who left us a rich legacy in the pursuit of truth, physical and moral courage, and man's insatiable thirst for freedom.

For those who desire an in depth examination of the life and times of the complex and controversial figure, Michael Scammell's *Solzhenitsyn: A Biography* makes a fundamental and essential contribution to our understanding of Solzhenitsyn up to 1984 when the book was published. The book not only illustrates the personal triumphs and crises of the writer and the man but also explains the "historical and cultural background against which Solzhenitsyn's life emerged as emblematic of the history of Russia in the 20th century."[2]

A free-lance writer himself, who specialized in Russian and East European affairs and translated widely from Russian into English other literary works, Scammell brings a unique perspective to the subject. Additionally, this book contains new material based on personal interviews with Solzhenitsyn and his family members.[2]

Solzhenitsyn was a towering figure in the 20th century. As political philosopher, memoirist, and historical novelist of the highest order, his contributions are enormous. Solzhenitsyn's achievements included helping dismantle the barbaric Gulag system, militating for the collapse of the "evil empire" of the Soviet Union, and most importantly perhaps, exposing the immorality of the communist system. All of this is eloquently recounted in both books—and specifically in Mahoney's book, recounting Solzhenitsyn's legacy to the Russia of Vladimir Putin.

Interestingly, in a personal interview while in exile in the United States, Solzhenitsyn stated:

> *I am firmly convinced…that I will return, that I will be in time for this business. You know, I feel so optimistic that it seems to me it is only a matter of a few years before I return to Russia….I have no proof of it, but I have a premonition, a feeling. And I have very often had these accurate feelings, prophetic feelings, when I know in advance what is going to happen, how things will turn out, and that's the way it is. I think—I am sure—that I will return to Russia and still have a chance to live there.*[2]

Solzhenitsyn's Reception in the West

Aleksandr Solzhenitsyn received well-deserved, superlative accolades early in his career following the publication of *One Day in the Life of Ivan Denisovich* in the Soviet literary magazine, *Novy Mir* on November 21, 1962.[3] The little novel was even used by Nikita Khrushchev to further dismantle Stalin's cult of personality. With Khrushchev's imprimatur, Western liberals had no qualms about embracing Solzhenitsyn from a distance. A few years later, in the Soviet Union of Leonid Brezhnev and KGB chairman Yuri Andropov, the international fame that Solzhenitsyn had attained from the publication of the novel protected his life, at least in part, from the Soviet security apparatus that continued to threaten and harass him.

However, Solzhenitsyn's adoration by the Western, particularly American, intelligentsia ended quickly after he was exiled from the USSR, and more precisely after he gave the 1978 commencement address at Harvard University. Western liberals decried his conservatism when he denounced Western decadence, moral relativism, and lambasted the anti-war protesters that forced the withdrawal of U.S. troops from South Vietnam, resulting in the communist takeover of that country. Solzhenitsyn has not been completely forgiven by the liberals ("progressives" and socialists) in the West. But it is fortunate that at least in Russia, a nation that experienced the collectivist evil firsthand, he has not been forgotten. Solzhenitsyn's masterpiece, *The Gulag Archipelago*, became required reading in Putin's Russia, at least as a literary masterpiece.[4,5] And

Solzhenitsyn's legacy of freedom and resistance to tyranny is seen by moderates in the Russian Federation as a bulwark against the return of communism.[6]

Figure 76: Russian writer Aleksandr Solzhenitsyn in 1974. Bert Verhoeff for Anefo, Dutch National Archives, The Hague

Modern liberals in the West—who are really progressive socialists and not classical liberals—abandoned Solzhenitsyn as soon as they discovered he was not one of them or a secular humanist liberal.[7] However, lasting praise for the Russian giant (both in intellect and physical stature) has come from more moderate and conservative sources in the West. The former U.S. Ambassador to the Soviet Union (1952) George F. Kennan, the architect of Truman's policy of communist containment in the late 1940s, called Solzhenitsyn's *Gulag Archipelago*, "the greatest and most powerful single indictment of a political regime ever to be leveled in modern times."[8] The conservative publication, *National Review,* described Solzhenitsyn as a man of moral splendor and the outstanding figure of the century.[9] Even Harrison Salisbury, a *New York Times* journalist and an admirer of Lenin and Mao Tse-tung, compared Solzhenitsyn to other great Russian writers, such as Tolstoy, Dostoevsky, Turgenev, Chekhov, Bunin, and Pasternak.[10]

But, for the most part since the Harvard address, Solzhenitsyn was maligned, criticized, or simply ignored by the liberal Western intelligentsia. That was one reason why Mahoney's book was needed; it supplemented Michael Scammell's 1984 authoritative biography. The two books help to combat the apathy and ignorance concerning the life and career of a man worthy of remembrance, not only for his legacy in the cause of freedom but also for his literary bequest in the cause of literature. Solzhenitsyn's struggle for freedom of thought and expression is recounted in his memoirs, *The Oak and the Calf*.[11]

Mahoney and Scammell defend Solzhenitsyn against the liberal critics and point out that despite the Russian's criticisms of the West, by in large Solzhenitsyn admired the Western intellectual tradition. Mahoney also cited Solzhenitsyn's 1993 address to the International Academy for Philosophy in Liechtenstein, where he lavishly recognized Western freedom and the "historically unique stability of civic life under the rule of law—a hard-won stability which grants independence and space to every citizen."[12]

Solzhenitsyn's Selected Works

Solzhenitsyn's autobiography, *The Oak and the Calf*, *The Gulag Archipelago*, and the installments or Nodes in *The Red Wheel* series of historical novels about events leading to the 1917 Russian revolution or as Solzhenitsyn described the work, "a narrative in discrete periods of time," (that is, *August 1914*, *November 1916*, *March 1917,* and *April 1917*), are perhaps the most celebrated of his literary achievements.[13]

The third node of *The Red Wheel* series, *March 1917*, deals with the historic events leading to the February Revolution that toppled Tsar Nicolas II and temporarily empowered the moderate revolutionaries led by Alexander Kerensky, and the subsequent more tragic events that ushered in the October Revolution and the military coup by Lenin's Bolsheviks.[13]

There is an element of permanence to Solzhenitsyn's works that transcend time. They remain as relevant today as they were when they were written decades ago. All of his major works have now been translated into English. They are genuine literary masterpieces.[14] At least on that account, Harrison Salisbury was totally correct.

Aleksandr Solzhenitsyn dedicated *The Gulag Archipelago* "to all those who did not live to tell it. And may they please forgive me for not having seen it all nor remembered it all, for not having divined all of it."[15] Toward the end of that work, he reminded us of the proverb, "Freedom spoils, and lack of freedom teaches."[16]

Figure 77: Detention cell ("penal isolator") of a camp in the Vorkuta Region, which was part of the Gulag system, in 1945. Russian Federation State Archive, Moscow

Solzhenitsyn made profound observations that had political and psychosocial implications. For our purposes, we will briefly mention a few that are particularly noteworthy and apropos to the current time—keeping in mind the wording of the dedication and the proverb mentioned above.

Lessons from *The Gulag Archipelago*

Aleksandr Solzhenitsyn experienced first-hand the suffering one endured in the Gulag of the Soviet Union. His journey began innocently enough through friendly correspondence with Nikolai Vitkevich. Solzhenitsyn biographer, Michael Scammell, related the circumstances:

At one point Nikolai had seemed to be changing his mind about Stalin— whom they referred to derogatorily in their letters as the pakhan, or 'big shot,' or as 'the moustachioed one'—and suggested that he might not be so bad as they had thought, but in that case, replied Solzhenitsyn, what conclusions should they draw about 'Vovka'? (that is, a playful diminutive of the name Vladimir, meaning Lenin).[17]

Shortly thereafter, Solzhenitsyn complained that he started receiving fewer and fewer letters from Nikolai; and Nikolai noted that he was receiving less from Solzhenitsyn. The Soviet censors were hard at work reading their correspondence.[18]

Solzhenitsyn described his first arrest by SMERSH during World War II:

> Mine was, probably, the easiest imaginable kind of arrest. It did not tear me from the embrace of kith and kin, nor wrench me from a deeply cherished home life. One pallid European February it took me from our narrow salient on the Baltic Sea, where, depending on one's point of view, either we had surrounded the Germans or they had surrounded us, and it deprived me only of my familiar artillery battery and the scenes of the last three months of war.
> The brigade commander called me to his headquarters and asked me for my pistol; I turned it over without suspecting any evil intent, when suddenly...two counterintelligence officers stepped forward...and shouted theatrically, 'You are under arrest!' Burning and prickling from head to toe, all I could exclaim was: 'Me? What for?'[19]

Solzhenitsyn was convicted and sentenced to eight years in prison for spreading anti-Soviet propaganda under paragraph 10 of Article 58 of the Soviet Criminal Code, and under paragraph 11 for "forming a hostile organization." In Stalin's Russia, two friends writing letters can constitute an organization.[20]

Thieves as "Socially-Friendly" Elements

Solzhenitsyn discussed the nature of common thieves and the paradoxical positions they held in Soviet Russia. This applied to thieves "in freedom" as well as those inside the Gulag corrective (destructive) labor camps. At the height of Stalin's reign of bloody purges, thieves were considered "socially friendly" elements, and deemed useful to the Soviet government. The government and the state security police used the thieves to terrorize the general population as haters and defilers of private property and as informants.[21]

In the Gulag, thieves and other criminal elements served as "instructors" in the cultural and educational sections or as assistants to officers of the internal security police (the MVD) to enforce hard labor and for the propagation of terror against ideological or political prisoners. And when needed, thieves worked hand in glove with the security forces in carrying out mass murder in the extermination camps of the Gulag.[21]

While Russian citizens were arrested, hauled off to the Gulag to be used as slave labor, and typically saddled with 10 to 25-year prison sentences, Solzhenitsyn noted:

Sentences [for the thieves] were bound to be reduced and of course for habitual criminals especially. Watch out there now, witness in the courtroom! They will all be back soon, and it will be a knife in the back of anyone who gives testimony! Therefore, if you see someone crawling through a window, or slitting a pocket, or your neighbor's suitcase being ripped open shut your eyes! Walk by! You didn't see anything! That's how the thieves have trained us—the thieves and our laws![22]

Figure 78: Political prisoners during a break inside a mine in the Soviet Gulag system. Second from left is Lithuanian Justinas Lebedžinskas, who was arrested in 1946 and sentenced to 10 years of hard labor. Kaunas 9th Fort Museum

In the destructive labor camps of the Soviet Union (1918–1956), the thieves robbed, tortured, and murdered political prisoners with impunity. Indeed, the thieves were rewarded with higher food rations, better living space, and other privileges for collaborating with the guards and fomenting terror.

Political prisoners, on the other hand, were treated the worse. Those who survived the torture and beatings were given the hardest jobs to perform and the most difficult and perilous assignments. For example, political prisoners dug the canals, felled trees in the forests, drained swamps, and worked in the mines. The Vorkuta coal mines, north of the Arctic Circle, and the Kolyma gold mines in northeastern Siberia, were notorious for harsh conditions. The prisoners were underfed and mistreated. It is not surprising that the life expectancy under those conditions was barely a few months, if not a few weeks. There is a story that of the initial group of 1,500 prisoners who were sent to Vorkuta, only 54 survived the ordeal.

And many of the prisoners sent to the Kolyma fields never completed the journey and died in transit.

Figure 79: Prisoners in the Gulag sentenced to hard labor working on a hillside during a moment of rest, 1936-1937

Soviet Citizens Should Have Resisted

During his confinement in the Gulag, Solzhenitsyn pondered the imponderable—namely, possible citizen resistance. He wrote:

And how we burned in the camps later, thinking: What would things have been like if every Security operative, when he went out at night to make an arrest, had been uncertain whether he would return alive and had to say good-bye to his family? Or if, during periods of mass arrests, as for example in Leningrad, when they arrested a quarter of the entire city, people had not simply sat there in their lairs, paling with terror at every bang of the downstairs door and at every step on the staircase, but had understood they had nothing left to lose and had boldly set up in the downstairs hall an ambush of half a dozen people with axes, hammers, pokers, or whatever else was at hand?... The Organs would very quickly have suffered a shortage of officers and transport and, notwithstanding all of Stalin's thirst, the cursed machine would have ground to a halt! If...if...We didn't love freedom enough. And even more—we had no awareness of the real situation.... We purely and simply deserved everything that happened afterward.[23]

The rude and abrupt knock on the door, the entrance, the typical KGB arrest, and the reaction of the hapless victims, are described in vivid details:

> *That's what arrest is: it's a blinding flash and a blow which shifts the present instantly into the past and the impossible into omnipotent actuality. That's all. And neither for the first hour nor for the first day will you be able to grasp anything else. Except that in your desperation the fake circus moon will blink at you: 'It's a mistake! They'll set things right!'*
>
> *And everything which is by now comprised in the traditional, even literary, image of an arrest will pile up and take shape, not in your own disordered memory, but in what your family and your neighbors in your apartment remember: The sharp nighttime ring or the rude knock at the door.*
>
> *The insolent entrance of the unwiped jackboots of the unsleeping State Security operatives. The frightened and cowed civilian witness at their backs. (And what function does this civilian witness serve? The victim doesn't even dare think about it and the operatives don't remember, but that's what the regulations call for, and so he has to sit there all night long and sign in the morning. For the witness, jerked from his bed, it is torture too—to go out night after night to help arrest his own neighbors and acquaintances).[24]*

Figure 80: "Week of Conscience" exhibition on the crimes of Stalinism held in 1988 at an electric factory in Moscow thanks to Perestroika. Dmitry Borko

No Right to Self-Defense: You Should Have Fled!

Astonishingly, Solzhenitsyn related that in the heavily militarized Soviet Union: "The State, in its Criminal Code, forbids citizens to have firearms or other weapons, but *does not itself undertake* to defend them."[25]

The Soviet Criminal Code of 1926 contained Article 139 that set "the limits of necessary self-defense."[25] Solzhenitsyn related:

You had the right to unsheath your knife only after the criminal's knife was hovering over you. And you could stab him only after he had stabbed you. Otherwise, you would be the one put on trial.[25]

However, the communist state defended itself ferociously with its famous KGB, the Sword and the Shield of the Soviet State, but it would not commit itself to defend Russian citizens from non-political criminals, particularly from the "socially friendly" thieves. Solzhenitsyn wrote:

The State turns its citizens over to the power of the bandits—and then through the press dares to summon them to 'social resistance' against these bandits. Resistance with what? With umbrellas? With rolling pins? First, they multiplied the bandits and then, in order to resist them, began to assemble people's vigilantes (druzhina), which by acting outside the legislation sometimes turned into the very same thing.[25]

Solzhenitsyn noted that "the fear of exceeding the measure of necessary self-defense led to total spinelessness as a national characteristic" on the part of the individual Russian citizen and total omnipotence on the part of the criminal state.[25] When a Red Army officer defended himself from an assailant and killed the hoodlum with a penknife, he was sentenced to 10 years in prison for murder. "And what was I supposed to do?" the officer asked, astonished. The Soviet prosecutor replied: "You should have fled!"[25]

"Flee!" That distant Soviet echo reverberates in modern society in most of the social democracies—"Scream, run, shout!"—not only in the United Kingdom but also in other territories of the British Commonwealth, Canada, and Australia. In those nations, there is no recognized or an untenable right to self-defense. And when citizens are in danger in the street or even in their homes, they are instructed to run and flee from criminal assailants. Human dignity, armed self-defense, and private property rights have been discarded when it comes to opposing criminals violating the rights of lawful citizens. Now thanks to Aleksandr Solzhenitsyn, one can trace this sad state of affairs in modern society all the way back to the repression and the lamentable political and societal situation in Stalin's Russia.[26]

Who Ran the Gulag?

From the time of the Cheka to the KGB, the security organs of the secret police ran the Gulag. And evil always begets evil. Gulag guards and officials included men like Naftaly Aronovich Frenkel (1883–1960), who played a major role in the re-organization of forced labor tasks in the Gulag system, beginning with one of the earliest sites of the destructive labor camps—that is, the Solovetsky Islands in the White Sea—and eventually encompassing the entire Gulag Archipelago that was so well-described by Aleksandr Solzhenitsyn in his monumental works.

Both Aleksandr Solzhenitsyn and journalist Anne Applebaum in their *magna opera*, assembled the pieces to the puzzle of Frenkel's elusive career.[27]

Figure 81: Naftaly Frenkel (1883–1960), circa 1930s, who reorganized the Gulag system so that the most labor could be attained in the short existence of the prisoners, which pleased Stalin

Frenkel was a mysterious individual. He began his known career as an obscure Turkish or Hungarian merchant of Jewish descent. He traveled from Haifa via the Austro-Hungarian Empire to Odessa and into Russia. He came to the attention of Soviet authorities in 1923 while working either as a merchant in a lucrative enterprise or as a profitable smuggler. He was arrested and sentenced to ten years of hard labor in the far north Solovetsky Islands.[28]

While confined to the prison camp, Frenkel demonstrated his ability in the reorganization of labor tasks. His idea was to make the Gulag more efficient by squeezing the most work out of the prisoners during their short existence in the labor camps. His reorganization of labor received the Vozhd's attention and protection.

Anne Applebaum related that when Frenkel arrived at the camp, he discovered shocking disorganization and the waste of human and material resources. Frenkel promptly wrote a precise description of what exactly was wrong with each of the camp's industries, including forestry, farming, and brickmaking, and placed his letter in the prison "complaint box."[28]

Appelbaum further related:

Even if Frenkel did not invent every aspect of the system, he did find a way to turn a prison camp into an apparently profitable economic institution, and he did so at a time, in a place, and in a manner which may well have brought that idea to the attention of Stalin.[29]

Figure 82: OGPU-chiefs responsible for construction of the White Sea-Baltic Canal, in July 1932. Right: Naftaly Frenkel; Center: Matvei Berman (head of the Gulag from 1932 to 1939); and Left: Afanasev (chief of the southern part of BelBaltLag). The White Sea-Baltic Canal was completed in summer 1933

Under Frenkel's management and ruthless efficiency, the Solovetsky camps were perceived to be profitable because of the "rational" distribution of food, the elimination of waste, and the fulfillment of production quotas. Frenkel rose through the ranks because of his results. His methods were duplicated throughout the rest of the Gulag labor system. He was promoted as chief of construction at the White Sea Canal, "the first major project of the Stalin-era Gulag, an extremely high post for a former prisoner."[30]

For the next two decades, the Gulag ran more efficiently and profitably at the expense of the enslaved prisoners. Frenkel's formula was "the supreme law of the Archipelago: 'We have to squeeze everything out of a prisoner in the first three months—after that we don't need him anymore.' "[31]

As previously stated, Stalin was pleased and protected Frenkel. He became a feared secret police official and security organ chief in the Gulag, who not only survived the Gulag and the purges but also survived Joseph Stalin.[32,33]

In Conclusion—A Personal Odyssey

February 12, 1974, began quite normally for Aleksandr Solzhenitsyn and his wife, Svetlova. They had spent the morning answering literary correspondence when they heard a knock at the front door. Upon opening it:

> *Two men burst inside, followed quickly by six others who had been waiting round a corner of the landing. Their leader took an official document from a folder, thrust it at Solzhenitsyn to inspect and sign, and informed him that he must accompany the assembled policemen to the prosecutor's office immediately. Solzhenitsyn was thunderstruck. He had described this very procedure in the opening pages of Gulag....Yet, when the actual moment came... 'I was in a state of witless shock, as though flames had suddenly enwrapped and paralyzed me.'...In short, he behaved just as distractedly, and made as many mistakes, as any other person would do on being arrested.[34]*

Solzhenitsyn was driven to Lefortovo Prison in Moscow and taken to the office of the deputy prosecutor general of the USSR, Mikhail P. Malyarov, who informed him "that he was being charged under Article 64 of the penal code with treason."[34] Despite having been arrested decades earlier and having spent eight years in the Gulag, he had not been ready to be rearrested now, and he spent a sleepless night confined to a cell.

The next morning, prison officers appeared and took Solzhenitsyn back to Malyarov's office where this time he was informed that he was being deported. The official document read:

> *By decree of the Presidium of the Supreme Soviet of the USSR for the systematic execution of actions incompatible with Soviet citizenship and harmful to the USSR, Solzhenitsyn A. I. is to be deprived of Soviet citizenship and evicted beyond the borders of the Soviet Union, today 13 February 1974.[35]*

Solzhenitsyn had "more than half expected it. The idea had been in the air...since the publication of *The Gulag Archipelago*.[36]

Suffice to say, Aleksandr Solzhenitsyn suffered oppression and survived against all odds. He confronted the pervasive evil that exercised nearly complete omnipotence over the individual and went on to defeat the totalitarian evil so thoroughly that it crumbled into dust. In the end, Solzhenitsyn lived to see himself vindicated and triumphant.

In 1990, the Soviet government dropped the charges of treason against Solzhenitsyn and restored his Soviet citizenship. In 1991, the Soviet Union collapsed. On May 27, 1994, the Nobel laureate returned to Russia after 20 years in exile.[37]

Figure 83: Alexander Solzhenitsyn (right), winner of the Nobel Prize in Literature 1970, and Russian cellist and conductor, Mstislav Rostropovich (left), at the celebration of Solzhenitsyn's 80th birthday in Moscow on December 17, 1998. Yuryi Abramochkin, RIA Novosti

The Other Solzhenitsyn and *Solzhenitsyn: A Biography* are mustread books for anyone interested in the legacy of this towering figure of the 20th century or those who relish inspirational works surrounding the legacies of great and courageous historical figures. Additionally, one must read Solzhenitsyn's own works, specifically the tomes mentioned in this chapter.

Those works will enrich your existence, give you a renewed sense of appreciation for life in freedom, and expand your historical and literary horizons beyond the constraining limitations of contemporary literature, progressive revisionist history, and the vacuity of popular culture.

Figure 84: Russian President Dmitry Medvedev and many Russian public figures attended Solzhenitsyn's funeral ceremony at the Donskoi Monastery, Moscow, August 6, 2008. Presidential Press and Information Office, Kremlin.ru

Part IV

Mao Tse-tung, the Mythic Long March (1934–1935), and China After Mao

CHAPTER 11

MAO TSE-TUNG—
THE CHAIRMAN WHO LED CHINA
INTO A COMMUNIST INFERNO

In 1978, a young assistant lecturer from Sichuan University left communist China for Great Britain and freedom. In 1982, Jung Chang was awarded a PhD in linguistics from the University of York and became the first person from the People's Republic of China to receive a doctorate from a British university. In 1991, her award-winning book, *Wild Swans*, was published.

Jon Halliday was a former Senior Research Fellow at King's College, University of London, and a noted author. He has written and edited eight previous books.

Jung Chang's collaboration with Jon Halliday produced *Mao: The Unknown Story*, a comprehensive biography of Mao Tse-tung (1893–1976) based on more than a decade of research and meticulous scholarship, including numerous personal interviews with many from Mao's close circle in China and those outside China who had significant dealings with him.[1] The authoritative biography, where 20th century Chinese communist history comes to life, provides enthralling reading with a fast-paced and flowing narrative.

The subtitle of the book is also very appropriate—namely, *The Unknown Story*—because much of the information and many of the new revelations contained in the book are not well known or found in other books on Mao or China.

Chang and Halliday not only revealed that the Chinese idol of communism was indeed rotten to the core and a brutal tyrant but also documented how Mao decimated China and exterminated the populace, including Communist Party cadres, entire Red Army regiments, and impoverished peasants.

Simon Sebag Montefiore, author of *Young Stalin* and *Stalin: The Court of the Red Tsar,* praised their book in *The Times* of London as "a triumph that exposes its subject as probably the most disgusting of the bloody troika of 20th-century tyrant-messiahs, in terms of character, deeds—and number of victims. This is the first intimate, political biography of the greatest monster of them all—the Red Emperor of China."[1,2]

Mao committed whatever crimes were necessary in order to attain and preserve supreme political power. For him, democracy, justice, equality, fraternity, and freedom were merely words to be used for propaganda purposes—not ideals to be pursued. And until the very end, only one predominate thought ever stirred in his mind: himself and his power.[3]

Figure 85: Mao Tse-tung (1893–1976), Chairman of the Communist Party of China (1943–1976), circa 1955

Chang and Halliday remind the reader that, "Today, Mao's portrait and his corpse still dominate Tiananmen Square in the heart of the Chinese capital. The current Communist regime declares itself to be Mao's heir and fiercely perpetuates the myth of Mao."[4]

Stalin and Mao—A Brief Comparison

As noted in the previous chapters, Joseph Stalin committed many atrocities and ruled Russia by terror. He shared some characteristics with Mao Tse-tung, yet there were differences. Therefore, a brief comparison between Stalin and Mao is instructive in understanding the enigmatic personality of Mao Tse-tung in all his savagery.

Stalin was noticed by Vladimir Lenin, who recognized his courage, his hard-working resourcefulness, and his usefulness—initially as a bandit who could obtain funds for the Communist Party but later, as a hardworking administrator who helped Lenin attain power and rule over a communist Russia. Stalin worked hard for the Bolsheviks behind the scenes and gradually achieved supreme power himself because his abilities were greatly underestimated by many comrades.

Stalin could inspire leadership, and at least had personal appeal as the Soviet Vozdh ("Great Leader")—that is, respect mixed with fear, a mixture of awe and even admiration as Stalin ruled the Soviet Union with a dictatorial iron fist and transformed a country of peasants into an industrialized nation that was not only feared by America but also made Western Europe tremble.

Figure 86: Mao Tse-tung (front row left) with Joseph Stalin (front row right) in December 1949 at Stalin's 71th birthday celebration in Moscow. Helsingin Sanomat

In contrast, Mao was lazy, insubordinate, and disliked by many who knew him personally. He was able to seize power only by duplicity and forced his subordinates to kowtow to him in abject submission. Mao turned the Red bases where he ruled into impoverished wastelands and was ultimately responsible for the death of 40 to 60 million Chinese.[5] At times, Mao even defied Stalin and the Soviets, who sustained him with money, arms, and other assistance through the years. By subterfuge, violence, atrocities, and propaganda in China as well as propaganda generated by Western writers abroad in the late 1930s, such as Edgar Snow's *Red Star*

Over China (1937), and, as we will see, with help from Stalin and the American moles in the Franklin D. Roosevelt (FDR) administration, Mao eventually came to rule all of Mainland China for 27 disastrous years. During the years in power, Mao never got into a bath or shower. "Instead, his servants rubbed him every day with a hot towel. He also enjoyed daily massages."[6]

Mao Tse-tung was hated and feared by all of his followers, including the subservient Chou En-lai. Mao ruled China by absolute terror and without any regard to the principles of government, strategic foresight, or judicious planning for the betterment of the country. Despite the mythic heroics of the Long March (1934–1935), the Chinese Civil War (1927–1949), and the Second Sino-Japanese War (1937–1945), the fact remained that Mao never inspired his troops. He was lazy and repeatedly used subterfuge or deceit to seize power from the Chinese Communist Party (CCP); and obtained the title of "Chairman" from Joseph Stalin, not from a plenum of the CCP. Therefore, Mao's power was not gained through merit or by recognition from the Party at large, but by fear, subterfuge, intimidation, and threats to the individual members of his inner circle Politburo.[1] Yet, as the head of state of the most populous nation on earth, he was respected as a communist statesman and great dignitary by Western politicians and academicians.

Beginning in 1937, Mao ruled the Yenan Red Base for the next decade. An ancient city and cultured city, Yenan was a hub of thriving commercial activity, and oil had been discovered in the region.[7]

However, under Mao's control, the province was devastated by communist mismanagement and plundered by the Chinese Red Army. "Living quarters built by Standard Oil were taken over by the Reds, who also appropriated substantial buildings owned by the Spanish Franciscans, including a just-completed cathedral."[7] Independent thought and action were punished. All goods and implements of labor were seized from the peasants to force them into compliance. Opium was cultivated and sold with all profits going to Mao's communists while the general populace starved. Yenan's population was decimated, a land where impoverishment became rampant, much worse than under the Nationalist rule of Generalissimo Chiang Kai-shek.[7] Mao's Yenan Red Base became a government from hell, and a prelude for what was to happen to the nation once the Chairman seized control of all of Mainland China.

Mao was also willing to sacrifice family members for political ends. Wives, brothers, sons, and daughters were left behind, either deliberately abandoned during China's Civil War to be shot by the Nationalists or condemned to die destitute in the poor villages throughout communist China.

Figure 87: Mao Tse-tung in Yenan (Yan'an), circa 1930s. The Yenan Red Base devastated the district, impoverished the people, and decimated the population

Mao would not hesitate to betray entire communist armies if they were led by military men he viewed as political rivals. Many Chinese Red soldiers were led to their death by irresponsible decisions or intentionally decimated based on Mao's need to attain power and eliminate competitors. For example, the most successful army in the Long March (1934–1935) was led by Chang Kuo-t'ao, a capable and competent military leader and political rival to Mao. Mao sent Kuo-t'ao's 80,000-man army to the desolate northwest district. Tens of thousands of soldiers succumbed from dysentery, typhus, infections, and freezing cold temperatures in the march through the inhospitable and swampy area. Supreme power was always paramount in Mao's decisions.[8]

Mao Received Soviet Assistance in the Conquest of China

Chang and Halliday described in graphic detail how China was delivered to Mao Tse-tung by active Soviet military assistance in northern China and with the tacit consent of Britain as well as the United States,

Mao Tse-tung—The Chairman Who Led China into a Communist Inferno   155

which was misled by moles like Owen Lattimore and Lauchlin Currie in the FDR administration.[9] Previously, little had been written about how Stalin attacked and ordered the Soviet Army to occupy Outer Mongolia, seized portions and important ports in Manchuria, and expropriated the strategic Eastern China Railway. Now, the story of how he did this and aided Mao in the Chinese Civil War that ensued immediately after Japan's surrender on August 15, 1945, has been coherently and convincingly related.

Figure 88: British Prime Minister Winston Churchill, U.S. President Franklin Roosevelt, and Soviet leader Joseph Stalin met at Yalta in February 1945 to discuss their joint occupation of Germany and plans for postwar Europe. National Archives and Records Administration

Chang and Halliday explained:

In February 1945, at Yalta in the Crimea, Stalin confirmed to Roosevelt and Churchill that Russia would enter the Pacific War two or three months after Germany's defeat. This meant the Soviet army would enter China, and thus give Mao his long-awaited chance to take the country. Mao had made a shrewd assessment as far back as 1923: communism, he had said then, 'had to be brought into China from the north by the Russian army.' Now, twenty-two years later, this was about to become reality.[10]

The Russo-Mongolian Soviet army, 1.5 million strong, swept through and invaded northern China across a 5,000-kilometer front, longer than the European front that stretched from the Baltic to the Adriatic Seas. Stalin ordered this army to continue to advance for several weeks after Japan's surrender, helping Mao take control of territories and large caches of arms left behind by the Japanese. The bases and the supplies would give Mao a boost in the continuing Civil War against Chiang Kai-shek. The occupied territories in northern China alone, were larger than those occupied by the Soviets in Eastern Europe.[10]

Figure 89: Chiang Kai-shek, Chairman of the National Government of China, during a visit to a U.S. Army air force base in March 1945. U.S. Army

Communist Moles in the U.S. Help Mao Gain Control of China

Mao received help from the United States.[11] Chiang Kai-shek, however, was sidelined by Washington and betrayed by several top generals in his Nationalist Army.[12] Recruited by the CCP while receiving officer training at the Whampoa Military Academy near Canton, the military officers essentially became "sleeper agents." At the proper moment—ten or twenty years later during the Civil War of 1946–1949—they were activated and betrayed the Generalissimo. They supplied vital military information to

Mao and either had entire armies deliberately massacred or surrendered them to Mao's forces.[12]

Figure 90: Chiang Kai-shek (center) and Chou En-lai (left) with cadets at Whampoa Military Academy in 1924

Communist moles in the FDR administration continued to act on the behalf of Mao and Stalin, and against the United States, by slandering Chiang Kai-shek and exalting Mao Tse-tung. Mao was supposed to have fought the Japanese, while Chiang was not doing any fighting. The opposite was closer to the truth. Except for one military campaign fought in 1940 by the Red Army Commander Peng Dehuai, who contravened Mao's order not to engage the Japanese, the Chinese Red Army did little against the Japanese since Mao wanted to keep his army intact for his ultimate confrontation with Chiang. Mao's order to his army had been "retreat when the enemy advances," which they did on almost all occasions.[13]

On the other hand, Chiang's Nationalist Army fought all the major engagements of World War II, while the Chinese Reds retreated and only occupied territories left behind by the Japanese. Even "in Burma, the

Nationalists had put more Japanese out of action in one campaign than the entire Communist army had in eight years in the whole of China."[14]

China in the Hands of Mao—A Travesty for the Chinese People

Mao was victorious in the Chinese Civil War not because he was a better military strategist or beloved by the people, but simply because he was more ruthless and vicious than Chiang Kai-shek. After the communist victory, Mao ruled China as the supreme leader. He used terror to keep the population subdued and fear to manage his underlings, just as he had done while building his power base in the various provinces prior to and during the great war.[13,15,16]

Tragically, the significant and historic events in communist China were not peaceful socio-economic advances, but militant initiatives begun by Chairman Mao to destroy the bourgeoisie, wipeout traditional mores, erase and re-write Chinese history, and construct a fully self-sufficient communist state with the Great Leap Forward (1958–1962) and the Cultural Revolution (1966–1976)—events that for China only brought social upheaval and violence, economic disaster, devastation, suffering, and death.[17]

The Fate of Mao's Lieutenants

Joseph Stalin carried out numerous purges during his communist rule in Russia; and in China, Mao Tse-tung was no different in that respect. "By November 1965, Mao was finally ready to launch the Great Purge he had long been planning…Mao proceeded in stages. He decided to fire his first shot at culture, and this is why the Great Purge was called the 'Cultural Revolution.' "[18]

To help run the Great Purge, Mao established the "Cultural Revolution Small Group," and put his fourth wife, Jiang Qing, "Madame Mao," in charge of it. Chen Boda served as the "nominal director," and Kang Sheng was an "advisor." Along with Lin Biao and Chou En-lai, these individuals made up Mao's inner circle.[19]

The Great Proletarian Cultural Revolution began in earnest in May 1966, becoming a "decade-long period of political and social chaos…that crippled the economy, ruined millions of lives and thrust China into 10 years of turmoil, bloodshed, hunger and stagnation…Historians believe somewhere between 500,000 and two million people lost their lives as a result of the Cultural Revolution."[20] According to historian Frank Dikötter, Chair Professor of Humanities at the University of Hong Kong and author of *The*

Cultural Revolution: A People's History (1962–1976), "Mao hoped his movement would make China the pinnacle of the socialist universe and turn him into 'the man who leads planet Earth into communism.' "[20]

Figure 91: Mao with loyal communist lieutenant Kang Sheng in Yenan in 1945

During the Cultural Revolution, "struggle sessions" or denunciation rallies were held throughout China. These mass rallies became violent spectacles against "public enemies." The accused ones were humiliated, tortured, and sometimes beaten to death, especially by people with whom they had been close, such as co-workers or students who had been incited by the fanatical "rebel" Red Guards. Students were pitted against teachers, spouses were pressured to denounce one another, friends were pressured to terrorize each other viciously, and children were urged and manipulated to expose parents by the Red Guards and Maoist agitators.

Perhaps for our purposes, it would be best to summarize what happened to a few of Mao's closest comrades-in-arms—those whom he had tamed, humiliated, and terrorized for nearly half a century, from the founding of the CCP in 1927 to his death in 1976.

Chou En-lai (1898–1976) was the servile assistant, the charming face Mao presented to the world for diplomatic and propaganda purposes.[21] Chou was probably Mao's most gifted and conscientious follower. He continued to serve Mao as a virtual slave, fawning over the

Chairman, always submissive, and frequently made to recant his "past mistakes." He served as Foreign Minister of the People's Republic of China (PRC) from 1949 to 1958 and as Premier from 1949 to 1976. Although he was ill, Chou tried to protect others and attempted to restrain the Red Guards during the Cultural Revolution. Somehow, he managed to survive the purges and violence. He was diagnosed with bladder cancer in 1974, but Mao refused to allow him to receive treatment. Mao wanted to make sure that Chou preceded him in death.[22] Chou continued to work even on his deathbed, trying unsuccessfully to moderate the Cultural Revolution, end the state of anarcho-tyranny, and keep the government of the PRC running. He died 8 months before Mao.

Figure 92: Chou En-lai in February 1972. Richard Nixon Library Oral History Collection

Lin Biao (1907–1971) was the youngest of Mao's henchmen and participated in the Long March as a military commander. He was Mao's strongest supporter throughout the Chinese Civil War and later headed the People's Liberation Army (PLA). Lin was instrumental in the communist victory during the Civil War, particularly in the northeast and Manchurian campaigns.[23] He ranked third among the Ten Marshals, just below generals Zhu De and Peng Dehuai. He helped foster Mao's Cult of

Personality, and as a reward, was designated his successor during the Cultural Revolution.[24] However, he mysteriously disappeared in 1971. Later, the world learned that Lin had been implicated in an unsuccessful plot to oust the Chairman. Reportedly, he had been denounced by his daughter while attempting to escape to the USSR. Lin, his wife, and son died in a plane crash in Mongolia.[25] To officially exonerate Mao, Lin Biao, Jiang Qing, and the "Gang of Four" were blamed by the PRC for the excesses of the Cultural Revolution.[26]

Figure 93: A public appearance of Chairman Mao (center left) and Lin Biao (center right) among Red Guards in Beijing during the Cultural Revolution in November 1966

Liu Shao-ch'i (1898–1969) participated in the Long March and supported Mao's leadership at the 1935 Zunyi conference. He helped Mao rule as second in command, assisted Mao in consolidating power and governing Yenan, and was appointed political commissar for the reconstituted New 4th Army.[27] After Mao's victory over Chiang Kai-shek and the establishment of Red China (PRC), Liu remained loyal to Mao and in 1959 was designated successor to Mao as "Closest Comrade in Arms."[28] But witnessing the suffering of the Chinese people in the provinces, Liu tried to moderate the viciousness of the Great Leap Forward (1958–1959), for which he paid a heavy price.[29] He was superseded by Lin Biao, and during the Cultural Revolution, Liu and his family were savagely persecuted. He was accused of "taking the capitalist road" and becoming "China's Khrushchev." He was imprisoned and tortured. In 1969, he died an agonizing death while still incarcerated.[30]

Figure 94: Liu Shao-ch'i (center) and Peng Dehuai (right) observing military exercises at the Liaodong Peninsula in 1955

Jiang Qing (1914–1991), "Madame Mao," was Mao's fourth wife and constant companion. She had been an actress in Shanghai and joined the underground CCP in 1932. She began living with Mao and then married him in 1938.[31] During the Cultural Revolution, she emerged as a leader and was the head of the notorious "Gang of Four," which was deposed by Deng Xiaoping.[32] She was arrested in October 1976, one month after Mao's death. She was prosecuted and at her trial she retorted in her defense, "I was Chairman Mao's dog. Whoever Chairman Mao asked me to bite. I bit." She was sentenced to death, but her sentence was commuted to life in prison. She was released in 1984 for medical reasons and committed suicide in 1991.[33]

Figure 95: Mao with his fourth wife, Jiang Qing ("Madame Mao"), in 1946

Chang Kuo-t'ao (1897–1979) was a founding member of the CCP and studied in the Soviet Union. He was the commander of the largest and most successful communist army during the Long March (1934–1935), acting independent of Mao. He was Mao's fiercest rival and contested him for the leadership of both the Red Army and the CCP. Before joining Mao in Yenan, his army was sabotaged and destroyed by Mao's treachery.[34]

In 1938, Chang renounced communism and escaped from Yenan to join the Nationalists. After the defeat of Chiang Kai-shek in the Civil War (1946–1949), Chang was fortunate to escape to Taiwan, and years later moved to Canada. Chang wrote vivid memoirs in exile that provided valuable information, became a Christian, and died in 1979 in Toronto at age 82.[35] The other Chinese military commanders, as we have seen and will see further, were not as fortunate as Chang.

Figure 96: Chang Kuo-t'ao, Peking University student leader and organizer of the CCP in the 1920s, later one of the best generals of the Chinese Red Army and rival to Mao in the 1930s

Zhu De (1886–1976), unlike most of the other Chinese leaders, came from a poor peasant background. Nevertheless, he obtained an education and traveled abroad. He was a leader of the Chinese Communist Party (CCP), participating in the Nanchang Uprising of 1927 that formed the Red Army. Zhu and Mao led the Zhu-Mao Army in the south. He supported Mao at the Zunyi conference in 1935, and with the advent of the Long March (1934–1935), Zhu was one of the military commanders. Later, he headed the 8th Route Army with Peng Dehuai during the Sino-Japanese War.[36] During the Civil War of 1946–1949, Zhu commanded the PLA. After the victory over Chiang Kai-shek and the Nationalists, and the formation of the PRC, he was awarded "Marshal of the People's Republic of China." He became Vice-Chairman of the PRC (1954–1959) and the CCP (1956–1966).[37] But Mao did not let bygones be bygones, and Zhu was later humiliated and disgraced during the Cultural Revolution because of "past mistakes," but he was reinstated in the CCP in 1973.[38] He died two months before Mao.[39]

Mao Tse-tung—The Chairman Who Led China into a Communist Inferno 165

Figure 97: Mao Tse-tung (right), Zhu De (second from right), Chou En-lai (second from left), and Bo Gu (left) in Yenan in 1937

Peng Dehuai (1898–1974), along with Chang Kuo-t'ao and Lin Biao, was one the best and most successful Red Army military commanders. Peng was already a soldier at the age of 16 and fought for various warlords in Hunan province. He joined and fought with the Kuomitang (Nationalist) Army in 1926 and participated in Chiang Kai-shek's Northern Expedition. By this time, though, he had become a communist, and he soon broke with Chiang to join the CCP. Allied with the Zhu-Mao Army, he fought against the Nationalists to preserve the Red bases. He also supported Mao at the 1935 Zunyi Conference and was a Red Army commander during the Long March (1934–1935). Peng was an advocate of a ceasefire with Chiang Kai-shek in order to fight the common enemy, the invading Japanese. He successfully re-energized the communist army during the ensuing Sino-Japanese War. Peng commanded the "Hundred Regiments," a victorious campaign and the only major battle the communists ever fought against Japan (between August and December of 1940).[40] He was to pay later for that victorious campaign, an engagement that had not been authorized by Mao. Peng was the commander of the Chinese forces fighting in the Korean War (1950–1953) and Defense Minister of the PRC from 1954 to 1959.[41] But Mao's long memory did not forget, and Peng became a target and victim of the Cultural Revolution. The former hero was dragged in the street and beaten to death by Maoist Red Guards in 1974.[42]

Figure 98: Peng Dehuai commanded the only serious communist offensive in the war against Japan in 1940

In short, Mao's legacy is one of unadulterated brutality and repressive dictatorship with no respect for life, liberty, or justice. Therefore, it is no coincidence that Mao's greatest disciples were notable psychopaths—namely, Pol Pot (1925–1998), who killed one million of his own people in Cambodia, and Abimael "Gonzalo" Guzman (1934–2021), who exterminated thousands of Peruvian indigenous peasants while leading the Maoist terrorist organization, *Sendero Luminoso*, the "Shining Path."

CHAPTER 12

THE MYTHIC LONG MARCH OF THE CHINESE RED ARMY

This chapter deals with a celebrated event in the turbulent life of Mao Tse-tung—that is, the mythic Long March—an event that was second only to his takeover of China. For the narration of this event in Western historiography, we will first cite the account written by Harrison E. Salisbury (1908–1993), author of *The Long March: The Untold Story*.[1]

Salisbury was an American journalist and an eloquent writer, who had a romantic, soft spot for young "idealistic," communist revolutionaries. His infatuation even persisted after the revolutionists showed their true colors and attained supreme power, ultimately discarding any sense of justice, imposing communism and totalitarianism, and using terror to rule the police states they created. Instead of the "workers' paradise" as promised, Vladimir Lenin and Joseph Stalin in the Soviet Union as well as Mao Tse-tung and his followers in communist China brought unspeakable horror to the people they claimed to have liberated.

Nevertheless, Salisbury seemed to have been wearing rose-tinted glasses that were super-imposed on blinders when writing about some of the communist dictators. That was the case with Salisbury's treatment of Vladimir Lenin, Leon Trotsky, and the rest of the Bolsheviks in his novelistic book, *Black Nights, White Snow*, about the October 1917 Russian revolution.[2] And, it seemed particularly true with his representation of Mao Tse-tung and the Chinese communists during the period 1934–1935 in *The Long March: The Untold Story*.

The Long March—Literary Storytelling by Harrison Salisbury

Salisbury was a fabulous storyteller, and his narrative is enthralling and mesmerizing. He admired these men; and in the case of Mao, Salisbury glossed over Mao's worst crimes and excused his excesses, attributing them to "his final years." There was no condemnation of the "Hundred Flowers

Campaign" and the "Anti-Rightist Campaign" (1957), the disastrous Great Leap Forward (1958–1962) or even the infamous Cultural Revolution (1966–1976), suggesting that these were errors (like breaking eggs to make omelets) or due to Mao's growing infirmity "in his final years." However, to his credit Salisbury summarized Mao's crimes against his former communist companions—that is, the heroes of the Long March whom Mao turned against with a vengeance during the Cultural Revolution. But there was no outrage for the crimes against the Chinese people or the 40 to 60 million victims who perished at the hands of Mao's communist government. Despite all the evidence available to Salisbury, *The New York Times* correspondent suggested that the Chinese people were better off during Mao's communist dictatorship than they had been under Chiang Kai-shek and the Nationalists' rule in China before the 1949 communist takeover. For those who have never lived under the yoke of tyranny, I suppose the collective equality of terror and misery somehow seems "better" than the freedoms inherent in individualism and the uncertainty of liberty.

Mao's Canonization and the Legendary March Retraced

Advancing the official version of the Long March propagandized by the historians of the People's Republic of China (PRC), who still venerate Mao and mythologize the heroic details of the Long March, Salisbury followed their lead and completely lost his objectivity. One can understand the veneration of Mao by Chinese academicians whose livelihood and maybe even lives depend on that veneration. But it is sometimes difficult to comprehend the admiration by those who live in freedom and have eyes to see the reality of living under Chinese communism, especially under Chairman Mao.

Like Edgar Snow before him, Harrison Salisbury crossed over from nonfiction history to revolutionary mythology and fantasy. But as previously stated, Salisbury was a master storyteller. The reader is taken on an interesting adventure but unfortunately the narration distorts the pages of the true and ghastly historic record.[1]

It was also disingenuous that in the middle of a page, Salisbury abruptly changed his narration of the "conspiracy of the litters" during the Long March to solemnly inform us:

Only with Mao's death on September 9, 1976, the arrest and destruction of the Gang of Four, and the rise of a new and more realistic scholarship under Deng Xiaoping is it becoming possible to disentangle the real Mao from the caricature created by the hagiographers.[3]

One expected Salisbury to then unveil the real historic Mao, but he does not. He goes on for the rest of his narrative to surpass the communist chroniclers of Beijing and the Marxist academicians in the West to create a supreme hagiography of his own, one that eclipses the others. Mao, who was ultimately responsible for the death of 40 to 60 million Chinese people, was virtually canonized by Salisbury, and his mistakes attributed to "his final years," when Salisbury suggested that the Chairman might have lost his grip on his faculties.

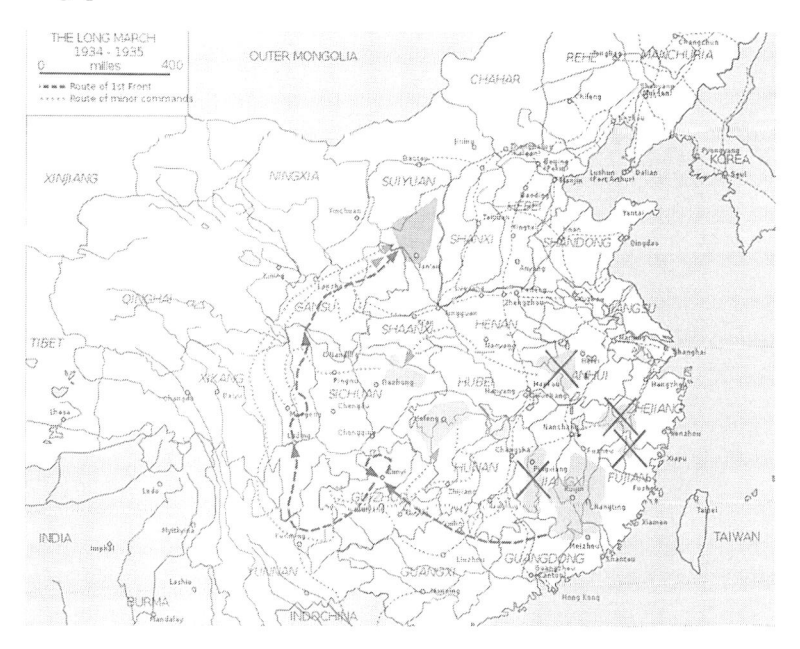

Figure 99: An overview map of the Long March (1934-1935) that began on October 16, 1934, lasted 368 days, and covered 6,000 miles

The reader must be cautious not to be seduced by the eloquent prose because, as previously stated, Salisbury was a master storyteller, and the unwary individual may be tempted to believe the highly embroidered tales. More accurate accounts of the Chairman were revealed in two authoritative tomes, *Mao: The Unknown Story* by Jung Chang and Jon Halliday that was discussed in chapter 11, and *The Long March: The True History of Communist China's Founding Myth* by Sun Shuyun.[4,5]

It is interesting to note that after obtaining permission from the PRC government and nearing age 75, Salisbury successfully retraced the route of the Long March. It was ironic, however, that he was not only accompanied by his wife but also by the former diplomat, John Stewart Service, an American communist sympathizer and "fellow traveler" who, while posted in China during World War II and like other the agents of influence previously cited, did his utmost to assist Mao Tse-tung and the communists instead of Chiang Kai-shek and the Nationalists.[6]

The Red Army "Supermen" of the Long March

To Harrison Salisbury, the Red Army men and women of the Long March were the Chinese version of Friedrich Nietzsche's *ubermensch*, enduring and heroic supermen and women who, purportedly, paid for everything they took from the oppressive landlords. But who were these "well-to-do" and "rich peasant" landlords, these Chinese "kulaks"? For the most part, they were not wealthy and were only slightly better off than other peasants. Strictly speaking, these "landlords" were peasants who aroused envy in their neighbors because they have risen above the rest to own more than a couple of acres of land or more than a couple of pigs or chickens.

However, the communists were the ones responsible for the incitement of envy through their revolutionary propaganda slogans that even encouraged and excused theft of private property. For example, one slogan advised, "Workers and peasants, rise up to kill the landlords' pigs and grab their grain for your new year!"[7]

Propaganda on the Long March was not only a major weapon but also a major enterprise. When the Red Army arrived in a new village, the "poster team" had to literally plaster the town with posters and slogans. "There was a minimum quota of 50 posters every day, and sometimes as many as 200…In Zunyi, the propaganda team wrote 18,400 slogans in two days."[7]

Shuyun related:

> *Even the Nationalists were overwhelmed. One bureaucrat reported to his superior that 'the Red Bandits pay particular attention to propaganda work. There were so many slogans that they covered every street and every lane, every window and every wall, occupying every inch of available space. No wonder people follow them like water flows downstream.'[7]*

Other propaganda slogans advocated "Down with Chiang Kai-shek," and urged the Chinese people to "Support the Red Army," telling them that "Only Communism can save China."[7]

Chiang Kai-shek's objective had been to herd the Red Army by forcing them to flee through desolate areas and finally corralling the survivors in the remote province of northern Shaanxi.

The Long March that began on October 16, 1934, lasted 368 days and covered 6,000 miles. The line of Long Marchers stretched over 50 miles in length.[8] They marched through harsh, mountainous terrain in the sweltering heat or freezing cold, despite their meager rations. For many of them, there was no turning back. There were tactical marches and countermarches over 18 mountain ranges, 24 river crossings, and skirmishes with the Nationalist Army.[8]

For the Red Army, the Long March was strategically a shameful and ignominious long flight as it mainly tried to avoid military engagement with Chiang Kai-shek's Nationalist Army. There were no brilliant, decisive battles in which the Reds smashed the Nationalists or military geniuses like Napoleon, Robert E. Lee, or even Leon Trotsky. The greatest wonder of the Long March was not the arduous, protracted retreat and escape, but the fact that for the most part, despite being hotly pursued by the Nationalists, the communist leaders, including Mao and Chou En-lai, continued to plan, intrigue, scheme, and give orders—directly from the litters in which they were being carried by the hapless porters.[9] Chang and Halliday wrote:

> *Bamboo litters were authorized for a few leaders, each of whom was also entitled to a horse and porters to carry their belongings. For much of the Long March, including the most grueling part of the trek, most of them were carried. Mao had even designed his own transportation…It had a tarpaulin awning…so [the passenger] would be shielded from the sun and the rain.[9]*

Additionally, one survivor noted that the Long March "was hardest for those who had to carry the leaders in their litters and the heavy loads. Some porters never got up again after they sat down to rest."[10]

The fact that the leaders "sat in sedan chairs" while the ordinary soldiers had to walk became a sore spot in the Red Army. Many of the Long Marchers took notice of this hypocrisy, and another survivor added, "The leaders talked about equality, but they lounged about in litters…" The flimsy explanation given to the soldiers was that "the leaders have a very hard life" even though they did not walk or carry any loads.[11] Chang and Halliday reported, "Not surprisingly, this low-level sophistry failed to assuage the rank-and-file."[11]

Figure 100: The leaders of the Chinese Communist Party during the Long March, from left to right, Chou En-lai, Mao Tse-tung, and Zhu De

During the Long March, the Red Army was plagued by disastrous mistakes and a serious desertion problem, often leaving desolation in its wake. It did not make planned, deliberate tactical maneuvers, but plainly outran the Nationalist Army. Circuitous routes were frequently followed, and in one particular episode "after two months of rushing further and further south with no end in view," the Long Marchers began asking, "Where are we going?"[12]

Moreover, while the mortality rate among the communist elite being carried in their litters was zero, the mortality rate for the common Chinese soldiers was 95 percent. Out of the 86,000 men who began the journey in the southern Soviet province of "Red Jiangxi," only 4,000 men and women survived to reach northern Shaanxi, their final destination.[8] The Fourth Army fared even worse and was completely annihilated.[13] Chang and Halliday summarized:

While the elite all survived, sheer exhaustion killed many of their much younger litter-carriers, nurses, and bodyguards, who were often in their teens—and some as young as twelve or thirteen. One statistic reveals the stony-hearted hierarchy and privilege under Mao's dominion: the Central Red Army now had almost more officers than soldiers.[13]

Chinese communist historiographers, supported by Western books such as those by Snow and Salisbury, like to elaborate on dramatic stories about Red Army military heroism during the Long March, led by the intrepid leader, Mao. They like to relate how the Red Army had to fight pitch battles to capture river crossings defended by warlords and Nationalist troops. The most famous of these episodes was the Battle for Luding Bridge, extolled in official history as a courageous triumph. Most historians now agree that the heroics and difficulties encountered in that battle were greatly exaggerated[14], if not outright fabricated for propaganda purposes.[15]

Documentary filmmaker Sun Shuyun had been indoctrinated about the purported glorious battle fought by the Red Army Long Marchers at the crossing of the Dadu River at Luding Bridge. In fact, the celebrated battle had been immortalized in a propaganda film she remembered watching as a youth. Before Shuyun set out on her journey, she recounted a conversation she had with a military historian in Beijing, who had been unusually candid. She asked him which battle she should concentrate on, and the following conversation ensued:

'Which one do you know best?' he asked. The Luding Bridge, I said, hardly thinking. 'You call that a battle? Just a couple of men fell into the river, and it was over in an hour. How can that be the biggest battle of the Long March?' I was stunned. I thought I knew it so well. 'Go and find out for yourself,' he added, 'and come back and tell me what you discovered.'[14]

Figure 101: Luding Bridge in Western Sichuan Province, where the famed battle supposedly took place. Rolf Müller

Indeed, Shuyun discovered that the historian had been correct. The gist of the battle, as succinctly related by him, was later confirmed to her by the Long March survivors she interviewed.[14]

How Mao and his hagiographers turned a disastrous retreating flight and decimation of the Red Army into a revolutionary triumph of legendary proportions was a masterstroke. And, although Salisbury's *The Long March* may be considered a literary masterpiece of mythic revolutionary propaganda, it is not objective history.

Chiang Kai-shek and Joseph Stalin

In *Mao: The Unknown Story*, Chang and Halliday also made an excellent case that part of the reason the heroic Long Marchers were not totally annihilated was simply because Chiang Kai-shek did not want to alienate Joseph Stalin, with whom he still enjoyed good relations.[16]

After the end of the Long March, Stalin urged cooperation between Mao and Chiang Kai-shek. He needed an undivided China to stave off the serious threat the Japanese posed to Russia's right flank, and the possibility that the USSR would be forced to fight on two fronts if war erupted in Europe as expected. On August 15, 1936, "Moscow sent the CCP a milestone order, telling them to stop treating Chiang as an enemy, and count him as an ally."[16] The order stated:

> *It is incorrect to treat Chiang Kai-shek the same as the Japanese…You must work for the cessation of hostilities between the Red Army and Chiang Kai-shek's army, and for an agreement…to struggle jointly against the Japanese.[16]*

Later in December 1936, Stalin saved Chiang Kai-shek's life, during the remarkable Xi'an incident when the Generalissimo was kidnapped by a renegade general, Chang Hsüeh-liang, known as the "Young Marshal."[16] While Mao schemed and plotted in the background to have Chiang killed, Stalin again stepped in, sending him a message on December 16 that condemned the kidnapping, saying it "can objectively only damage the anti-Japanese united front and help Japan's aggression against China…The CCP must take a decisive stand in favour of a peaceful resolution."[16]

Essentially, the message constituted an order from Moscow to "secure the release and reinstatement of the Generalissimo." Needless to say, "when the cable arrived, Mao flew into a rage…" but eventually, he "brought his goals back into alignment with Stalin's."[16]

In short, for the time being, Joseph Stalin deemed it strategically advantageous to Russia for China to remain as a united front against the Japanese thereby protecting his right flank.

Another Account of the Long March by Chinese Historian Sun Shuyun

Sun Shuyun was born in communist China in the 1960s, reared and schooled there and later at Oxford, England, where she won a scholarship. She became a documentary filmmaker and television producer who created documentaries aired on PBS and the Discovery Channel, and "divided her time between London and Beijing." Shuyun's father was a hardline communist, who bitterly resented the more moderate course China took in more recent years. Upon his death, he was cremated in his Mao uniform with his medals.

This short biographical vignette of Sun Shuyun is essential to explain her "conflicted" and seemingly ambivalent views on Mao and his legacy—vis-à-vis, the People's Republic of China (PRC). Evidently, at the time of the writing of her book, she had not completely broken away or totally freed herself from her communist childhood indoctrination. Criticism of Mao and China's communist history is obliquely alluded to and only indirectly uttered from the mouths of some of the elderly survivors of the Long March who she interviewed.

Figure 102: A communist leader addressing Long March survivors, 1930s

Shuyun's book, *The Long March: The True History of Communist China's Founding Myth*, was dedicated "to all the men and women on the Long March," and appropriately so. Shuyun relied on historic archives and the personal accounts related to her by several of the forty survivors that she found who had not only participated in the Long March but also had settled along the routes the Long March followed between 1934 to 1935.

However, during the Cultural Revolution, those octogenarian and nonagenarian survivors of the Long March were abused and persecuted by the Red Guards—treated as pariahs, deserters, and even traitors by the PRC, which they had helped to bring about. Shuyun related:

> *Mao had almost all of the veterans of the Long March purged in the Cultural Revolution—they were too old, and too unwilling, to do his bidding. The Red Guards were the new Marchers.[17]*

Recently, though, the Long March survivors have been rehabilitated, finally acknowledged as loyal Red Army men and women, and given pensions as participants in the Long March. The veterans' tales are heartrending and not always flattering to Mao or to the communist government he ushered in. Nevertheless, for the most part and despite their travails and the persecutions, they remained faithful to the Revolution and proud of their role in the Long March.

The Forgotten Saga of the Western Legion of the 4th Army

Connoisseurs of Chinese communist history in general and the Long March in particular will be struck by at least two salient aspects of Sun Shuyun's book. The first aspect of her book, which was based on the true accounts of Long March survivors, is how much those accounts are in accord with and confirm the information contained in *Mao: The Unknown Story* by Jung Chang and Jon Halliday, including the stories of starvation, disease, and desertion. The second aspect is the disclosure of the mysterious course and, heretofore, the untold story and ghastly fate (forbidden in communist history) of the 4th Army of General Chang Kuo-t'ao (or Zhang Guotao)—namely, the Western Legion or the "Legion of Death."

The Red Army's Western Legion was deliberately sabotaged by Mao and sent to their death. The Legion was massacred by the formidable cavalry of the Muslim army of the Mas, the tribesmen operating in the remote and barren province of Gansu in northwestern China and allied to Chiang Kai-shek.

Chang and Halliday blamed the loss of the Western Legion on Mao's deliberate machinations and political plotting against his rival, General Chang Kuo-t'ao. Sun Shuyun's survivor accounts all but confirm those conclusions without actually making definitive statements about that fact. Shuyun added:

All but 400 of the 20,800 men and women were either killed or captured, yet this tragic story has been virtually left out of Long March history, except for a brief denunciation... For the next fifty years anyone who questioned this would have been challenging Mao—an unthinkable crime. The few memoirs that referred to it were suppressed; veterans of the Legion were treated as traitors; scholars who dared to ask questions were warned by the Party and followed by police... In 2002, the new History of the Communist Party carried a brief revised entry, saying the Western Legion was not carrying out Zhang Guotao's scheme, as Mao had claimed, but was fully under the command of the Central Committee.[18]

In short, Mao's "erratic stop-and-go orders" proved lethal for the Western Legion.[18] Shuyun's account of the saga of the Western Legion of the 4th Army will remind readers of another great book from antiquity—namely, Xenophon's *Anabasis*, except that in the *Anabasis*, the ancient warriors were not betrayed by their leader.

Sun Shuyun also corroborated the fact that Mao and the communists lost support of the people and even some Communist Party leaders after the political intrigues and bloody purges that followed in the wake of the Futian incident, which was "the first open challenge to Mao."[19] Twenty thousand party functionaries were denounced, purged, and summarily executed on Mao's orders as "enemies of the people" or "Nationalist spies," purportedly members of the non-existent Anti-Bolshevik (AB) faction within the Communist Party.[19] Shuyun noted:

Mao's purge was not copied from Moscow's tactics; It came before Stalin was to employ such means on any scale. It is estimated that over 20,000 people from the army, the Party, and the Jiangxi Soviet government died in the purge, which lasted just over a year. That was more than the casualties suffered by the Red Army in Chiang's first three campaigns. The purge weakened the Party at a time when it was most vulnerable, and it shook the people's faith in the man they thought was their leader.[19]

Initially, Mao's purges were confined to the Communist Party and the Red Army. Now, they "moved into wider society and helped to undermine support for the Jiangxi Soviet."[19] Three elderly Chinese men intriguingly told Shuyun, "the water began to flow upstream," meaning people fled from Mao's Jiangxi Red base, fearful for their lives and escaping the desolation.[19] That was the reason Mao was marginalized and lost power within the Communist Party at this time, forcing the party to plan the Long March in order to flee from the Nationalists. Mao's barbarity and disastrous policies turned Chiang Kai-shek's Fifth Campaign into a Nationalist victory and necessitated the abandonment of the Jiangxi Soviet base in the rout the Long March really was.

Figure 103: Chang Kuo-t'ao (Zhang Guotao) and Mao Tse-tung in Yenan (Yan'an) in 1937

However, Mao was not solely to blame for every mistake, and he was not the only bloodthirsty Chinese communist. Just before setting out on the Long March, the Communist Party ordered its own purge to cleanse the Red Army and ensure the loyalty of those left behind in the Jiangxi Soviet.

Thousands more were executed. And General He Long's 2nd Army, just before embarking on its own long march, exterminated most of its own soldiers, so that from 1932 to 1934 its number dropped from 30,000 to 3,000.[20] Shuyun related:

> *They killed so many people, they did not have to wait for Chiang's campaigns; they had to leave their base in 1932, two years before the Central Army went on the Long March, because they lost the support of the local people.[20]*

Not surprisingly, the people of the Red Jiangxi Soviet lost faith in the communists as the purges and mass killings took place and resources were squandered. Chiang Kai-shek took advantage of the opportunity and began his Fifth Campaign that forced the communists to leave Jiangxi in the massive retreat that Mao and his propagandists later turned into the "victorious" and "epic" Long March.[21]

This was one of the many revelations Shuyun brought to light, debunking the official histories of the Chinese Communist Party archives and the various heroic myths that lionized Chairman Mao and bolstered his image as the infallible leader of Chinese communism. In a moment of introspection, Sun Shuyun remarked that, "Twenty years of communist upbringing had left their stamp on me, when all I was told, heard, and read was the good things the Party did."[19] She realized that the Communist Party had told her many lies, but in freedom, she had prospered.

Conclusion

In the previous section, we mentioned the formidable cavalry of the Muslim army of the Mas, the tribesmen allied to Chiang Kai-shek who operated in the remote province of Gansu in northwestern China and decimated the Western Legion of the 4th Army. In connection with this, we will mention the plight of another Muslim minority in China that has not easily submitted to the communist successors of Mao. They are the Uighurs, a Turkic ethnic minority that has been persecuted for their intransigency, their love of liberty, and their devotion to Islam and not communism.

A BBC report explained:

> *The Uighurs are a Muslim Turkic-speaking minority based in the northwest Xinjiang region of China, which has come under intense surveillance by Chinese authorities. Their language is close to Turkish, and a significant number of Uighurs have fled to Turkey from China in recent years. So far, few Muslim-majority countries have joined in public*

international condemnation of the allegations. Analysts say many fear political and economic retaliation from China.[22]

Perhaps remembering the feat of the Muslim Mas cavalry and knowing the Uighur's tenacious adherence to their way of life, the Chinese communist government in recent years has ferociously persecuted them. The Uighurs have been corralled and placed in detention centers and concentration camps. Turkey has complained, but to no avail. And the persecutions continue. This is the way of communism.

Figure 104: The Uighurs protesting in Amsterdam in 2011. Paul Keller

The BBC report went on to quote a complaint voiced by a spokesman in the Turkish Foreign Ministry:

It is no longer a secret that more than a million Uighur Turks exposed to arbitrary arrests are subjected to torture and political brainwashing... The reintroduction of concentration camps in the 21st century and the systematic assimilation policy of Chinese authorities against the Uighur Turks is a great embarrassment for humanity.[22]

As we should see in the next chapter, the crimes of Chinese communism have impaired Chinese relations with the West, although not always. From time to time, some government administrations in the United States, for example, have chosen to look the other way at these crimes for political considerations as well as economic expediency—or just plain corruption and ineptitude.

CHAPTER 13

CHINA-UNITED STATES RELATIONS SINCE THE 1990S

In 1998, United States national security experts, Edward Timperlake and William C. Triplett, II, alleged that the administration of U.S. President Bill Clinton (1993–2001) sold national security secrets to communist Red China in return for illegal campaign contributions.[1] The allegations that were outlined in graphic detail in their book, *Year of the Rat: How Bill Clinton Compromised U.S. Security for Chinese Cash*, provoked an outcry in Washington D.C. at the time. But incredibly, only a handful of the individuals were indicted. Apparently, the U.S. Department of Justice, under the control of Clinton's Attorney General, Janet Reno, was not asking too many questions.

Figure 105: Official White House photo of President Bill Clinton, 42nd President of the United States (1993–2001). Bob McNeely, The White House

The authors also reminded the world that the Clinton administration sold those secrets to the butchers of Tiananmen Square where, on June 4, 1989, the communist Chinese government brutally squelched the pro-democracy protests that had been taking place in China over the previous seven weeks. According to newly declassified British documents, the death toll for the Tiananmen Square massacre was 10,000 Chinese students killed in cold blood.[2] The implications of the Clinton-Gore administration welcoming those responsible for the massacre to Washington, D.C. with 19-gun salutes did not pass unnoticed by the authors either.[1]

The Bill Clinton and Al Gore team would do anything for money to gain power in 1992 and to retain power in 1996. A U.S. Commerce Department employee and Chinese spy John Huang, working for the Indonesia-based Lippo Group moguls, Mochtar and James Riady, who the U.S. Central Intelligence Agency (CIA) confirmed had a long-standing association with Chinese intelligence, all played pivotal roles.

Figure 106: James Riady, deputy chairman of the Lippo Group, at the World Economic Forum on East Asia on June 7, 2010. Sikarin Thanachaiary, World Economic Forum

Likewise, a Clinton-Arkansas crony and "Four Seas" Triad member Yah Lin aka "Charlie Trie" and Macau criminal syndicate and prostitution ringleaders Ng Lapseng and Ted Sioeng were all purportedly involved in the transfer of cash for U.S. national security secrets, including the sale of highly sophisticated, satellite technology—"a prime focus of China's military buildup."[3,4]

Year of the Rat also introduced four intriguing and determined Chinese women who had what could be characterized as "improper relations" with the president (and the vice president). The relations were not sexual in nature but treasonous. One of the women, Lieutenant Colonel Liu Chaoying, a People's Liberation Army (PLA) intelligence agent who had insisted on meeting Bill Clinton, later made substantial contributions to the Democratic Party coffers, and thereafter, received considerable help from the president's lobbying efforts to obtain the needed concessions for the China Ocean Shipping Company (COSCO) to lease a naval base in Long Beach, California.[5]

Figure 107: Photo of PLA Lt. Col. Liu Chaoying from 1996 testimony hearings concerning Johnny Chung and noted "Lippo-Gate." U.S. Government

At this time, President Clinton was frequently criticized by some in the media for being hypocritical—namely, for preaching draconian gun control laws that affected law-abiding American citizens while entertaining Chinese arms dealers, such as Wang Jun of Polytechnologies, at a White House coffee that was part of a Democratic National Committee (DNC) fundraising event.[6] Timperlake and Triplett explained:

In 1996, a COSCO ship called the Empress Phoenix was caught carrying two thousand automatic weapons into the port of Oakland, California. The cargo was seized by U.S. Customs agents. The Empress Phoenix was manned on that voyage by Wang Jun's arms dealership, Polytechnologies. The cargo was destined for Los Angeles gang members.[7]

Although Mr. Wang was subsequently indicted in the United States, apparently President Clinton remained undaunted. On May 30, 1998, he approved the launch of a Lockheed Martin telecommunications satellite by China Orient Satellite Telecommunications (COSAT).[8] Timperlake and Triplett added:

According to published reports, COSAT is a joint venture between the Chinese Ministry of Posts and Telecommunications and Polytechnologies…. Polytechnologies is…owned by the General Staff Department of the PLA and headed by Deng Xiaoping's son-in-law. Poly is China's leading arms smuggler and the conduit for Russian arms transfers to China. Poly was also one of two Chinese arms smugglers caught by U.S. Customs agents trying to sell fully automatic machine guns to U.S. drug gangs in 1996.[8]

Not all of the characters in this nefarious story were communist Chinese though. Several American capitalists placed corporate profits ahead of America's national interest. The corporations they headed donated millions of dollars to the DNC to help the Democrats regain Congress in the 1996 and 1998 elections. In return, the Clinton-Gore team signed waivers allowing U.S. companies to transfer the most sensitive satellite (that is, missile launching) technology to Red China, obliterating the safety margin and technological edge the U.S. previously had on China and other potential enemies.[9] Gary Milhollin, director of the University of Wisconsin Project on Nuclear Arms Control, confirmed that, "The danger is that we are giving away the technical edge that we've always relied upon for our security."[10]

Dr. William Graham, former deputy administrator of the National Aeronautics and Space Administration (NASA) testified during a U.S. Senate hearing on May 21, 1998, and explained that, "Intercontinental ballistic missiles can be considered space launch vehicles whose orbits intersect the earth at the target…In the case of China, the Long March 3 [space launch vehicle] is based on DF-5 ballistic missile technology."[11] According to Dr. Graham, ICBMs and space launch vehicles share the same propulsion, structure, staging, guidance and control, and payload deployment. Timperlake and Triplett added:

The principal national security argument against allowing United States or European satellites to be launched by Chinese space launch vehicles is the possible transfer, even inadvertently, of technology to the PLA's missile and space launch development. The key point is reliability. If we have made Chinese space launch vehicles and missiles more reliable, we have enhanced their missile force and their ability to get into space consistently.[11]

Figure 108: Donfeng (DF-5B) intercontinental ballistic missile operated by the Chinese PLA Army Rocket Force developed in the 1990s. If launched from eastern China, they could reach the entire United States. Voice of America

According to American intelligence and the Cox Committee Report, before the year 2000, China had 20 reliable ICBMs targeted at U.S. cities, and although not à la par with the U.S., they still posed a serious threat to American national security.[9] Given what we now know, President Clinton was lying when he stated: "For the first time since the dawn of the nuclear age, there is not a single solitary nuclear missile pointed at an American child tonight. Not one. Not a single one."[12]

Subsequently, China transferred the sensitive U.S. technology to Pakistan, Iran, and North Korea—the last two nations are enemies of the United States. And since that time, China has continued to make serious and perilous threats towards Taiwan. It is beyond human understanding.

In an exclusive interview with newsletter editor David Bossie, U.S. Representative Dan Burton (R-IN), Chairman of the U.S. House Committee on Government Reform and Oversight, summarized:

We had 79 people involved in fundraising for the Democratic Party invoke the Fifth Amendment protection to avoid incriminating themselves. And there are another 23 witnesses, like James Riady of the Lippo Group and Liu Chaoying of China Aerospace, who live in other countries, and we have been unable to interview them. I asked FBI director [Louis] Freeh if he had ever been involved in any investigation in which so many witnesses took the Fifth or fled. He said the only time he remembered such a situation was during an investigation of organized crime in New York.[12]

It is now known that both Riadys, and their associate, Democrat operative Johnny Chung, a former owner of a "blastfaxing" business, made illegal donations to the Democratic Party between 1994 and 1996 for the Clinton administration. Moreover, all three men had communist connections as well as ties to Chinese intelligence.[13,14]

In fact, "Chung testified under oath to the U.S House Committee in May 1999 that he was introduced to Chinese General Ji Shengde, head of Chinese military intelligence, by Liu Chaoying. Chung said that Ji told him, "We like your president very much. We would like to see him reelected. We would like to give you 300,000 U.S. dollars. You can give it to the president and the Democrat Party."[14]

For his part, in 1998 Chinese-Indonesian James Riady was indicted and plead guilty to campaign finance violations by himself and his corporation. "He was ordered to pay an 8.6 million U.S. dollar fine for contributing foreign funds to the Democratic Party, the largest fine ever levied in a campaign finance case."[15] Years later, in January 2010, the *Washington Post* revealed how the "disgraced" Riady had received a visa waiver by the current Obama Administration to re-enter the U.S., despite having been banned by the previous Bush administration. Riady's old friend, U.S. Secretary of State Hillary Rodham Clinton claimed she had no knowledge of the visa waiver. A State Department official, embarrassed by the *Post's* revelation, stated, "the reality of his past remains a significant obstacle for future travel to the United States." Riady received a "waiver from a rule that forbids entry to foreigners guilty of 'a crime involving moral turpitude,' a term that government lawyers generally interpret to include fraud."[15]

Several U.S. corporations were also later charged with a total of "123 violations of export laws in connection with the Chinese data transfers" and successfully prosecuted by the federal government. Loral, Hughes Electronics, Lockheed Martin, and Boeing were fined and the companies paid multi-million dollar penalties to "settle civil charges that they unlawfully transferred rocket and satellite data to China in the 1990s."[15]

The many revelations that came out of the Cox Committee Report—of which one third were censored by the Clinton-Gore administration as deemed "too sensitive" for public consumption—showed the frightening extent of Red Chinese corruption permeating the Democratic administration of Bill Clinton and Al Gore as well as espionage with the consequent loss of the United States' most sensitive nuclear and technological secrets.

Taiwan, U.S. and China Relations

In 1996, a Taiwan Strait crisis developed in which China attempted to intimidate Taiwan by launching a series of missile tests. This time the Clinton administration responded appropriately and sent the U.S. 7th Fleet to the region to discourage any thought of a communist invasion of Taiwan. At the same time, however, a leading Chinese general threatened to nuke Los Angeles, adding with great assurance that "such an attack against Los Angeles would be in prospect if the United States interfered in China's campaign of intimidation against Taiwan."[16,17]

For over four decades, the United States has had a "one China" policy, which meant "the U.S. government has maintained official relations with the People's Republic of China (PRC or China) and unofficial relations with self-governed Taiwan."[18]

To a significant degree, the U.S. abides by its "one China" policy. Most of the historic antecedents for the policy have been correctly ascribed to Republican U.S. President Richard M. Nixon and his Secretary of State Henry Kissinger. Nixon visited China and was greeted by Chairman Mao in 1972 with the opening of relations between the two nations that astounded the world. Taiwan was essentially left hanging.[11]

Many patriotic and conservative Americans looked upon President Nixon's trip as a very disheartening betrayal of Taiwan. However, the move was also viewed as a strategic one that widened the rift between the two communist superpowers during the dangerous Cold War—that is, the Soviets and the Red Chinese.

While Nixon received credit for opening up China, on January 1, 1979, Democrat U.S. President Jimmy Carter further trampled on the honor of America by kowtowing excessively to the communist Chinese and establishing full diplomatic relations with Red China. On that same date, diplomatic relations with Taiwan were terminated and the former U.S. ally was cast aside. Many in Congress considered Carter's move to be one more submissive gesture to left-wing dictatorships and communist regimes among a long list of foreign policy failures and disasters during his administration. So, on April 10, 1979, both Houses of the United States

Congress passed the Taiwan Relations Act (TRA).[18] On December 31, 1979, the previous Sino-American Mutual Defense Treaty between the United States and the Republic of China (on Taiwan), which had been in place since 1955, was allowed to expire.

Figure 109: Mao Tse-tung with Henry Kissinger and Chou En-lai in Beijing in 1972. Oliver Atkins, U.S. Government

In July 1982, President Ronald Reagan issued "Six Assurances" to "faithfully enforce all existing United States Government commitments to Taiwan."[18] Currently, the Taiwan Relations Act, three U.S.-China joint communiqués issued in 1972, 1978, and 1982, and Reagan's Six Assurances, form the framework for U.S. relations between Taiwan and Red China.[18]

It should be noted that although the PRC claims sovereignty over Taiwan, "taking no position on Taiwan's sovereignty has been longstanding U.S. policy."[18] As recently as September 17, 2020, a U.S. State Department spokesman reaffirmed that the United States "will not take a position on [Taiwan's] sovereignty," and added, "the question of sovereignty was…left undecided and to be worked out between the two parties, Taiwan and the PRC."[18]

Figure 110: Official presidential portrait of Ronald Reagan, 40th President of the United States (1981-1989). Michael Evans, Executive Office of the President of the United States

Even though the question of sovereignty over Taiwan remains diplomatically "undecided," the rest of the Six Assurances do not seem quite as pusillanimous:

> The United States "did not agree to set a date certain for ending arms sales to Taiwan"; "the [1982 joint communiqué] should not be read to imply that we have agreed to engage in prior consultations with Beijing on arms sales to Taiwan"; "we see no mediation role for the United States"; "we have no plans to seek any revisions to the TRA"; "there has been no change in our longstanding position on the issue of sovereignty over Taiwan"; "nor will we attempt to exert pressure on Taiwan to enter into negotiations with the PRC."[18]

In accordance with the TRA, the United States has long provided arms and military equipment to Taiwan. In 2023, the Biden administration in Washington, D.C., approved two arms sales to the island totaling $440 billion. A U.S. State Department spokesman noted that the proposed sale served "U.S. national, economic and security interests by supporting the recipient's continuing efforts to modernize its armed forces and to maintain a credible defensive capability."[19] While the Taiwanese Defense Minister thanked the United States, the Chinese, of course, voiced their objection to the sale stating that the United States should abide by the "one China policy and the three joint communiqués," conveniently omitting any mention of the Taiwan Relations Act, which they know full well gives America the "agreed upon concession" to sell arms to Taiwan.[19]

Today, Taiwan remains one of America's vital trading partners. In 2021, the United States accounted for 15% of Taiwan's exports. Interestingly, mainland China and Hong Kong accounted for 42% of the exports. In other words, mainland China does more trade in goods and services with Taiwan than the United States.[20]

President Donald Trump Enters the Scene in the 21st Century

On December 2, 2016, Donald Trump, the newly elected U. S. president, received a congratulatory telephone call from Taiwan's President Tsai-Ing-wen, triggering a thunderstorm of media clatter and protestations. Some mainstream media analysts were "aghast" at the incident. I personally believe Trump was correct, and that it was proper to take the call from the diminutive, determined, and democratically elected Taiwanese president. The Taiwanese have lived under the threat of invasion or nuclear attack from the communist Chinese for decades.[21]

Mellifluous-voiced David Wright, a broadcast journalist on *ABC News* said, "It is difficult to tell if Trump's conversation was a rookie mistake or a deliberate provocation"; while *ABC News* political analyst Matthew Dowd further expounded stating that either way Trump's posture was "problematic."[21] The Sunday morning *ABC News* show was reminiscent of the egregiously biased coverage on election night when Trump was elected in November 2016.[22]

The media predicted a massive, angry, and destabilizing Chinese response, already blaming Trump for his "rookie mistake" or "deliberate provocation."[23] Moreover, Trump had previously not minced words during his campaign, accusing the communist nation of terrible business and trade practices and for manipulating their currency to the detriment of the United States. But the feared and expected destabilizing response from China did not materialize. The diplomatic protest—if we can even call it a protest—was a very measured response, only lodging "solemn representations" with the United States.[24]

The Chinese foreign minister informed reporters in Beijing that China urged the relevant parties in the United States to handle Taiwan-related issues "cautiously and properly" to avoid "unnecessary interference" in the China-U.S. relationship. The minister added that, "there is only one China in the world, and Taiwan is an inseparable part of Chinese territory."[24]

Figure 111: Xi Jinping, paramount leader of the PRC (2012–). Alan Santos

The U.S. remains China's largest trading partner, and China has a big economic interest in maintaining that partnership, a trading partnership that actually resulted in an American trade deficit of nearly $340 billion in 2015.[21] Corporativist China was not about to endanger that lucrative trade and chance a military confrontation with the U.S. for a "runaway province" of Imperial China, especially when the American president-elect was Donald Trump, and not a more submissive-president like Jimmy Carter.[21]

The roles were switched in 2020 when Democrat Joe Biden became U.S. president, and he had to confront the formidable and paramount leader of China Xi Jinping, General Secretary of the Chinese Communist Party since 2012 and President of the PRC since 2013. Biden had to confront Xi in relation to acts of intimidation against Taiwan that have continued in violation of Taiwan's air space and territorial waters by the air and naval forces of the PLA.

We will have more to say about China-U.S. relations in the next chapter, which deals with espionage, computer systems hacking, continued theft of technology, military advances and capabilities, the Huawei technologies, and the Wuhan laboratories and Institute of Technology.

In Remembrance—The Tiananmen Square Massacre, June 3-4, 1989

The Tiananmen Square demonstrations were student-led, pro-democracy protests held in Beijing and other parts of China between April 15 and June 4, 1989. The protests were precipitated by the April 15 death of reformist Hu Yaobang. Hu was a veteran of the Long March and served as General Secretary of the Chinese Communist Party (CCP) from 1980 to 1987. However, in 1987, "after several weeks of student demonstrations demanding greater Western-style freedom, Hu was forced to resign for 'mistakes on major issues of political policy.' "[25]

Reforms had brought economic improvement to China but also uncertainty, as well as a recognition that a one-party political system was incompatible with many of the freedoms the students expected, given the rapid changes taking place in Europe with Mikhail Gorbachev's implementation of glasnost and perestroika and other developments questioning the legitimacy of communist repression and totalitarianism.

The Chinese students wanted freedom of the press, freedom of speech, participation in government, and recognition of other basic human rights and civil liberties. Some Chinese workers joined the protests because of increasing high prices and low wages, and the wish for the government to grant more political and economic rights. It was estimated that, at the height of the demonstrations upward of one million people assembled in the square.

As the protests became generalized during May, involving students and workers in hundreds of Chinese cities, the CCP top leadership called for the government to use harsh measures to suppress the protestors. Top party leaders—including Deng Xiaoping, who had been up to that time a reformer, and Chinese President Yang Shangkun—went along with martial law and the crackdown, which was led by General Yang Baibing.[26]

As many as 300,000 troops were mobilized and massed in Beijing for the crackdown. People's Liberation Army troops advanced into central Beijing and in the early morning hours of June 4, 1989, began killing both the demonstrators and the bystanders. The PLA fired at the students with assault rifles and tanks, specifically the protestors who tried to block the military's advance into Tiananmen Square. A photo of one student trying to stop a tank has become a symbol of what one individual could do to halt repression, if only momentarily.[27] Estimates of the death toll varied in the past but, as previously stated, recently declassified British documents indicate the death toll for the Tiananmen Square massacre was 10,000 Chinese students killed in cold blood.[2]

Figure 112: Deng Xiaoping, paramount leader of the PRC (1978–1989), who presided over the Tiananmen Square massacre and was weakened politically because of it. National Archives and Records Administration

Throughout the rest of China, the Chinese government arrested thousands more of the protesters and their supporters. Human rights organizations condemned the government for the massacre, foreign journalists were expelled, and many Communist Party functionaries, who were deemed sympathetic to the protestors, were demoted or purged.

China had no intention of following the same path the Soviet Union had taken with glasnost, perestroika, and the general liberalization of communist political power concomitant with its firm hold on the population.

From now on, journalists and the press would be strictly controlled; the police and internal security forces would be strengthened; and the political reforms that begun in 1986 with Deng Xiaoping would be halted.

The Tiananmen Square massacre is considered a crucial event that set the limits on political expression and liberty, and re-established political repression in China that has lasted up to the present day. The Tiananmen "incident," remains a forbidden, taboo, and censored topic of discussion in China.[28]

Figure 113: Tiananmen Square protest and massacre, July 1989. Photo taken from U.S. diplomatic compound showing Chinese tanks preparing to squelch protests in Beijing. Pete Campolongo, U.S. Department of State

Chapter 14

Chinese Espionage Against the U.S. and the West

David Wise, a former journalist and leading American writer on intelligence and espionage, asserted that even in the 21st century, the communist Chinese continue to follow the advice contained in the 5th century B.C. Chinese manuscript, *The Art of War*, by the military strategist Sun Tzu.[1]

Figure 114: Representation of Sun Tzu from the Qing Palace Dynasty Collection Picture Book. Palace Museum Press, Beijing

Sun Tzu advised that espionage should be conducted by obtaining small and innumerable pieces of information from vast numbers of individuals sent as armies of spies against the enemy. This type of intelligence gathering methodology was described as a "thousand grains of sand" approach by Paul D. Moore, a former China analyst for the Federal

Bureau of Investigation (FBI).[1] Moore illustrated that intelligence collection method in the following way:

> *If a beach was an espionage target, the Russians would send in a sub, frogmen would steal ashore in the dark of night and with great secrecy collect several buckets of sand and take them back to Moscow. The U.S. would target the beach with satellites and produce reams of data. The Chinese would send in a thousand tourists, each assigned to collect a single grain of sand. When they returned, they would be asked to shake out their towels. And they would end up knowing more about the sand than anyone else.[1]*

Furthermore, Wise asserted that unlike the Soviets, the communist Chinese were not interested in recruiting agents with vulnerabilities or misfits or even people motivated by revenge, but "good" people, who are naively convinced of the humanitarian nature of their actions. Theoretically, foreigners recruited by Chinese spymasters genuinely want to assist China and help it improve technologically, to modernize and achieve parity with the West. For example, Wise stated that the Chinese might "pitch" foreign contacts with statements such as, "Scientific information should recognize no political boundaries."[1]

John F. Lewis, Jr., a former head of the FBI national security division, further illustrated how this approach could work when dealing with Chinese operations. Lewis stated:

> *You may be talking about a different kind of espionage, where scientists get together and there may not even be an exchange of documents. An exchange of ideas and ways to solve problems. There is the heart of the problem. With unfettered travel back and forth to mainland China, in many cases scientists may not even be aware of what the hell is happening.[1]*

Therefore, students studying aboard, academicians working abroad, scientists attending conferences, tourists, corporate executives, and especially government employees could potentially be targeted, since the Chinese often seek to "develop general relationships with people that may have an intelligence dimension."[1]

In 98 percent of the cases, though, actual recruitment usually translates to ethnic, first-generation Chinese immigrants with cultural and familial ties to China. Sometimes the Chinese government reciprocates by helping those part-time spies create or proceed with commercial business ventures in the United States. This is called *guanxi*.

Thus, supposedly, the Chinese spymasters do not offer money for information, and they do not accept walk-in cases—that is, volunteers who may be "dangles" (namely, double agents sent by the enemy). And China, "like many other countries, has used sex for purposes of espionage or blackmail." Most Chinese espionage activities are coordinated by the Ministry of State Security (MSS) or the military intelligence arm of the People's Liberation Army (PLA).[1]

"Sexpionage" and Cyber Warfare Against America Since the 1990s

Not all spies fit neatly into just one category, as we shall see throughout the chapter. Wise related several cases of Chinese espionage that challenged the notion of the "thousand grains of sand" information gathering approach, and instead resembled complex and lengthy, large-scale espionage operations similar to the horrendous theft of the atomic bomb secrets by the Soviets in the 1940s or the heinous betrayals by American traitors Aldrich Ames and Robert Hanssen in the 1980s and 1990s.

Take for instance, the case of PARLOR MAID, the code name of the Chinese-American double agent, Katrina Leung. This incredible story was immersed in betrayal and as much sex as espionage—that is, "sexpionage." It cast a dark shadow of shame, ineptitude, and negligence on the FBI and two of its top Chinese counterintelligence (CI) experts—namely, James J. Smith and William B. Cleveland, Jr.[2]

Chinese Agent Katrina Leung (PARLOR MAID)

Katrina Leung not only spied for China for 20 years but also managed to seduce two FBI agents in the process. In turn, they unwittingly—and sometimes, unfortunately, willingly—collaborated in her deception and betrayal. In the United States, the Federal Bureau of Investigation is the agency charged with catching spies. If the FBI had been more vigilant, Leung's betrayal would have been deduced and exposed much earlier, thereby limiting the damage she did to American and Western security.

Katrina Leung was recruited by FBI agent James J. Smith in Los Angeles, California, in 1982. Smith gave Leung the code name PARLOR MAID, and unwisely began an affair with her. For the next two decades, Leung would serve as the FBI's premier intelligence source on China, the Chinese Communist Party (CCP) leadership, and the MSS. Smith also introduced Leung to William "Bill" Cleveland, chief of the FBI's Chinese counterintelligence group in San Francisco, California. Soon after that introduction, Cleveland and Leung began an affair.

Then in December 1990, an audiotape of an intercept recorded by the National Security Agency (NSA) in Fort Meade, Maryland, and forwarded from FBI headquarters in Washington, D.C., landed on Bill Cleveland's San Francisco desk. "Most of the bureau's Chinese translators were based in San Francisco" at that time. The unanalyzed tape consisted of a recording of a "conversation in Mandarin between a woman in Los Angeles, who used the code name Luo, and her MSS handler in Beijing, named, of all things, Mao."[2] Cleveland, who was fluent in Mandarin, immediately recognized the woman's voice. It was Katrina Leung. Cleveland's heart sank because the shocking implication was only too obvious—"PARLOR MAID had been doubled back against the FBI and was working for Beijing."[2]

Several red flags that indicated Katrina Leung had turned against the United States were missed; and protected by her two FBI agent-lovers, the clues were ignored by those higher up in the chain of command. The FBI launched its own counterespionage operation against PARLOR MAID, but that case also amounted to nothing. The case was simply astonishing, and Wise performed a great service in bringing the incredible "sexpionage" case to light—in sizzling and blood boiling detail.[2]

Even though the bungling by FBI agents in a few cases was highly disturbing, the ineptitude did not stop with the FBI. The pusillanimity of the United States Department of Justice in prosecuting the spies that actually got caught, was likewise troubling and disturbing, as was the leniency extended by the federal judges presiding over the trials of the few defendants who were prosecuted. Many of the convicted defendants, in the end, received light sentences that seemed more like a simple slap on the wrist.[2]

Much of the Chinese espionage was, and continues to be, conducted to obtain technology, defense, or intelligence secrets from the United States. The FBI operation KINDRED SPIRIT was undertaken to identify a Chinese spy in Los Alamos who had revealed the secret design of the W-88 warhead of the Trident submarines in the 1990s. The warhead was not only one of the most powerful but also one of the most advanced nuclear weapons in the U.S. arsenal. Additionally, as part of the submarine strike force, the W-88 warhead was one of the most survivable of the retaliatory triad of nuclear deterrence strike capabilities of the United States. In KINDRED SPIRIT, the FBI investigated Wen Ho Lee and his wife Sylvia Lee, but unfortunately the operation was bungled and led nowhere. Wen Ho

Lee became a suspect in the case not only because he "had worked on the W-88 warhead in the most secret division of Los Alamos" but also because he had lied to the FBI about telephoning an individual who was the main suspect in another FBI investigation and failing to "report that he had been questioned about key U.S. nuclear secrets when China's top bomb designer visited him privately in a hotel room in Beijing."[3]

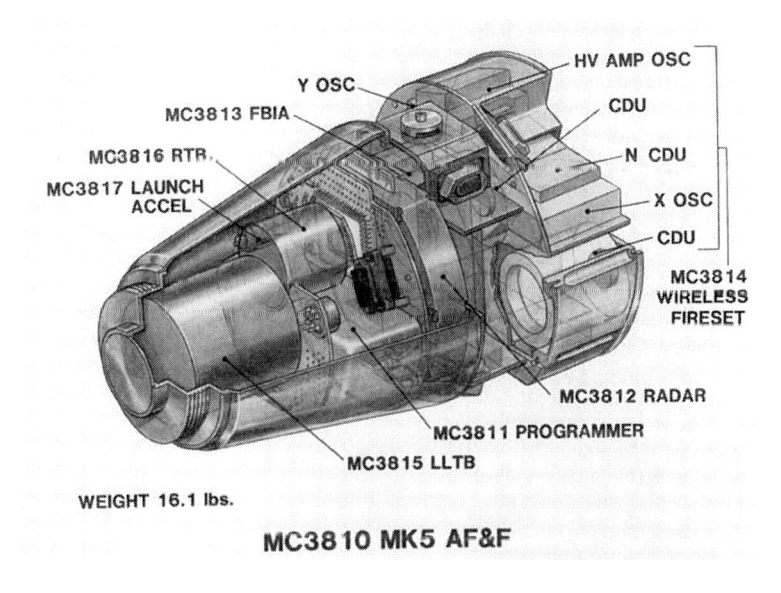

Figure 115: The MC3810 arming, fusing and firing (AF&F) system for the W-88 nuclear warhead used on Trident II submarines. U.S. Department of Energy

KINDRED SPIRIT was later expanded into operation SEGO PALM, but the investigation led to no arrests.[3] Operation TIGER TRAP (after which the David Wise book was titled) was another CI operation in which the guilty culprit once again got away with U.S. nuclear secrets.[4]

However, "the PARLOR MAID case was not first time China had penetrated an American intelligence agency."[5] The successful FBI operation EAGLE CLAW was launched against a CIA employee and American traitor, Larry Wu-Tai Chin, who spied for China for 30 years and finally made a mistake that led to his arrest in 1985. Chin was successfully prosecuted and committed suicide in prison.[5]

In conclusion, it should be noted that "when the FBI investigates or arrests a Chinese national or an American of Chinese background, it inevitably opens itself up to charges of racism"…but the "record of Chinese espionage against defense and intelligence agencies in the United States demonstrates that it is China, rather than the FBI, that targets ethnic Chinese."[3] As previously stated, in 98 percent of the cases, China targeted ethic Chinese for recruitment.

Historical Background of Espionage

Chinese espionage against the West is not a new phenomenon. It has been going on and increased throughout the entire Cold War period. And it has become amplified in scope, effectiveness, and seriousness in the last several decades.

Amerasia was a pro-communist magazine on Far Eastern affairs that was run by several communist "agents of influence" and numerous overt American and Western communists, who were involved in espionage against the West or who could subtly influence American or British policy in favor of communist nations, especially China.

On March 11, 1945, agents from the Office of Strategic Services (OSS; precursor to the CIA) secretly broke into the New York City offices of the magazine and discovered "photographs of top-secret documents from the British and U.S. navies, the U.S. State Department, and the OSS and files from the U.S. Office of Censorship."[6] The FBI began an investigation and found dozens of Soviet agents and communist agents of influence involved not only in the *Amerasia* magazine itself but also in the U.S. State Department, the OSS, and the U.S. diplomatic corps.[7,8]

After extensive investigations by various American agencies and congressional committees, several individuals on the *Amerasia* staff were charged with espionage and unauthorized possession of classified government documents, and the serious affair became known as the *Amerasia* scandal.[7,8]

Despite the mountains of documentary evidence, *The Encyclopedia of Cold War Espionage, Spies, and Secret Operations* asserted that U.S. diplomat John Stewart Service, a major player in the *Amerasia* affair, had been a victim of the Red Scare.[9] Service was not an innocent victim, but a full-fledged communist fellow traveler rooming in Chungking with two other spies, the Chinese communist propagandist and intelligence agent, Chi Chao-ting, and FDR administration official, Solomon Adler.[10] All three men spread disinformation about alleged venal conditions in the Nationalist government, calumniated Chiang Kai-shek, and praised Mao Tse-tung.

By lionizing Mao, they helped to pave the way for the United States government to turn its back on Chiang, depriving him of needed funding to carry on the war effort, and thereby contributing to Mao's takeover of China.[7,8,10]

Figure 116: Chiang Kai-shek, Franklin D. Roosevelt, and Winston Churchill at the Cairo Conference, December 1, 1943. National Archives and Records Administration

Other agents of influence, who also helped in the betrayal of China to the communists, included Lauchlin Currie, a leading presidential aid to FDR, the Chinese scholar Owen Lattimore, and FDR's closest confidant and adviser, Harry Hopkins.[11 13]

And yet, like *The Encyclopedia of Cold War Espionage, Spies, and Secret Operations*, which attempted to exonerate John Stewart Service and blamed his prosecution on McCarthyism, *History.com* tried to whitewash the historical role played by Owen Lattimore.[14] In fact, Joseph McCarthy was correct.[15] Professor Owen Lattimore, a Chinese scholar, may not have been a full-fledged Soviet spy, but he was an agent of influence working for the Soviets, like Harry Hopkins. Lattimore used his power of influence to help the Soviets and the Red Chinese against the interests of the United States and the West.[12,13]

As demonstrated by Professor Christopher Andrew and the Mitrokhin Archive, as well as the various sources previously cited in this chapter, agents of influence can be as harmful to a nation as conventional espionage agents. *History.com* and many other sources still deny that these men were traitors; and instead, refer to them as naive intellectuals, who sympathized with the Soviets and the Chinese. But Service, Lattimore, Adler, Currie, and Hopkins were conscious agents of influence whose damage to the United States was immense with the loss of China to the communists, surpassing the damage inflicted by some of the full-fledged Soviet spies.[7,8,10-13]

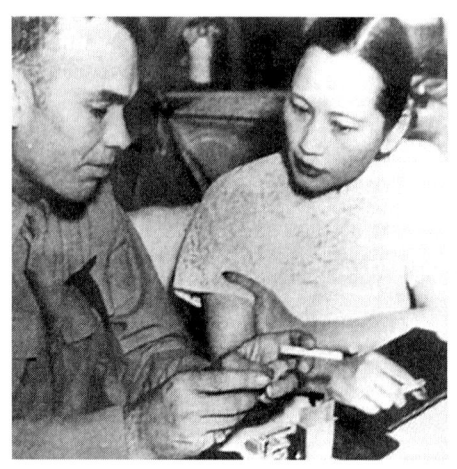

Figure 117: Conscious agents of influence who helped betray China to Mao and the communists. Photo left: John Stewart Service talking with Soong Ching-ling in 1944. Ching-ling, the third wife of Sun Yat-sen, the "Red Sister" opponent of Chiang Kai-shek and later one of Mao's vice-chair. Photo right: Owen Lattimore in 1945. Truman Library

Moreover, the fact that some of the agents of influence were not mentioned in the Venona files does not confirm their innocence. Most of Venona remains encrypted and undeciphered, and only a small fraction of the Soviet traffic collected over a short period of time has been decoded. And yet, information obtained from defectors and the decoded Venona files has largely exposed the identity of many of those traitors, and in the case of China in particular, corroborated that the concerted campaign by the Soviet agents of influence in the FDR administration against Chiang Kai-shek was Soviet-created disinformation, propagated to tilt American opinion away from Chiang. At the same time, the agents of influence blocked the American government from rendering the needed assistance to the Nationalists, while

Mao continued to get immense support in arms and ammunition from Stalin and the Soviet Union. During the FDR administration and the subsequent Truman administration, that betrayal helped Mao immensely to ascend to power and to seize China in 1949.[1,7,8,10-13]

China Uses Cuba as Base for Espionage Against the United States

China has been using Cuba, another communist nation, as a theater for espionage operations against their main enemy, the United States. Today, in our increasingly perilous world, Cuba could furnish Beijing with a strategic operational base against America during a political or military crisis. More than a decade ago, Toby Westerman, editor and publisher of *International News Analysis* (*INA*) wrote:

> *China's intelligence operations are the 'core arena' for achieving the superpower status that the Communist oligarchy in Beijing so passionately desires. Central to its spy activities is the island of Cuba, which is strategically located for the interception of U.S. military and civilian satellite communications. China's spy services also cooperate closely with Havana's own world-class intelligence services. Inexplicably, the U.S. mass media are ignoring both the existence of the spy base as well as the Cuban-Chinese alliance responsible for it.[16]*

Westerman also interviewed Chris Simmons, a retired counterintelligence special agent with 28 years of service in the Army and the Defense Intelligence Agency. Simmons testified before the U.S. House Foreign Affairs Committee on Cuban espionage and explained why China needed Cuba in the increasingly confrontational relations between China and the United States:

> *The value Beijing places upon the information acquired via Havana can be seen in the October 2011 visit to the island by Gen. Guo Boxiong, Vice Chairman of China's Central Military Commission. Guo's presence in Cuba underscored that China has a special military commitment in addition to a sizable economic investment in Cuba.[16]*

As far back as the first decade of the 21st century, China began replacing and updating Cuba's obsolete "non-lethal" technical equipment on the island, but the degree and nature of that technological transfer was difficult to assess. Westerman observed: "The U.S. prohibits 'lethal' assistance to Cuba, and Beijing is risking U.S. sanctions if that prohibition is known to be violated."[16] No sanctions were imposed by America for China's assistance to Cuba at that time. However, sanctions would be imposed a few years later in the case of China's Huawei Technologies, as we will see. Ties continued to grow between Cuba and Red China in both military aid as well as improving Cuba's spying capabilities:

> *General Guo's trip to Cuba follows a December 2010 military agreement, signed by top ranking PLA General Fu Quanyou, insuring needed military aid to the Castro regime. Simmons pointed out that China's electronic intelligence activities in Cuba are particularly interesting, because China claims they don't exist.[16]*

Figure 118: Guo Boxiong, General of the PLA (2002–2012). Department of Foreign Affairs and Trade, Australia

The mainstream American media, especially the main three television broadcast networks—CBS, NBC, and ABC—have been slow to recognize and cover the threat China poses to U.S. economic and strategic interests by forging closer ties with Latin American nations in America's own backyard. In Central America, for example, "Chinese companies have positioned themselves at either end of the Panama Canal through port concession agreements," thereby boosting China's footprint in the Canal zone.[17] Moreover, of the goods moving through the Canal, "over 60 percent originate in or end up in U.S. markets, intrinsically tying free and fair Canal access to U.S. national security and economic interests in the country."[17]

In the Caribbean, Beijing has spread its tentacles in Puerto Rico, Haiti, the Dominican Republic, and now Cuba with its intelligence gathering operations. Westerman wrote:

> *The base at Bejucal, however, is still operating. While the Cubans technically run it, some 50-100 Chinese intelligence officers are at Bejucal gathering and interpreting information, according to Simmons. In sharp contrast to Moscow, there is no political cost to China. 'It took us years to find out [the Chinese Communists] were operating there. We found out through émigrés, defectors, and travelers to Cuba,' Simmons told INA Today. Unlike the Soviets, China has not constructed a facility, and only with the greatest of difficulty can the Chinese be connected with Cuban electronic spy base activities. In this way, China can plausibly deny both the use of the base and the transference of information from its Havana embassy to Beijing.[16]*

In addition to Bejucal, China reactivated the Lourdes Radio Electronics Center (REC), an old Soviet SIGINT base near Havana, and three other intelligence stations in Cuba in 2019. It is likely that China will share gathered SIGINT information with Russia.[18] According to a *Fox News* report:

> *These facilities likely have the capability to monitor cellphone and internet traffic, including financial transactions throughout much of the U.S. Southeast. Modern AI is probably being employed to sift through hundreds of millions of daily communications, looking for information of interest to convert into intelligence. Depending on the availability of electric power, there may even be electronic jamming systems as well.[19]*

In *Cuba's Eternal Revolution through the Prism of Insurgency, Socialism, and Espionage,* two chapters discussed Cuban espionage and its foreign intelligence capabilities. This issue remains momentous given the tensions between China, Russia and Iran, on the one hand, and the U.S. and the British Commonwealth, including Canada and Australia, on the other. Cuba remains in a very strategic position for human intelligence (HUMINT), signals intelligence (SIGINT) and cyber espionage against the United States.[20]

Another reason for Xi Jinping's interest and Beijing's involvement in Cuba—that is, establishing bases and forging closer ties with Havana—is likely for subversion in Latin America:

First, the base will likely serve to train security forces for Latin America's socialist leaders who know they may be one fair election away from losing power. Second, the Chinese may start to train insurgents to overthrow some of the remaining seven U.S.-aligned governments in the region.[19]

There is no longer any question as to whether China's control of the Cuban facilities poses a serious national security threat to the United States or not. That fact is now undeniable.

Chinese Hackers Steal American Advanced Weapons Designs

Tensions between China and the United States have continued to escalate since the 1990s. In 2013, Chinese hackers stole two dozen American weapon systems designs—a serious and dangerous development that could have endangered the lives of American soldiers if a conflict with China had arisen. A *United States Naval Institute* (*USNI*) article reported:

> *Chinese hackers have obtained designs for more than two dozen U.S. weapon systems—including the Aegis Ballistic Missile Defense System, the F-35 Lighting II Joint Strike Fighter, the Littoral Combat Ship and electromagnetic railguns.[21]*

The *USNI* article also cited a *Washington Post* national security feature article that stated:

> *China, which is pursuing a comprehensive long-term strategy to modernize its military, is investing in ways to overcome the U.S. military advantage—and cyber-espionage is seen as a key tool in that effort, the Pentagon noted this month in a report to Congress on China. For the first time, the Pentagon specifically named the Chinese government and military as the culprit behind intrusions into government and other computer systems.[22]*

According to *USNI*, the Pentagon report to Congress stated:

> *China utilized its intelligence services and employed other illicit approaches that involve violations of U.S. laws and export controls to obtain key national security technologies, controlled equipment, and other materials not readily obtainable through commercial means or academia.[21]*

The *USNI* article went on to advise that the hacking and stealing of American sensitive technologies continue and that "the breaches were part of a growing espionage effort that targets defense contractors."[21] While many of the larger defense contractors have taken needed cyber security measures, smaller contractors and subcontractors remain vulnerable to hackers and cyberattacks.

Cyberattacks that stole information from over 100 targets in the U.S. and other countries have been traced to a Chinese military cyber unit that is part of China's People's Liberation Army. It is housed in a building on the outskirts of Shanghai.[23]

Ongoing Chinese Cyber Espionage

Perhaps the most troubling of all the aspects of espionage, as we have seen, remains the silent, ongoing cyber wars launched by the communist Chinese against the U.S. and the West. This undeclared war proved that "the end of history" mentality, which prevailed immediately after the collapse of Soviet communism in 1991, was dangerous to the security of the free world.

China's invisible cyber spies threaten a nation's survival; and yet, few Americans and Westerners understand that fact. The Chinese military experts in cyber warfare or their proxies, including hacker units and espionage cells, pose a serious security risk to the free world. In America, the Chinese have unleashed this potential menace against the federal, state, and municipal governments, government agencies, industry, and various other targets like banking, infrastructure, and computer networks.[1,23]

In 2006, Peter Yuan Li, a Chinese-American computer technologist in Atlanta, Georgia, was beaten by a gang of Asian men and his computer stolen. Li had been working to expose China's cyberattacks on U.S. agencies. The attacks persisted of course. In a 2012 BBC article, a cyber expert warned about the seriousness of international hackers. But what many articles fail to state is that China was the main culprit, followed by Russia and Iran. Western experts are finally taking notice, and at least the BBC is reporting the dangerous trend.[24]

Unless the U.S. and its allies rise to the challenge, this up-to-now silent but ominous Chinese cyber war portends a dark future for the survival of the institutions of freedom. America and the West will need to forge ahead with research and development not only to combat cyber warfare but also to survive the ongoing Chinese onslaught of conventional and cyber espionage, not to mention the potentially more intense and destructive cyber wars of the future.[1,16,21,23,24]

WANTED BY THE FBI

Conspiring to Commit Computer Fraud; Accessing a Computer Without Authorization for the Purpose of Commercial Advantage and Private Financial Gain; Damaging Computers Through the Transmission of Code and Commands; Aggravated Identity Theft; Economic Espionage; Theft of Trade Secrets

Huang Zhenyu   Wen Xinyu   Sun Kailiang   Gu Chunhui   Wang Dong

Figure 119: FBI poster of five PLA Unit 61398 military officers indicted and charged in 2014 with cyber espionage, including the thief of confidential business information and planting malware on computers of U.S. commercial firms. U.S. Department of Justice, Office of Public Affairs

U.S. President Donald Trump Bans China's Huawei Technologies

In 2019, U.S. President Donald Trump imposed sanctions on Red China for exporting gadgets to the United States that could be used as espionage equipment. "China's Huawei Technologies Co Ltd was banned from buying vital U.S. technology without special approval and its equipment was effectively barred from U.S. telecom networks on national security grounds."[25]

American telecommunications experts contended that Huawei's handsets and network equipment could be used by the Chinese government to spy on Americans, thus posing a risk to national security.[25]

The communist Chinese threatened to retaliate:

Huawei denies its products pose a security threat and says it is ready to engage with the US. Beijing accused President Trump of engaging in industrial sabotage by using state security 'as a pretext for suppressing foreign business. We urge the US to stop this practice and instead create better conditions for business co-operation.'[26]

Figure 120: Official White House portrait of President Donald J. Trump, 45th President of the United States (2017–2021). Shealah Craighead, Executive Office of the President of the United States

In the wake of President Trump's sanctions on Huawei, Sir Richard Dearlove, a former Chief of MI6 in Great Britain, stated that "giving the Chinese telecoms firm Huawei a role in building the United Kingdom's 5G network posed an unnecessary risk to national security," adding, "The fact that the British government now appears to have decided to place the development of some of its most sensitive critical infrastructure in the hands of a company from the People's Republic of China (PRC) is deeply worrying."[27]

In 2022, the British wisely took heed of Dearlove's advice and followed the lead of the United States by banning Huawei telecommunication equipment from the United Kingdom's 5G network core.[28]

U.S. Senator Ben Sasse (R-NE) succinctly summarized the outlook and explained:

China's main export is espionage, and the distinction between the Chinese Communist Party and Chinese 'private-sector' businesses like Huawei is imaginary.[25]

Figure 121: U.S. Department of Justice and others, including Acting U.S. Attorney General Matthew Whitaker (center rear), Homeland Security Secretary Kirstjen Nielsen (center front), Commerce Secretary Wilbur Ross (left), and FBI Director Christopher Wray (right), announce 23 criminal charges (Financial Fraud, Money Laundering, Conspiracy to Defraud the United States, Theft of Trade Secret Technology and Sanctions Violations, et cetera) against Huawei and its CFO Wanzhou Meng in 2019. U.S. Department of Justice

Since that time, U.S. relations with Red China have not improved, not even with the election of Democrat President Joe Biden and the change of administrations in Washington. In fact, tensions have escalated over the issue of Taiwan's independence, America's continued pledge to abide by the Taiwan Relations Act, and the ongoing contention over the South China Sea Islands and surrounding territorial and international waters. Taiwan, U.S., and China relations were discussed in greater detail in chapter 13.

U.S. President Joe Biden and Chinese President Xi Jinping remain at odds on a variety of issues, and U.S.-China relations are not expected to improve in the foreseeable future. For his part, Xi Jinping has amassed more power than any Chinese politician since Mao Tse-tung. Xi is presently General Secretary of the Chinese Communist Party, Chairman of the Central Military Commission, and President of the People's Republic of China.

Charles Lieber, PhD, Espionage, and the Wuhan Laboratory

Charles Lieber, PhD, the Chair of Harvard University's Chemistry and Chemical Biology Department, was arrested on January 28, 2020, by the FBI and charged with conducting espionage for China against the United States. Professor Lieber had been receiving more than $50,000 per month from the Chinese Communist Party (CCP) for his efforts "as a 'Strategic Scientist' at Wuhan University of Technology (WUT) in China and as a contractual participant in China's Thousand Talents Plan."[29] According to court documents:

> *China's Thousand Talents Plan is one of the most prominent Chinese talent recruitment plans designed to attract, recruit, and cultivate high-level scientific talent in furtherance of China's scientific development, economic prosperity and national security. These talent programs seek to hire Chinese overseas talent and foreign experts to bring their knowledge and experience to China and reward individuals for stealing proprietary information.[29]*

Lieber and two Chinese nationals, who were posing as his students, had traveled freely back and forth many times between Boston and Wuhan, China, conducting their illegal activities and trading vital U.S. scientific secrets for financial gain.[29]

On January 28, the two Chinese nationals were also formally charged. Yanqing Ye was "charged in an indictment with one count each of visa fraud, making false statements, acting as an agent of a foreign government and conspiracy."[29] Fortunately for Ye, he was in China at the time of the indictment.

On December 10, 2019, Zaosong Zheng, the other Chinese national, had been arrested at Boston's Logan International Airport "attempting to smuggle 21 vials of biological research to China."[29] On January 21, 2020, Zheng was "indicted on one count of smuggling goods from the United States and one count of making false, fictitious or fraudulent statements."[29] He had been in federal custody since December 30, 2019.[29]

Was there any connection between Lieber's research and what happened at the Wuhan Institute of Virology lab with the outbreak of the COVID pandemic? Was there an association between Lieber and Anthony Fauci, the former director of the National Institute of Allergy and Infectious Diseases from 1984 to 1922 and chief medical advisor to President Joe Biden between 2021 and 2022? Fauci had connections to the Wuhan laboratory. These are reasonable questions still begging for answers.

212 Chapter 14

Figure 122: Charles M. Lieber, American chemist, nanotechnology expert and convicted felon, in 2006. Kris Snibbe, Harvard Public Affairs & Communications

Figure 123: Wuhan Institute of Virology, research institute of the Chinese Academy of Sciences in Jiangxia District, Hubei province, December 2016

Some authorities do not believe that the release of the virus was strictly unintentional. Perhaps, *The China Virus: What is the Truth?* by James I. Ausman, M.D., PhD and Russell L. Blaylock, M.D. came the closest to putting the pieces of the puzzle together concerning the mystery of the COVID pandemic. But the book was independently published and did not receive the attention it deserved.[30]

Nevertheless, on December 22, 2021, after a six-day jury trial, Lieber was convicted of "lying to federal authorities about his affiliation with the PRC's Thousand Talents Program and the Wuhan University of Technology in Wuhan, China, as well as hiding the income he received from the WUT."[31] Lieber not only lied to the Internal Revenue Service (IRS) about the income he received but also "concealed his Chinese bank account from the United States."[31] After the guilty verdict was announced, the United States Attorney's Office, District of Massachusetts, released a statement that noted that Lieber's research had been funded at U.S. taxpayer expense in a federal grant while Lieber was "conducting research for the Department of Defense."[31]

The Chinese Surveillance Balloon Incident

A great hullabaloo occurred in February 2023 when a giant Chinese surveillance balloon, which the Chinese insisted was a weather balloon, was seen cruising leisurely over the United States. The BBC reported the incident as follows:

> *A suspected Chinese surveillance balloon shot down off the US coast was about 200 ft (60m) tall and carrying an airliner-sized load. A US Defense Department official said the size and make-up of the object informed the decision not to shoot it down while it was over land. 'Picture large debris weighing hundreds if not thousands of pounds falling out of the sky,' General Glen VanHerck said. The US is still working to recover debris off the coast of South Carolina. Remnants of the object—which the US believes is a spy balloon, but China says is a weather monitoring device blown astray—have been collected...[32]*

Multiple U.S. fighter jets were scrambled to track the surveillance balloon, which was finally shot down by a U.S. Air Force F-22 jet days after it first appeared over the United States.

There were no plans to return the balloon remnants to China. The retrieved debris was analyzed by intelligence experts who eventually confirmed America was dealing with an instrument of espionage. No further action was taken by the Biden administration, despite heavy criticism from many Republicans about the incident. Biden was accused of dereliction of duty, while the Chinese government responded by the amusing accusation

of America "using indiscriminate force in downing the balloon and overreacting and seriously violating the spirit of international law."[32]
The BBC report further noted:

General VanHerck said the US was still working to determine whether the debris includes potentially dangerous materials, such as explosives or battery components...Republican politicians have accused US President Joe Biden of a dereliction of duty for allowing the balloon to traverse the country unhindered. The decision to shoot it down also triggered a diplomatic spat between the US and China and prompted Secretary of State Anthony Blinken to cancel a scheduled trip to Beijing that had been aimed at easing tensions.[32]

Several more Chinese balloons were sent over U.S. territories in the ensuing weeks with similar results and no further action taken by the U.S. government other than unceremoniously and sometimes leisurely shooting down the balloons and retrieving the debris.

Figure 124: Chinese surveillance balloon observed by U.S. Air Force U-2 pilot as it hovered over the Central Continental United States on February 3, 2023. Recovery efforts began shortly after the balloon was downed. U.S. Department of Defense

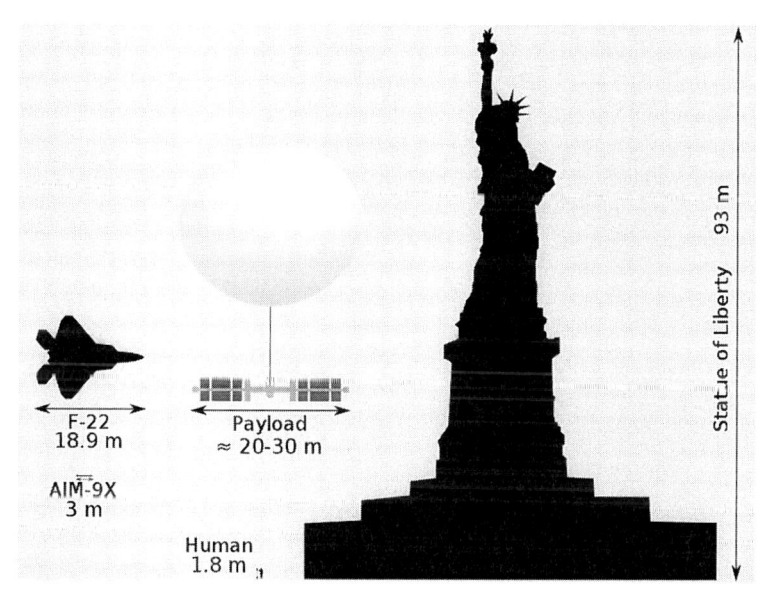

Figure 125: Estimated size of the February 2023 Chinese balloon (described by some sources as "3 school buses" in length) compared to the dimensions of a human, an F-22, and the Statue of Liberty

The Closing Act in the Chinese Espionage Drama

The balloon incidents seem almost acts of a comical farce with surrealistic images of festivities surrounding them, especially at Myrtle Beach, South Carolina, on the east coast of the U.S. where throngs of beachgoers assembled to watch them fly over. But this type of espionage should not delude the American public of its seriousness in terms of national security. In fact, as we close the final chapter on China, it is apropos that we close with two most recent incidents. *Newsmax.com* and other American media outlets reported that two U.S. Navy sailors were arrested, charged with "providing sensitive military information to China—including details of wartime exercises, Naval operations, and critical technical material."[33]

The cases underscore the fact that China, like the former Soviet Union, may also use monetary reward to obtain desired information, but it still largely relies, as we stated previously, with acceptance or actual recruitment of ethnic Chinese or Americans with a Chinese ancestral background or cultural ties to China. The report further stated:

> *Jinchao Wei, a 22-year-old sailor assigned to the San Diego-based USS Essex, was arrested Wednesday on a charge related to espionage involving conspiracy to send national defense information to Chinese officials, according to the U.S. officials. The Justice Department also charged Navy service member Wenhen Zhao, 26, accusing him of taking bribes in exchange for giving sensitive U.S. military photos and videos to a Chinese intelligence officer between August 2021 through at least this May.... The two sailors were charged with similar crimes, but they were charged in separate cases. It wasn't clear Thursday if the two were connected or if they were courted or paid by the same Chinese intelligence officer.[33]*

The two cases are still under investigation and details as to how these betrayals were detected will remain undisclosed for the foreseeable future as to protect HUMINT and SIGINT sources.

In conclusion, we should stress that China continues to advance on all fronts, and gathering intelligence against the West, particularly the United States, is a major priority. In the event or threat of hostilities with the United States, China would have enough intelligence gathering capability and collected information, not to mention control of sea routes through the Caribbean and on both sides of the Atlantic and Pacific oceans with its position in the Panama Canal, to pose a great military challenge to the United States and its allies around the world.

Moreover, militant communism in China is not dead. China has quietly sought allies in other militant nations, such as the increasingly bellicose and authoritarian Russia and Iran. And, one must not forget that totalitarianism, in its most overtly malevolent form, also survives in Cuba and North Korea. Red China, the giant of the Far East, saves face with Mao's legacy of collectivism and authoritarianism by claiming that politically and economically it is a nation governed by unadulterated communism. Yet, the fact remains that China has progressed in science and technology due to increased trade with and profits from the West, as well as by stealing technology, defense, and intelligence secrets from its trading partners. Although China still calls itself a communist state, some authorities argue that its variety of totalitarianism is more akin to a behemothic fascist state than to the typical inefficient communist state of the 20th century.

Be that as it may, China has become a dangerous superpower; and the West must remain alert. China's espionage activities, growing military might, and technological capabilities, require renewed diligence and vigilance on the part of the United States and the West.

PART V

ESPIONAGE—
THE KGB AND CIA BATTLES
DURING THE COLD WAR

CHAPTER 15

FOUR SEMINAL BOOKS CHRONICLING KGB ACTIVITIES IN THE COLD WAR

In the former Soviet Union, the Committee for State Security—that is, the *Komitet Gosudarstvennoy Bezopasnosti* or simply, the KGB—was the "Sword and Shield" of the communist Soviet state from 1954 to 1991. Foreign intelligence and counterintelligence, internal security and repression, and the general work of Soviet secret agents were all functions of the various directorates and departments within the KGB.

And, four essential books are necessary reading for students, scholars, researchers, and specialists interested in the political history of Soviet espionage during the period known as the Cold War.

KGB: The Secret Work of the Soviet Secret Agents

The brilliantly written *KGB: The Secret Work of the Soviet Secret Agents* by John Barron not only sets the stage for the Soviet espionage saga during the Cold War but also is crucial to understand the history of espionage and intelligence collection as well as the chronology of events that unfolded during the period. The book describes the methods, organization, and goals of Soviet espionage—namely, the KGB modus operandi, especially the First Chief Directorate (foreign intelligence) and the Second Chief Directorate (internal security operations).[1]

John Barron (1930–2005) was an American investigative journalist, a Senior Editor at *Reader's Digest*, and one of the foremost scholars on Soviet espionage during the Cold War. Previously, Barron served in the United States Navy as a naval intelligence officer specializing in the Russian language until 1957. And, it should be noted that subsequent to the book on the KGB, Barron wrote the 1996 tome that dramatically detailed the highly successful, FBI counterintelligence operation, *Operation Solo: The FBI's Man in the Kremlin*.[2]

Nevertheless, the 1974 publication of *KGB: The Secret Work of the Soviet Secret Agents* sent shock waves through the entire KGB and Soviet hierarchy and dealt a crushing blow to worldwide KGB operations.[3]

In the book, Barron exposed all of the KGB officers posted around the globe who were known at the time to Western security services. British professor and author, Christopher Andrew, confirmed that and added:

> The Mitrokhin Archive gave a vivid indication of the ferocity with which the Centre (KGB headquarters) has traditionally responded to intelligence leaks about its past foreign operations. The publication in 1974 of John Barron's KGB: The Secret Work of Soviet Secret Agents, based on information from Soviet defectors and Western intelligence agencies, generated no fewer than 350 KGB damage assessments and other reports.[3]

The KBG countered the publication of the book with a disinformation campaign, directed primarily against Barron personally but even "employed against some of the journalists who wrote articles based on Barron's book."[3] Christopher Andrew explained:

> The resident in Washington, Mikhail Korneyevich Polonik (codenamed ARDOV), was instructed to obtain all available information on Barron, then a senior editor at Reader's Digest, and to suggest ways "to compromise him." Most of the "active measures" used by the KGB in its attempts to discredit Barron made much of his Jewish origins, but its fabricated claims that he was part of a Zionist conspiracy (a favorite theme in Soviet disinformation) appear to have had little resonance outside the Middle East.[3]

During the decade of the 1970s, the publication of *KGB: The Secret Work of Soviet Secret Agents* was considered one of the major Western intelligence successes against the Soviets. And to emphasize the point, Professor Andrew added, "The files noted by Mitrokhin list other KGB countermeasures against Barron's book in countries as far afield as Turkey, Cyprus, Libya, Lebanon, Egypt, Iran, Kuwait, Somalia, Uganda, India, Sri Lanka and Afghanistan."[3]

Appropriately, Robert Conquest, the British-American historian and noted scholar on the Soviet Union, wrote the Introduction to Barron's book. And, the author's Preface described the interesting circumstances leading to the compilation of information that was published.

The following partial list of the chapter titles will give the reader a glimpse into some of the information covered in Barron's all-encompassing yet extremely readable book. In "Instrument of Power," Barron outlined the organization and function of the various KGB directorates and departments and their operations around the globe. "Secrets From the Desert" recounted the dramatic story of a sensitive KGB officer stationed in the Middle East

220 Chapter 15

who becomes a double agent for the West. "Sword and Shield," which was also the emblem for the KBG, related a brief history of the Cheka, the Bolshevik security force and secret police forerunner to the KGB, and the chapter leads to momentous events in the USSR in the 1960s. "Behind the Guarded Gates" exposed the methods behind foreign and internal KGB operations that were further expounded in the other descriptive chapter titles, including "How to Run a Tyranny"; "Surveillance and Seduction"; "Disinformation: Poisoning Public Opinion"; "The Art and Science of Espionage"; and finally, "The Dark Core," which described "wet affairs"—that is, assassinations.

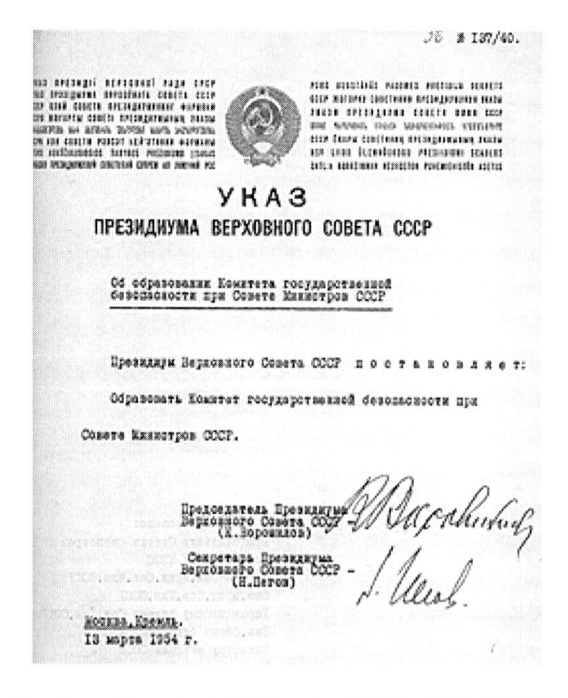

Figure 126: The ukase (decree) establishing the KGB in 1954. K.E. Voroshilov

Kaarlo Tuomi, KBG "Illegal" Agent

An informative and revealing dialogue took place between a KGB instructor in the philosophy of intelligence and his student. The student was receiving training as a KGB "illegal" agent prior to being sent to America as a spy. The student's name was Kaarlo Tuomi. The dialogue provides a window into not only how the KGB trained their agents but also how the

Soviet intelligentsia (expressed by the instructor Aleksei Galkin), viewed America:

> '*You must absolutely understand the morality of socialist intelligence,*' the instructor began. '*Occasionally we must perform unpleasant acts, even kidnapping and liquidation. But none of this is immoral. All acts that further history and socialism are moral acts.*'
> There were aspects of America the teacher frankly admired. '*Over there if you want to go somewhere, you just get in a car, bus, train, or plane and go, and nobody asks any questions,*' he informed Tuomi with wonder in his voice. '*The highway system is unbelievable, and they're about to spend billions more to improve it.*'
> '*Capitalism has nothing to do with this, does it?*' Tuomi asked jokingly.
> '*In a way it does,*' the teacher replied seriously. '*Just as feudalism had a place in history, so did capitalism. But its time is past. The American economy owes its strength to three primary factors that have nothing to do with capitalism. First, the United States has immense natural resources. Second, its territory has escaped the devastation of war for nearly a century. Third, America was settled by the bravest and most industrious people of Europe. Americans today are descendants of good stock, and they remain industrious and tough. It would be folly to pretend otherwise.*'[4]

In "The Spy Who Changed His Mind," John Barron related the entire poignant story about Kaarlo Tuomi, the KGB "illegal" agent. Tuomi was picked up by the FBI almost immediately upon entry into the U.S. Through the gentle treatment and patience of the FBI agent assigned to him, Tuomi was turned into a valuable double agent and transformed into a genuine American hero and patriot.

Although Tuomi had been born in Michigan in 1916, his family returned to the Soviet Union in 1933, where he was raised. Kaarlo noted that, "all his life in the Soviet Union, he had accepted communist promises of free and decent tomorrows. He had believed that the summary arrests, purges, and massacres engineered by the KGB were unpleasant yet essential means to a noble end."[5] But once Tuomi experienced the "undeniable realities of America," his faith in the old Soviet promises was destroyed. In America, "rights, liberties, and opportunities unimaginable in the Soviet Union already existed" and "freedom was not a theoretical abstraction but a reality."[5]

In 1962, shortly after the successful resolution of the Cuban Missile Crisis, Kaarlo Tuomi picked up the telephone and dialed the FBI agent he had known. "Jack, you remember when I said that there were a lot of things

I wouldn't tell you?" Tuomi asked. "Well, I'm ready now to tell you everything…."[5] And with that step, Tuomi revealed all the KGB secrets he knew and became an American patriot.

Barron concluded the chapter with the following notation:

> *In 1971, after the Reader's Digest had published in slightly different form an excerpt from [my book's] manuscript containing the story of Tuomi, the FBI warned him that the KGB now was hunting him. His name had been added to the official list of those upon whom the KGB seeks, by any means it can, to inflict the 'highest measure of punishment.'[6]*

"Dangerous Little Brothers" and Other Secrets

In the chapter, "Dangerous Little Brothers," Barron exposed the methods used by the highly competent, well trained, and still active Cuban DGI (*Dirección General de Inteligencia*) in the area of foreign intelligence.[7,8] During the 1960s and 1970s, Cuban DGI officers, working in conjunction with the KGB, scored several spectacular successes against the U.S. because of the romanticized aura and revolutionary mystique that appealed to many students and professors of the "New Left." Barron related a human-interest story that illustrated the naiveté of a young female Western student who volunteered to work for the Cuban DGI, to which the KGB referred to as "dangerous little brothers."[7,8]

And while we are discussing Cuba, allow me to digress momentarily and interject an analogy gleaned from "Disinformation: Poisoning Public Opinion" that is still applicable to tourists traveling to communist countries today, particularly those traveling to Cuba. Since the Cuban DGI worked so closely with the KGB as noted, the reader can easily substitute DGI and Cuba for KGB and Moscow to understand the point Barron related:

> *Yuri Nosenko stated that while he was helping direct operations against Americans in Moscow, the Central Committee expressly ordered the KGB to intensify efforts to influence the opinions of visiting foreigners. Today performance of this mission is greatly facilitated by the basic controls that allow the KGB invisibly to restrict the lodging, travel, and contacts of visitors. Simply by ensuring that the foreigner talks to the right officials, by determining what he may and may not see, the KGB can shape his impressions without mounting a complicated operation. Respectable foreigners who come away from the controlled Soviet society with erroneous impressions, whether fostered directly by the KGB or not, sometimes affect attitudes in their own countries. Occasionally it is possible to trace the effects of misinformation purveyed in good faith by honorable but misled men.[9]*

Many foreign visitors not only to Cuba but also to other communist nations sometimes forget that what they are shown or see during their trip is probably not the full picture. For example, the "Potemkin villages" that surround the Cuban tourism industry ensure that foreign tourists do not bear witness to the disagreeable features of Revolutionary Cuba. Large international hotel chains built the hotels and resort communities—not the communist Cuban government. Likewise, there is "medical apartheid" and a two-tier system of health care in Cuba. In other words, tourists are treated at select hospitals or clinics that are "off-limits" to ordinary Cubans.[10]

Therefore, when the misled individuals return to their own countries, the misinformation is circulated. Because the tourist was told that medical care in Cuba is "free" and available to every citizen, the public accepts that at face value, assuming the *free* medical care equates to *quality* medical care, when in fact that is not the case. The public rarely scrutinizes the government's statement or statistics, but repeat them without question.[10]

Returning to John Barron's book, "Treasures From the Vault" described the sordid treason and espionage committed by a depraved U.S. Army Sergeant, Robert Lee Johnson. In the mid-1960s, Johnson repeatedly sold U.S. secrets and NATO defense plans to the Soviets. An interesting observation regarding KGB recruitment of a Johnson accomplice was also instructive:

> *Contrary to popular supposition, the KGB is not primarily interested in homosexuals because of their presumed susceptibility to blackmail. In its judgment, homosexuality often is accompanied by personality disorders that make the victim potentially unstable and vulnerable to adroit manipulation. It hunts the particular homosexual who, while more or less a functioning member of his society, is nevertheless subconsciously at war with it and himself. Compulsively driven into tortured relations that never gratify, he cannot escape awareness that he is different. Being different, he easily rationalizes that he is not morally bound by the mores, values, and allegiances that unite others in community or society. Moreover, he nurtures a dormant impulse to strike back at the society which he feels has conspired to make him a secret leper. To such a man, treason offers the weapon of retaliation.[11]*

"The Plot to Destroy Mexico" described the efforts made by the KGB to wreak havoc, overthrow the Mexican government, and convert Mexico into a Soviet satellite, which would have been a significant coup due to Mexico's proximity to the United States.[12] For the CIA's successful effort to prevent that from happening, one must read Jefferson Morley's 2008 magnum opus, *Our Man in Mexico: Winston Scott and the Hidden History of the CIA*. Interestingly, the Foreword to Morley's book was written by Michael Scott, the journalist son of Winston Scott, the CIA station Chief in Mexico at the time.[12]

Komitet Gosudarstvennoy Bezopasnosti

KGB overview

Formed	March 13, 1954
Preceding agencies	Cheka (1917-1922) GPU (1922-1923) OGPU (1923-1934) NKVD (1934-1946) NKGB (February-July 1941/1943-1946) MGB (1946-1953)
Dissolved	December 3, 1991

Figure 127: The symbol of the KGB was the sword and the shield: The shield to defend the Bolshevik Revolution, and the sword to smite its foes

Of all the chapters in Barron's book, my two personal favorites were "The Spy Who Changed His Mind" and "Secrets From the Desert." In "Secrets From the Desert," Barron recounted the dramatic story of Vladimir N. Sakharov, an intelligent and sensitive KGB officer stationed in the Middle East, who recognized the oppression of the people living under communism, discerned the evil falsifications of communism, and realized the blessings of liberty in free countries. Sakharov defected in situ and spied for the West. His information exposed the treasonous espionage ring led by

Egyptian communist and KGB agent, Sami Sharaf, and prevented the overthrow of Egyptian President Anwar Sadat. Under Sadat's presidency, Egypt bolted from the Soviet camp and joined the side of freedom and the West.[13]

As stated, the chapter titles previously listed comprise only a partial list. Barron covered additional information about the history of the state security apparatus; the GRU, which is Soviet Military Intelligence; the Soviet practice of recruiting Americans in the U.S. and third countries; as well as Soviet citizens engaged in clandestine operations abroad.

Suffice to say, fifty years after the publication of *KGB: The Secret Work of the Soviet Secret Agents*, John Barron's comprehensive book remains a historic classic of Cold War espionage and an informative thriller.

KGB: The Inside Story of Its Foreign Operations from Lenin to Gorbachev

If the Soviet KGB had a conniption fit following the publication of John Barron's book, it came close to going apoplectic with the 1990 publication of *KGB: The Inside Story of Its Foreign Operations from Lenin to Gorbachev* by Christopher Andrew and Oleg Gordievsky.[14]

This second essential book "drew on KGB documents and other information obtained by Oleg Gordievsky while working as a British agent inside the KGB from 1974 to 1985"; and predictably, the Centre "responded with active measures against both the book and its authors."[15]

From the time of the Tsarist Okhrana to the Soviet KGB, the stories of agents, double agents, and betrayals, is superbly told by the firsthand experience of one of the greatest heroes of the Cold War, Oleg Gordievsky, in collaboration with the most knowledgeable scholar of Cold War secret intelligence, Cambridge professor Christopher Andrew.

Oleg Gordievsky, an ex Colonel in the KGB, was the head of the KGB's London Residency. He was unexpectedly recalled to Moscow at a time when the KGB was secretly investigating internal leaks. Nevertheless, he obeyed the summons, returned to Moscow, was placed essentially under house arrest, taken to a dacha and intensely interrogated. But Gordievsky did not break, despite being drugged and harshly questioned. He was released but placed under extensive surveillance. He was able to signal the British Secret Intelligence Service (SIS; better known as MI6) about the need to be rescued and exfiltrated. Fortunately, MI6 had planned for such a contingency and had arranged a daring escape plan that, incidentally, remained secret for many years. Gordievsky was scooped up from a busy city street in Moscow in midday, eluding KGB surveillance and escaping through Finland to the West and freedom.[16]

Despite the book's breadth and scope, this enthralling volume on the history of Russian and Soviet espionage and their intelligence services is very readable and will hold the reader's attention. The collaboration of Andrew and Gordievsky produced a book packed with captivating stories, fascinating real-life characters, and astonishing revelations.

Figure 128: U.S. President Ronald Reagan (left) meets with MI6 asset Oleg Gordievsky (right) in Washington, D.C. on July 21, 1987. Mary Anne Fackelman, Ronald Reagan Presidential Library

The Sword and the Shield: The Mitrokhin Archive and the Secret History of the KGB

The Sword and the Shield: The Mitrokhin Archive and the Secret History of the KGB by Christopher Andrew and Vasili Mitrokhin is a treasure trove of KGB intelligence secrets that came to light thanks to the courage and determination of Vasili Mitrokhin, a KGB officer and senior archivist in the First Chief Directorate (foreign intelligence) of the KGB.

Mitrokhin and his family were exfiltrated from Russia by the British Secret Intelligence Service (SIS) on November 7, 1992.[17] The defector brought with him six large cases containing the voluminous top-secret notes that he had copied from the KGB files on a daily basis for twelve years, from 1972 to 1984. The files went as far back as 1918 and contained all of the information available to the KGB's First Chief Directorate up to Mitrokhin's retirement in 1984.

The American FBI described the contents of Mitrokhin's cases as "the most complete and extensive intelligence ever received from any source."[17] And, as a result of his defection with the cache of top-secret files, hundreds of Soviet agents, Russian spies, and American traitors were uncovered. Many were finally brought to justice.

Furthermore, as Christopher Andrew noted:

> *Mitrokhin's archive contains much material from KGB files, which the SVR is still anxious to keep from public view. Unlike the documents selected for declassification by the SVR, none of which are more recent than the early 1960s, Mitrokhin's archive covers almost the whole of the Cold War. Most of it is still highly classified in Moscow. The originals of some of the most important documents noted or transcribed by Mitrokhin may no longer exist... In a number of cases, Mitrokhin's notes on them may now be all that survives.[18]*

Scholars and Western intelligence services are still studying Mitrokhin's archive. This third essential book contains an enormous amount of material, code names, intelligence files, and probably will continue to be savored by serious espionage scholars, Sovietologists, and perhaps by a few Cold War aficionados.

The World Was Going Our Way: The KGB and the Battle For the Third World

The World Was Going Our Way: The KGB and the Battle For the Third World by Christopher Andrew and Vasili Mitrokhin is the fourth essential book. Once again, the collaboration of Andrew and Mitrokhin resulted in another magnificent contribution, detailing Russian Cold War secrets involving the espionage battles waged between the CIA and KGB and their proxies in the Third World. The chapters are divided by geographical regions, and include Latin America, the Middle East, Asia, and Africa.[19]

Chapter 15

The world was seemingly going the way the Soviets intended, particularly in the intelligence wars in the Third World; and the KGB was as astounded as the West when the Soviet Union suddenly collapsed. The truth was that Soviet communism and its collectivist policies were rotten to the core, and not even the all-powerful KGB could prevent the collapse. This tome is even more reader friendly than *The Sword and The Shield*, and should garner a wider audience.

The World Was Going Our Way: The KGB and the Battle For the Third World will be an important reference for espionage researchers, modern historians, and scholars of Third World foreign policy and international studies.

Figure 129: Christopher Andrew, Emeritus Professor of Modern and Contemporary History at the University of Cambridge, at an event in 2008. Andrew produced three seminal works in collaboration with Oleg Gordievsky and Vasili Mitrokhin, the former KGB officers who defected. Tanya Hart

Plate 1: The "Big Three" (seated, left to right): British Prime Minister Clement Attlee, U.S. President Harry S. Truman, and Soviet Premier Joseph Stalin pose with their principal advisors at Potsdam, Germany, 1945. Courtesy: National Archives and Records Administration

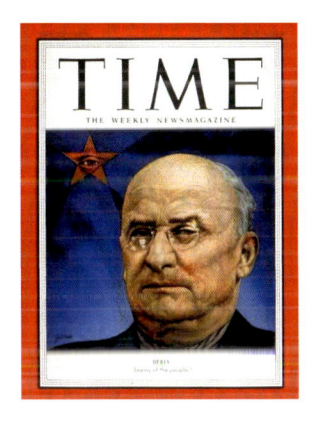

Plate 2: Lavrenti Beria, branded "enemy of the people," on the July 20, 1953, cover of *Time* magazine. Courtesy: Time, Inc.

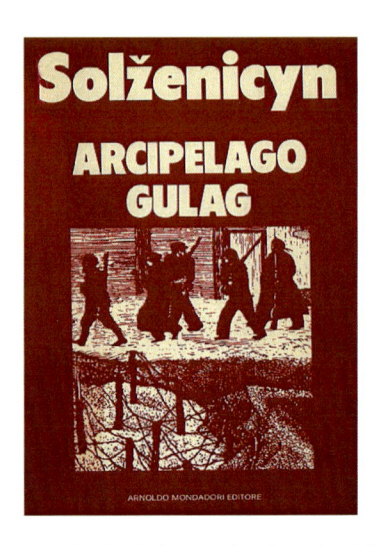

Plate 3: Italian translation of *The Gulag Archipelago* by Aleksandr Solzhenitsyn published in Milan in 1974. Courtesy: Archivi Mondadori

Plate 4: U.S. President Ronald Reagan says goodbye to Soviet General Secretary Mikhail Gorbachev after the last meeting at Hofdi House, Reykjavik, Iceland, October 12, 1986. Courtesy: White House Photographic Collection

Plate 5: View of the Berlin Wall in 1986 from the West showing graffiti art on the Wall. The "death strip" lies on the East side of the Wall. Courtesy: Thierry Noir

Plate 6: President Ronald Reagan at Brandenburg Gate West Berlin on June 12, 1987, urging General Secretary Gorbachev to "tear down this wall." Courtesy: White House Photographic Collection

Plate 7: President Ronald Reagan's July 21, 1987, meeting with MI6 asset, Oleg Gordievsky. Courtesy: Mary Anne Fackelman, Ronald Reagan Presidential Library

Plate 8: President Ronald Reagan's November 16, 1988, meeting with British Prime Minister Margaret Thatcher in the White House Oval Office. Courtesy: National Archives and Records Administration

Plate 9: A contingent from the Communist Party of Great Britain (Marxist-Leninist) carrying a banner of Joseph Stalin at a May Day march through London, 2008. Courtesy: Wikimedia Commons

Plate 10: March in Hong Kong on July 15, 2017, in memory of Liu Xiaobo, Nobel Peace Prize laureate, who called for the end of communist one-party rule in China. Courtesy: Voice of America

CHAPTER 16

ESPIONAGE—
THE WILDERNESS OF MIRRORS
DURING THE COLD WAR

As the Cold War continued to heat up from the 1960s through the 1970s, two men stood out in the annals of American intelligence—namely, James Jesus Angleton (1917–1987), the chief of counterintelligence in the Central Intelligence Agency (CIA), and Anatoliy M. Golitsyn (1926–2008), the KGB officer who defected to the West. Thus, began "one of the most extraordinary relationships in the history of the secret war between the CIA and the KGB."[1]

The Soviet Defector

Anatoliy M. Golitsyn, codenamed AE LADLE, had been a formidable major in the First Chief Directorate of the KGB.[2] In December 1961, while stationed in Helsinki, Finland, he defected along with his family and was exfiltrated to the United States.[3]

In the West, Golitsyn provided information that was invaluable in understanding the Soviet system and used his photographic memory to help uncover a number of Soviet agents infiltrating the West. He described Soviet intelligence operations and their methods of recruitment as well as practices in handling and running agents.[3] James Jesus Angleton called Golitsyn, "the most valuable defector ever to reach the West."[4]

From the time of his defection and through the Cold War, Golitsyn worked with the CIA and other Western governments, including Great Britain, where he received the title of Honorary Commander of the Order of the British Empire (CBE). In 1984, Golitsyn became an American citizen. Nevertheless, with a price placed on his head by the KGB, he remained under deep cover until his death in 2008.

Christopher Andrew noted:

Chapter 16

Deep concern in the Centre at the damage done by Anatoliy Golitsyn's defection...strengthened its determination to deter future defectors...His case prompted a major review...of its procedures for liquidating traitors outside the Soviet Union... An approved plan for 'special actions' that was drawn up by the heads of the First and Second Chief Directorates...stated, 'As these traitors, who have given important state secrets to the opponent and caused great political damage to the USSR, have been sentenced to death in their absence, this sentence will be carried out abroad.'[3]

Golitsyn was very respected in the West. After years of debriefings, he became a consultant for the CIA and, as one agency officer noted, "the prime interpreter of counterintelligence."[1] But Golitsyn was not omniscient and infallible as some in counterintelligence believed. In fact, he submitted several analyses that turned out to be incorrect. The CIA suffered for almost two decades because of those errors and Golitsyn's firm belief in his own infallibility, an opinion shared by Angleton.[5]

Figure 130: Soviet defector Anatoliy M. Golitsyn (left) and James Jesus Angleton (right), chief of CIA counterintelligence who considered espionage a "wilderness of mirrors." Mémoires de Guerre/U.S. Government

Since Angleton believed in the infallibility of Golitsyn's judgment, the counterintelligence unit launched a hunt for a super-mole, an active, deep penetration spy, codenamed SASHA. However, the spy no longer existed as a viable agent, and the mole hunt was counterproductive—sowing distrust, dissension, and wreaking havoc in the agency.[1-3] The problems created were only partially Golitsyn's fault. The lion's share of blame should be assigned to the head of the CIA counterintelligence unit, James Jesus Angleton.

The Spy Hunter

Jim Angleton was a brilliant intelligence officer, who was also endowed with a photographic memory and a superior intellect. He was a dedicated spy hunter, head of the CIA counterintelligence unit from 1954 to 1975, and an American patriot.

Angleton had been born in Boise, Idaho. At age 12, he contracted tuberculosis and the family moved to Arizona to help his recovery. In 1933, while his father was working for the National Cash Register Corporation (NCR), the family relocated to Italy. Angleton was 16 years old and, consequently, educated at a series of schools in England. He returned to the U.S., graduated from Yale University in 1941, and briefly studied law at Harvard Law School. Following America's entry into World War II, Angleton entered the Office of Strategic Services (OSS), and became "totally devoted to the craft of counterintelligence."[6]

The most promising OSS recruits were routinely "sent to England for training by the topflight officers of the British Secret Intelligence Service (SIS), better known as MI6 (Military Intelligence, Department 6)."[6] In London, Jim Angleton met MI6 officer Harold "Kim" Philby (1912–1988).

Kim Philby was greatly impressed with Angleton. Angleton later admitted that he came to view Philby as an older brother. Philby "took the young American under his wing and began to teach him everything he knew about counterintelligence—everything, that is, except its most basic precept: *Trust no one.*[6]

In *The Secret History of the CIA*, Joseph Trento added:

> This training turned James Angleton into one of the greatest, and most deeply flawed, intelligence officers of the twentieth century.[6]

During World War II, Angleton's ability to catch Axis spies made him a star in the OSS. After the war, he returned to Washington, D.C. and went to work for the CIA, the successor organization to the OSS. In 1954, Angleton was appointed head of counterintelligence by Allen Dulles, the new Director of Central Intelligence (DCI).

However, when Kim Philby was finally exposed as a communist and British traitor, Angleton was deeply hurt psychologically and emotionally by the betrayal of his friend and colleague.[7] Psychologically, Angleton never quite got over his friend's betrayal, and it haunted him. As one CIA officer noted, "Philby was the greatest blow Angleton ever suffered."[8] Perhaps because of that and the guilt associated with his professional failure to detect the ideological betrayal, the counterintelligence chief saw Soviet spies where there were only shadows, and deduced the existence of complex, long-term deception where there were only coincidences, incompetence, and outright errors made by his adversaries or the CIA.[7,8]

Figure 131: USSR postage stamp from the 1990 series "Soviet Intelligence Agents," honoring Kim Philby, one of the Cambridge Five

In Anatoliy Golitsyn, "Angleton found a defector whose dire warnings of Soviet machinations conformed to his own vision of fiendishly subtle KGB plots."[1] Angleton shared Golitsyn's belief in the near omnipotence of the Soviet KGB and far overestimated its capability for mounting strategic long-term deception plans against the U.S. and the West.[9,10] The two men were convinced that Soviet spies were everywhere—infiltrating, deceiving, and stealing secrets from the CIA and the Western intelligence services. Spy hunting in the "wilderness of mirrors" was obsessive. And as previously stated, during the 1960s and 1970s, the CIA became immersed in turmoil, making the agency irresolute and ineffective.[1-3]

Golitsyn even managed to convince Angleton that the Sino-Soviet split (1960–1989) was another strategic deception plan designed to deceive the West.[3] In this instance, Golitsyn was wrong. In fact, the split was real and exploitable, and the Nixon administration (1968–1974), for better or for worse, took advantage of it to deepen the rift between the Soviets and the communist Chinese.

Despite the Nixon administration's successful overtures to China, on many other fronts, the Soviet KGB was perceived to be gaining ground over the American CIA and the British MI6. Angleton continued to press the hunt for the nonexistent CIA mole.[1]

A Counterintelligence Conundrum— Separating the Wheat from the Chaff

In the 1960s, Golitsyn had helped uncover a number of Soviet agents who had infiltrated Western governments. With great confidence, he not only warned about CIA infiltration by the deep cover Soviet mole but also insisted that he was the last true defector, and those who would come after him would be "dangles" or double agents sent to deceive the U.S. and the West.

Within six months following Golitsyn's defection, three more Soviet intelligence officers offered their services to the CIA as "agents in place." Two of them made their approach in New York, and were codenamed SCOTCH and BOURBON. The third officer was Yuri Nosenko in Geneva, Switzerland. "Another 'walk-in,' Colonel Oleg Penkovsky of the GRU, was busy handing over 10,000 pages of highly classified documents on Soviet missiles."[1] David Martin wrote:

Suddenly, in the spring of 1962, the CIA was awash with penetrations of Soviet intelligence—more at one time than during its entire history. It strained credulity to think that all of these volunteers were genuine, particularly if the CIA was as deeply penetrated as...Golitsyn said.[1]

In the world of counterintelligence, in the "wilderness of mirrors," one must sort out the legitimate defectors from "dangles" and double agents—like separating the wheat from the chaff. This, of course, takes time; and the bona fides of a potential agent must be verified and their motivation assessed. A minor mistake in the recollection of a date, time or place, or other slight contradiction was often enough to create doubt about a defector's bona fides.

The atmosphere of distrust produced by Golitsyn's theory that every defector after him was a "dangle" or double agent continued to hamper the CIA. Most damaging of all, a slate of legitimate Soviet KGB defectors were thought to be "dangles," or Soviet double agents. It took years, veritably until the collapse of the Soviet Empire, to ascertain with certainty that some of those men—specifically, Yuri Nosenko (1927–2008)—were legitimate KGB defectors.[11]

In Nosenko's case, he ran into trouble mainly because he was not as smart as his CIA debriefers expected, nor did he possess an incredible memory like Golitsyn.[11] That was enough for James Jesus Angleton to doubt Nosenko's legitimacy as a true defector. He was not to be trusted, despite the good information he revealed. Accordingly, Nosenko was interrogated endlessly, kept isolated, and incarcerated for years.[11,12] He was treated as a hostile double agent, when, in fact, he was not.

Figure 132: Dmitri Polyakov (1921–1988), Major General in the Soviet GRU and double agent for the American CIA and FBI (codenamed BOURBON and TOPHAT). Patrick Caproni

One should not be surprised to learn that even GRU Colonel Oleg Penkovsky (code name: HERO)[13,14]; GRU Major General Dmitri Polyakov (CIA code name: BOURBON; FBI code name: TOPHAT)[15]; and Oleg Gordievsky (CIA code name: TICKLE; MI6 code name: SUNBEAM[16] had briefly come under suspicion as well. To this day, doubts remain about the mysterious FBI agent FEDORA (CIA code name: SCOTCH), a KGB officer at the United Nations.[12]

As we know, the other men were all genuine defectors—heroes who helped the West immensely by containing the advance of communism and risking their lives in the cause of freedom. Colonel Penkovsky and General Polyakov paid with their lives. They were tortured and executed. As previously mentioned, Oleg Gordievsky, barely escaped the grasp of the KGB.[17] These defectors not only helped the West but also helped bring about a greater freedom for Russian citizens today—even under Vladimir Putin's calculated and relentless drive towards authoritarianism.[18]

By the 1970s, however, Golitsyn's intelligence was no longer timely. Yet he wanted to remain the star defector. He began to deduce information based on global political assessments and analyses of more current events. Golitsyn, who had mistakenly argued that the Sino-Soviet split was a long-term deception ploy, went so far as to assert years later that the collapse of Soviet communism (1989–1991) was not real but more disinformation and long-term deception.[19]

Golitsyn thought he could distinguish between true Soviet intent and disinformation and unravel Soviet long-term strategic deception plans to conquer the West. Unfortunately, he was no longer privy to human intelligence as he had obtained while operating within the Soviet bloc as a KGB officer. What he was now providing was not specific information but erroneous analyses based on circumstantial intelligence and his own developing political beliefs as they formed while living in the West.

The CIA is Defanged

Throughout the 1970s, the CIA was virtually under assault. Various congressional investigative committees damaged the intelligence and spy detection capabilities of the agency, and succeeding presidential administrations carried out veritable governmental persecutions of the agency. The world was also in political turmoil. The following brief synopsis will provide a panoramic view of the global situation.

From 1972 to 1974, the Watergate political scandal, which occurred during the administration of President Richard M. Nixon, rocked the U.S. government and shook the American nation. By 1973, America had lost the Vietnam War. On August 9, 1974, President Nixon became the first U.S. president to resign while in office; but not before he had replaced "the man who kept the secrets," Richard Helms (1913–2002), a veteran spymaster who had served as the 8th Director of Central Intelligence from 1966 to 1973.

During this time, the CIA counterintelligence (CI) unit was severely hampered by the prevailing culture of paranoia engendered by the unproductive search for the mole SASHA. In December 1975, CI chief James Jesus Angleton was dismissed by the Director of Central Intelligence, William Colby (DCI, 1973–1976).

As if the turmoil in the CIA was not enough, also in 1975 during the presidency of Gerald Ford (1973–1977), the agency's intelligence activities were investigated by various governmental committees. The United States President's Commission on CIA Activities within the United States, or more commonly referred to as the Rockefeller Commission, was officially sanctioned by President Ford and led by Vice President Nelson Rockefeller. Another hostile, congressional investigative committee was headed by Idaho Senator Frank Church. "The Church investigation in the Senate had been paralleled by an equally damning [U.S.] House investigation lead by New York Congressman Otis Pike."[20] The CIA was accused of violating its charter, conducting domestic surveillance of U.S. citizens, and sanctioning assassinations in the 1960s and early 1970s. The Church Committee came dangerously close to completely dismantling the operational and intelligence gathering capabilities of the CIA.[21]

Figure 133: Richard Helms, Director of Central Intelligence (1966–1973). Central Intelligence Agency

In the presidency of Jimmy Carter (1977–1981), the CIA suffered even more serious setbacks. Admiral Stansfield Turner (DCI, 1977–1981) made drastic cutbacks in personnel, like the "Halloween massacre" of 1977.[20] Joseph Persico explained:

When Jimmy Carter became President, he sent a technocrat admiral to run the CIA. Stansfield Turner was the administration's chosen instrument to rein in the Agency, which Turner did by eliminating 820 essentially clandestine positions and notifying the incumbents of their removal through a computerized form letter.[20]

The agency's powers were severely trimmed, virtually defanging the intelligence and counterintelligence (CI) capabilities.[20] Robert M.

Gates, an executive assistant to Admiral Turner at the time, and who, years later during the Reagan administration, would be confirmed as the youngest Director of Central Intelligence, remembered:

With the people fired, driven out, or lured into retirement, half of our analysts had less than five years' experience. And our analysis wasn't at all sharp, forward looking, or relevant. Our paramilitary capability was clinically dead. What covert action we did carry out was super-cautious and lacked any imagination. The CIA was hunkered down in a defensive crouch.[20]

As a result, America would suffer humiliations and defeats unparalleled in its history. And Gates' description about covert actions being "super-cautious and lacking any imagination," fits the Carter administration's aborted hostage rescue mission to a tee.

By comparison, the Soviets and their surrogate warriors, the Cubans, were playing for high stakes. Like toppling dominoes, country after country on three continents fell prey to communism and revolution. For the Soviet KGB, it must have certainly seemed like "the world was going our way."[22]

In 1974, Ethiopia fell to a Marxist-Leninist junta, the Derg, and the revered Emperor of Ethiopia, Elect of God and Conquering Lion of the Tribe of Judah, Haile Selassie I, was deposed, arrested, and assassinated one year later in 1975.[23] Mozambique and Angola fell to the communists in 1975 followed by civil wars.[24]

The year 1979 was extremely turbulent globally. On January 16, the Shah of Iran, Mohammad Reza Pahlavi, left Iran for Egypt, hoping the military would seize control and allow him to return.[25] Instead, the Ayatollah Khomeini returned to Iran from exile in Paris and by February 10, the Shah's government had resigned and pro-Khomeini forces had taken control.[26] In July, the Sandinista National Liberation Front (FSLN), backed by the Cubans and the Soviets, overthrew the government of Anastasio Somoza in Nicaragua. In October, when the exiled Shah of Iran "came to America for cancer treatment, the Ayatollah incited Iranian militants to attack the U.S."[27] On November 4, the American Embassy in Tehran was stormed by militant Iranian students. Fifty-two American diplomats and citizens were taken captive. The Iran hostage crisis lasted for 444 days.[27] On Christmas Eve 1979, the Russians invaded Afghanistan and murdered its president, turning the country into a puppet nation and its mountainous terrain into Russian killing fields for the next ten years.[28]

238   Chapter 16

Figure 134: His Imperial Majesty Emperor Haile Selassie I (1892–1975), Emperor of Ethiopia (1930–1974) until he was overthrown in a military coup by the Derg, a Marxist-Leninist junta

Figure 135: Mohammad Reza Pahlavi in 1973, Shah of Iran (1941–1979), who was overthrown in the Islamic revolution

Espionage—The Wilderness of Mirrors During the Cold War   239

America also faced serious economic problems in the 1970s, such as high unemployment and high inflation—that is, stagflation. Those economic problems, coupled with the Iran hostage crisis and the failure of the attempted rescue mission, triggered a complete and general demoralization of the United States. President Carter called it a "general malaise." The Carter administration "had governed in malaise, and ended in humiliation."[29]

The CIA regained its bearings in the 1980s, under the administration of President Ronald Reagan (1981–1989) and his Director of Central Intelligence, William J. "Bill" Casey (DCI, 1981–1987).[21,29] On January 20, 1981, Reagan's first inauguration day, Iran released all remaining American hostages. Soon after taking over as DCI, Bill Casey summoned his covert-actions chief. "I want to see one place on this globe, one spot where we can checkmate them and roll them back. We've got to make the Communists feel the heat," Casey demanded.[29] America and the CIA were on their way back!

Figure 136: Official portrait of William J. Casey, DCI (1981–1987). Under Casey's direction, the CIA once again became an effective and powerful agency. Central Intelligence Agency

The KGB and The Mitrokhin Archive

As we have seen in chapter 15, Vasili Mitrokhin brought with him the "family jewels" of foreign intelligence secrets from the KGB's First Chief Directorate. The files had recorded all major agents and operations from the inception of Soviet foreign intelligence up to the year 1984, when Mitrokhin defected. The papers were so extensive that they became known as the Mitrokhin Archive.

In association with British historian, Christopher Andrew, the treasure trove of material was released to the world. Many traitors and double agents from the labyrinthine wilderness of mirrors were exposed, and mysteries from the Cold War were solved. One could posit that in the hands of Vasili Mitrokhin, the KGB's sword was used to sever the Gordian knot of Soviet secrets and expose the truth in an incredible number of cases.[30]

In addition to Vasili Mitrokhin, Oleg Gordievsky, and other valiant Soviet defectors, the United States also had an American who was working as a deep undercover agent for the FBI. For many years, Morris Childs, who had known Vladimir Lenin personally, continued to sit with the top Kremlin leadership and was privy to their discussions. Seated as an honorary Bolshevik with leaders, such as Khrushchev, Brezhnev and Andropov, agent SOLO, reported directly to J. Edgar Hoover and the American presidents.[31] Thus, the world now has information with corroborated facts illuminating the wilderness of mirrors, the true scope of Soviet power, the extent of what Soviet espionage really did and did not accomplish.

The KGB's First Chief Directorate was a powerful foreign intelligence agency. However, despite its tremendous power and resources—resources that dwarfed those of the CIA—it was not omnipotent or omniscient. The police state directorates were overburdened with corruption and failures, not to mention the overall immorality of communism and the Soviet system, rotting from the top. It could not carry on a grand design of deception that KGB Chief Alexander Shelepin (1958–1961) envisioned, and that the KGB defector, Anatoliy Golitsyn, believed was firmly in place as Soviet policy during the 1960s to the 1980s.[10]

One cannot totally disprove that *the idea* of long-term deception against the West never existed in the minds or actions of the KGB and Soviet leadership. Soviet disinformation was rampant. An entire department was dedicated to falsifying data and documents, and spreading disinformation to discombobulate the enemy. In fact, the concept may have been applied and carried out in part at various stages or strategic points, like when the

USSR used deception to bolster its flagging economy because it was in need of economic assistance from the West.

Figure 137: The Lubyanka building where the KGB headquarters were located in Moscow, 2010. Now the Federal Security Service of the Russian Federation (FSB) has offices in the building. A. Savin

Soviet Premiers, such as Nikita Khrushchev and Leonid Brezhnev, instituted their own deceptive periods of glasnost and perestroika before the terms were divulged to the world. For example, consider Khrushchev with his denunciation of the cult of personality of Stalin and his program of peaceful coexistence with the West; and Brezhnev with his policy of détente and his many photo sessions while wining and dining with President Richard Nixon. Nevertheless, the unrelenting Cold War continued worldwide, just as the espionage books described.

In conclusion, disinformation, betrayals, double agents, "Trust" operations, and "dangles" were all part of the great game. But a grand design of long-term deception that consisted of a series of false defectors, no; a faked Sino-Soviet split, definitely not; a feigned collapse of the Soviet empire and its satellites, certainly not. A radical plan like that would never have been possible. Instead, in 1991, the Soviet Empire collapsed.

CHAPTER 17

CATALOGING THE SPIES OF THE COLD WAR

The Encyclopedia of Cold War Espionage, Spies, and Secret Operations provides a suspenseful narrative of the espionage contest between the American eagle and its allies, on the one hand, and the Russian bear and its satellites, on the other. Consisting of nearly 300 entries, the encyclopedia encompasses a greater time span than just the Cold War period, beginning in 1917 before World War II and ending in 2003, well after the collapse of the Soviet Empire in 1991. There is a helpful chronology of events for the reader, a useful glossary of terms, and an index. The encyclopedia used previously published material and secondary sources. Therefore, this chapter will catalogue the salient points and a few main characters in this historical drama.[1]

Given the passage of time since the crumbling of the USSR in 1991 and the publication of additional espionage material, there are two welcomed threads of information stemming from this tome. The information goes beyond the disclosure of secrets revealed by the Soviet defector, Oleg Gordievsky, who worked in collaboration with British historian Christopher Andrew[2]; and the fantastic archive material smuggled out by Russian defector Vasili Mitrokhin (1922–2004). As previously discussed, the Mitrokhin Archive covered mostly foreign activities of the USSR's First Chief Directorate up to 1984—the year Vasili Mitrokhin defected. Mitrokhin's archive material was studied extensively by the British Secret Intelligence Service (SIS) and first published in 1999.[3,4]

Although Trahair relied heavily on those authors, he also included entries about other Soviet spies as well as the various security directorates of the KGB and the GRU (Soviet military intelligence). Moreover, Trahair utilized noted published sources to fill in the gap between 1984 and 2003. One can only speculate about the information Vasili Mitrokhin would have gathered if he had remained at the Russian archives until the collapse of the USSR in 1991. For one thing, it would have cut short the careers of the two most heinous American spies in U.S. history—namely, CIA agent Aldrich "Rick" Ames[5,6] and FBI agent Robert Hanssen (1944–2023).[7,8]

Heroes and Villains

As a result of the expanded coverage in the encyclopedia, Trahair included entries relating to the heroes and villains in the annals of Western intelligence. For example, one learns about Vladimir Vetrov (1928–1983), a KBG officer in Department T who, at great personal risk, remained a defector in place and gave his life in the process.[9] Working through the French secret service, the Directorate of Territorial Security (DST), Vetrov helped the West curb the theft of technology by the Soviets and fight the modus operandi of the KGB espionage activities.[9] The strain took a great toll on him; he made grave mistakes, was detected by the KGB, and executed in 1983. We will have more to say about Vladimir Vetrov in the next chapter of this book.

Little known spies, who are rarely mentioned in the spy literature, such as South African naval officer, Dieter F. Gerhardt, are included in the encyclopedia. Gerhardt spied for the USSR for 20 years. His motives were simple: ubiquitous greed and revenge for the alleged mistreatment of his German father by the pro-British government of South Africa during World War II.[10] And one will find it interesting that it was Vladimir Vetrov who informed the American Central Intelligence Agency (CIA) about Gerhardt's espionage activities for the Soviets.

Figure 138: Heroes—American cryptanalyst Meredith Gardner (left) and FBI agent Robert Lamphere (right). National Security Agency (NSA)

Another hero from the annals of Western intelligence, this time an American, was the linguist and mathematics genius, Meredith Gardner (1913–2002). Gardner was the American cryptanalyst who, in 1948, first broke the code to the Venona files, specifically the secret 1944 to 1945

Soviet communications against America when the Russians were supposedly America's allies in fighting the Nazis. The young Gardner also helped FBI agent Robert Lamphere (1918–2002) catch American traitors like Judith Coplon.[11,12] Gardner, who became the chief of the Venona project, remembered a visit his team received from the MI6 British liaison officer, Kim Philby, at Arlington Hall Station, the headquarters of the National Security Agency (NSA). As Philby looked over their shoulders, Gardner later recalled "the strange intensity with which the Englishman had observed the decryption team at work."[13] Meredith Gardner retired from the National Security Agency (NSA) in 1972 to pursue personal endeavors.

The Venona intercepts identified or confirmed the treasonous espionage activities of Judith Coplon; Julius and Ethel Rosenberg (the only nuclear spies executed in 1953); Donald Maclean (1913–1983), the British foreign diplomat and one of the Cambridge Five; and two known nuclear physicist traitors in the Manhattan Project—namely, Ted Hall (1925–1999) and Klaus Fuchs (1911–1988).[14]

Figure 139: Another hero—Michael Goleniewski in 1965, a Polish officer and deputy head of military counterintelligence. Goleniewski spied for the CIA from 1959 to 1961, exposing dangerous Soviet agent George Blake

Another unsung hero was the defector in place and triple agent Michael Goleniewski (1922–1993). The "powerfully built" Pole had a "commanding presence" and had been a KGB agent as well as deputy chief of Polish military intelligence before he "crossed over" in 1959. Appropriately codenamed SNIPER by the CIA, Goleniewski exposed the treason of the infamous George Blake (1922–2020), who not only caused the death of many Western agents but also revealed secret operations to the Soviets like the Berlin Tunnel, a joint CIA and MI6 effort used to tap telephone conversations of the Soviet military.[15] Blake was such a valuable agent for the Soviets that the tunnel was allowed to remain operational for nearly a year in order to protect his identity. In other words, Blake was more important to the Soviets than their military conversations.

Needless to say, Blake was arrested and received "the longest sentence in British criminal history, 42 years."[15] But in 1966, five years into his imprisonment at Wormwood Scrubs Prison, Blake escaped with the help of a suspected IRA man and two antinuclear activists. He made his way to Russia where he lived as an unrepentant hardline communist until his death in 2020.

Figure 140: George Blake of MI6 was a double agent for the Soviet Union and a real villain. He not only betrayed the Berlin Tunnel operation used to tap telephone conversations of the Soviet military but also dozens of British spies, most of them executed by the Soviets

Goleniewski also identified the equally atrocious German double agent, Heinz Felfe (1918–2008), the KGB's man in West German intelligence who subverted the Gehlen Organization after World War II (1951–1961).[15]

After Goleniewski "crossed over" to the American CIA, he exposed Polish and Soviet operations and identified hundreds of other spies who were working for either the Polish (SB) or Soviet intelligence services

(KGB or GRU). Goleniewsky died in 1993, not in 1972 as listed by Trahair.[15]

Caveat Lector—The *Encyclopedia's* Tilt to the Left in the Political Spectrum

Although the *Encyclopedia of Cold War Espionage, Spies, and Secret Operations* is extensive and well researched, there are significant shortcomings that should be pointed out. Trahair has a penchant for relating with obvious delight not only the peculiarities, which may be understandable, but also the gossipy eccentricities displayed and possible errors that might have been committed by some of the heroes of the West. As a trained psychologist, however, Trahair should have recognized the incredible strain Soviet defectors in place experience while working behind the Iron Curtain at great risk to themselves and similarly to the lives of family members. Any consequent change in personality due to the enormous strain they shoulder may not even subside after reaching relative safety. Moreover, many receive "death in absentia" sentences; therefore, they continue to live in constant fear of assassination by the KGB. So, who is to judge from the armchair comforts of academic life these eccentricities and then cast aspersions on the invaluable service provided to the West, for example, by Goleniewski, referring to his "curious unreliability" extending to a vague and probably spurious claim he was descended from Tsar Nicholas II.[15]

In the case of Anatoliy Golitsyn and James Jesus Angleton, their eccentricities were more profound and seriously affected the intelligence and counterintelligence (CI) capabilities of the West. Therefore, mentioning them was not only necessary but also critical to the narrative. However, that was not the case with Goleniewski, Elizabeth Bentley, or even Moise Tshombe (1917–1969) and several others, who ultimately ended on the side of freedom. Inserting gossipy comments in their entries was misleading, disparaging, and gratuitous.[1]

Another irksome observation was that Trahair followed the well blazed and politically correct path established by others in describing the "Red Menace" and the career of U.S. Senator Joseph McCarthy (1908–1957; McCarthyism). The intimation was that both of those events—that is, the "Red Menace" and McCarthyism—produced unwarranted, "irrational fears."[16] Yet, the encyclopedia described in incredible detail the vast Soviet espionage network that was being conducted when Senator McCarthy was making his denunciations. Soviet espionage was indeed undermining the West, despite Trahair's cavalier statements that it took place "in a fear-ridden background, between 1950 and 1953," as Senator

McCarthy was investigating "with irrational fears" communist infiltration of the U.S. government.[16]

Figure 141: FBI mugshot of Colonel Rudolf Abel in 1957, a Soviet "illegal" and case officer sentenced to 30 years. In 1962, Abel was exchanged to American U-2 pilot Francis Gary Powers. Federal Bureau of Investigation

In previous chapters in this book, we documented the infiltration of the U.S. government by agents of influence and Soviet and Chinese spies. The reader should consider the following partial list of spies and their activities primarily in the United States and judge for himself if those anti-communist fears were "irrational": Soviet "illegal" master spy, Colonel Rudolf Abel (1903–1971), who was also the case officer for the duet of Soviet spies Lona Cohen (1913–1992) and Morris Cohen (1905–1995); the Portland spy ring in Great Britain headed by Soviet "illegal" Konon Molody (aka, Gordon Lonsdale; 1922–1977) and, incidentally, exposed by Michael Goleniewski; the treason committed by high U.S. government officials, such as Alger Hiss, Harry Dexter White, and several other spies or agents of influence in the FDR administration as later confirmed in the Venona intercepts, not to mention the greatest espionage of all, which was the theft of atomic secrets from the Manhattan Project at Los Alamos by Soviet spy rings, including the Rosenbergs, and involving several noted nuclear scientists, just a few years before.

Trahair also took singular pleasure in describing CIA operations conducted in an attempt to fight the offensive KGB and the Soviets on a more equal footing, when they failed or embarrassed the agency, specifically Operations Chaos, Congress, Artichoke, and Corona.

Figure 142: Konon Molody (aka, Gordon Lonsdale) in 1961, Soviet "illegal" and head of the Portland spy ring in Great Britain sentenced to 25 years. In 1964, Molody was exchanged in a spy-swap for Greville Wynne, the British businessman apprehended in Moscow for his contacts with Oleg Penkovsky. Associated Press

In discussing the mysterious death of Frank Olsen (1910–1953) and Operation Artichoke, the author meandered into "conspiracy theories" and added a subjective and unconfirmed note that "Olsen's son does not plan to let the matter rest."[17]

In deriding Operation Congress, Trahair used sarcasm to describe the CIA's attempt to court conservative intellectuals and ended the section by quoting (or paraphrasing) a CIA critic, Francis Saunders, at length:

In her account of the CIA's influence on intellectuals, Saunders (1999) writes, with irony, that it was the same set of people who had been raised on classical literature and educated at America's foremost universities who, after World War II, recruited Nazis, manipulated democratic elections in foreign lands, administered LSD to subjects without their consent, opened their citizens' mail illegally, funded dictatorships and plotted assassinations—all in the interest of securing an empire for the United States. This use of irony for criticism meets resistance in the work of CIA apologists Richard Bissell (1996) and William Colby (1987).[18]

Because quotation marks were not used in the paragraph, the reader cannot discern which words belonged to Trahair and which words were quoted from Saunders. Suffice to say, Trahair did not use the same cutting sarcasm when describing the Soviet or KGB's astounding blunders. And, there are other examples of subtle and not so subtle instances of leftist ideological bias and anti-Americanism that seemed brewing just under the surface, especially in the treatment of Soviet defectors or Russian double agents working for the West. Their personal defects were spotlighted while their anti-communist and ideological preferences for liberty were downplayed. In Trahair's mind, the defectors were enamored of the good life in the West or invariably afflicted with the usual character flaws like greed and lust. Take for instance, General Dmitri Polyakov (FBI code name: TOPHAT), the GRU defector in place, who came over to the West because the Soviets denied his eldest son access to life-saving medical treatment in the United States. Instead, according to Trahair, Polyakov "became disillusioned with the Russian system and the inadequate salary he received."[19] The Russian patriot died with a bullet to the back of his head after courageously denouncing the Soviet system during interrogation and torture. One might consider this example a minor error or simply a difference of opinion, but these errors, misleading statements, and derogatory descriptions occur in almost all of the personal descriptions about the Russian defectors.

Figure 143: Press photos of three of the Cambridge Five spies (from left to right), Kim Philby, Guy Burgess, and Donald Maclean. Not pictured are Anthony Blunt and John Cairncross. United Press International

Conversely, consider the treatment of American traitors working in the U.S. State Department and other government agencies during the FDR administration. Alger Hiss (1904–1996), George Silverman (fl. 1916–

1943), and Harry Dexter White (1892–1948) were "young and ambitious idealists who believed they were fighting a secret war against fascism."[20] With more subtlety, the Cambridge Five spies were usually referred to by their sobriquet, "The Magnificent Five," as they were dubbed in admiration by the KGB's First Chief Directorate.[20]

Figure 144: The passenger steamer SS *Falaise* that Guy Burgess and Donald Maclean boarded as they fled to the Soviet Union in May 1951

The intelligence services of the West were usually described in terms of moral equivalence to the KGB and their associates, as if the Western services had similar modus operandi with the repressive Soviet intelligence and security organs. We have already discussed the treatment of the CIA. There were more subtle intimations like the brief glossary description of "sleeper agents." According to Trahair, "the practice was used more by the Russians than the British."[21] And yet, he failed to give any examples of "illegal" agents trained by the British and sent to Russia as sleeper agents.

Indeed, the Russians had many famous "sleeper agents" sent to the West, such as the spy couple Lona and Morris Cohen, Willie Fisher (aka, Colonel Rudolf Abel) and Konon Molody (aka, Gordon Lonsdale), all of who had entries as mentioned. But the Soviet "illegal" agent Kaarlo Tuomi, who became an FBI double agent and ultimately an American patriot[22], was not even mentioned in the encyclopedia.

Trahair's abbreviated definition of the Spanish Civil War in the glossary again showed his bias. According to Trahair, "the militarists" and "German Nazis and Italian fascists" supported General Franco. No mention was made of Soviet support for the loyalists or the communists in the International Brigades or the NKVD troops and the assassination squads sent by Joseph Stalin—only "unofficial British and Soviet support." Trahair ended by stating that "the militarists won."[21]

Figure 145: Press photo of communist spies Lona and Morris Cohen on their way to Moscow after being exchanged in a 1969 spy-swap for a British subject. Associated Press

Let us consider when and how the Cold War began. Most authorities agree that the early Cold War period began in 1945 after the astounding disclosure of Soviet espionage against their Western allies made by the Soviet defector and GRU cipher clerk Igor Gouzenko (1919–1982) in Ottawa, Canada. Instead, Trahair noted that "according to some observers," it was when U.S. President Harry Truman "announced he would give aid to Greece and Turkey" in 1947 to resist communist expansion.[23] Gouzenko's astounding defection was labeled "the first major espionage event of the Cold War"[24], as if Gouzenko's act triggered the espionage war, when in fact the Soviet documents he disclosed to the West proved that the Russians had already been spying on their allies during World War II.

And finally, British Prime Minister Margaret Thatcher's views "were clearly right-wing"[25], but no British Labor leader was described as having "left-wing" views.

Figure 146: Igor Gouzenko in 1946, cipher clerk for the Soviet embassy in Ottawa, Canada, who defected and exposed Soviet espionage against their Western allies during World War II

Obscure Moments, Bizarre Incidents, and Notable Omissions

To its credit, the *Encyclopedia of Cold War Espionage, Spies, and Secret Operations* describes many obscure and bizarre incidents of espionage, which otherwise would have escaped public notice, such as the Berlin Spy Carousel, The Crabb Affair, various KGB Honeytrap and Romeo operations[26], the strange 1954 defection of the West German counterintelligence (CI) chief Otto John and his mysterious return in 1955 to West Germany[27], and other peculiar incidents.

Another welcomed addition was the notation of the year of birth and death of the figure being discussed and the approximate dates of their espionage activities. The author also made an effort to bring each entry up to date and find out what became of the spy or their whereabouts. We surmise that at the time of publication, the following spies were still alive but are now deceased: CIA traitor Philip Agee (1935–2008) died in Cuba; communist agent Judith Coplon (1921–2011) died in New York; double agent George Blake (1922–2020) died in Russia; and East German spy Günter Guillaume (1927–1995), who in 1974 brought down the government of West German Chancellor, Willy Brandt (1913–1992), was awarded the Order of Lenin, and given a villa in East Germany.[28]

Figure 147: West German Chancellor Willy Brandt (left) and East German (Stasi) spy Günter Guillaume (right) at a Party conference between 1972 and 1974 in Düsseldorf, Germany

Nevertheless, the encyclopedia is not exhaustive and had notable omissions. There were no entries for Boris Yuzhin, Valery Martynov, or Sergei Motorin, who were KGB officers working for the FBI as double agents. They were betrayed by Aldrich Ames and Robert Hanssen. Martynov and Motorin, who were referred to as "M&M" by the Americans, were lured back to Moscow and executed by the Soviets. Yuzhin was sent to the Gulag and later emigrated to the United States. Adolf G. Tolkachev, a Soviet engineer and super-spy double agent for the CIA, was only mentioned in passing with no formal entry created under his name. These names represent but a few of the significant omissions.

There were minor errors of facts. We mentioned Goleniewski's dates, and Günter Guillaume was thought to be alive, when, in fact, he died in 1995. But there were also complex errors of facts due either to wrong sources or incorrect interpretation of facts stemming from political bias. For example, in the *Amerasia* affair, Trahair asserted that the diplomat John Stewart Service was a victim of the Red Scare when, in fact, he was a full-fledged communist fellow traveler, rooming in Chungking with two other traitors, the Chinese Chi Chao-ting, and FDR administration official Solomon Adler.[29] All three men spread disinformation about alleged venal conditions in the Nationalist government, calumniated Chiang Kai-shek, and praised Mao Tse-tung. Information from defectors and the Venona files verified the concerted campaign was Soviet-created disinformation, propagated by Soviet spies and agents of influence to tilt American public opinion away from Chiang and the American government from rendering the needed assistance to the Nationalists, while helping Mao seize control of China.[30]

One final detraction, there were no photographs of the spies or illustrations of any kind in the encyclopedia. A series of photographs of individuals on the front cover were not even identified, which was unconscionable, and the only photo credit given was to Corbis.

Nevertheless, with the aforementioned important caveats, the *Encyclopedia of Cold War Espionage, Spies, and Secret Operations* is still recommended for espionage researchers and as a quick reference guide for the student of espionage history. At the end of each entry, Trahair listed the sources he used to create the entry. The researcher or student would find those lists of sources to be a helpful starting point in locating additional information on the topic.

CHAPTER 18

THE STORY OF FAREWELL—
THE PATRIOT WHO GAVE HIS LIFE
FOR RUSSIA'S FREEDOM

The disintegration of the USSR was inextricably entwined and intimately related to the life and times, failures and accomplishments, paradoxes and contradictions of the KGB analyst and courageous Russian patriot—who was the subject of *Farewell: The Greatest Spy Story of the Twentieth Century* by Sergei Kostin and Eric Raynaud—Colonel Vladimir Ippolitovich Vetrov (1932–1985; codenamed FAREWELL).[1]

Vetrov was a man with tenacious clarity of purpose and the steely determination to carry out and accomplish his goal at any price. Vetrov crossed over to the West as a defector in place and spied against the KGB and his former Soviet comrades. What were the motivating factors? Vetrov was sickened not only by the nepotism of the apparatchiks and the abuses, corruption, and injustices that plagued the KGB specifically but also by the lack of individual freedom, the hypocrisy of the nomenklatura, and the inequalities and abuses sustained by the citizens in the entire Soviet system where family connections were more important than merit or hard work.

What were Vetrov's goals? He wanted to break the machinery of repression in the corrupt KGB and bring down the Soviet system, even if the task led to his own destruction and death. So, as we shall see, Vladimir Vetrov became the main protagonist in one of the most important espionage cases of the Cold War, and along the way, changed history.

But to comprehend the dimensions of Vetrov's accomplishment and the global implications of the Farewell Dossier, one must understand the dismal geopolitical situation in the West vis-à-vis the USSR from the 1970s up to 1981, the year of Vetrov's defection in place and his work for France and the United States.

The Situation in America: 1972 to 1981

During the seventies, the situation in America as well as globally was critical. As noted in chapter 16, from 1972 to 1974, the Watergate political scandal rocked the U.S. government and shook the American nation. By 1973, America had lost the Vietnam War. In 1974, President Richard M. Nixon became the first American president to resign while in office. During the Carter administration from 1977 to 1981, America suffered more global humiliations and defeats unparalleled in the annals of its history as well as faced serious economic problems, such as high unemployment and high inflation—that is, stagflation.

On the global scene, the situation was just as dismal as country after country fell prey to communism and revolution. Perhaps this recapitulation from chapter 16 is worth recounting:

> *The Soviets and their surrogate warriors, the Cubans, were playing for high stakes. In 1974, Ethiopia fell to the communists and one year later, the revered King of the Ethiopians, Haile Selassie I, was deposed and later assassinated. In 1975, Mozambique and Angola also fell to the communists, followed by civil wars. The year 1979 was a watershed year, as the communist Sandinistas overthrew the government of Nicaragua; the Russians invaded Afghanistan, murdered its president, turned the country into a puppet nation and its mountainous terrain into Russian killing fields; the Shah of Iran, Mohammad Reza Pahlavi, fell from power, Iranian militants stormed the U.S. Embassy in Tehran, and took 52 Americans hostage. The Iran hostage crisis would last for 444 days.*

America's domestic economic problems coupled with the dire global situation triggered a complete and general demoralization in the United States that U.S. President Jimmy Carter called a "general malaise."

The Situation in France: 1950 to 1981

The situation in France was not any better. During the fifties and sixties, France lost most of its overseas colonies and territories following bloody or humiliating defeats in French Indochina (1954), Tunisia (1956), and Algeria (1962). When France was part of NATO, Georges Pâques (1914–1993), a Soviet mole, wormed his way into the administration of French President Charles de Gaulle (1890–1970; President of France, 1959–1969). NATO headquarters were located in Paris at the time, and in 1962, Pâques "started work as Deputy Head of the NATO Press Service."[2] His position gave him access to high-level French government and NATO officials. Pâques revealed secret French and NATO defense plans to the Soviet Union, including "NATO documents with plans related to psychological warfare, force posture, military exercises and defense plans for Berlin."[2] He also provided the Soviets with "extensive biographies of prominent officials at NATO and within Allied governments."[2] With the Cold War in full swing at the time, the potential damage to France and NATO was extraordinarily grave. Pâques was apprehended in 1963 by the French intelligence service, thanks in part to the information revealed by Anatoliy Golitsyn, who had defected to the West in 1961.[2] At his trial, the world learned that Pâques had been spying for the Russian communists for 20 years, further shaming France and embarrassing de Gaulle.

Figure 148: François Mitterrand, leader of the French Socialist Party from 1971 to 1981

By the seventies, France was no longer part of NATO and had been drifting leftward in the political spectrum for some time. French president Valéry Giscard d'Estaing (President of France, 1974–1981) had been unsuccessful in fighting inflation and climbing unemployment. France, it seemed, had lost her nerve in facing domestic problems or meeting the Soviet threat.

The Socialist Party was on the rise in France, led by the debonair François Mitterrand (1916–1996). As the elections of 1981 approached, they were ready, well organized, and counting on the support of all of the leftist parties, including the Communist Party of France. One socialist goal was to prune or completely dismantle and abolish the *Direction de la*

Surveillance du Territoire (DST), France's domestic counterintelligence service, the equivalent of the American FBI. The socialists claimed the DST "was an instrument of the political right rather than a tool to defend the nation."[3]

Mitterrand was very skeptical of the DST. While serving as a minister years earlier, he had been investigated for suspicion of being a Moscow agent. Moreover, the French foreign intelligence service, the SDECE, the equivalent of the American CIA, did not even have a presence in the Soviet Union, with virtually no significant espionage or counterintelligence (CI) activity recorded against the Soviets in the late seventies and early eighties.

On May 10, 1981, the socialist candidate, François Mitterrand, was elected President of France (1981–1995) and vowed to appoint his communist allies to the French government. The Western alliance threatened to crack. When the Reagan administration protested and sent Vice President George H.W. Bush (a former Director of Central Intelligence, 1975–1976) to the Elysée Palace, the French president publicly invoked France's sovereignty and sent the American envoy packing.

Mitterrand pleased the French public with the political gesture. He did not worry about the Americans. He knew he had an impressive trump card he would soon share with the ebullient, anti-communist U.S. president.

Why France was Chosen as a Vehicle for Deception

Two months earlier, a high-ranking Soviet KGB analyst, Colonel Vladimir Ippolitovich Vetrov contacted the French. To compound the situation, the defector in place was recruited in the midst of French elections by officers in the DST, namely the urbane Jacques Prévost, a Thomson-CSF company executive and DST liaison, who introduced Vetrov to the DST; the resourceful Raymond Nart, USSR section head of the French DST; and Marcel Chalet, the politically savvy and security-minded DST chief. In order to maximize secrecy and protect their new asset, the three DST officials decided to act on their own initiative without advising the administration of President Giscard d'Estaing. The DST officials also decided that they would wait at least two months after the election to brief the new President of France, whoever he might be.

To the relief of the three Frenchmen, President Mitterrand was delighted when informed about the DST intelligence operation. He immediately authorized its continuation under the aegis of the trusted French Interior Minister—and not under the SDECE, which was headed by a minister who had been identified as a Soviet agent.

Why did Vladimir Vetrov choose France to be his vehicle for betraying his comrades in the KGB and destroying the Soviet system? As a KGB agent, Vetrov was well aware that the Soviets believed they had little to fear from a progressive France since the nation had been moving decisively toward the left in the political spectrum. France was viewed as not much of a threat by the Soviets. Moreover, the KGB had penetrated the French foreign intelligence service, the SDECE. The Soviets would be alerted in advance about any betrayal or espionage activity conducted against the USSR. Additionally, Vetrov knew that CIA officers stationed in France were carefully watched and kept under constant surveillance by the KGB's Second Chief Directorate, which was in charge of Soviet counterintelligence. Therefore, Vetrov cautiously approached the DST, the French internal security service, which was not involved in foreign operations. Besides, he had worked in France and admired French culture immensely.

U.S. President Ronald Reagan Meets French President François Mitterrand

The confident François Mitterrand waited until the G7 economic summit held on July 20-21, 1981, in Quebec and nearby Ottawa, to play his trump card. Elected as a socialist, Mitterrand was initially considered a bit of the black sheep among the summit participants since the American president, Ronald Reagan, had set the tone of getting tough with the Soviets. But when Mitterrand and Reagan met for the first time, the President of France showed his trump card and shared the superb Farewell Dossier with the U.S. president.

Mitterrand removed any shadow of a doubt as to where he and France stood. He was squarely in the freedom camp, and the two presidents became instant allies. From that time on, until the collapse of Soviet communism in 1991, France stood shoulder to shoulder with America.

During his active but brief espionage career that lasted from March 1981 to January 1982—less than a year but longer than most agents operating inside a communist police state—Vladimir "Volodia" Vetrov identified and neutralized 422 KGB officers and 54 Western agents or Soviet moles working for the KGB and the USSR bloc.

Previously, Volodia had worked in both Canada and France under the cover of a trade representative for the USSR. His main tasks were to recruit spies but most importantly, to steal technological and electronic secrets from the West to facilitate research and military applications for the Soviet Military Industrial Commission (VPK). During the Cold War, and especially in the seventies, "Soviet intelligence carried out a substantial and successful clandestine effort to obtain technical and scientific knowledge from the West."[4]

Figure 149: President François Mitterrand of France and U.S. President Ronald Reagan attend a wreath-laying ceremony at the American cemetery at Omaha Beach in 1984 to commemorate the 40th anniversary of the D-Day invasion. SPC 5 James Cavalier, U.S. Military

Gus W. Weiss, a Special Assistant to the U.S. Secretary of Defense and the Director of International Economics for the National Security Council, explained that the Americans had viewed détente as a means of easing U.S.-Soviet relations, and "moving the superpowers from confrontation to negotiation. Arms control, trade, and investment were the main substantive topics."[4] But the Soviets, on the other hand, had conceived of détente as "peaceful coexistence" and "an avenue to improve their inefficient, if not beleaguered economy using improved political relations to obtain grain, foreign credits, and technology."[4] Leonid Brezhnev, General Secretary of the Communist Party of the Soviet Union

The Story of FAREWELL—The Patriot Who Gave His Life   261
for Russia's Freedom

(1964–1982), outlined this Soviet strategy in his 1971 remarks to the Politburo when he stated:

We communists have to string along with the capitalists for a while. We need their credits, their agriculture, and their technology. But we are going to continue massive military programs and by the middle 1980s we will be in a position to return to a much more aggressive foreign policy designed to gain the upper hand in our relationship with the West.[4]

Figure 150: Leonid Brezhnev, General Secretary of the Communist Party of the Soviet Union, photographed in 1972. Anefo, Dutch National Archives, The Hague

The Soviet leadership moved rapidly implementing the strategic policy. Within the KGB's First Chief Directorate, Soviet authorities established a new unit, Directorate T, and called its operational arm, Line X. The KGB and the GRU, Soviet military intelligence, would perform the bulk of information collection with "extensive support from the East European intelligence services."[4] Beginning in 1972, Soviet trade and scientific delegations were arriving on visits to corporations and laboratories in the United States. Line X took full advantage of the opportunity and "populated these delegations with its own people."[4]

After the years of working abroad, Vetrov was transferred back to the Center in Moscow at Yasenevo. Although he was not allowed to travel to the West, Volodia was placed at a key nexus point of scientific and technological information collation of the KGB. When he decided to spy for the West and became agent FAREWELL, Vetrov was privy to the Soviet state's requirements for technological, electronic, and scientific information—the "family jewels" of secret information the Russians needed from the West, including the United States and France. Vetrov "photographed and supplied 4,000 KGB documents on the program," which French intelligence labeled the "Farewell Dossier."[4] Additionally, Vetrov exposed the vast network of Soviet and Eastern Bloc organizations that with innocuous names were front organizations also involved in pilfering science and technology from the West for the VPK.

Duping the Soviets and Precipitating the Collapse

Thanks to the Farewell Dossier, the Reagan administration learned and estimated that by the theft of such vast amounts of information the Soviets were able to fund their entire intelligence gathering apparatus (KGB and GRU espionage) and a large amount of their military capabilities. President Reagan's Secretary of Defense, Caspar Weinberger, stated the fact very clearly, "The United States and other Western nations are thus subsidizing the Soviet military buildup."[5] This knowledge "led to a potent counterintelligence response by CIA and the NATO intelligence services."[4]

President Reagan and his National Security Council (NSC) team, including Robert MacFarlane, Gus Weiss, Richard V. Allen (who wrote the Foreword to the book), and William Casey (Director of Central Intelligence), were able to put together a group of intelligence officers, defense analysts, economists, and scientists who, using the Farewell Dossier, fed erroneous technical and dead-end scientific information to the KGB spies, and duped the Soviets.[4] And Thomas Reed, who worked with Reagan's NSC team and assisted on the Strategic Defense Initiative (SDI) project, wrote in his memoirs:

> *[As a grand finale] in 1984-85, the United States and its NATO allies rolled up the entire Line X connection both in the U.S. and overseas. This effectively extinguished the KGB's technology collection capabilities at a time when Moscow was being sandwiched between a failing economy on the one hand and an American president—intent on prevailing and ending the Cold War—on the other... Its ultimate bankruptcy, not a bloody battle or a nuclear exchange, is what brought the Cold War to an end.[6]*

And it worked. When President Reagan, along with Lieutenant General Daniel O. Graham, announced SDI, referred to as "Star Wars" by the media, the bankrupt USSR, led by Mikhail Gorbachev (General Secretary of the Communist Party of the Soviet Union, 1985–1991), knew the game was over. To make the story short, the Soviet "evil empire," as Reagan called the USSR in 1983, began to crack and finally came tumbling down, beginning in 1989 with the fall of the Berlin Wall. By the end of 1991, the Soviet state had crumbled.

FAREWELL—The Man, His Fall, and His Final Days

If one still has any doubt about what motivated Vetrov to spy for the West, the following statement he wrote to the French and transmitted by Patrick Ferrant, the French Embassy military attaché and Vetrov's DST case officer in Moscow, should remove that doubt:

> *Dear Maurice [presumably President François Maurice Mitterrand], Thank you for worrying about my safety. I will do everything I can in this regard. You are asking why I took this step. I could explain as follows. Sure, I like France very much, a country that marked my soul deeply, but apart from this, I detest and am appalled by the regime in place in our country. This totalitarian order crushes individuals and promotes discord between people. There is nothing good in our life; in short, it's rotten through and through.[7]*

By January 1982, Vetrov was psychologically exhausted from the risk he had been taking and his double existence. His personal life was also in shambles. On the evening of February 22, 1982, Volodia and his mistress, Ludmilla Ochikina, were parked in his Lada just off a major Moscow highway drinking champagne. He had been estranged from his mistress, who was a KGB translator. They had worked together at Yasenevo. Apparently, by a slip of his tongue due to the champagne, Volodia must have revealed he was a double agent spying for the West. He panicked, lost control, and furiously stabbed his mistress. An off-duty policeman came to the window of the Lada, and Volodia got out of the car and stabbed him too, killing the man. Vetrov was arrested for killing the policeman and attempting to kill his mistress.

He was confined to a prison cell while an ongoing investigation took place. It would only be a matter of time before his espionage activities were discovered. The KGB was suspicious of the strange circumstances surrounding the crime and continued to investigate. That suspicion only increased as stool pigeons inside the prison reported on Vetrov's unguarded political remarks.

Vetrov and his son Vladik had always been close. Now Volodia and his wife Svetlana, who had been very close at one time, grew closer in adversity. Even while in prison, Vetrov wanted desperately to continue to spy for the West. But he and Svetlana made grave mistakes. Concrete evidence was uncovered and Vetrov was made to confess. He was executed on January 23, 1985.

It was not until August 1985, when the head of Soviet counterintelligence, KGB officer Vitaly Yurchenko, defected to the West and shortly thereafter re-defected to the USSR, that the CIA learned what had happened to Volodia. The sad information was relayed to the French.

A Patriot or a Traitor in Moral Terms?

Before execution, the KGB made Vetrov write out a confession of his "treason."[8] Instead, the handwritten, sixty-page document was a scathing condemnation of the Soviet system and the KGB. In a gripping account, Vitaly Yurchenko related the end of the Farewell affair to the CIA. Vetrov died a hero. His allegiance had been to freedom and to serving his motherland for the betterment of the Russian people—not to the KGB and the repressive Soviet system. Russia would be better served by following the ideals of liberty and the West. According to Yurchenko, Vetrov "went to his death with only one regret, that he could not have done more damage to the KGB in his service for France."[8]

Was Vetrov a hero or a traitor? Patrick Ferrant, Volodia's DST case officer, agreed to break his long silence, and in 2009, summed up the situation as follows:

> *True, he committed treason, but to me he is, in fact, a patriot… Here we have a guy with his dacha, his friends, his Russian homeland. His grudge was against the KGB. He was a patriot who wanted to protect his country, the population of his country, against evil people. Was Klaus von Stauffenberg accused of being a traitor after his assassination attempt of Hitler?[9]*

Indeed, one must answer the key question: Is a patriot the one who knowingly partakes of a national evil or the one whose allegiance is to goodness and what he knows to be just for his homeland, such as life, liberty, and the pursuit of happiness?

In conclusion, to our pantheon of heroes, the name of Vladimir Vetrov now joins the ranks. The list of the men and women who most immediately helped bring about the collapse of the evil empire of Soviet communism already included: U.S. President Ronald Reagan; Director of

Central Intelligence, William Casey; British Prime Minister Margaret Thatcher; French President François Mitterrand; Nobel Prize Winner, Aleksandr Solzhenitsyn; St. Pope John Paul II; Polish Solidarity leader, Lech Walesa; Russian President Boris Yeltsin; Russian defectors in place—Vladimir N. Sakharov[10]; Kaarlo Tuomi[11]; Aleksandr D. Ogorodnik[12]; Oleg Penkovsky[13]; Dmitri Polyakov[14]; Oleg Gordievsky[15]; Adolf Tolkachev[16]—and many others.

Epilogue

The French film, *L'affaire Farewell*, was based on the Farewell Dossier and released in 2009. The English version of the movie was released in 2010.[17] The film received excellent reviews and starred Guillaume Canet (playing Patrick Ferrant, as "Pierre Fremont") and Emir Kusturica (playing Vetrov, as "Sergei Gregoriev"). The film was well done and for the most part encapsulated the substance of the Farewell Dossier. The movie avoided making a psychological profile of Vetrov and interjecting itself into his mental state or speculating on ulterior motives. Vetrov was correctly portrayed as an educated Russian patriot, who was fearful of the growing might of the Soviet state, felt he had the means to contribute to its destruction and, as a devoted father, wanted a better future of freedom for his son. Inexplicably, however, the movie left out the most poignant part of the story, namely how the KGB caught Vetrov and how his espionage career ended. Instead, the producers sadly chose to use the final moments in the movie as left-wing propaganda to disparage the United States and suppress the truth by omitting the most dramatic episode of the saga. The outlandish ending marred the denouement, and truth and content were subordinated to bashing the United States and the Reagan administration. The mendacious and totally fabricated ending, which had no basis in fact, was a shameful and lamentable way to conclude an otherwise excellent movie.

CHAPTER 19

TWO MAJOR INTELLIGENCE OPERATIONS: ONE HELPED PREVENT AND THE OTHER ALMOST CAUSED WORLD WAR III

The FBI's Operation SOLO

Operation SOLO was a sensitive operation against the Communist Party of the USA (CPUSA) that rapidly evolved into a deep penetration of the leadership of the Soviet Union conceived by the Federal Bureau of Investigation (FBI) and carried out by three patriotic and determined Americans: Morris Childs, his wife Eva, and his brother Jack.

Over a 27-year period, Morris Childs, "Agent 58," conducted 52 clandestine missions into communist nations like the Soviet Union, China, and Cuba, as well as to parts of the Soviet empire in Eastern Europe. The missions usually lasted several weeks at a time. "Nikita Khrushchev, Leonid Brezhnev, Yuri Andropov, Mao Tse-tung, Fidel Castro, and Nicolae Ceausescu trusted him as both a friend and confidant."[1]

As a member of the CPUSA since 1919, Morris was considered a reliable "old Bolshevik," and was made advisor to the International Department of the Central Committee (Comintern). He was so esteemed by the Soviet leadership that Leonid Brezhnev awarded him the Order of the Red Banner, for impeccable service. During those 27 years of service, his loyalty to international communism was never questioned; nor did the communist leaders ever learn that Morris was working for the FBI.[1]

Historians Harvey Klehr and John Earl Haynes wrote that, "Operation SOLO was a long-running FBI program to infiltrate the Communist Party of the United States and gather intelligence about its relationship to the Union of Soviet Socialist Republics, China, and other communist nations."[2] Officially, Operation SOLO began in 1958 and concluded in 1977. However, "two of the principal agents in the operation had been involved with the Bureau for several years prior"[2]; and one of them, since 1952.[1]

Morris Childs (codenamed "58"), his wife Eva, and his brother Jack Childs had been active members of the CPUSA. When the trio became

Two Major Intelligence Operations: One Helped Prevent and the Other Almost Caused World War III

disillusioned with communism and the CPUSA, the FBI recruited them, and they agreed to work with the Bureau.[1,3] The three courageous Americans became deep penetration FBI agents into the leadership of the Soviet Union and other communist nations.

Figure 151: FBI file photo of Morris Childs, covert FBI agent and deep penetration informant on the American communist party and Kremlin leadership. Federal Bureau of Investigation

While on missions, Morris enjoyed unparalleled access to the Soviet leadership, including two prominent Soviets—namely, Boris Ponomarev, head of the International Department of the Central Committee, and Mikhail Suslov, chief of Ideology for the Central Committee.[4]

Eva Lieb Childs, Morris' second wife, became a spy in her own right. Eva proved to be a great asset to Morris, traveling with him, providing cover, and transcribing messages and documents. Eva and Morris would "hide underneath bed covers in Moscow copying secret Soviet documents, one holding a flashlight while the other wrote," and then "smuggle out the copies encased in plastic wrapped around their bodies."[1]

Jack Childs became the conduit for the transfer of funds from the USSR to the CPUSA. Over the years, the CPUSA "received more than $28 million from Moscow, which the FBI counted down to the penny."[1] Subsequently, Jack Childs was also awarded the Order of the Red Banner by the Soviets.[5]

The intelligence gathered through Operation SOLO provided American presidents, including Richard Nixon, Gerald Ford, and Jimmy Carter, as well as secretaries of state and national security advisors, like Henry Kissinger, with a virtual "window into the Kremlin."[6] From 1958 to 1977, the U.S. knew what discussions took place in the Kremlin; what the political and economic situation really was in the Soviet Union; and what foreign policy initiatives would be undertaken.

Figure 152: Mikhail Suslov, chief Soviet ideologist, in Moscow in 1964 and a good friend and confidant of Morris Childs. Dutch National Archives, The Hague

In short, the U.S. knew what was brewing in the minds of the Soviet leadership and their worries and fears. Moreover, because of the intelligence, American leaders understood how to respond, how to negotiate, and how to exploit Soviet vulnerabilities, but also how to assuage the leaders' minds when tensions escalated.

Exploiting the Very Real and Dangerous Sino-Soviet Split

From intelligence provided by Operation SOLO, Nixon and Kissinger learned that the Sino-Soviet split was real and deepening, reaching dangerous levels of confrontation between Russia and China. In August 1963, upon his return from Moscow and Prague, Morris reported that the July negotiations between the Chinese and Soviet delegations had been calamitous for the Soviets. Mikhail Suslov, chief ideologist for the Kremlin and chief Soviet negotiator, had even allowed Morris to review the documents.[7] China and the Soviet Union had become implacable enemies.[8]

The Chinese demanded that the Russians "recant their repudiations of Stalin, abandon the policy of 'peaceful coexistence' with the West, and renounce the doctrine that World War III was not inevitable... In essence, [the Chinese] demanded that the Soviet Union, 'domestically and internationally,' revert to Stalinism."[8] The Chinese negotiators insulted the Russians, accusing them "of cowardice for not looking forward to nuclear war."[8] The Russians were astounded. They believed in the Doctrine of Correlation of Forces—that is, that they should not fight a war unless they were certain of victory. The report went on to state:

> In a nuclear war with the United States, victory was far from certain; obliteration of all Soviet cities and basic industry was. Soviet strategists comprehended that whatever the other outcomes, nuclear war would leave them with a depopulated, primitive agrarian society vulnerable to hordes of Chinese. The Chinese professed not to fear nuclear war. They did not understand that it would return them to the Stone Age, and they believed they could afford to lose a few hundred million people, people being the one thing they had in abundance. Hence, the Soviets, in defiance of what the Chinese considered fundamental rules of fraternal Marxism, refused to share nuclear weapons and withdrew technical assistance.[9]

Moreover, Mao refused to help the Soviets in the Vietnam War or to allow Soviet aircraft to fly over Chinese territory to aid the communist Vietnamese. On April 25, 1965, within a plastic wrapping, Eva carried secret intelligence that had been submitted by the Soviet analysts to the Kremlin leadership. The Soviets complained that Mao wanted to "encourage the conflict and worsen both the military and economic position of Vietnam. They want to embroil the Soviet Union in a military conflict with the United States and, to further this overall policy, want to force Soviet ships with supplies to Vietnam into direct confrontation with U.S. military forces."[10]

Mao Tse-tung's hatred of both Nikita Khrushchev for abandoning Stalinism and Leonid Brezhnev for pursuing détente with the West provided the optimal time for the U.S. to approach China. The SOLO files "offered a clear road map to China," and "made clear that the Chinese would likely welcome American overtures."[11]

Because of Operation SOLO, Nixon and Kissinger were able to exploit the Sino-Soviet split. And following Morris Childs' advice, they visited China, befriended Mao and Chou En-lai, and, in effect, developed a geopolitical alliance against the Soviets.[11] The Russians were so frightened by the warming of international relations between China and the United States that they pursued détente even more avidly than before.[12]

Given the uneasy political climate that existed in the United States following President Nixon's resignation from office in 1974, the FBI felt it necessary to inform the new president, Gerald Ford, and Secretary Kissinger "about the origins of the 'Special Source.' "[6] After the briefing on the source of the intelligence, Henry Kissinger told the FBI agents, "This is a window not only into the Kremlin but into the minds of the men in the Kremlin. This is fabulous."[6] President Ford and Secretary of State Kissinger continued to use the information gathered and analyzed by Morris Childs to exploit Soviet foreign policy fears and vulnerabilities.

Perfidious Congressional Investigations Threaten SOLO

Unfortunately, in the wake of the Watergate scandal, congressional investigative committees almost destroyed Operation SOLO and its "window into the Kremlin." The Church Senate Select Committee and other congressional investigations drilled U.S. intelligence agencies and threatened to expose and derail the entire operation, endangering the lives of Morris, Eva, and Jack Childs.[13] When the FBI advised terminating Operation SOLO for security reasons, Henry Kissinger objected. He stated that he had to have SOLO's intelligence for his dealings with the Soviets. Kissinger concluded his remarks to the FBI, explaining that, "while he respected the judgment of the FBI, SOLO must go on and it would go on. Though Kissinger made no threats, the FBI comprehended that if it did not comply with his dictate, it doubtless would receive a comparable, and possibly less genial, one from the president."[14]

Morris Childs could deal with Moscow, but the investigations and recriminations going on in Washington against America's security agencies worried him intensely. After returning from a four-week mission to Moscow in March 1976, it was obvious that "anxiety about what might happen in Washington had added to the physical stress imposed by a business and social routine that would have exhausted a much younger and healthier man."[15]

In his last trip to the Soviet Union at the end of 1977, when Morris and Jack were awarded the Order of the Red Banner, Morris had reported to his FBI handler, "Right now, we're alright in Moscow. It's Washington we have to worry about."[5]

In fact, as a result of the unending investigations, leaks to journalists and other officials and further danger to their mission, the FBI terminated Operation SOLO after decades of astounding intelligence results.

The trio was exhausted after nearly thirty years spying for America. "In 1987, the brothers became the first spies to be decorated by both the Soviets and the United States when Ronald Reagan (1911–2004) awarded them the Presidential Medal of Freedom."[3]

Two Major Intelligence Operations: One Helped Prevent and the Other Almost Caused World War III

The Delusional KGB's Operation RYAN

Oleg Gordievsky had just briefed MI6 and British Prime Minister Margaret Thatcher on a "worldwide KGB operation codenamed 'RYAN' (*Raketno-Yadernoe Napadeni*, 'nuclear missile attack')." Now, on September 16, 1985, the British were bringing the Americans into the loop by informing William Casey, President Ronald Reagan's Director of Central Intelligence.[16]

In May 1981, Yuri Andropov, Chairman of the KGB, had announced to the Soviet leadership in the Kremlin that, "The new U.S. administration [the Reagan administration] is actively preparing for a nuclear war and a surprise attack upon the Soviet Union is a distinct possibility."[17] Before the stunned Politburo, Andropov instituted Operation RYAN, the "biggest peacetime Soviet intelligence operation ever launched."[18]

To confirm their fears, in early 1982, the Soviets repeatedly sent messages to all the *Rezidenturas* (KGB headquarters in Western capitals) instructing them to be on the alert and to search for evidence of preparations by Western governments in anticipation of nuclear war. The KGB and GRU were to promptly report any alterations in patterns to the Center, the KGB headquarters in Moscow. No item was too insignificant or should be overlooked—including, changes in banking practices, goods available or unavailable in supermarkets, fewer vehicles in parking lots, a marked increase in church attendance, a decrease in the number of lights left on in government buildings overnight, and the monitoring of the level of blood held in blood banks—because Operation RYAN's motto declared: Don't Miss It! (*Ne Prozerot!*).[18]

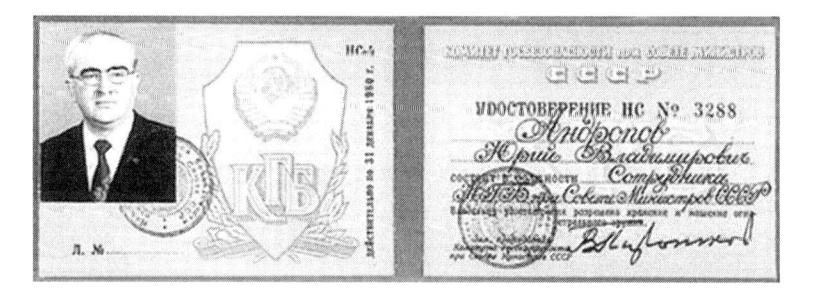

Figure 153: KGB identification card of Yuri Andropov, Chairman of the KGB (1967–1982) and General Secretary of the Communist Party of the Soviet Union from 1982 until his death in 1984

During Operation SOLO in the seventies, Morris Childs had warned the FBI about the danger of paranoia in the Kremlin leadership. In a report, Morris noted the following:

> The old men in the Soviet Union were increasingly isolating or insulating themselves from reality... Consequently, they could ignore or misinterpret authentic information... They read little from the Western press, and what they did read about political or military affairs they distrusted as propaganda. They were congenitally conspiratorial...and could misconstrue ordinary and unrelated events into a horrific conspiracy. This is very dangerous because they act on their thoughts. They are susceptible to dangerous delusion.[19]

Yuri Andropov's paranoia and Operation RYAN confirmed Morris Childs' assessment of the Kremlin leadership.

Bill Casey wasted no time in passing the British intelligence report to President Reagan. Reagan immediately realized the danger, and to assuage the Soviets, he toned down the rhetoric in his foreign policy speeches.[20]

Figure 154: Ronald Reagan, U.S. President (left), and Mikhail Gorbachev, Soviet General Secretary (right), at The First Summit in Geneva, Switzerland, in 1985. Balmore A. Ramos, National Archives and Records Administration

When Mikhail Gorbachev came to power in the Soviet Union, Prime Minister Thatcher recorded her impressions of Gorbachev for Reagan, writing:

I certainly found him a man one could do business with. I actually rather liked him—there is no doubt that he is completely loyal to the Soviet system, but he is prepared to listen and have a genuine dialogue and make up his own mind.[20]

In November 1985, President Reagan and General Secretary Gorbachev met for the first time in Geneva, Switzerland, and Reagan personally assured him that there were no such plans for nuclear war.[21] Reagan befriended the Soviet leader and de-escalated the threat of war. Instead, they came to the negotiating table.

One fact remained clear: "Had Operation SOLO still been alive, RYAN never would have been born."[21]

Part VI

The New Russia After the Fall of Communism

CHAPTER 20

AN INTRODUCTION TO THE NEW RUSSIA

Soviet leader Mikhail Gorbachev (1931–2022) popularized glasnost and perestroika in the Soviet's final attempt to deceive the West. While propping up and trying to keep the collapsing communist regime afloat, Gorbachev sought to reform communism, not destroy it. The amiable and cooperative General Secretary of the Communist Party of the USSR (1985–1991) claimed that he only wanted to follow the European social democrat model similar to the Spanish socialist government of Felipe Gonzalez. Gorbachev remained General Secretary until the Soviet Union's dissolution in 1991. Although he instituted some reforms, the problem for the Soviet leadership was that the desperate gamble undertaken was of such a degree with its new openness and the taste of freedom that once it was put into effect, there was no way to control it and it spiraled out of their control.

Boris Yeltsin and the New Russia

Boris Yeltsin was the real hero. The Russian patriot, who was the first President of Russia (1991–1999), climbed on top of a Soviet tank during the attempted coup by communist hardliners in August 1991 and addressed the crowd gathered outside the parliament in Moscow.[1] Fearless and defiant, Yeltsin would not allow Russia to return to communism. Two months earlier in a speech on June 1 in Moscow, Yeltsin acknowledged:

> *Our country has not been lucky…It was decided to carry out this Marxist experiment on us…It has simply pushed us off the path the world's civilized countries have taken…In the end, we proved that there is no place for this idea.[2]*

Russian President Boris Yeltsin presided over the dissolution of the Soviet empire and the dismantling of nuclear arsenals in former Soviet Republics. In 1994, he signed the Budapest Memorandum, making Russia one of the three signatories to the agreement along with the United States and the United Kingdom (UK). The agreement provided assurances to

An Introduction to the New Russia 277

Ukraine "in consideration of Ukraine relinquishing their nuclear arsenal."[3] Russia, the U.S., and the UK pledged to:

Respect the independence and sovereignty and the existing borders of Ukraine; Refrain from the threat or use of force against the territorial integrity or political independence of Ukraine; Not to use nuclear weapons against any non-nuclear weapon state party to the Treaty on the Non-Proliferation of Nuclear Weapons.[3]

The agreement was straightforward. More importantly, it was designed to deter any future military aggression against Ukraine and assure Ukraine's territorial integrity. In fact, new archival records from the early 1990s, ironically reveal that the threat of "border revisionism by Russia was the single gravest concern of Ukraine's leadership when surrendering the nuclear arsenal."[4]

Figure 155: Official portrait of Boris Yeltsin, the first President of Russia (1991–1999). Presidential Press and Information Office, Kremlin.ru

But despite bringing freedom to the Russian people, Yeltsin was not a very popular president. He was criticized for accelerating the process of both Soviet dissolution and Russian democratization, which caused temporary hardship and misery. It has been forgotten that he played the pivotal role in giving Soviet totalitarianism the *coup de grace*. Yeltsin has not received the proper credit he deserved for bringing peace, freedom, self-government, and eventually prosperity to the Russian people.

The fact that in the new Russia under Vladimir Putin the world has seen a regression of liberty and a growth in authoritarianism cannot be attributed to Yeltsin. The blame should be assigned to the Russian populace, who miss Russia's former "glory" and condone Vladimir Putin's aggressive posture, including the 2008 Russo-Georgian War[5], the 2014 annexation of the Crimea and the seizure of Eastern Ukraine[6], and his "special military operation"—that is, the February 2022 full-scale Russian invasion of Ukraine.[7] Clearly, when Vladimir Putin rolled Russian forces into Ukraine in 2014, he was in direct violation of the 1994 Budapest Memorandum.

A Very Dangerous World

Dr. Russell L. Blaylock, a political science scholar on the Soviet Union, the Cold War and communism, postulated that the Soviets had deceived the world, that the Cold War was not over and, likewise, communism had not been consigned to the dustbin of history. These sentiments were also expressed by the KGB defector, Anatoliy Golitsyn, and disclosed in his books, *New Lies for Old* and *The Perestroika Deception*.[8]

Blaylock asserted that Russia would likely continue the same path regardless of what transpired after the fall of the Berlin Wall in 1989 and that the KGB had worked closely with organized crime in the international narcotics trade, like Joseph Douglass documented in *Red Cocaine* and others confirmed.[9,10] Additionally, the old KGB's entrenchment in American and European governments would continue.[11]

Douglass also insisted that flooding the West with drugs and terrorism was a ploy not only to destroy the fighting ability of the United States and its allies but also to bankrupt nations by their efforts to protect their citizens from drugs and terrorism. The evidence for this was overwhelming. In short, the United States and Europe had been fooled by glasnost and perestroika, and the Western powers needed to remain vigilant.[9]

In articles written after the assumption and consolidation of power by Vladimir Putin in the new Russia, Blaylock noted:

> *With the fall of the Soviet empire, the KGB merged into the Federal Security Service (FSB) and sank into the shadows—that is, it is rarely discussed or examined today by the West. Yet, a number of intelligence-minded people have concluded that the FSB and SVR (Foreign Intelligence Service) continue their old tricks of undermining the United*

States—something that I believe is being continued by President Putin.[11]

He further opined that to better understand the link to the Soviet methodology for destroying a country from the inside, one should study the books and audiotapes of another KGB defector, Yuri A. Bezmenov, who carefully outlined the methods used by his bosses in the KGB to undermine the United States and the West. Bezmenov, wrote:

The main emphasis of the KGB is not in the area of intelligence at all. Only about 15 percent of time, money, and manpower is spent on espionage and such. The other 85 percent is a slow process which we call either ideological subversion or active measures...or psychological warfare.[12]

Although the twin evils of socialism and communism are not dead, one must remember that the fall of the Berlin Wall in 1989 and the collapse of the Soviet communist empire in 1991 were real pivotal events in the course of history in which fundamental changes occurred.

Communism, in its most overtly malevolent form, survives in Cuba and North Korea. Even China, in order to save face with Mao's historical legacy, still calls itself communist, whereas China's economic policies and productive output are more consistent with that of a fascist giant. Despite their historical adversarial political posture, communism and fascism are birds of a feather that flock together in the political firmament, and China could easily fit into either one of those molds.

There also remains a persistent crude mixture of socialism and corruption ubiquitous in many Third World countries of Africa and Asia as well as in a few Latin American countries, such as Nicaragua, Bolivia, Ecuador, Brazil, and Venezuela, where the political and economic results have been uniformly catastrophic.

Russia's Tsarist legacy of autocracy and authoritarianism should not be confused with Soviet communism and totalitarianism, which were much worse. The Russian people's legacy of submission to arbitrary rule began in the 13th century with the conquering Mongol hordes. Barbarism followed with Ivan the Terrible and did not soften considerably through the centuries even with the reforms of Peter the Great. Consequently, Russia's flirtation with "Tsarist rule" under Vladimir Putin must not be regarded as the same as Soviet communism.

In Russia today, the pre-1991 Soviet-style communism is dead—as it is in Central and Eastern Europe. Unfortunately, subversion, espionage, and the role of spies and spying in "the world's second oldest profession," continue, just as rivalry among the world's most powerful nations will continue.

There is much truth in the fact that during the Cold War, the drug trade was partly handled by communist intelligence services in various countries, intending to use it to subvert the West and to make profits to carry out further subversion.[10] This was true of the Soviet KGB, and Cuba's foreign intelligence service, the *Dirección General de Inteligencia* (DGI), working through third countries such as Colombia and Panama.[9,10,13]

Today in Russia, the Foreign Intelligence Service of the Russian Federation (SVR) and the Federal Security Service of the Russian Federation (FSB) are the two successor organizations of the Soviet KGB. After the August 1991 communist coup attempt that involved many KGB units, Russian President Boris Yeltsin dismantled and dissolved the Soviet organization in December 1991. The SVR assumed the functions of the KGB's First Chief Directorate. "Tasked with intelligence and espionage activities outside the Russian Federation," it is headquartered in the Yasenevo District of Moscow.[14]

In early 1992, the internal security functions of the KGB's Second Chief Directorate were reconstituted in a newly created Ministry of Security, and shortly thereafter, "placed under the control of the President of Russia."[15] In 1995, Russian President Boris Yeltsin renamed the state service the Federal Security Service (FSB) and "granted it additional powers."

Today, the FSB is responsible for internal and border security, counterterrorism, and surveillance within the country. It can also "enter private homes and conduct intelligence activities in Russia or abroad in cooperation with the SVR."[15] The FSB emblem incorporated an image of an updated sword and shield, and the service's headquarters are located in Moscow's Lubyanka Square, in the main building of the former KGB. The director of the FSB is appointed by and directly answerable to the President of Russia.

In recent years, the agency's mission expanded to include offensive cyber operations, such as theft of intelligence information and malicious cyberattacks.[16] Moreover, "the FSB has been known to task criminal hackers for espionage-focused cyber activity," including destructive malware, disruptive ransomware, denial-of-service attacks, and phishing campaigns.[17]

Needless to say, the SVR and FSB remained formidable police and espionage apparatuses of the new Russia.

Evidence of Espionage and Attempted and Completed Assassinations

As mentioned elsewhere in this book, there have been Westerners not only in government but also in economic and business circles that have succumbed to betraying their country by serving the interests of other nations – even nations hostile to their homeland. At times, individuals have been naïve or ignorant about the inherent danger of traveling into these unfriendly regions and attempting to render assistance in one form or another out of altruistic motives. Citizens have been kidnapped and held as hostages in Iran, Lebanon, and in other countries. Other individuals succumbed to conscious spying either because of blackmail by seduction or sexual misconduct, affinity of political philosophies, such as communism or socialism being concordant with personal political views, or simply venal reasons like financial gain. For example, one person who satisfied the latter two conditions was the American business mogul, Armand Hammer.[18]

Likewise, an example of espionage between nations was the deceptive unity of the allies during World War II, which ended quickly toward the end of the war. It took the valiant efforts of a Russian defector, GRU cipher clerk Igor Gouzenko, to awaken America and England to the fact that their other ally, the Soviet Union, was conducting serious and devastating espionage against them and stealing American atomic bomb secrets in the process. Never mind the fact that the United States was providing vital economic and military aid to the Soviets for the "Great Patriotic War" against the Nazis at the time.

But as we know, the Berlin Wall came crashing down in 1989 and the Soviet Union collapsed in 1991. Professor Francis Fukuyama wrote enthusiastically that this was "not just ... the passing of a particular period of post-war history, but the end of history as such: That is, the end-point of mankind's ideological evolution and the universalization of Western liberal democracy as the final form of human government."[19] Fukuyama's definition of Western liberal democracy was "a soft blend of global socialism and capitalism."[19]

Then in October 2000, Russia's master spy in America, Sergei O. Tretyakov, the highest-ranking SVR operative at the New York City *rezidentura*, defected. His story was not a rehash of KGB Cold War material but freshly "ripped from the front pages of the Boris Yeltsin and Vladimir Putin presidencies."[20] Moreover, his revelations rained down heavily on the globalist "end of history" hypothesis. As First Secretary of the Permanent Mission of the Russian Federation to the United Nations and deputy *rezident*, Tretyakov was "in charge of running *all* SVR intelligence day-to-day operations. Every SVR intelligence officer stationed in Manhattan reported directly to him—all sixty of them."[21] He was the first SVR officer actively spying for the new Russia to defect to the United States. According to a senior FBI agent involved in the case, Sergei Tretyakov "has been by far the most important Russian spy that our side has had in decades...I can tell you this man saved American lives."[22]

Perhaps Tretyakov expressed it best himself when he stated his purpose:

> *I want to warn Americans. As a people, you are very naïve about Russia and its intentions. You believe because the Soviet Union no longer exists, Russia now is your friend. It isn't, and I can show you how the SVR is trying to destroy the U.S. even today and even more than the KGB did during the Cold War.[23]*

Once again, it took a courageous Russian defector to reawaken America and the West to the fact that, in addition to the Global War on Terrorism (GWOT) launched after the September 11, 2001, Islamic attack on American soil, the rest of the world was just as dangerous.

The West learned the painful lesson that the new Russia had not shed its expansionist and militant tendencies. Tretyakov's revelations provided many geopolitical insights into the surrounding southern countries of Russia, particularly those that abound with oil. Russia's subtle intimidation of former Soviet Republics like Georgia, Ukraine, and Azerbaijan over natural resources and "privileges in the area" remained serious threats to global peace and security. Turkey, which is a member of NATO, had been drifting away from the West over the years because of shortsighted diplomacy on the part of many Western European politicians. Tretyakov provided information about regional attitudes that were worth studying by Western diplomats to preserve peace and maintain friendship and alliances in the region.

In November 2006, the assassination of a former Russian intelligence officer, Alexander "Sasha" Litvinenko, drew international attention. The sudden onset and rapid progression of illness in the former agent turned dissident and his mode of death were reminiscent of the 1978 KGB assassination of Georgi Markov in London. Within a few short weeks, the 43-year-old Sasha deteriorated in both personal appearance and health, seemingly aging rapidly and finally dying in a hospital bed. The British investigated and discovered that the radioactive isotope Polonium-210 had been used to poison Litvinenko. He had been virtually the hapless victim of an internal "tiny nuclear bomb."[24]

Figure 156: The grave of Alexander Litvinenko at Highgate Cemetery, London, in 2017. Ethan Doyle White

Russian President Vladimir Putin and the FSB were implicated. Litvinenko had been very critical of Putin's policies in Russia's internal affairs as well as of his aggression and the war in Chechnya. Moreover, Litvinenko had been an intelligence officer and knew secrets that the Russian regime would not want known. When traces of polonium radiation were also found in Germany and on British Airways planes that suggested a travel route originating in Russia for the carriers of the poison, it became evident that agents from the Putin regime were responsible.[25]

Two weeks before the Litvinenko poisoning, Anna S. Politkovskaya, a 48-year-old Russian journalist and human rights activist, had been assassinated in Moscow on October 7, 2006. Although five men were charged with her murder and sent to prison, the assassination implicated the Putin regime. For seven years, Politkovskaya had reported on the political situation and increasing repression in Russia as well as the sanguinary events in the Second Chechen War (1999–2005), an aggressive and atrocious war which had also been criticized by Litvinenko.[26,27]

Figure 157: Anna S. Politkovskaya, Russian journalist and human rights advocate, in 2005. Blaues Sofa

Politkovskaya had been threatened, but she refused to be intimidated. While reporting on the war, she was arrested by Russian military forces in Chechnya and subjected to a mock execution. She had also been poisoned in 2004 and required medical attention and recuperation. Yet, she continued to write and report on events in Russia and achieved a well-deserved international reputation. But her merit and achievements did not protect her. She was gunned down in the elevator of her block of apartments and the details of her murder remain murky.[28]

One must also consider the case of Sergei V. Skripal, a former Russian military intelligence (GRU) officer who became a double agent for the British during the 1990s and 2000s. Skripal was arrested by the FSB in 2006, convicted of "high treason in the form of espionage," for "passing the identities of Russian secret agents in Europe to the UK's Secret Intelligence Service (MI6)," and sentenced to 13 years in prison.[29] The former GRU colonel was later pardoned by Russian President Dmitry Medvedev, and exchanged in a spy swap in 2010. He moved to Great Britain where he settled with dual Russian and British citizenship.[29]

Now let us move forward to March 4, 2018, when Skripal and his 33-year-old daughter Yulia, who was visiting from Russia, were found semi-conscious in a public park in Salisbury, Wiltshire, England. They were hospitalized and placed in intensive care in critical condition. British experts determined that a "military-grade nerve agent developed by the Soviet Union" was used to poison them. The agent was in a "class of extremely dangerous secret toxins known as Novichok."[29]

Figure 158: A forensics tent covers the bench where Sergei and Yulia Skripal fell unconscious after being poisoned. Peter Curbishley

Several detectives involved in the investigation also became ill from exposure to the agent. The British intelligence service concluded the case had been one of attempted murder. Both Skripal and his daughter recovered enough after two months of hospitalization to be discharged, but they required outpatient treatment for some time thereafter.

On March 14, 2018, British Prime Minister Teresa May announced that Russia had been responsible for the incident and 23 Russian diplomats were expelled from Great Britain.[30]

During the first two presidencies of Vladimir Putin, events that occurred presaged the coming years. The resurgence of espionage wars abroad, an increase in political repression and loss of civil liberties at home, the vicious murders of Russian dissidents like Alexander Litvinenko and independent journalists like Anna Politkovskaya as well as attempted assassinations of former Russian citizens living abroad like Sergei Skripal, did not bode well for the future of Russia or the tranquility of the world.

The Russian Election of 2012

Let us turn back the clock six years and examine the Russian presidential election of 2012. For Russia and the rest of the world, the March 4, 2012, election raised concerns about how the turbulent but still burgeoning Russian democracy and the stability of Europe would be affected—that is, Russia vis-à-vis the West. The previous November, Russian Chief of Staff General Nikolai Makarov and Russian President Dmitry Medvedev had threatened to deploy Russian missiles against the proposed U.S. missile shield in Europe.

Moreover, the waves of protests in Russia over the December 2011 parliamentary elections were disturbing, not only because of its potential impact on foreign affairs but also after the world learned of the troubling nature of Russian politics, such as the various dangerous political factions and the powder keg of special interest groups fueling unrest. At the time, both U.S. Secretary of State Hillary Clinton and a leading Republican presidential candidate, Mitt Romney, expressed dissatisfaction with Putin's political regime.

Protesters accused the Medvedev-Putin administration of electoral fraud, and the protest rallies called for fresh parliamentary elections. According to the BBC, "The parliamentary elections on 4 December were criticized by observers from the Organization for Security and Co-operation in Europe (OSCE), who asserted there had been 'severe problems with the counting process.' They said the poll was slanted in favor of Mr. Putin's party, United Russia, and that there had been irregularities including the stuffing of ballot boxes."[31]

A report in *The Atlantic* claimed:

> *Putin's United Russia party lost 25 percent of its seats in the election but hung onto a majority in parliament through what independent observers said was widespread fraud. United Russia, seen as representing a corrupt bureaucracy, has become known as the party of 'crooks and thieves,' a phrase coined by Alexei Navalny, a corruption-fighting lawyer and popular blogger and leader of the demonstrations.[32]*

Since that time, Navalny has been politically persecuted, his organizations banned for alleged extremism, and poisoned. He nearly died in August 2020 from a Novichok poisoning attempt that took place in Siberia. Novichok was the same toxic nerve agent used against Sergei Skripal. Navalny was treated in Berlin but upon returning to Russia a few months later in January 2021, he was arrested, prosecuted, and given a 19-year sentence. He remains in prison at the time of this writing.[32]

Figure 159: Alexei Navalny at a rally in Moscow in 2011. Dmitry Aleshkovskiy

Eighty-year-old Mikhail Gorbachev, who presided over the collapse of the USSR on December 25, 1991, twenty years earlier, asked Putin to step down and follow his example toward openness and democracy. Former World Chess champion and Russian activist, Garry Kasparov, joined the protesters in support of the pro-democracy movement. He called for more use of the Internet for the dissemination of information and coordination of the protest movement. He criticized the Medvedev-Putin regime for human rights violations and the systematic trampling of civil liberties in Russia.[31,32]

Who were the Russian presidential candidates, what political parties did they represent, and how much support did they command in the polls conducted in mid-December 2011:

1. Vladimir Putin of the United Russia political party was considered an almost complete shoo-in as the next president. United Russia was the successor organization to Boris Yeltsin's democrats and was established in the late 1990s to counterbalance the communists and prevent them from taking over after Yeltsin stepped down. Although Russian President Dmitry Medvedev was an Independent, he supported Putin's United Russia political party. Putin, who was serving as Prime Minister at the time, had agreed to run for an unprecedented third term as president in

the 2012 elections. Polling data suggested that the United Russia party and Putin would garner 42 percent of the vote and gain a plurality of votes.

2. Gennady Zyuganov was the leader of the Communist Party of the Russian Federation that sought to bring back communist repression, totalitarianism, and even Stalinism to Russia. Zyuganov emphasized his "commitment to the renationalization of resources and banking and called for a reduction in influence of international organizations such as the North Atlantic Treaty Organization and the World Trade Organization."[33] Polling data gave the Communist Party second place with 11 percent of the vote.

3. Vladimir Zhirinovsky of the Liberal Democratic Party (LDP; allegedly formed as a sham party by the Soviet Communist Party and the KGB in 1991 as the USSR was disintegrating) was the third leading candidate. Despite the party's deliberately misleading name, the LDP was a nationalistic, chauvinistic Russian party with large doses of collectivism, statism, authoritarianism, and fascism in its incendiary and bombastic political philosophy. Yet, the LDP commanded 9 percent of the electorate.

4. Sergei Mironov was the presidential candidate of the A Just Russia (a pro-democracy) party. He was the Chairman of the Federation Council, the upper house of the Russian parliament (2001–2011). In the 2004 elections, he admitted, "We all want Vladimir Putin to be the next president"[34]; Mironov received less than 1 percent of the vote in that election. Moreover, he had socialistic tendencies, and made repeated calls for more government intervention in the Russian economy. In the 2012 election as "leader of the liberal opposition," he was polling 5 percent of voter support.

5. Grigory Yavlinsky, leader of the Yabloko Party, polled 1 percent of the vote, preaching an anti-corruption reform message. Representation in the Duma required at least 5 percent of the popular vote.

6. Much hope was pinned on the influence of Mikhail Prokhorov, the highly visible candidate of the Independent Party. He was a self-made billionaire, but he barely commanded 1 percent of the vote, despite the wide coverage his candidacy received from the international press. In *Forbes* magazine, Prokhorov was ranked as Russia's third richest man with a fortune worth $18 billion in 2011.[31] Regardless of his charisma, ordinary Russians resented the 46-year-old successful entrepreneur because of his wealth; and thus, he was not expected to garner enough support for the necessary grassroots movement needed to make an impact in Russian politics.

Similar to Mironov, Prokhorov had previously stated that Vladimir Putin was the only man who "can manage this inefficient state machine."[35]

More recently, though, Prokhorov stated that Putin must change and move Russia to democracy quickly to avoid the bloody path of revolution. The report in Reuters noted, "Prokhorov made clear he considers revolution equally unacceptable for a country with grim memories of a century of hardship, war, and upheaval starting with Vladimir Lenin's 1917 Bolshevik Revolution, instead calling for 'very fast evolution.' "[35] Despite the hostility and protests against Prime Minister Putin, exactly how much support Mikhail Prokhorov and the other pro-democracy candidates were going to be able to generate remained unclear.

Russia's tiny democratic opposition—that is, the parties of Mironov, Yavlinsky, and Prokhorov—barely presented a challenge to Putin or to the menacing and massive authoritarian flank—namely, the parties of Zyuganov and Zhirinovsky. The freedom opposition did not seem to stand a chance in the contest. And the Communist Party leader, Gennady Zyuganov, who commanded the strongest "threat" to Putin, joined the administration by disparaging the protests and supporting the Kremlin. In short, the closeness of the political philosophies of the authoritarian parties of Zyuganov and Zhirinovsky reveal the intrinsic kinship of collectivism and totalitarianism in any of its incarnations.[36]

A Perilous Future Portended

The March 4, 2012, Russian elections confirmed that the autocratic legacy of Joseph Stalin still lurked in the shadows. Communism, for all its latter-day Marxist apologists, cannot be reformed.[37,38] But the grim Russian authoritarian past does not seem to allow the new Russia to move irresolutely forward toward a future of freedom.

The election was not a new beginning, but a worsening of the situation for Russia and its neighbors. Election results reflected expectations, and Vladimir Putin was re-elected; unfortunately, he has not listened to voices of reason or the dictates of freedom. He has become more authoritarian and repressive. This was sadly demonstrated in the geopolitics and foreign policy of Putin in the Caspian Sea region and the Caucasus. From the attempted intimidation of Azerbaijan, the bloody suppression of the separatist Chechnya insurrections in the 1990s, and the invasion of Georgia in the South Ossetia War of 2008, to the initial bullying and subsequent aggression and annexation of the Crimea and the eastern part of the nation, followed by the full invasion of Ukraine in 2022—all ominously reminds one of the belligerent imperialism of the Russian Tsars or the brutal militarism of the Soviet Union.

Figure 160: Vladimir Putin, a former KGB intelligence officer, and President of Russia since 2012. Press Service of the President of the Russian Federation, Kremlin.ru

One can only hope that the Russian people break away from the authoritarian spell and divest themselves of the mistaken notion of the "good old days" of communism and nostalgia for "Stalin's greatness." Likewise, the elected leaders must rid themselves of their imperial and authoritarian legacy. They must follow the rule of law, serve the people they represent, respect civil liberties, and promote economic liberty and the free market—not rebuild the Soviet empire.

The world situation has become more precarious with two resurgent powerful nations—Russia and China—trampling human rights at home and threatening further aggression. However, hope springs eternal and miracles can still happen. After all, who expected the 1991 collapse of Soviet communism.

CHAPTER 21

RUSSIAN GEOPOLITICS

The world was hoping for wiser policies from Vladimir Putin in his third term as Russian president, and better times for the emerging "democracy" of the Russian Federation that, like a phoenix, might rise triumphantly from the ashes of the communist Soviet Union. Instead, in 2014, Putin and his allies in the Ukraine invaded the Crimean peninsula and threatened to start another war.

One might wonder which figure from Russian history was Putin imitating. Tsar Peter the Great wanted the Russian fleet to have access to the Baltic Sea in the north. "After winning access to the Baltic Sea through his victories in the Great Northern War (1700–1721), which significantly expanded the Russian empire," he founded St. Petersburg and made the city the new capital of Russia.[1] Tsarina Catherine the Great continued empire building and "annexed much of what is now Ukraine through wars with the Ottoman Empire" gaining access to the Black Sea in the warmer waters of the south.[2] Or was Putin imitating the calculating and sinister Joseph Stalin, who first used Sochi as his private resort and, more ominously, helped to start World War II by signing the Molotov-Ribbentrop Pact, invading Eastern Poland, and swallowing up the Baltic states in 1939? The world had hoped that the imperialist expansion of Peter the Great and Catherine the Great was over and that the times of the brutal Stalin and the gulags were long gone.

Russian Aggression Against Ukraine and Crimea— Tsarist Imperialism or Stalinist Conquest

The imperialistic designs of Tsarist Russia in the 18th and 19th centuries and the murderous, authoritarian legacy of Joseph Stalin still seemed to lurk in the shadows of the Russian nation with the consent of a large proportion of the Russian people. Was communism, for all the assurances of Western politicians, journalists and academicians, truly dead, or was it going to rear its ugly head once again behind the former Iron Curtain? The grim Russian authoritarian past does not seem to allow Russia to move irresolutely toward a future of individual freedom, prosperity, and peace.

As previously stated, the geopolitical maneuvers and tactics of Putin in the Caspian Sea region and the Caucasus, and the invasion of Ukraine and occupation of the Crimea—remind us of the imperialism of the Russian Tsars or the use of brutal force by the Soviet Union with the occupation of Eastern Europe and part of Central Europe after World War II. It was hoped that there would be time for Putin and his advisers to listen to the voices of reason, restraint, and peace; and that there would not be another Cold War, with or without communism.

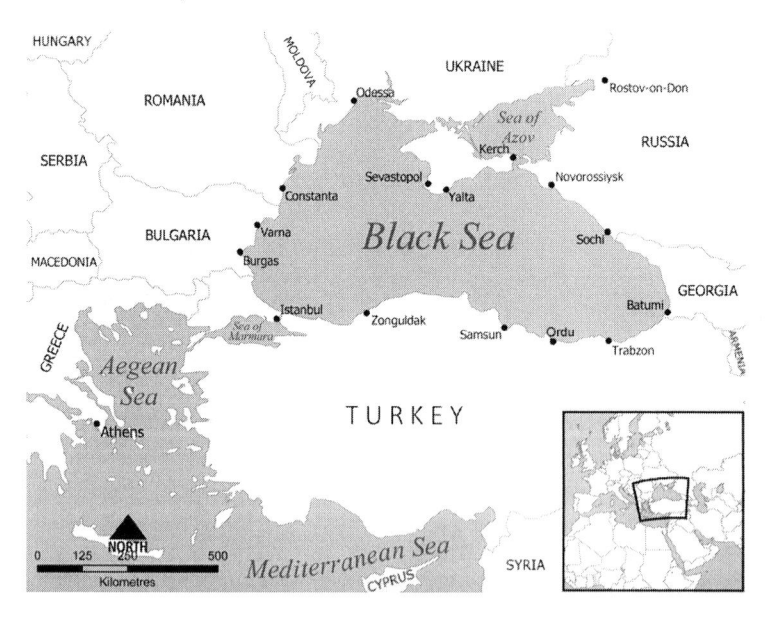

Figure 161: Map showing the eastern Mediterranean, the Sea of Azov, and the Crimea, hanging like a jewel pendant in the Black Sea. The Sea of Marmara joins the Black Sea to the Aegean Sea via the Bosporus Strait and the Dardanelles. Some of the important ports, such as Sevastopol and Odessa, in those bodies of water are noted. Norman Einstein

Instead, a perilous situation arose in 2014 when Putin and the Russians (assisted by proxy troops) invaded and seized the Crimean Peninsula. The Russians seriously destabilized Ukraine and seized a large segment of the eastern part of that nation, where the majority of the population were of Russian descent and largely Russian speaking, like in the Crimea.[3] Although the Russian and Ukrainian neighboring states, such as the former Soviet Republics of Kazakhstan, Belarus, Moldova and Azerbaijan, do not have ethnic Russian majorities, they do possess large Russian-speaking populations. Consequently, if that was the motivating reason, then they too might be at risk and vulnerable to a Russian offensive. So, even nations like Romania and Poland, which were never Soviet Republics and already NATO members, worried.

The Western Response

In response, NATO mobilized some forces to counteract the threat to the eastern Ukraine. A report dated April 16, 2014, stated:

> *NATO is strengthening its military footprint along its eastern border immediately in response to Russia's aggression in Ukraine, the alliance's chief said Wednesday. Secretary General Anders Fogh Rasmussen said NATO's air policing aircraft will fly more sorties over the Baltic region and allied ships will deploy to the Baltic Sea, the eastern Mediterranean and elsewhere if needed.*
> *'We will have more planes in the air, more ships on the water and more readiness on the land,' Fogh Rasmussen told reporters in Brussels, declining to give exact troop figures. Moscow must make clear 'it doesn't support the violent actions of well-armed militias or pro-Russian separatists' in eastern Ukraine, he added.*
> *NATO's eastern members—including Lithuania, Estonia, Latvia, and Poland—have been wary following Russia's annexation of Ukraine's Crimean Peninsula, demanding a more robust military deterrence to counter neighboring Russia.[3]*

Once again, the situation looked grim as the report went on to state:

> *The NATO chief did not mention naval deployments to the Black Sea—which Russia would likely see as a direct aggression even though NATO members Bulgaria, Romania and Turkey also border the sea. He insisted, however, that 'more will follow if needed.'*
> *NATO estimates Russia has amassed some 40,000 troops on Ukraine's eastern border and could invade parts of the country within days if it wished. Fogh Rasmussen urged Russia to pull those troops back.*
> *The 28-nation alliance has already suspended most cooperation and talks with Russia. The United States has dispatched fighter planes to Poland and the Baltics, enabling NATO to reinforce air patrols on its eastern border. NATO also performs daily AWAC surveillance flights over Poland and Romania.[3]*

The entire scenario brought back dark memories of 1938–1939. After orchestrating the Anschluss of Austria into the Third Reich in March of 1938, Adolf Hitler claimed that the Sudetenland was also part of Greater Germany. Among the reasons, he insisted those parts of Czechoslovakia were mostly German-speaking and the populace of German descent. As discussed in chapter 7 in this book, Great Britain and France, which were allied to Czechoslovakia, yielded. British Prime Minister Neville Chamberlain flew to Munich to placate Germany and thought he had "brought peace in our time." French Prime Minister Edouard Daladier agreed with the German annexation (Munich Agreement, September 1938). Thus, Czechoslovakia was betrayed in an attempt to placate Hitler.

Placated but not yet satiated, Hitler ordered the Wehrmacht to invade and occupy the Sudetenland, which the German army promptly did; and one month later in October 1938, the Third Reich duly annexed that part of Czechoslovakia. Of course, this was not enough for Hitler. Subsequently Germany invaded and seized the rest of Czechoslovakia in March 1939. Nazi Germany then signed the Molotov-Ribbentrop Pact with the Soviet Union (August 1939), and Hitler, who was now allied with Stalin, ordered his Panzers to invade western Poland (September 1, 1939), while the USSR in a concerted action invaded and seized eastern Poland. World War II in Europe began.

With those historic comparisons in mind, it was obvious what Vladimir Putin envisioned the re-establishment of Russian hegemony in the region, and perhaps even the military reconquest of some of the former territories of the USSR, regardless of the consequences.

Never mind that geographically Russia was already the largest nation in the world, with no other nation a close second. Russia had plenty of citizens and natural resources as well as access to the seas in the north, east, and in the south, the Black Sea. But reason was not invoked in these events. Vladimir Putin's aggression and conquest would not be fully satiated, and the danger of history repeating itself with grave consequences never vanished.

Despite the saber rattling by NATO and the West to deter Russian aggression, Ukraine was left out in the cold, much like Czechoslovakia had been in 1938–1939. And so Russia, which had taken over and occupied the Georgian provinces of Abkhazia and South Ossetia in 2008, now turned to the Crimea and eastern Ukraine in 2014.

The U.S. and Great Britain had some responsibility for protecting Ukraine. As we have noted in the previous chapter, under the 1994 Budapest Memorandum, Ukraine gave up its nuclear arsenal in return for protection from the U.S., Russia, and Great Britain and given "assurances of territorial integrity."[4] However, no protection was provided. The United States discussed sending additional troops to Europe to discourage further aggression from Russia. A report stated:

Army Chief of Staff Gen. Mark Milley told the Journal that he would like to send attack helicopter units and artillery brigades to Europe as well as more rotating brigades. Gen. Philip Breedlove, the supreme allied commander of NATO, told the Journal that decisions on the proposals would be made 'in the next couple of months.' Any plans for a troop increase must be developed by the Pentagon, approved by President Obama, and funded by Congress. The paper reported that funding for the troop increase would be included in a budget request sent to Congress early next year.[5]

Figure 162: North Atlantic Treaty Organization (darker areas) in orthographic projection, 2009. Finland, not shown, joined in 2023

Figure 163: The Russian Federation (darker areas) in orthographic projection, 2023. The Crimea and eastern Ukraine are disputed. Jamie Eilat

In the spring of 2014, months after Russian troops had rolled into the Crimea, U.S. President Barack Obama and Secretary of State John Kerry imposed mild sanctions, not on Russia per se but against 11 Russian oligarchs and oil company executives along with a few visa restrictions. Thus, the United States and much of Europe thought the storm, which they had treated as nothing more than a tempest in a teapot, would pass. But, as we know, there was a more serious storm forming on the horizon.

Nevertheless, Vladimir Putin spent the remainder of 2014 and most of 2015 strengthening the Russian military with increased training and deployment of troops, and generally expanding the military build-up. The same report noted:

> *Under President Vladimir Putin, Russia is challenging the U.S. in many arenas, including the Arctic, where last year Moscow said it was reopening 10 former Soviet-era military bases along the Arctic seaboard that were closed after the Cold War ended in 1991. Russia also is flying*

more long-range air patrols off U.S. shores and increasing submarine patrols and exercises...[5]

A Little History Regarding Ukraine

The Soviets placed the Crimea within the "Ukraine Republic" under the USSR, from the time Lenin appointed Stalin as Commissar of Nationalities (1917-1922), based on expertise gained when Stalin authored his famous report on nationalities in 1914 titled "Marxism and the National Question." Stalin used his power and the bureaucracy to convert the union of nationalistic republics into a totalitarian Soviet state. Before that, the Crimea was part of the Tsarist Russian Empire, as were Georgia, Byelorussia, all of the Ukraine, and most of the so-called Soviet Republics.

Ironically, the Crimea was the last stronghold of White Russians fighting in 1919-1920 against the advancing Red Army. Admiral Alexander Kolchak's armies disintegrated in Siberia, and General Anton Denikin retreated to the Crimea. In that peninsula, a demoralized Denikin resigned his post to Baron Pyotr Wrangel, the White Army general who had the unenviable task of evacuating the Crimea, the last anti-communist stronghold, leaving it to the advancing Red Army of seasoned Bolsheviks. Wrangel successfully evacuated 150,000 anti-communist freedom fighters in 1920.

Since that time, Ukraine, including the Crimea, was a place of sorrow, famine, and death under Soviet communism. Nikita Khrushchev presided over a virtual genocide of the Ukrainians, massacring kulaks and forcing collectivization of farms for Stalin. All of this was well recounted by British-American historian Robert Conquest in his books and documentaries.[6]

Ukraine was the somber nation that suffered under the Soviet yoke. Political leaders seeking independence and freedom, such as Stepan Banderas, were assassinated by Soviet intelligence agents[7]; anti-communist leaders and freedom fighters were exterminated[8]; workers as well as rebellious peasants resisting Stalin and later Khrushchev were harshly suppressed. The collective Soviet leadership under Malenkov and Khrushchev—borrowing a page from Stalin's book on persecuting and fomenting divisiveness and discord among minorities—ceded the Crimea to the "Ukrainian Soviet Republic" in 1954 precisely to keep the nation divided not only among tribal and ethnic differences but also by the fifth column of Soviet Russians who settled there.

Figure 164: Portrait of Pyotr Wrangel, the Black Baron, circa 1920

Geopolitics in the Caspian Sea Area and the Caucasus

Ukraine was not the only area threatened, invaded, or occupied by Russia. We mentioned Georgia and its provinces of Abkhazia and South Ossetia, which were occupied by Russia after the 2008 Russo-Georgian War. Those provinces then seceded from Georgia, became sovereign states, and Russian military bases were established. The territories were integrated with Russia in both military and economic spheres. Russia does not allow the European Union Monitoring Mission to enter the occupied provinces. Most of the international community—including the EU, the United States, Canada, Turkey, Australia, et cetera—consider Abkhazia and South Ossetia occupied territories and have condemned Russia's military presence there.

Georgia and Azerbaijan straddle the area south of Russia in the Caucasus region between the Black and Caspian Seas. This region, which was formerly part of the USSR, has been historically an area of trouble and contention, where several former Soviet Republics border each other and exist with suppressed animosities. As previously mentioned, Joseph Stalin took advantage of ethnic rivalry to divide and rule, leaving a legacy of discord among the various ethnic minorities—while the Russian boot suppressed them all.

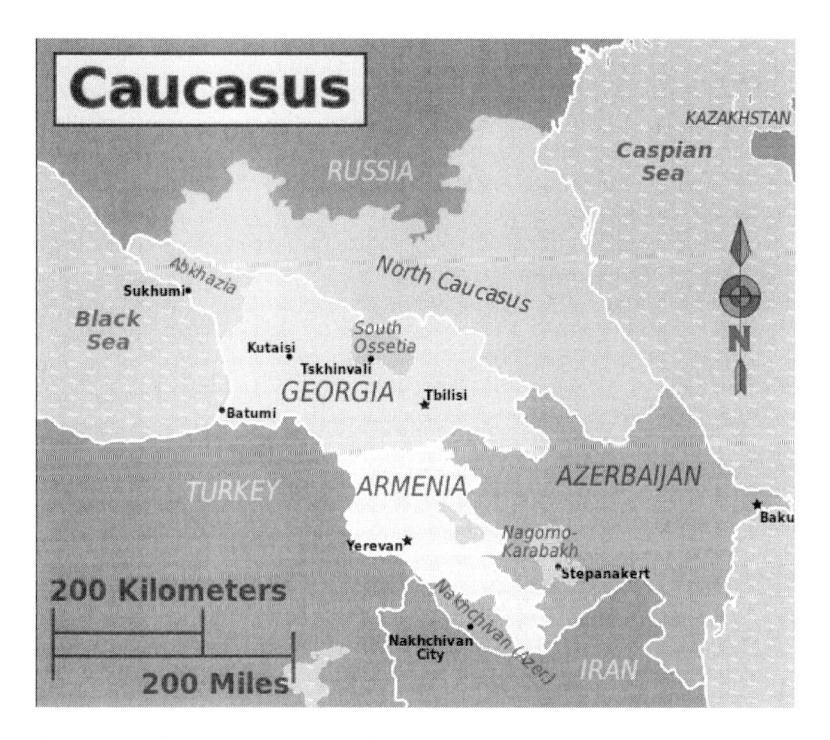

Figure 165: The Caucasus, the very important geopolitical and mountainous region between the Black and Caspian Seas. Abkhazia and South Ossetia were seized from Georgia by Russia. Armenia, Azerbaijan, southern Russia, Georgia, and northeastern Turkey are also noted

Today, Stalin's policy lives on with Azerbaijan remaining at odds with Armenia, and Georgia with its provinces of South Ossetia and Abkhazia now occupied by Russia. Azerbaijan is actually split in two by a strip of Armenian land and remains in conflict with the latter over the highly disputed Nagorno-Karabakh region.

Instability remains in this strategic geopolitical area, which is rich in oil and other natural resources. If Russia were to again seize or even establish hegemony over the rest of Georgia, Azerbaijan, and the Baku oil field region, it would be a major setback for its neighbor Turkey and the European Union (EU). Turkey, a traditional enemy of Russia, has more recently established an excellent rapport with its gigantic neighbor to the north, but it is still theoretically allied to the EU and the United States as part of NATO.

A look at the oil pipelines going through Georgia in the Caucasus tell the story of the importance of the region to all nations in the region, not to mention Turkey, Russia, and the EU. From the Baku oil fields, pipelines run from Azerbaijan to Russia as well as through Georgia and Turkey to the West. Oil is an important commodity not only to the West but also to developing nations.

China and India need coal, natural gas and oil for their ever-increasing population. And energy supply is a growing concern for the entire world, including the United States.

The Syrian Crisis

In the early morning hours of April 7, 2018, U.S. President Donald Trump ordered, and the American military launched, a devastating missile strike on a Syrian air base. The strike was in retaliation for the Syrian chemical attack on a rebel-held town in northwestern Syria a few days before in which 80 Syrians, including dozens of women and children, had been killed. The BBC reported the U.S. missile launch:

Fifty-nine Tomahawk cruise missiles were fired from two US Navy ships in the Mediterranean. At least six people are reported to have been killed. It is the first direct US military action against forces commanded by Syria's president. The Kremlin, which backs Bashar al-Assad, has condemned the strike.[9]

Previously, President Trump and President Putin had tried to collaborate in Syria, at least against the areas held by the terrorist ISIS (Islamic State of Iraq and Syria). Putin reacted cautiously to the American unilateral action, which was devastating for his protégé and main ally in the region, Syrian dictator Bashar al-Assad. China released a neutral message calling for restraint. The United Kingdom, Japan, and NATO supported the American action, while Iran, Syria, and Russia condemned it.

In the Middle East, Israel, Saudi Arabia, and Turkey strongly supported the American missile strike. Israel's Prime Minister Benjamin Netanyahu stated: "President Trump sent a strong and clear message today that the use and spread of chemical weapons will not be tolerated. Israel fully supports President Trump's decision and hopes that this message of resolve in the face of the Assad regime's horrific actions will resonate not only in Damascus, but in Tehran, Pyongyang and elsewhere."[10]

Turkish President Tayyip Erdoğan, who had been a strong opponent of the Assad regime and had denounced the Syrian chemical attack a few days earlier, also supported the American action as "strongly positive" and his foreign ministry spokesman stated that "Turkey would fully support steps that would ensure accountability for the Syrian regime."[11]

Figure 166: Official portrait of Israel's 9th Prime Minister, Benjamin Netanyahu. Avi Ohayon, Government Press Office

What did these developments mean for Putin and Russia's aspirations in the Middle East? Putin had his sights on building an eastern Mediterranean power base centered in Syria, relying on the acquiescence and assistance of his ally, Syrian dictator Bashar al-Assad.

The Russian Special Forces—Spetsnaz

Spetsnaz are Russian "special forces" that were developed in the Soviet era and expanded in the new Russia and in some of the former Republics. Russian military forces assigned to special tasks have also been referred to as Spetsnaz.

Soviet Spetsnaz forces assisted the Vietcong and the North Vietnamese during the Vietnam War, helping defeat the South Vietnamese and their American allies. They also took part in the Soviet-Afghan War of 1979–1989.

On December 27, 1979, in Operation Storm-333, Spetsnaz forces stormed the Tajbik Palace in Kabul and killed Afghan president Hafizullah Amin and more than 300 guards in a savage encounter that lasted less than an hour.[12] The conquering Soviets then installed another communist president more to their liking, Babrak Karmal, as Amin's successor. Thereafter Russian forces, including Spetsnaz troops, fought side by side with their communist Afghan army allies against the Mujahideen.

The West learned about the existence, purpose, and methods of the Spetsnaz from the revelations of GRU agent Viktor Suvorov, who defected to the British in 1978.

Figure 167: Soviet Spetsnaz forces prepare for a mission in Afghanistan in 1988. Mikhail Evstafiev

Following the breakup of the Soviet Union, Spetsnaz developed celebrity status in the new Russia, captivating the imagination of the populace and participating in numerous intelligence and military operations against Russia's neighbors, such as Georgia and Ukraine. Spetsnaz forces were directly involved in the seizure of the Crimea in 2014.

In 2015, after Russia's conquest of the Crimea and eastern Ukraine, Putin redirected Spetsnaz forces to the Syrian civil war. Putin sent ground forces and used the Russian Aerospace Forces to support the flagging authoritarian regime of Syrian President Bashar al-Assad. Air strikes followed that were supposedly directed to support the Syrian army in their war against Islamic State (IS) forces, but those claims were disputed.

In fact, Russian forces attacked other Syrian rebels, such as the Free Syrian Army militias, that were also fighting IS but were being assisted by the West and the United States.[13]

Spetsnaz performed sniper missions, sabotage, and reconnaissance against all of Assad's enemies, and supported the Iranian Quds Force under General Qasem Soleimani on the ground. The Quds Force is one of the five branches of the Islamic Revolutionary Guard Corps (IRGC), and its "elite clandestine wing."[14] The IRGC-QF is "responsible for conducting covert lethal activities outside of Iran, including asymmetric and terrorist operations...IRGC-QF uses its intelligence and military capabilities to support not only its own terrorist operations but also those of its partners and proxies."[15] The Quds Force was very active in the Syrian civil war and has been active in other parts of the Middle East as well.[14] One of the Quds Force's missions reportedly was to gain Iran access to the Mediterranean Sea, and this necessity was one reason for Iran's assistance to Syria and Russia in this civil war contest. Soleimani's involvement in Middle East clandestine military activities and terrorism cost him his life. He was targeted in an American drone attack in Iraq on the orders of U.S. President Donald Trump in January 2020 and killed.

Along with Russian Aerospace Forces, Spetsnaz troops were instrumental in pushing back rebels, who until that point were gaining the upper hand in the fight against the Syrian government forces that maintained President Assad in power.[16]

The Wagner Group, referred to as a "private military company" (PMC), was also reported to be operating in Syria to help prop up Assad. Although the group's involvement was not confirmed officially, sources at the FSB and the Russian Defense Ministry admitted, unofficially, that the Wagner Group was supervised by intelligence and military GRU officials.[17]

Russian forces did remarkably well in Syria. A friendly source report concluded:

The VKS [Russian Aerospace Forces] flew more than 9,000 sorties using precision weapons, with targets including energy infrastructure, weapons, and supply routes. Russian bombers assisted in reclaiming 400 settlements and 10,000 square kilometers of Syrian territory. Furthermore, Russian aircraft destroyed 209 Syrian [IS-controlled] oil facilities and over 2,000 means of delivery of petroleum products.[18]

Russian Mercenaries Collide with American Commandos in Syria

But in February 2018, a much-feared clash, which both sides had tried to avoid, took place between Free Syrian Army forces and American commandos on one side and Syrian government forces and Russian mercenaries on the other. The clash turned out to be one of the bloodiest battles American forces had participated in since deployment to the Middle East to fight the militant Islamic State. The American force consisted of Delta Force soldiers, Green Berets, Marines, and Rangers from the Joint Special Operations Command, which was operating alongside friendly Arab and Kurdish rebels next to a Conoco oil field outpost near Deir al-Zour by the Euphrates in eastern Syria. *The New York Times* reported:

> *WASHINGTON—The artillery barrage was so intense that the American commandos dived into foxholes for protection, emerging covered in flying dirt and debris to fire back at a column of tanks advancing under the heavy shelling. It was the opening salvo in a nearly four-hour assault in February by around 500 pro-Syrian government forces—including Russian mercenaries—that threatened to inflame already-simmering tensions between Washington and Moscow.[19]*

Despite American efforts to communicate with the hostile advancing force, Russian and Syrian forces continued the attack and refused to stop the armored advance and artillery bombardment of the American position. At this point, the tiny American force of 40 commandos called for air support:

> *American warplanes arrived in waves, including Reaper drones, F-22 stealth fighter jets, F-15E Strike Fighters, B-52 bombers, AC-130 gunships and AH-64 Apache helicopters. For the next three hours, American officials said, scores of strikes pummeled enemy troops, tanks, and other vehicles. Marine rocket artillery was fired from the ground.[19]*

The Russian mercenaries and their allies suffered heavy losses:

> *In the end, 200 to 300 of the attacking fighters were killed. The others retreated under merciless airstrikes from the United States, returning later to retrieve their battlefield dead. None of the Americans at the small outpost in eastern Syria—about 40 by the end of the firefight—were harmed.[19]*

According to American intelligence officials, the Russian mercenaries were likely part of the Wagner Group, the paramilitary company that "the Kremlin often used to carry out objectives that officials do not want to be connected to the Russian government."[19] We will have more to say about mercenary forces and the Wagner Group in the Epilogue of this book.

Geopolitics in the Volatile Middle East and Turkey

Russia not only had plans to build military bases in Egypt but also had received the go-ahead from Syrian President Bashar al-Assad to build an offensive submarine and naval base in Tartus, Syria—a development that would have tilted the balance of power in the Mediterranean towards Russia. Those with knowledge of geopolitics and history would recognize that Vladimir Putin's actions in the eastern Mediterranean have been unprecedented for the Russians.

In centuries past, Tsarina Catherine the Great and her all-powerful minister and lover, Grigory Potemkin (1739–1791), and Tsars Nicholas I and Alexander II, could only have dreamt of projecting Russian power in the Mediterranean with the building of naval bases to challenge the West. The Ottoman Turks, supported by England and France, prevented the fulfillment of this dream—a dream that would have been a nightmare for the British fleet, French possessions in the Mediterranean, and the European balance of power.

The Soviets attempted to build major bases in the Mediterranean, but their efforts in Egypt and Libya ultimately failed.

Putin has attempted to fulfill the role of statesman in the Middle East by increasing Russian influence in the region, projecting Russian power in Syria, and planning to do the same in Egypt and Libya—of course, with the help and connivance of Syria and Iran.

He also prudently eased tensions with Russia's traditional enemy, Turkey, after the downing of a Russian jet by a Turkish F-16 fighter on November 24, 2015, which many feared might have ominous repercussions for the NATO alliance. Turkey asserted that the Su-24 Russian jet was shot down while violating Turkish airspace; and the Russians maintained that their jet had not strayed from Syrian into Turkish airspace. Turkey, a member of NATO, was supported by the Western alliance that backed the Turkish claim that the Russian warplane had violated Turkish airspace while flying over a tongue of land stretching into Syria. Initially, both the Russian and the Turkish presidents fumed about the incident.[20] But Putin and Erdoğan soon recognized that their countries stretched into hotbeds of terrorist activities directed by ISIS, the common enemy. Both Turkey and Russia were then being assailed and destabilized by ISIS and terrorism. Just the previous month, a Russian plane had been blown up by Islamic terrorists in Egypt. So, both leaders calmed down, and the situation was defused peacefully. In fact, in time both leaders seemed to grow closer and more isolated from the rest of Europe.

Figure 168: Hassan Rouhani (President of Iran 2013–2021), Vladimir Putin, and Recep Tayyip Erdoğan in 2017. Kremlin.ru

At the same time, Iran's Supreme Leader, Ali Khamenei, continued to court Putin and offered the Russians an airbase in Iran. This generosity, of course, was a quid pro quo arrangement for Iran to continue to exert power in Syria through Hezbollah, as well as asking for Russian acquiescence in building a railroad passing through Syria allowing Tehran access to the Mediterranean Sea.

After the American missile strike in Syria, the U.S actually made reinvigorated allies in the region besides some old friends like Israel and Jordan. Turkish President Tayyip Erdoğan was for a time at the forefront of that alliance, despite the capricious animosity of the European Union (EU) towards the Turkish president.

Conflicting Powers in the Middle East

The development of closer ties between the U.S and Turkey was practical not only because of the common fight against ISIS but also because of Turkey's traditional fear of Russia, which went as far back as Tsarist times. For centuries, Russia had been a natural enemy of Turkey for geopolitical and historic reasons—namely, the attempted use of power in the region and the Russians' repeated efforts for unconditional passage, if not outright possession and even annexation, of the straits between the Black Sea and the Mediterranean.

In the Crimean War (1853–1856), France and England had supported the flagging Ottoman Empire, or as Tsar Nicholas I called it, "the sick man of Europe," and fought Tsarist Russia to preserve the littoral area and straits in the Black Sea and the Sea of Marmara from falling in the hands of the expansionist Russians.

In 2018, U.S. President Donald Trump capitalized on that bit of history and managed to force a wedge between Erdoğan and Putin with the U.S. missile attack on the Syrian airfield.

It was hoped that the Trump-Putin cordiality, in general, and the close military cooperation in Syria against ISIS, in particular, would continue, but that was not to be the case. ISIS and Islamic terrorism targeted America and the West as well as Russia. Take for instance the metro suicide-bombing attack in St. Petersburg on April 4, 2017 by a young Moslem Kyrgyz terrorist.[21] The Russian underbelly is surrounded by Islamic nations and territories and not all of them are friendly to the Russian Federation. Moreover, both Trump and Putin along with Theresa May of Great Britain and Turkey's Tayyip Erdoğan had been at the forefront in opposing the New World Order of forced secularization, regimentation, and globalization campaign of the European Union. European nationalism was in ascendancy. Many EU member nations were noticing the political trend and taking steps in opposition to the globalization and regimentation.[22]

The American missile strike in Syria sent a message to that and other rogue nations that violation of treaties to which both the violator and the U.S. were signatories—such as the Chemical Weapons Convention of 1993, as well as committing war crimes in the process—will not be tolerated and would have dire consequences in a conflict in which the U.S. is also involved. With the EU globalization drive and new Syrian developments, Putin once again saw himself and Russia surrounded by hostile powers.

Unfortunately, Putin ignored the message that further aggression toward his neighbors or seizure of territories by force, as he did in the Crimea, would lead to untoward ramifications for Russia.

Thus, Putin's continued aggressive posturing and hostility toward his neighbors did not cease. North Korea and its dangerous *enfant terrible*, Kim Jong-un, took notice especially after U.S. President Donald Trump was not re-elected to a second term in 2020. Kim Jong-un resumed his tantrums with his restless fingers threatening nuclear war. He continued missile launchings and other provocations towards South Korea and Japan, both American allies. And to some extent, the same can be said of China and its belligerent actions in the disputed islands of the South China Sea and Taiwan, as discussed in previous chapters.

Epilogue

The 2022 Russian Invasion of Ukraine and Its Aftermath

In a major escalation of the conflict that began in 2014, Russia invaded Ukraine and quickly occupied part of Ukrainian territory on February 24, 2022. For months prior to the invasion, Russian troops had been massing along Ukrainian borders. Vladimir Putin commenced his "special military operation" ostensibly to support the Russian-occupied breakaway republics of Donetsk and Luhans. These former Ukrainian provinces that were controlled by Russia had been fighting Ukraine in the Donbas conflict since 2014. Russia thought the invasion would be a walk in the park—that is, rapid and decisive in their favor—but the war turned out not to be an easy contest for the Russian military.

The Russian aggression was met with almost unanimous condemnation worldwide, and various European nations and the United States immediately mobilized to send aid to Ukraine in the form of monetary assistance, supplies, and arms.

Putin insisted the invasion was necessary to "demilitarize" and "denazify" Ukraine. Using rhetoric that distorts history, he also claimed that Ukraine was governed by neo-Nazis who persecuted the ethnic Russian minority.[1]

The Russian attack on Ukraine can be summarized as consisting of air strikes and a ground invasion: a Kiev Offensive consisting of a Northern Front from Belarus to Kiev; a Northeastern Ukraine Campaign pushing towards Kharkiv, a Southern Ukraine Campaign advancing from the Crimean Peninsula; and an Eastern Ukraine Campaign invading from Donbas.[2]

The invasion resulted in thousands of casualties on both sides and provoked the largest refugee crisis since World War II with millions of Ukrainians either fleeing their country or displaced in their native land. Nevertheless, the Ukrainian military and civilians fought bravely and proved to be a surprising match for the Russians. After initially occupying several areas of Ukrainian territory, the Russian army encountered strong and serious opposition from the Ukrainian defensive forces and was stopped in its tracks on the various fronts. For months, the war remained hotly contested and fiercely fought with the Ukrainian civilian population enduring untold hardships and privations.

On July 22, 2022, in an important diplomatic and geopolitical move, Turkey and the United Nations formulated an agreement with Russia and Ukraine to allow for the safe transport through the Black Sea of grain from Ukraine, a major exporter of foodstuffs. The Black Sea Grain Initiative was important because Russia's invasion of Ukraine had led to a complete halt in shipments of the much-needed grain to global markets. Russia was accused of "weaponizing" food supplies and threatening famine, especially in Third World nations. Because of this initiative, by the summer of 2023 more than one thousand ships had left Ukrainian ports carrying over 33 million tons of grain and other foodstuffs to 45 countries.

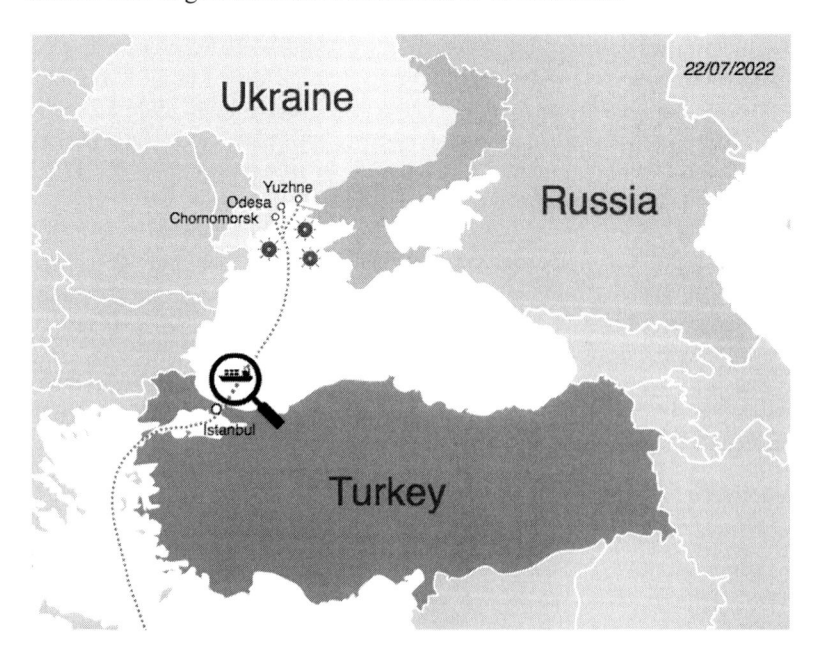

Figure 169: Map showing the route of the Black Sea Grain Initiative, an agreement formulated for the safe transport and passage of grain and foodstuffs from Ukrainian ports following the Russian invasion

Unfortunately, after repeatedly threatening to withdraw from the agreement, Russia refused to sign an extension for the Black Sea Grain

Initiative by the July 17, 2023, deadline because its impossible demands had not been met.[3] The collapse of the initiative meant the "withdrawal of safety guarantees for shipping, and the ending of a maritime humanitarian corridor" that allowed foodstuffs and other products, including fertilizer, to reach global markets.[3]

In June 2023, Ukraine finally launched its counteroffensive against Russian forces and began to slowly retake territories Russia had gained, particularly in the eastern Donetsk region. With its army stopped on all fronts, Russia continued its offensive with missile and drone attacks. In August 2023, Russia began moving tactical nuclear weapons to Belarus, its ally.[4] The war continues.

Figure 170: The President of Ukraine, Volodymyr Zelenskyy (center), with members of the Ukrainian Army on June 18, 2022. President.gov.ua

Those Excusing and Defending Putin

Curiously in the United States many conservative groups and individuals have defended Putin's aggression against the Ukraine because they believed Putin's false claims.[1] They also admired his nationalism, praise for traditional values, and opposition to the New World Order (NWO) regimentation and the internationalist and socialistic agenda that the European Union (EU) wanted to impose not only upon Union members but also, and with subtlety, upon the rest of the world.[5]

Speculation that Vladimir Putin's invasion of the Ukraine was due to the fact that he feared NATO encirclement and aggression was not based on any evidence or historical probability. NATO has never invaded or even threatened any nation, unlike Russia or worse, the Soviet Union. In fact, during the Cold War, if it had not been for the U.S., Russian tanks would have rolled all over Central and Eastern Europe. If NATO did not exist with the United States support behind it, it is more likely that Putin's Russia would have already invaded many other nations—including Georgia (Ossetia), eastern Ukraine, Crimea, the rest of Ukraine, as well as Poland, Romania, Bulgaria, et cetera—to reconstitute the Russian empire with its satellites like it was during the USSR, communism or not. This is evident by what has happened in Georgia and is happening in Ukraine.

Russian state media and communist Chinese media have promulgated the Russian state-sponsored, disinformation campaign that falsely claimed Ukraine had been sheltering "16 U.S. biological (biowarfare) labs." The naive readership on social media fell for this fictitious assertion and item of state propaganda, passed it along, and transmogrified it into the falsehood that "drugs were being sent to Russia, and that was a reason for the invasion."[6]

Although Putin was admired for his nationalism and independence from the EU by many individuals, Russia's invasion and the threat of nuclear war proved, as the Cuban proverb says, "He has undone with his feet what he had done with his hands." Power corrupts and absolute power corrupts absolutely. The fact is that Vladimir Putin has become a despot, a brutal dictator with his suppression of political opposition at home, the intimidation of Russian neighbors abroad, and the outright brutal invasion of Ukraine.

As for the "denazification" claim, this too is a falsehood, a propaganda ploy, and only a pretext to justify Russia's aggression. Putin it seems went back to his KGB days and used Lenin's communist dictum:

We can and must write in language which sows among the masses hate, revulsion, and scorn toward those who disagree with us and when certain obstructionists become too irritating, label them, after suitable build ups, as Fascist or Nazi or anti-Semitic.... In the public mind constantly associate those who oppose us with those whose name already have a bad smell. The association will, after enough repetition, become 'fact' in the public mind.[7]

After all, the President of Ukraine Volodymyr Zelenskyy is Jewish. And if many Ukrainians collaborated with the Nazis during World War II, then why did they do this? Perhaps, because through his dekulakization and collectivist policies, Joseph Stalin oppressed and killed millions of Ukrainians, starving them to death with government orchestrated famines to the point that many people were forced to resort to cannibalism to prevent their own demise.[8]

As for corruption in Ukraine today, we now know the Bidens hoodwinked them into it. The Ukrainians are now actively exposing the corruption of the Bidens and the Democrats and documenting how allegedly they stole millions from the Ukrainian people.[9] The Ukrainians are doing this courageously in their hour of peril as they continue to face a relentless and barbaric war.

Figure 171: President Volodymyr Zelenskyy delivers an official address to the nation on March 16, 2022, regarding the Russian invasion of Ukraine. President.gov.ua

Putin had more nonviolent options available to him. The scenario of NATO attacking Russia was another pretext without precedence. Instead, Putin made an unholy alliance with communist China against the West and the United States. As noted in previous chapters, China is an adversary of the West and Western democracies. Even Turkish President Tayyip Erdoğan, who was courting Putin and called him a friend, soon recognized the aggressive posture of Putin's Russia, gradually pulled away from his increasingly belligerent and hostile neighbor to the north and gently returned to the side of the NATO alliance to which Turkey belongs.[10]

Figure 172: Ukrainians have countered with an effective defense. Depicted is a destroyed Russian armored vehicle near Mariupol in 2022. Ministry of Internal Affairs of Ukraine, Mvs.gov.ua

True, Turkey has played a delicate balancing act, but it has proven diplomatically successful—carefully supporting Ukraine politically and militarily, without upsetting Russia on the economic front.[11]

Former U.S. President Donald Trump stated at the 2022 Conservative Political Action Conference (CPAC) that Putin did wrong with the invasion and noted:

> *The Russian attack on the Ukraine is appalling. It's an outrage and an atrocity that should never have been allowed to occur, Trump told the gathering in Orlando. I have no doubt that President Putin made his decision...only after watching the pathetic withdrawal from Afghanistan. Thirteen U.S. service members were killed in a bombing at the Kabul airport during the Biden administration's withdrawal this summer from Afghanistan, which has since fallen under Taliban control.[12]*

Trump's contention possessed more than a grain of truth, considering the historical fact that perceived weakness is an invitation for aggression, as observed in Czechoslovakia in 1938, Poland in 1939, and numerous other historical examples.

Figure 173: The Russian Black Sea flagship Moskva was sunk on April 14, 2022, reportedly after being hit by two Ukrainian Neptune anti-ship missiles. Ministry of Defence of the Russian Federation, Mil.ru

Finally, if Putin and Russia are pacifists that pose no threat to their neighbors—except providing for Russia's defense and national security—then one must ask why are neighboring countries, such as Ukraine, Georgia, Moldova and others, seeking to join NATO? Why did Poland, Romania, and the Czech Republic join NATO? And why are traditionally neutral nations like Finland (which joined) and Sweden seeking to join NATO?

Just and moral people in the West, politically conservative though they might be, should have a difficult time supporting Vladimir Putin's aggression. They will have to find a new champion to oppose the socialism and globalism of the EU and the NWO.

Yevgeny Prigozhin and the Wagner Group

Yevgeny Prigozhin was a Russian oligarch, formerly very close to Vladimir Putin, and who controlled a number of restaurant businesses in addition to his well-known paramilitary activities in the service of Putin's Russia. It was also known that his military activities for the Wagner Group were "tightly integrated with Russia's Defense Ministry and its intelligence arm, the GRU."[13] Prigozhin and his business dealings had been sanctioned (banned) by the United States, Great Britain, Switzerland, and the European Union.[14]

Figure 174: Yevgeny Prigozhin, Russian oligarch and former restaurateur, in 2010. Government of the Russian Federation

In 2022, prompted by a video that went viral in which Prigozhin was caught on camera recruiting prisoners from Russia's extensive penitentiaries, he admitted that he had founded the Wagner Group in 2014 to support separatist and Russian proxy forces in eastern Ukraine in the Donbas War (2014–2022). The prisoners, most of them hardened criminals, were recruited for frontline combat in Ukraine.[15]

Prigozhin promised the convicts money and plunder as well as their freedom after purportedly serving six months with the Wagner Group. Not surprisingly, the mercenary force in Ukraine ballooned from 1,000 to 50,000 by the end of 2022.[16]

But in 2023, the use of Prigozhin and private Russian paramilitary mercenaries to carry out missions the Russian government wished to disclaim misfired, at least temporarily. In an astounding move, the Wagner Group leader called for an open rebellion against the leaders of the Russian military, particularly the Minister of Defense, Sergei Shoigu, and the Chief of the General Staff of the Russian Federation, Valery Gerasimov, whom Prigozhin accused of corruption and mismanagement in the Russo-Ukrainian War.

The uprising began on June 23, 2023, in the southern Russian city of Rostov-on-Don, near the Ukrainian border. By 7:30 am the next morning, the Wagner Group had assumed control of the military facilities and an airport in the Russian city. Prigozhin was threatening to march on Moscow against Russia's military leadership and "destroy anyone who stands in our way." Wagner forces then began their drive through the Voronezh region about 300 miles south of Moscow towards the capital of the Russian Federation in a long column.[17]

After being briefed on the rebellion, Putin appeared on Russian television at 10:00 am and stated that the rebellion mounted to "a stab in the back."[17] Putin said that "necessary orders have been given" to defend Russia and that military forces had been moved to defensive positions. Neither Putin nor Prigozhin had mentioned the other by name.

Ukrainian President Volodymyr Zelenksyy observed that there was a "deafening" silence from Russian elites and claimed, "Russia used propaganda to mask its weakness and the stupidity of its government. And now there is so much chaos that no lie can hide it."[17]

Then inexplicably, the rebellion fizzled. Prigozhin halted his military column's drive toward Moscow and ordered the advancing Wagner convoy to return to their field camps. He claimed that he "wanted to avoid shedding Russian blood." *ABC News* stated, "As part of a deal struck with Putin, Prigozhin would relocate to Belarus and would not be prosecuted."[17]

Although the rebellion lasted less than 48 hours, it left a bad impression of Putin's leadership and the Russian military, especially regarding the Ukrainian War and the stability of the Putin regime. The attempted rebellion and its short duration remain a mystery.

However, one doesn't cross Vladimir Putin and get away with it. Prigozhin had been allowed to come and go in Russia as he pleased, take care of his businesses, and run the Wagner Group, which had ostensibly been resettled and run from Belarus—until August 23, 2023, exactly two months after the aborted coup, when Prigozhin and the top leadership of the Wagner Group were killed in a plane crash.[18]

According to Russia's Federal Air Transport Agency, the crash of the Embraer aircraft took place in the Tver region of Russia. Ten people died in the crash, three crewmembers and seven passengers. Among the seven dead passengers listed on the flight manifest were Yevgeny Prigozhin, a Russian oligarch and founder of the Wagner Group; Dmitry Utkin, a special forces (Spetsnaz) GRU officer, cofounder and military commander of the Wagner Group, who was referred to by the military alias, "Wagner" (also the name of the group, reportedly, an approving reference to Adolf Hitler's favorite composer, Richard Wagner); Valeriy Chekalov, a businessman and senior official in Prigozhin's business empire; and two senior mercenary officers, Evgeniy Makaryan and Sergey Propustin, who had fought in Syria and the Second Chechen War, respectively.[19] In short, the Federal Air Transport Agency report seemed to confirm that the Wagner Group had been decapitated from the top.

Ukrainian President Zelenskyy denied any Ukrainian military involvement but alluded to the culprit by stating, "We had nothing to do with it. Everybody realizes who has something to do with it."[20] For his part, U.S. President Joe Biden admitted he did not know all of the details about the incident, but he had no qualms in fingering Putin as being behind the crash. *The Guardian* noted:

> *'I don't know for a fact what happened, but I'm not surprised,' the US president said after a briefing after the crash of Prigozhin's private jet between Moscow and St Petersburg. 'There's not much that happens in Russia that Putin's not behind. But I don't know enough to know the answer.'[20]*

The Polish and Estonian government spokesmen had no difficulty in naming Putin as the person behind the assassination. Both of those neighboring countries, which suffered under the Russian yoke for centuries and the very recent past, felt Putin was the responsible party. Both spokesmen expressed in different words the same sentiment—that the Russian president does not tolerate dissension and eliminates anyone who becomes a threat to his power or has an opinion different from his.[20]

Similarly, British Member of Parliament Alicia Kearns, Chair of the Foreign Affairs Select Committee, tweeted:

> *The speed at which the Russian govt has confirmed Yevgeny Prigozhin was on a plane that crashed on a flight from Moscow to St Petersburg should tell us everything we need to know. Reports Russian air defence shot down the plane suggests Putin is sending a very loud message. For Putin there is one unforgivable sin: the betrayal of Putin and Russia. He hunts down those he perceives to be traitors, [including] on British shores, such as Alexander Litvinenko and Sergei Skripal. Now Yevgeny Prigozhin has been added to that list, ending Putin's humiliation.[20]*

Russia: A Final Adieu

In 2018, Agence France-Presse carried a news item that noted how many young Russians today "admit to only a passing knowledge" of the highly acclaimed Russian author, Aleksandr Solzhenitsyn.

Alexander Altunyan, a journalism professor at Moscow's International University confirmed the unfortunate trend and explained that, "Out of a class of 30 students, no more than two or three will have read a book by Solzhenitsyn. Most of them don't know a thing about him."[21]

Several teachers also expressed the opinion that the younger generation needed to read Solzhenitsyn's works because his moral and political teachings were important and still very relevant.

Olga Mayevskaya, an instructor of Russian language and literature, remarked that today "there are more and more attempts to deny the Stalin-era repressions," with some people saying "nothing terrible happened in that era."[21]

Mayevskaya succinctly concluded her comments by stating, "What's unbelievable is that they are not told about this in history lessons. This is the history of our country. They have to know it so it does not happen again."[21]

The next news item did not receive the attention it deserved and was essentially neglected by the Western media. It is recorded here for the travesty that this happening portends, which is reminiscent of Stalin's policy of revising or erasing history and creating non-persons.

In 2018, *The Moscow Times* reported:

> *Russian officials are reportedly destroying the records of gulag prisoners under a secret order passed in 2014, Russian media have reported. An estimated 3-12 million victims of Soviet repression were imprisoned in the gulag network of prisons and forced labor camps in the former Soviet Union. Registration records kept by the Museum of the History of the Gulag, now threatened with destruction, include the permanent records of those killed, as well as archival files detailing those who survived the gulag and when they were released.[22]*

The reason for this erasure of records was not clear, but since Russian security agencies were involved, the order must come from very high up in the government power structure. The report went on to state:

> *A 2014 inter-agency order labeled 'for internal use' instructs files to be destroyed once the former prisoner reaches the age of 80, Russia's Kommersant business daily cited a regional police official as saying Friday. 'This information is forgotten once it's destroyed,' gulag historian Sergei Prudovsky, who revealed the practice, was quoted as saying. The internal order was signed by 11 Russian state agencies, including the KGB's successor agency, the FSB, the Foreign Intelligence Service (SVR), the Interior Ministry, Justice Ministry, and the General Prosecutor's Office, Kommersant reported.[22]*

The Moscow Times article revealed that Gulag Museum director, Roman Romanov, had even approached presidential Human Rights Council head, Mikhail Fedotov, "to prevent the destruction of records that...could curb research into the history of Soviet political repression."[22]

Fedotov promised to defend keeping the archive material as a way to "counter the falsification of history" because "when there's no document, you can make up anything you want," he warned.[22]

We close with a communication from a friend. After learning about the writing of this book, she wanted to relieve her soul of painful ancestral memories and reveal some experiences her Polish father and grandfather endured. She wrote me:

> *My father was in Gulag for over 2 1/2 years north of the Arctic Circle, Kola Peninsula labor camp, taken by cattle car after Russia invaded Poland from the East. He was arrested by NKVD. While he was still in Gulag his father, a Polish officer, was seen in one of the three main holding camps of Polish 'intelligentsia.' While in Gulag prisoners continually rotated in to replace the dead, often left in the cells as my father explained. Some new prisoner knew my grandfather and father and advised him. There was an amnesty granted to some prisoners because Russians needed help fighting Germany. Stalin offered transport to the Western Front, my father said no thank you as did others as well and they made their way on foot to Persia to connect with the British Eighth Army and fight with Allied forces against Germany in North Africa. These were descriptions told to me by father regarding his experiences about himself and his family. He came to this country in 1952 and met my mother. I was born here in Detroit.[23]*

To which I responded:

> *I consider the Polish and the Irish the most abused people in European history, and part of it stems from their staunch Catholicism and patriotism. I especially have great admiration for the Polish people and all they suffered under the German Nazis and the Russian communists, and for centuries before that under Austria, Prussia, and Tsarist Russia—and yet, they kept their religion, their culture, their language, and their dignity.[24]*

Recent events in Vladimir Putin's Russia do not bode well for the future of Russia or the tranquility of the world. We can only hope for better times for the Russians and, especially, for the Ukrainian people.

Appendix A

Cuba's Adventurism as Soviet Proxy in Africa (1961–1991)

Cuba: An African Odyssey is a 2007 documentary directed by Jihan El Tahri. The documentary description reads:

> The Soviet Union wanted to extend its influence into a new continent; the U.S. lusted after Africa's natural resources; former European empires felt their grip on the area weaken; and newly formed African nations fought to defend their recently won independence. When the latter called on Cuban guerillas to aid them in their struggle, Castro and Cuba stepped in to build a new offensive strategy, which would have long-lasting influence on developing countries in their battles against colonialism... Cuba: An African Odyssey tells the story of those internationalists who won their battles but ultimately lost the war.[1]

Many viewers were enchanted by the documentary and posted positive reviews on Amazon. Some reviewers even lambasted a critical review, which was, in fact, the most accurate. I decided to enter the fray with my own review, which follows. I know something about the subject since it is in an area of my historical expertise and because an uncle of mine was conscripted in the communist Cuban army and participated in Cuba's African adventure, serving honorably in Angola.

The documentary is interesting, informative, and well done, and uses good video footage. Nevertheless, it is terribly biased and one-sided, and glorifies communist Cuba and its heroes in the repressive pantheon of the workers' paradise.

Part 1 of the documentary relates to the Congo and its war for independence from Belgium, proceeding with the struggle for power between communist leader Patrice Lumumba, who was idolized in the documentary, and his successor, Laurent Kabila, against Mobutu Sese Seko (1930–1997), who eventually won and ruled with an iron hand as a socialist dictator.

Che Guevara enters the picture in the Congolese civil war, and despite a hero-worship tribute to the communist icon, the producers are forced to admit that Che's misadventure was a disastrous and colossal failure with which I concur.[1,2]

Figure 175: Che Guevara (seated right) listening to shortwave receiver in the Congo, 1965

Viewers are not told that if there was a real communist hero in the Congo, it was Cuban General Arnaldo Ochoa. Ochoa was sent by Fidel Castro to rescue Guevara in 1965, while the Argentinean was in full retreat from the claws of his enemies. Che got lost and nearly perished on his desperate escape to Lake Tanganyika. General Ochoa, who later became a potential political opponent to Fidel Castro, was falsely accused of drug smuggling, used as a scapegoat by the Castro regime in a 1989 kangaroo trial, and executed in Cuba.[3]

The producers endeavor to provide a semblance of balance to the documentary by using token CIA operatives, like Larry Devlin, who admits to his cloak and dagger operations. But the glorification of the war against neocolonialism and the exaltation of Cuban and African communist heroes—not only big fish, like Patrice Lumumba and Che Guevara, but also smaller heroes, such as Víctor Dreke and Harry Villegas, both assistants to Che and who actually do some of the narration—is all pervasive in the documentary.

It is highly ironic, although the producers fail to see the irony, that when the Cuban revolutionaries entered the Congo, Víctor Dreke, a black Cuban, was given the nom de guerre "Moya." The Congolese rebels were also told that "Moya" was the supreme "commander of the Congo mission." They were astounded and in awe because Moya was black and ranked higher than two white Cubans. Of course, this was not true because one of the two whites was Che Guevara, nom de guerre "Tatu." After Che's identity was ascertained, the astonishment passed. Che was then worshiped almost as a demigod, and the Congolese were afraid for his safety and that "something" might happen to him. However, the documentary says nothing about the cruelty of Cuba's African comrades, the brutal tribal warfare, and the atrocities committed by their African confreres—to the point that Che was revolted by the barbarism he witnessed.[2]

Part 2 of the documentary covers Cuban involvement in the collapse of the Portuguese colonies in Africa, specifically in Angola and Mozambique. Once again, the viewer is not informed about the major role played by the left-wing Portuguese military junta, which was actually the largest player in the collapse. Withdrawal of colonial troops from the Portuguese colonies by the sympathetic junta actually facilitated the work of the African national liberation movements in Cabo Verde, Mozambique, and Angola in 1975. Selective omissions such as this favor leftist revisionism and, unfortunately, haunt the documentary.

In the Angolan war, the troops of the communist-backed People's Movement for the Liberation of Angola (MPLA) are treated like heroes, but the freedom fighters of the National Union for the Total Independence of Angola (UNITA) are insufficiently covered, intimating instead that the U.S.-supported UNITA troops were merely U.S. puppets. The viewer never learns that Dr. Jonas Savimbi had been not only a great military leader in the Angolan war for independence but also in the civil war that ensued, and that he was assassinated in 2002 while still fighting.

The venial situation of the MPLA communist regime of Agostinho Neto, which allowed Western oil companies to prop it up and accepted protection from the Cuban army in the oil fields, was abhorrent. This was not mentioned in the documentary, I suppose, so as not to taint the revolutionary image of Neto, who was the head of the MPLA and later, the communist dictator of Angola.

Figure 176: National Union for the Total Independence of Angola (UNITA) leader, Dr. Jonas Savimbi, 1989

In short, the documentary is well researched and includes good video footage, but it is tremendously one-sided and biased, exalting the heroes of the communist pantheon and at times omitting inconvenient facts that would oppose the leftist perspective of the producers.

The documentary fails to tell the viewers about the corruption (Angola), depredation (Mozambique), and even genocidal perversity (Ethiopia, the Derg, and Mengistu Haile Marian) that the African socialists and communists left in their wake. The viewer will not learn about the atrocities committed by the African communists but exaltation of Cuba's adventurism in Africa during the Cold War.

By all means watch the documentary, but only after doing some preparatory reading on the subject. That way, you will be able to separate the wheat from the chaff. (Reading this review was a good start.—MAF.)

Miguel A. Faria, Jr., M.D., "*Cuba: An African Odyssey*, a review," *HaciendaPublishing.com*, August 25, 2021. Revised and updated: July 15, 2023

APPENDIX B

AN ABBREVIATED HISTORY OF THE CIA TO THE 2011 DEATH OF OSAMA BIN LADEN

The United States of America owes a great debt of gratitude to the men and women of the Central Intelligence Agency (CIA). This government agency has been at the forefront of untold battles in the defense of the nation's freedom, and yet, has remained almost unacknowledged and unappreciated by many U.S. citizens and even derided by some Americans.

Along with the men and women of the United States military, the CIA functions as a preserver of liberty and a guardian of freedom, a protective shield of U.S. national security (and indirectly, the West), while routinely remaining in the background.

From 1942 to 1945, the Office of Strategic Services (OSS) served as America's intelligence gathering agency under the control of the U.S. military's Joint Chiefs of Staff (JCS). President Franklin D. Roosevelt chose the "highly decorated World War I officer" and attorney, William J. "Wild Bill" Donovan, to head the OSS in the fight against the Nazi juggernaut. After the Allied victory, the OSS was dissolved. Two years later, in 1947, the Central Intelligence Agency was created as a civilian agency and successor to the OSS when President Harry Truman signed the National Security Act.[1]

The mission and vision of the Central Intelligence Agency is summarized as follows:

> *At its core, our mission is to gather and share intelligence to protect our Nation from threats. Our highest principles guide our vision and all that we do: integrity; service; excellence; courage; teamwork; and stewardship.[2]*

The Central Intelligence Agency places the American nation first. The men and women of the CIA do not shy away from executing "difficult, high-stakes, or dangerous tasks" when required.[2]

But for years, critics in the media, academia, and Hollywood have castigated the CIA for a few real but more often imagined offenses—

offenses that even when real, were pursued for defense or national security reasons, including covert operations, which are "conducted as directed by the president."[2]

While it was true the CIA conducted some testing on LSD, ending the program in 1963, the charge that the agency tested the drug in the New York subway system was ludicrous and fictitious.[3] An even more absurd calumny was the accusation that the CIA "manufactured the AIDS virus" for biological warfare and to carry out genocide of African Americans. We learned—from the archive of KGB defector Vasili Mitrokhin and confirmed by the Russian government in 1987—that this gruesome and false allegation had been KGB disinformation, or an "active measure" conducted to discredit the CIA and as psychological warfare against the U.S.[4]

The critical and largely hypocritical attitude of America's liberal establishment toward the Central Intelligence Agency had been developing for years. Whereas the legality of some of the earliest CIA operations may be questioned and debatable, the intention was always to protect the nation's security and thereby the freedoms enshrined in the U.S. Bill of Rights, including the liberties exercised by the armchair pundits, who from the comfort and safety of their homes criticize the actions of the men and women who routinely place themselves in harm's way abroad.

Besides, if the media, academia, or the Hollywood movie industry need a proverbial punching bag, instead of the CIA, might I suggest the Bureau of Alcohol Tobacco and Firearms (ATF)? On many occasions this roguish agency has run roughshod over the constitutional rights, not of hostile aliens or foreign enemies within the nation, but of law-abiding American citizens. The ATF has forcefully entered the wrong homes in dynamic entries and launched attacks on U.S. citizens, like the atrocious raid in Waco, Texas, and other lesser known but no less reckless raids carried out in the 1990s.[5]

While the CIA has protected U.S. national security abroad, the Federal Bureau of Investigation (FBI) has provided security within the country. The services provided by the FBI have been widely publicized and popularized from its inception to the present day, particularly under the leadership of legendary FBI Director J. Edgar Hoover. Additionally, the FBI has been favorably portrayed in movies and in serialized American television programs. One can easily find movies that portray the FBI and the U.S. military in a favorable light, but one is hard pressed to find movies in which the CIA is portrayed in a complimentary light. *Time* magazine in its listing for the "top 10 CIA movies" admitted, "Ever notice how movies almost always make the Central Intelligence Agency the bad guy?"[6] Watch any one of the recommended movies on their list, and you will find double-dealings, cowardice, mistrust, criminal behavior, lust, greed, et cetera, in the portrayal of the cloak and dagger characters, the supposed men and women of the CIA. Fiction it is, but, unfortunately, in the zeitgeist of our time, life imitates art and perception becomes reality. Bad publicity can also be lethal, particularly for an intelligence agency that requires funding and congressional blessing to properly perform its duties.

Allen Dulles, Director of Central Intelligence (1953–1961)

During the early years of the Cold War, under Director of Central Intelligence (DCI), Allen Dulles, the agency fought the militant expansionism of communism, in accordance with the dictum of diplomat and historian, George F. Kennan, and the need for "containment" of communism, which was implemented as U.S. policy by President Truman. Throughout the 1950s, the CIA scored notable successes in Iran and Guatemala—even if only a few writers describe them as victories.[7] Never mind the fact that the U.S. was engaged in a Cold War against an opponent that was bent on world conquest, had nuclear weapons, and was acting like a big bully in the world neighborhood.

In the sixties, the failure of CIA clandestine operations in Cuba has been written about extensively, including the fiasco of the Bay of Pigs invasion in April 1961 and the iniquity of Operation Mongoose to assassinate Fidel Castro in the years from 1961 to 1963. The fact remains that it was U.S. President John F. Kennedy who ordered the operations, and not rogue actions initiated by the agency without presidential sanction.

Moreover, in the case of the Bay of Pigs invasion, Kennedy doomed the mission by his insistence on "plausible deniability."[8] In the case of Operation Mongoose, Kennedy was persistent—as was his brother, Attorney General Robert Kennedy—that even though the "special task" might be feasible, it needed to be carried out with secrecy and political deniability. The culpability for the failure of the CIA clandestine operations in Cuba rested solely with the President and Commander-in-Chief, John F. Kennedy.[9]

And when President Kennedy, who was beginning to enjoy the cloak and dagger intrigue, inquired if America had a "James Bond," the answer was yes, he was CIA officer William K. ("Bill") Harvey. The American 007, although rough and ready and overweight, was devoted to his presidential-assigned missions. Harvey won some CIA battles in Berlin in the midst of the Cold War. However, he failed in Cuba, but not for lack of trying.[10]

Figure 177: President John F. Kennedy presenting the National Security Medal to Allen Dulles (DCI) at the CIA building in Langley, Virginia. Central Intelligence Agency

The leftwing faction in the American Democratic Party had never been a friend of the CIA. Since the days of the failed Bay of Pigs invasion, the Democrats blamed the CIA for every malfeasance imaginable and did what it could to generally defang the agency. It should be stated that with the end of the Cold War and the collapse of the Soviet communism, Democrats and many liberal academicians have downplayed the role of the CIA and the threat that Soviet communism had posed to the free world.

Admiral Stansfield Turner, Director of Central Intelligence (1977–1981)

In the wake of the Watergate Scandal and the resignation of President Richard Nixon in 1974, the Democrats, led by Senator Frank Church (D-Idaho), finally got their chance, and during the Jimmy Carter administration, largely dismantled the U.S. security and intelligence apparatus. The CIA was defanged. Richard Helms, the DCI from 1966 to

1973, was convicted of "lying to Congress" about covert activities. In reality, Helms was protecting vital U.S. national security secrets as well as the agency. Helm's successor, William Colby, the DCI from 1974 to 1975, revealed all secrets to the world, and Carter's DCI from 1978 to 1980, Admiral Stansfield Turner, lent a hand in dismantling the agency's intelligence apparatus with horrifying consequences worldwide.

The Shah of Iran fell from power in 1979, and the West lost Iran to the Ayatollah Khomeini. Afghanistan was invaded by the Soviets that same year. Communist regimes were set up in Angola, Ethiopia, Somalia, and Mozambique. The Russians, East Germans, and their Cuban surrogates made Africa their playground for communist aggression and militarism.[11] In Ethiopia, the legendary Lion of Judah, Emperor Haile Selassie I, was overthrown and unceremoniously strangled by the communist Derg, led by Mengistu Haile Mariam.

In the Western hemisphere, where Cuba was already a Soviet satellite, the U.S. was threatened with communism in Nicaragua, Chile, El Salvador, and Guatemala. Soviet power and prestige were growing worldwide at the expense of American influence and security.

American hostages had been taken in Iran, and the U.S. had been humiliated by a failed rescue attempt and multiple other foreign policy fiascos. President Jimmy Carter noted a malaise in American society. But the malaise really stemmed from his presidency and his lack of leadership.

William J. Casey, Director of Central Intelligence (1981–1987)

Beginning with the presidency of Ronald Reagan in 1981, and the appointment of William J. Casey as Director of Central Intelligence from 1981 to 1987, the CIA became resurgent.[12] Ultimately, President Reagan would be able to "boast that *his* had been the first *administration* since World War II that had *not* given up an inch of territory to the communists."[13] In the meantime, though, there were still problems. Not only did the CIA and FBI have to contend with the explosive "1985 Year of the Spy," but even after the fall of Soviet communism, two acts of supreme betrayal rocked America and had repercussions for both the CIA and the FBI.

In 1994, an extensive government investigation revealed that Aldrich "Rick" Ames, a CIA counterintelligence officer, had been spying for the Soviets since 1985. After the collapse of the Soviet Union, Ames had continued to spy for the Russians up to the time of his arrest. Ames' betrayal had resulted in the execution of at least ten Russian agents, who had been working for the CIA.[14,15] His arrest and conviction for espionage were a serious blow to the prestige of the CIA.[16] As a result, the FBI gained prestige over the CIA during the years President Bill Clinton was in the White House.

Figure 178: Plaque honoring the late Director of Central Intelligence William J. Casey in the CIA headquarters lobby. Central Intelligence Agency

However, the FBI's ascendancy was not long lived. The tables turned again in 2001, when Robert Hanssen, an FBI counterintelligence officer, was exposed and convicted of spying for Russia from 1979 to 2001. Hanssen's treason has been categorized "as possibly the worst intelligence disaster in U.S. history."[17,18]

Like a phoenix rising from the ashes, the CIA rose again. Despite the ominous and vast powers of the Soviet KGB, the sword and the shield of Soviet communism, the CIA ultimately triumphed over the KGB. The CIA survived. The Soviet extensive, repressive and intelligence apparatus, the KGB, which vastly surpassed the CIA both in funding and manpower resources, won many battles supported by the totalitarian government of the USSR, but lost the war.[19-21] The USSR and its Central and Eastern European, Warsaw Pact allies began to crack in 1989, and as we know, the great Soviet bear fell in 1991.

Osama bin Laden, 1st General Emir of al-Qaeda (1988–2011)

Felicity over the collapse of Soviet communism was short-lived despite the prematurely proclaimed "end of history." The tragedy of September 11, 2001, unfolded and shocked the world. In fact, a new conflict arose, brought about by religious and cultural hatred and Islamic terrorism, al-Qaeda, and Osama bin Laden. In the meantime, quietly the CIA worked assiduously to root out and defeat al-Qaeda terrorists and to bring justice to Osama bin Laden.

At the U.S. base in Guantanamo Bay, the CIA used harsh interrogation techniques and waterboarding to obtain information from terrorist prisoners. The administration of President George W. Bush justified its use in the name of U.S. national security. Nevertheless, the Bush administration and the CIA were castigated for the practice in the media, which considered it torture. A few years later, U.S. government agencies vowed to "abide by interrogation limitations in the Army Field Manual, which bans waterboarding."[22]

Another brouhaha erupted in 2003, when columnist Robert Novak revealed the public identification of Valerie Plame (aka Valerie Wilson) as a CIA operative in one of his *Washington Post* columns. Suddenly, the liberals in the media and in the U.S. government were uncharacteristically outraged that a CIA operative had been "outed," and blamed the Bush administration for "blowing the cover of a CIA covert officer." Indeed, a leak had occurred, and as serious as the exposure may have been, there was no sudden love expressed for the CIA by Washington's liberal establishment, which, more characteristically, would have applauded the exposure of a CIA agent.[23]

But Mrs. Wilson had never been in danger of life or limb. Soon it was learned that her husband, Joseph Wilson, was an official in the Democratic Party. The liberal Democrat establishment had thought it was expedient to defend Mrs. Wilson to score political points against the Bush administration. A mistake had certainly been made, but the way the "Plame affair" had been promulgated and repeatedly reported on showed that the end game had always been about politics.

It took the CIA ten years of painstaking intelligence work to locate Osama bin Laden in Pakistan. On May 1, 2011, under orders from President Barack Obama, members of U.S. Navy Seal Team Six conducted an intrepid raid on a compound that ended in the death of bin Laden, who was later buried at sea.[24]

Figure 179: Pakistani journalist Hamid Mir interviewing Osama bin Laden in 1997. Hamid Mir

Today, the CIA functions as the main intelligence collection organization for U.S. intelligence, assisted by the National Security Agency (NSA) and working under the Office of the Director of National Intelligence (ODNI). The Department of Homeland Security was created in the wake of 9/11 to protect the U.S. homeland from terrorism, while the ODNI became the top managing agency for the U.S. intelligence community in 2004.

Moreover, the CIA remains America's shield, the main source of human intelligence and foreign counterintelligence, as well as general research and analysis of national security information gathered overseas about friendly and hostile nations. We need not dwell on the overt mistakes committed by the CIA over the years because that has been done repeatedly and extensively in the electronic mass media and in printed publications. Professor and British historian Christopher Andrew remarked:

While the Soviet Union tried hard to keep its failings secret, the United States exposed its own to public view... No intelligence service had ever been exposed to such public examination of its failings... Though the abuses of the KGB were at a greater level of iniquity than those of the CIA, they were also far less publicized and attracted far less global attention.[25]

In conclusion, as long as America and the West have enemies, freedom will require and need the men and women of the Central Intelligence Agency. Those of us fortunate to live in liberty should tip our hats to the men and women of the CIA—not only for the elimination of a terrorist and mass murderer but also for all they do to preserve the peace and security of the West.

Miguel A. Faria, Jr., M.D., "A History of (and tribute to) the CIA and the hunting down and death of Osama bin Laden," *HaciendaPublishing.com*, May 9, 2011. Revised and updated: July 22, 2023

APPENDIX C

IS AMERICA A STAUNCH FRIEND AND ALLY OR A NATION THAT FORGETS FRIENDS WHEN THEY ARE NO LONGER USEFUL?

On a graduate-level International Studies website, I came across a lengthy debate over that question as well as the student discussion about which nation—that is, Russia or the United States—made a better friend?

Not surprisingly, perhaps, the Indian and Pakistani commentators expressed opinions that Russia made a better friend, citing the example of cordial Indian-USSR relations during the Cold War and beyond, despite recently improved relations between India and the United States.

Regarding U.S.-Pakistani relations, the opposite was noted; relations had soured since the Cold War. The arguable conclusion was that America abandoned its friends and allies when they were no longer politically useful or when it was no longer politically expedient to continue the relationship.

The fate of America's anti-communist friend, Pakistani strongman, General Mohammad Zia-ul-Haq, killed in a 1988 plane crash that remains shrouded in mystery, was an example noted in the online discussion. It was even speculated that the CIA had had a hand in the horrible event; when, in reality, the KGB was the more likely culprit.[1]

It may be true that America and the CIA have not been as efficient as Israel and the Mossad, but America never forgets its friends. The CIA did not give up its search for moles that penetrated the CIA and the FBI in the 1980s and 1990s—like Aldrich "Rick" Ames (CIA) and Robert Hanssen (FBI), American traitors who sent dozens of courageous Russian double agents to their deaths.[2-6].

But given that the discussion centered on Middle Eastern and Indian politics, I submitted the story of a brave Pakistani, known as Colonel Imam, who worked as a CIA agent for America and was assassinated in the cause of freedom. After laborious CIA intelligence work and tracking, Colonel Imam's assassination was avenged when the assassin was obliterated, as if struck by Zeus's thunderbolt or pierced by one of Apollo's

Is America a Staunch Friend and Ally or a Nation that Forgets Friends 335
When They Are No Longer Useful?

celestial arrows. This was an untold story that needed telling, even if briefly so.

Brigadier Amir Sultan Tarar, better known as Colonel Imam, was a former Inter-Services Intelligence (ISI) officer, a loyal subject of Pakistan, a staunch ally of the U.S. during the Cold War, and a hero of the Afghanistan Mujahideen during the 1980s and 1990s.

Always a proponent and adherent of cordial relations with the U.S. and the West, Colonel Imam was a courageous Pakistani fighter for freedom, and—like Ahmad Shah Massoud, the Lion of Panjshir, and Hero of the Afghan Nation[7]—an anti-communist and friend of the U.S. through thick and thin.[8]

Figure 180: A picture of Ahmad Shah Massoud (left) on display during a conference in Kabul, Afghanistan, 2010. Mass Communication Specialist 2nd Class David Quillen, U.S. Navy

Declan Walsh, a correspondent for the British daily newspaper, *The Guardian*, wrote a lengthy and truly investigative piece of journalism in 2011 about the mysterious but highly respected Pakistani Inter-Services Intelligence (ISI) officer. Walsh's article on Colonel Imam was the best piece of journalism that I have read on the subject. Walsh was trying to determine if the ISI was still a friend to the United States or if it had succumbed to Islamic fundamentalism and become a cryptic enemy intelligence service. Although ISI's loyalty was put in question, the career of its former agent, Colonel Imam, a Brigadier General and Pakistani diplomat, was not.[8]

Figure 181: Brigadier Amir Sultan Tarar, aka "Colonel Imam," a veteran Pakistan Army officer and Pakistan Inter-Services Intelligence (ISI) operative in 2010. Like Ahmad Shah Massoud, Colonel Imam was a friend of the United States and the West. Tamir Eshel, Defense Update

Walsh personally interviewed Colonel Imam at his Rawalpindi home, and found him to be a friend of America. One of the Colonel's treasured possessions was a piece of the Berlin Wall that had been given to him by U.S. President George H.W. Bush and donated by the CIA as a memento of the Cold War, a war that the Colonel had helped to bring an end to in Afghanistan. In Afghanistan during the 1980s, the Mujahideen, led by warriors like Colonel Imam and Ahmad Shah Massoud, decisively defeated the Soviets militarily.[9]

In 2011, although still working on and off as a diplomat for Pakistan, Colonel Imam remained involved as a commando-guerilla warfare specialist in the civil war in Afghanistan. In the spring of 2010, Hakimullah Mehsud (1979–2013), an emir of the militant Taliban of Pakistan and former deputy commander to the elder Baitullah Mehsud, kidnapped Colonel Imam, an associate in the ISI, a journalist, and their driver. Both Mehsuds were militant leaders of the Islamic group, the Fedayeen al-Islam.

Colonel Imam's ISI associate was summarily executed, but the Colonel remained in custody for months. He was finally executed in January

2011. His assassins released a horrific video of the execution, which I viewed shortly after reading Walsh's article. It showed the Colonel being shot while refusing to sit down, standing tall and defiant. When the Colonel was shot again, he fell but then tried to stand up. When shot what seemed to be the third time, his body remained still. The graphic video has since been edited, but its sanitized version is still available.[10] It should also be mentioned that the Afghan Taliban, which included former Mujahideen members, reportedly opposed Colonel Imam's execution.

America did not forget its friend, Colonel Imam. The elder Mehsud had been killed in a 2009 drone attack. Terrorists lost 40 "holy warriors" in that attack.[11] In retaliation for the death of Colonel Imam, the CIA hunted down the younger Hakimullah Mehsud quietly, presumably using both HUMINT and SIGINT sources. Hakimullah Mehsud paid the price and, like the elder Mehsud, was killed in a U.S. drone strike in November 2013.[12]

In 2014, the BBC reported that Asmatullah Shaheen, who had followed the younger Mehsud as head of the Pakistani Taliban, was ambushed, shot, and killed as he drove through a village near Miranshah in North Waziristan in Pakistan. Three aides in the vehicle also died. The BBC further commented, "Since then, there have been a series of attacks in which unidentified gunmen have targeted militants in the tribal areas, puzzling observers about who could be behind them…"[13] Here we can only speculate. But let us end with the fact that, regardless of where the enemy might try to hide, America and the CIA possess a very long memory, won't forget their friends, and will avenge them.

Miguel A. Faria, Jr., M.D., "The good CIA—Avenging a friend of America and a Cold War hero," *HaciendaPublishing.com,* December 3, 2020. Revised and updated: August 5, 2023

APPENDIX D

A CIA AGENT IN THE IRANIAN REVOLUTIONARY GUARDS

One of the most heartrending and enthralling accounts I have ever read of bravery, dissimulation, and personal suffering in the genre of espionage memoirs was the story of Reza Kahlili, a courageous man, who risked his life to fight surreptitiously against the cruelties and injustices of the ruling government in his native country—Iran.[1]

A Time to Betray: The Astonishing Double Life of a CIA Agent Inside the Revolutionary Guards of Iran also struck a personal chord with me, reminding me of painful and regretful similarities that beset my family in Cuba prior to and following the 1959 Cuban Revolution that brought the communist Castro brothers to power.[2,3] I recall various family members arguing passionately but amicably for and against the dictatorial government of Cuban President Fulgencio Batista, his 1952 coup d'état concomitant with the trampling of the legendary Constitution of 1940, and his subsequent dictatorship with the lack of political rights; and the cruel imprisonment and systematic torture of rebels captured while fighting against his regime—an opposition in which my parents played a clandestine part. I also remember a favorite uncle warning my family about the malevolent changes that a victory for the revolutionary *barbudos* ("The bearded ones") would bring—but my parents did not listen and came to regret it.[2]

Following the triumph of the Revolution and the establishment of communism in Cuba, there were indeed drastic "changes," but those militated changes were for the worse, like the inception of a culture of deception, oppression, and terror. And there would no longer be friendly political discussions among family members—only mistrust, dissimulation, and fear.[2,3]

A similar event took place in 1979 in Iran. The Shah of Iran, Mohammed Reza Pahlavi (1919–1980), fell from power and the Iranian government was taken over by the mullahs, and the Ayatollah Khomeini. Young Reza Kahlili (a pseudonym) had been brought up in a close-knit and prosperous family in Tehran. He remembered engaging family conversations in the "good old days" with festivities, gatherings, and his loving grandfather defending the ruling Shah and his dynasty as well as traditional Persian mores. Living in such a warm and jovial atmosphere, Reza could not imagine the horrific changes that would rapidly occur in Iranian society with the establishment of an Islamic Republic. After returning to Iran from studying abroad in California, Reza excitedly joined the Iranian Revolutionary Guards. Little did he know that soon most of his family and closest childhood friends would be devoured by the Revolution or persecuted by the organization he compliantly served.

Figure 182: Ayatollah Ruhollah Khomeini, first Supreme Leader of Iran from 1979 to 1989, pictured in a pre-1989 photo

One might recollect the saying, "Be careful what you wish for; you might just get it." Alas, that is what happened to those who wanted change in Cuba and Iran, deriding and helping to overthrow Batista and the Shah of Iran by revolution. Many of those citizens themselves would end up crushed by Castro or the Ayatollah—both significantly worse tyrannical figures than their predecessors. And the tragic concatenations that followed in their wake have not ended in either country.

Let us now depart from the comparisons between the two nations and focus on Iran and the subject of the book. *A Time to Betray* is an excellent tome, expertly written, personal, passionate, and although it reads like a suspense thriller, it is also interspersed with background material, recounting brief episodes in the history of Iran that are necessary to the narrative. For example, we learn the Iranians had mixed feelings (and many resented) the British and American governments' interference in national affairs. This resentment dated from 1953, when both governments, using the Central Intelligence Agency (CIA) as the vehicle, helped to overthrow the democratically elected President of Iran, Muhammad Mossadegh, a militant nationalist. Mossadegh had nationalized the Iranian oil industry and forced the Shah, a friend of the West, to flee the country.

It was also of historic interest that in 2007, Iranian President Mahmoud Ahmadinejad, while defending his country's right to a nuclear program, remarked, "The country of Iran was heir to a great empire and home to a 2,500-year civilization."[4] I remember my surprise at the statement since I thought the conquests of Mohammed and the religious and cultural revolution of the 7th century—imposed by the victorious Arabs on the conquered Sassanid Persians—had resulted in a new Islamic nation. Moreover, with the fall of the Pahlavi Dynasty in 1979, the last Persian monarchy, the drastic changes brought about by the Islamic Revolution and the inception of an Islamic Republic, a virtual theocracy, gave rise to an even more distinct nation.

The Iranians have a long cultural history as Persians and speak Farsi. The Arabs, who attained historical distinction with the conquests of Mohammed, have a more recent civilization and speak Arabic. Reza's loving grandfather and many other more secular Iranians, cognizant of their heritage, confirmed that cultural interpretation. Iranian nationalists and traditionalists think of themselves as heirs to a distinct but vanishing Persian civilization that has been suppressed culturally by Arab Islamism, and more recently, politically, by the tyranny of the mullahs and the ayatollahs.

The heartrending stories of cruelty and betrayal, as well as dissimulation and bravery, revolve precariously around Reza, who, as a member of the feared Iranian Revolutionary Guards, courageously spied against the ruthless regime he ostensibly served for more than a decade. Suffice to say, the brutality of the regime toward his friends and the Iranian people drastically changed his perspective. Among the information Reza provided to the CIA was vital intelligence that probably prevented the collapse of the Saudi government.

The Iranians had planned to use the Hajj, the religious pilgrimage that Muslims must make to Mecca, to stage a coup d'état in Saudi Arabia. They sent armaments to the Hajj, but most of these were intercepted and many of the militants arrested beforehand, foiling the insurrection. Other information was communicated to the U.S., but not necessarily acted upon by the American government, which through various administrations was bent on placating and not offending the mullahs.

Figure 183: Pilgrims praying near the Kaaba during the Hajj in Mecca, Saudi Arabia, 1907

Although leading a double life took its toll, Reza persisted in his clandestine espionage with the thought of bringing about genuine change for the betterment of his countrymen. How Reza performed his self-appointed mission, and how he survived spying at great personal risk from within the belly of the infernal beast are engrossing topics in *A Time to Betray*.

I would recommend the book not only to scholars of Iranian history but also readers who enjoy nonfiction, recent history, or passionate espionage accounts.

Miguel A. Faria, Jr., M.D., "Spying from the belly of the beast in the Revolutionary Guards of Iran, a book review," *HaciendaPublishing.com*, December 1, 2013. Revised and updated: August 15, 2023

APPENDIX E

TURKEY—
RUSSIA'S NEIGHBOR TO THE SOUTH (2016)

The attempted coup against Turkish president Recep Tayyip Erdoğan in July 2016 demonstrated the perilous state of affairs in Turkey, an important member of NATO and Russia's neighbor and historic traditional enemy. According to the BBC, the coup attempt was a serious one with over 6,000 people detained, particularly army personnel and high-ranking officers: "The sweep included high-ranking soldiers and 2,700 judges... and at least 265 people were killed in clashes as the coup failed."[1]

Part of the problem for Turkey has been the contemptuous attitude of the European Union (EU) that has impeded Turkey's entrance into EU membership. The imperious attitude stems ostensibly from Turkey's authoritarian streak in repressing freedom of speech, prosecutions of militant opponents of the government and the established Turkish order.[2] In other words, the European Union wants Turkey to behave like other liberal (progressive or socialistic) social democracies of Western Europe with political liberalization, political correctness, approved speech, and socially-liberal mores—as if every globalist measure implemented by France and Germany would work in Turkey.

Although Turkey is an Islamic nation, it has been traditionally secular until recently. In the last several decades with resurgent Islam, Turkey has moved toward a more Islamist culture and government. Erdoğan has been forced to walk a tight rope and perform a delicate balancing act between the secular militarists on the one hand and the increasingly stronger Islamists on the other. The EU should take notice of the humbling Brexit act that came from Great Britain and respect Turkey and accept the cultural differences among nations.

But returning to the 2016 coup attempt, the question remained, who was behind it? Erdoğan implicated the Turkish Muslim cleric, Fethullah Gulen, as being behind the plot. In fact, the plot was carried out by a large number of Gulen's followers in Turkey and elsewhere. But Gulen has denied any involvement. Be that as it may, and I believe Erdoğan on this issue, the U.S. should send Mr. Gulen back to Turkey.[3] Gulen came to the United States in 1999 for medical treatment and has remained here ever since. He is no friend of the United States and hampers U.S. relations with Turkey, which has been a reliable NATO ally.

Figure 184: Recep Tayyip Erdoğan, President of the Republic of Turkey, during visit to Lviv, Ukraine, in 2022. President.gov.ua

Instead of investigating the attempted coup and who was responsible, the West listened to the complaints of Noam Chomsky against Erdoğan and the Turkish crackdown. Chomsky not only criticized the Turkish government but also stirred up other "intellectuals" to do the same, at just about the time of the failed coup. Chomsky condemned Turkey's government for violating human rights and cracking down on subversive liberal professors.[4]

Chomsky is treated with great respect and his work is quoted and published in numerous mass media outlets, academic newspapers, and literary journals. His "scholarship" in philosophy and social politics has been widely celebrated, and praise has been heaped on him because of his liberal and progressive leanings—that is, authoritarian socialism, which today is in accord with the left-wing mass media and academia.

However, if one were interested in another Jewish perspective on the Middle East, in particular, and politics, in general, I would recommend the writings of David Horowitz as a balancing act to Chomsky. Horowitz is an impressive Jewish conservative writer, and his biographical and political books are the most perspicacious and brilliant works of literature.

In short, the EU's policies have proven to be disastrous vis-à-vis Western relations with Turkey. Erdoğan has had to reach a historic rapprochement with Vladimir Putin out of necessity, given the adversarial attitude of the EU to Turkey's internal politics. The EU needs to quit rebuffing Erdoğan and Turkey with their uppity demands and outrageous criticisms of a political situation and culture they do not seem to understand.

European Union leaders are a pusillanimous and arrogant bunch, which seem to lack knowledge of geopolitics and the variegated cultures of Eastern nations. Likewise, U.S. President Barack Obama, Secretary of State John Kerry, and the U.S. State Department were no match for Vladimir Putin and Recep Tayyip Erdoğan when it came to an understanding of the geopolitics of the Middle East. Besides, Putin and Erdoğan are nationalists, and both will do what they deem to be in the best interest of their countries.

The rift that developed between Barack Obama and Vladimir Putin was real and unneeded. Obama kowtowed to the EU as well as to militant Islamic and communist leaders. He was very much part of the socialist and internationalist New World Order (NWO) that President Donald Trump and other nationalist European leaders abhorred, such as Viktor Mihály Orbán. For his part, in 2016, Putin delivered a scathing attack on the NWO, and let it be known that any enemy of the NWO was a friend of his.[5]

Unfortunately, Putin's recent turn to despotism and imperialism has deservingly damaged his image, and his counsel today is of little value for most Western leaders. For Erdoğan, the opposite seems to be the case. In recent years, he has conducted himself like a great statesman, and not as the caricature that the globalist media tries to portray.

Miguel A. Faria, Jr., M.D., "The Turkish-Russian conflict—Converting adversity into opportunity," an editorial opinion. *HaciendaPublishing.com*, December 1, 2015. Revised and updated: September 16, 2023

APPENDIX F

LIST OF FIGURE CREDITS

Figure 1 credit: Batum Gendarme Administration/Georgian MIA Academy Archive, II Division (former IMEL Archive)/Public Domain via Wikimedia Commons, https://tinyurl.com/fauynuxm

Figure 2 credit: Gori photographer/Georgian MIA Academy Archive, II Division (former IMEL Archive)/Public Domain via Wikimedia Commons, https://tinyurl.com/46hw4sjz

Figure 3 credit: Eleazar Langman/Public domain via Wikimedia Commons, https://tinyurl.com/mmmkt3m4

Figure 4 credit: Stalin Digital Archive/Mondadori Publishers/Public domain via Wikimedia Commons, https://tinyurl.com/2ru6745a/ https://tinyurl.com/4b9ds3vx

Figure 5 credit: Maria Ulyanova/Public domain via Wikimedia Commons, https://tinyurl.com/yu86vue5

Figure 6 credit: Public domain via Wikimedia Commons, https://tinyurl.com/wkufwwu2

Figure 7 credit: Public domain via Wikimedia Commons, https://tinyurl.com/57nya5au

Figure 8 credit: Grigory Mikhailovich Vayl/RIA Novosti Archive, image #7781/CC-BY-SA 3.0 via Wikimedia Commons, https://tinyurl.com/44nys7ns

Figure 9 credit: Public domain via Wikimedia Commons, https://tinyurl.com/4ju8kutj

Figure 10 credit: Dmitry Rozhkov/CC-BY-SA 3.0 via Wikimedia Commons (image converted to black and white), https://tinyurl.com/ex2nj2n7

Figure 11 credit: Nikolai Petrov/Public domain via Wikimedia Commons, https://tinyurl.com/yeypvfpb

Figure 12 credit: Public domain via Wikimedia Commons (image converted to black and white), https://tinyurl.com/5h2y4x93

Figure 13 credit: CC-BY-SA 4.0 via Wikimedia Commons, https://tinyurl.com/mryurxm6

Figure 14 credit: Public domain via Wikimedia Commons, https://tinyurl.com/2ktkry9d and https://tinyurl.com/ju4jjfjf
Figure 15 credit: Public domain via Wikimedia Commons, https://tinyurl.com/2dpjzmcf
Figure 16 credit: Public domain via Wikimedia Commons, https://tinyurl.com/2p8bwy7d
Figure 17 credit: Public domain via Wikimedia Commons, https://tinyurl.com/4h2v2mns
Figure 18 credit: Public domain via Wikimedia Commons, https://tinyurl.com/bdzzwjfd
Figure 19 credit: Ivan Dubasov/Public domain via Wikimedia Commons (image converted to black and white), https://tinyurl.com/49mkzea5
Figure 20 credit: Associated Press/Public domain via Wikimedia Commons, https://tinyurl.com/2mstmasz
Figure 21 credit: Public domain via Wikimedia Commons, https://tinyurl.com/mrxwsh5x
Figure 22 credit: Public domain via Wikimedia Commons, https://tinyurl.com/pwtj7e69
Figure 23 credit: Public domain via Wikimedia Commons, https://tinyurl.com/5937x52z
Figure 24 credit: George Grantham Bain/Library of Congress, https://tinyurl.com/2h5tt3nv
Figure 25 credit: RIA Novosti Archive, image #6464/CC-BY-SA 3.0 via Wikimedia Commons, https://tinyurl.com/yckbwzma
Figure 26 credit: Public domain via Wikimedia Commons, https://tinyurl.com/yfhz9t7r
Figure 27 credit: Public domain via Wikimedia Commons, https://tinyurl.com/2ufk6e98
Figure 28 credit: Public domain via Wikimedia Commons, https://tinyurl.com/3k5nfe4k
Figure 29 credit: Dutch National Archives, The Hague/Public domain via Wikimedia Commons, https://tinyurl.com/7cd6db3k
Figure 30 credit: Time, Inc./Public domain via Wikimedia Commons (image converted to black and white), https://tinyurl.com/6x52zn5f
Figure 31 credit: German Federal Archives/Public domain via Wikimedia Commons, https://tinyurl.com/yr8mcm68
Figure 32 credit: Eric Koch for Anefo/Dutch National Archives, The Hague/CC-BY-SA 3.0 via Wikimedia Commons, https://tinyurl.com/y376rbbh
Figure 33 credit: Public domain via Wikimedia Commons (image converted to black and white), https://tinyurl.com/32sypmxx

List of Figure Credits 347

Figure 34 credit: Biblioteca Virtual de Defensa, Madrid/Public domain via Wikimedia Commons, https://tinyurl.com/2sjsuh7r
Figure 35 credit: Public domain via Wikimedia Commons, https://tinyurl.com/36m27cjf
Figure 36 credit: Public domain via Wikimedia Commons, https://tinyurl.com/5c9hcs4m
Figure 37 credit: Kurt Alber/Heinrich Hoffmann/German Federal Archives/Public domain via Wikimedia Commons, https://tinyurl.com/34pt353w and https://tinyurl.com/4temtvh8
Figure 38 credit: BBC/Public domain via Wikimedia Commons, https://tinyurl.com/53nmv9fx
Figure 39 credit: Vincenzo Laviosa/Getty Center/Public domain via Wikimedia Commons (image converted to black and white), https://tinyurl.com/3pvsuw4j
Figure 40 credit: Associated Press/Library of Congress/Public domain via Wikimedia Commons, https://tinyurl.com/3hesut8p
Figure 41 credit: Harris & Ewing Photographs/Library of Congress/Public domain via Wikimedia Commons, https://tinyurl.com/twkdnush
Figure 42 credit: Harris & Ewing Photographs/Library of Congress/Public domain via Wikimedia Commons, https://tinyurl.com/yc39p3y7
Figure 43 credit: Dōmei Tsushin/Empire of Japan/Public domain via Wikimedia Commons, https://tinyurl.com/4ukxnrxb
Figure 44 credit: Abbie Rowe/National Archives and Records Administration/Public domain via Wikimedia Commons, https://tinyurl.com/t75jxm3m
Figure 45 credit: New York World-Telegram & Sun Collection/Library of Congress/Public domain via Wikimedia Commons, https://tinyurl.com/2curjmuk
Figure 46 credit: Los Alamos National Laboratory/U.S. Department of Energy/Public domain via Wikimedia Commons (image converted to black and white), https://tinyurl.com/y68yvku2
Figure 47 credit: Ministry of Defence of the Russian Federation/Mil.ru/ CC-BY-SA 4.0 International via Wikimedia Commons, https://tinyurl.com/5n8txzzw
Figure 48: credit: Central Intelligence Agency/Public domain via Wikimedia Commons (image converted to black and white), https://tinyurl.com/6nbmpmyu
Figure 49 credit: U.S. Army/Public domain via Wikimedia Commons, https://tinyurl.com/3sv2ayw3

Figure 50 credit: National Archives and Records Administration/Public domain via Wikimedia Commons, https://tinyurl.com/2anuu5fm
Figure 51 credit: German Federal Archives/CC-BY-SA 3.0 via Wikimedia Commons, https://tinyurl.com/2r4xc552
Figure 52 credit: German Federal Archives/CC-BY-SA 3.0 via Wikimedia Commons, https://tinyurl.com/r2y9fz33
Figure 53 credit: German Federal Archives/CC-BY-SA 3.0 via Wikimedia Commons, https://tinyurl.com/3zp6ua6r
Figure 54 credit: German Federal Archives/CC-BY-SA 3.0 via Wikimedia Commons, https://tinyurl.com/mswxntfu
Figure 55 credit: German Federal Archives/CC-BY-SA 3.0 via Wikimedia Commons, https://tinyurl.com/mr23nybn
Figure 56 credit: German Federal Archives/CC-BY-SA 3.0 via Wikimedia Commons, https://tinyurl.com/52t5z68j
Figure 57 credit: German Federal Archives/CC-BY-SA 3.0 via Wikimedia Commons, https://tinyurl.com/3j53x8bt
Figure 58 credit: U.S. Army Signal Corps/Public domain via Wikimedia Commons, https://tinyurl.com/u46945eh
Figure 59 credit: Library and Archives Canada/Public domain via Wikimedia Commons, https://tinyurl.com/3c9376rs
Figure 60 credit: German Federal Archives/CC-BY-SA 3.0 via Wikimedia Commons, https://tinyurl.com/bddrcjch
Figure 61 credit: TASS/Public domain via Wikimedia Commons, https://tinyurl.com/3mzzstev
Figure 62 credit: Carlosrodriguesw235/CC-BY-SA 4.0 International via Wikimedia Commons, https://tinyurl.com/mpjbptpy
Figure 63 credit: Public domain via Wikimedia Commons, https://tinyurl.com/y4nbnshn
Figure 64 credit: National Archives and Records Administration, https://tinyurl.com/yhvbmzra
Figure 65 credit: German Federal Archives/CC-BY-SA 3.0 via Wikimedia Commons, https://tinyurl.com/4yz3xvha
Figure 66 credit: Ministry of Defence of the Russian Federation/Mil.ru/ CC-BY-SA 4.0 International via Wikimedia Commons, https://tinyurl.com/2s4jdbxv
Figure 67 credit: Ministry of Defence of the Russian Federation/Mil.ru/ CC-BY-SA 4.0 International via Wikimedia Commons, https://tinyurl.com/y6zbsxf4
Figure 68 credit: U.S. Army//Public domain via Wikimedia Commons, https://tinyurl.com/vdnhbuac

List of Figure Credits

Figure 69 credit: Mondadori Publishers/Public domain via Wikimedia Commons, https://tinyurl.com/mr33xahk
Figure 70 credit: Ministry of Defence of the Russian Federation/Mil.ru/ Public domain via Wikimedia Commons, https://tinyurl.com/mrta63uj
Figure 71 credit: Public domain via Wikimedia Commons, https://tinyurl.com/msm2hmwh
Figure 72 credit: Public domain via Wikimedia Commons, https://tinyurl.com/567pbwcc
Figure 73 credit: Public domain via Wikimedia Commons, https://tinyurl.com/4ryad9r6
Figure 74 credit: FSB of the Russian Federation/Public domain via Wikimedia Commons, https://tinyurl.com/mvreev6t
Figure 75 credit: Russian Information Bureau, New York, 1918/Public domain via Wikimedia Commons, https://tinyurl.com/yckfum64
Figure 76 credit: Bert Verhoeff for Anefo/Dutch National Archives, The Hague/Public domain via Wikimedia Commons, https://tinyurl.com/4368t894
Figure 77 credit: Russian Federation State Archive, Moscow/CC-BY-SA 3.0 via Wikimedia Commons, https://tinyurl.com/53ks8rb4
Figure 78 credit: Kaunas 9th Fort Museum/CC-BY-SA 4.0 International via Wikimedia Commons, https://tinyurl.com/2vyakuek
Figure 79 credit: Public domain via Wikimedia Commons, https://tinyurl.com/yxfhstjf
Figure 80 credit: Dmitry Borko/CC-BY-SA 4.0 International via Wikimedia Commons, https://tinyurl.com/5rw8ww89
Figure 81 credit: Public domain via Wikimedia Commons, https://tinyurl.com/5n6vrf9t
Figure 82 credit: Public domain via Wikimedia Commons, https://tinyurl.com/53x4wtuc
Figure 83 credit: Yuryi Abramochkin/RIA Novosti/Public domain via Wikimedia Commons, https://tinyurl.com/23haah63
Figure 84 credit: Presidential Press and Information Office, Kremlin.ru/CC-BY-SA 4.0 International via Wikimedia Commons, https://tinyurl.com/3nhbw7ye
Figure 85 credit: Public domain via Wikimedia Commons, https://tinyurl.com/mu5fs2d4
Figure 86 credit: Helsingin Sanomat/Public domain via Wikimedia Commons, https://tinyurl.com/5n6k85b3
Figure 87 credit: Public domain via Wikimedia Commons, https://tinyurl.com/mubm3huj

350   Appendix F

Figure 88 credit: National Archives and Records Administration/Public domain via Wikimedia Commons, https://tinyurl.com/ycknhdhc
Figure 89 credit: U.S. Army/Public domain via Wikimedia Commons, https://tinyurl.com/3ypbynw3
Figure 90 credit: Public domain via Wikimedia Commons (image converted to black and white), https://tinyurl.com/bddjmcb2
Figure 91 credit: Public domain via Wikimedia Commons, https://tinyurl.com/y9jphzum
Figure 92 credit: Richard Nixon Library Oral History Collection/Public domain via Wikimedia Commons, https://tinyurl.com/63v6sfk9
Figure 93 credit: Public domain via Wikimedia Commons, https://tinyurl.com/38yvs4ee
Figure 94 credit: Public domain via Wikimedia Commons, https://tinyurl.com/mrzkvty7
Figure 95 credit: Public domain via Wikimedia Commons, https://tinyurl.com/42u9djxt
Figure 96 credit: Public domain via Wikimedia Commons, https://tinyurl.com/4m6696zj
Figure 97 credit: Public domain via Wikimedia Commons, https://tinyurl.com/nsh9says
Figure 98 credit: Public domain via Wikimedia Commons, https://tinyurl.com/44ene52j
Figure 99 credit: CC-BY-SA 3.0 via Wikimedia Commons (image converted to black and white), https://tinyurl.com/4rkxpd56
Figure 100 credit: Public domain via Wikimedia Commons, https://tinyurl.com/yf93hfvm
Figure 101 credit: Rolf Müller/CC-BY-SA 3.0 via Wikimedia Commons (image converted to black and white), https://tinyurl.com/44fcb3r7
Figure 102 credit: Public domain via Wikimedia Commons, https://tinyurl.com/2ywtd37w
Figure 103 credit: Public domain via Wikimedia Commons, https://tinyurl.com/ydcwe77x
Figure 104 credit: Paul Keller/CC-BY-SA 2.0 Generic via Wikimedia Commons (image converted to black and white), https://tinyurl.com/4tzprn36
Figure 105 credit: Bob McNeely, The White House/Public domain via Wikimedia Commons (image converted to black and white), https://tinyurl.com/2vkkwycj
Figure 106 credit: Sikarin Thanachaiary/World Economic Forum/CC-BY-SA 2.0 Generic via Wikimedia Commons (image converted to black and white), https://tinyurl.com/mr3r88p9

Figure 107 credit: U.S. Government/Public domain via Wikimedia Commons (image converted to black and white), https://tinyurl.com/4r9na2ax
Figure 108 credit: Voice of America/Public domain via Wikimedia Commons (image converted to black and white), https://tinyurl.com/3wcahpvp
Figure 109 credit: Oliver Atkins, U.S. Government/Public domain via Wikimedia Commons (image converted to black and white), https://tinyurl.com/ycykprrx
Figure 110 credit: Michael Evans, Executive Office of the President of the United States/Public domain via Wikimedia Commons (image converted to black and white), https://tinyurl.com/e8fwz22a
Figure 111 credit: Alan Santos/Retouching by Roman Kubanskiy/CC-BY-SA 4.0 via Wikimedia Commons (image converted to black and white), https://tinyurl.com/2s4c5x48
Figure 112 credit: National Archives and Records Administration/Public domain via Wikimedia Commons (image converted to black and white), https://tinyurl.com/yrthdnnz
Figure 113 credit: Pete Campolongo/U.S. Department of State/Public domain via Wikimedia Commons, https://tinyurl.com/mmxybdve
Figure 114 credit: Palace Museum Press, Beijing/Public domain via Wikimedia Commons (image converted to black and white), https://tinyurl.com/ypyc6vr2
Figure 115 credit: U.S. Department of Energy/Public domain via Wikimedia Commons (image converted to black and white), https://tinyurl.com/2ykvn3ck
Figure 116 credit: National Archives and Records Administration/Public domain via Wikimedia Commons, https://tinyurl.com/25hny746
Figure 117 credit: Public domain via Wikimedia Commons (image converted to black and white)/ Truman Library, https://tinyurl.com/ypbmtj2w and https://tinyurl.com/4nj5te4k
Figure 118 credit: Department of Foreign Affairs and Trade, Australia/CC-BY-SA 4.0 International via Wikimedia Commons (image converted to black and white), https://tinyurl.com/4dyz7kmc
Figure 119 credit: U.S. Department of Justice, Office of Public Affairs/Public domain via Wikimedia Commons, (image converted to black and white), https://tinyurl.com/yvfzaefu
Figure 120 credit: Shealah Craighead, Executive Office of the President of the United States/Public domain via Wikimedia Commons (image converted to black and white), https://tinyurl.com/34e3xn4f

Figure 121 credit: U.S. Department of Justice/Public domain via Wikimedia Commons (image converted to black and white), https://tinyurl.com/5n8cw9u7
Figure 122 credit: Kris Snibbe, Harvard Public Affairs & Communications/ CC-BY-SA 4.0 International via Wikimedia Commons (image converted to black and white), https://tinyurl.com/mrx67v9d
Figure 123 credit: Ureem2805/CC-BY-SA 4.0 International via Wikimedia Commons (image converted to black and white), https://tinyurl.com/44rjxttf
Figure 124 credit: U.S. Department of Defense/Public domain via Wikimedia Commons (image converted to black and white), https://tinyurl.com/d8wz2f6f
Figure 125 credit: Osunpokeh/CC-BY-SA 4.0 International via Wikimedia Commons, https://tinyurl.com/ymby3dns
Figure 126 credit: K.E. Voroshilov/Public domain via Wikimedia Commons (image converted to black and white), https://tinyurl.com/yckesfud
Figure 127 credit: Public domain via Wikimedia Commons (image converted to black and white), https://tinyurl.com/yc7cnyyy and https://tinyurl.com/2udxcuuc
Figure 128 credit: Mary Anne Fackelman, Ronald Reagan Presidential Library/Public domain via Wikimedia Commons (image converted to black and white), https://tinyurl.com/y8nxpb87
Figure 129 credit: Tanya Hart/CC-BY-SA 2.0 Generic via Wikimedia Commons, https://tinyurl.com/34v2uncs
Figure 130 credit: Mémoires de Guerre/U.S. Government/Public domain via Wikimedia Commons, https://tinyurl.com/yc7jb47w and https://tinyurl.com/ynbckyh5
Figure 131 credit: Public domain via Wikimedia Commons (image converted to black and white), https://tinyurl.com/428mbuuf
Figure 132 credit: Patrick Caproni/CC-BY-SA 4.0 International via Wikimedia Commons, https://tinyurl.com/4vjm5tdp
Figure 133 credit: Central Intelligence Agency/Public domain via Wikimedia Commons (image converted to black and white), https://tinyurl.com/wrdpt985
Figure 134 credit: Public domain via Wikimedia Commons (image converted to black and white), https://tinyurl.com/4rxe3rxz
Figure 135 credit: Public domain via Wikimedia Commons (image converted to black and white), https://tinyurl.com/35fxvdy4

Figure 136 credit: Central Intelligence Agency/Public domain via Wikimedia Commons (image converted to black and white), https://tinyurl.com/4vya3jxt
Figure 137 credit: A. Savin/CC-BY-SA 3.0 via Wikimedia Commons (image converted to black and white), https://tinyurl.com/323bcuy7
Figure 138 credit: National Security Agency/Public domain via Wikimedia Commons, https://tinyurl.com/2tt428mk and https://tinyurl.com/37bmy35s
Figure 139 credit: Public domain via Wikimedia Commons, https://tinyurl.com/5fc7dx7h
Figure 140 credit: Public domain via Wikimedia Commons, https://tinyurl.com/muhzdh35
Figure 141 credit: Federal Bureau of Investigation/Public domain via Wikimedia Commons, https://tinyurl.com/4yebbwb4
Figure 142 credit: Associated Press/Public domain via Wikimedia Commons, https://tinyurl.com/mw9tjshn
Figure 143 credit: United Press International/Public domain via Wikimedia Commons, https://tinyurl.com/bdpstbpn, https://tinyurl.com/yc7hdavj and https://tinyurl.com/yh5tv8eb
Figure 144 credit: Public domain via Wikimedia Commons, https://tinyurl.com/3yn77ezf
Figure 145 credit: Associated Press/Public domain via Wikimedia Commons, https://tinyurl.com/5jmrxtjy
Figure 146 credit: Public domain via Wikimedia Commons, https://tinyurl.com/39v9kncw
Figure 147 credit: Pelz/CC-BY-SA 3.0 via Wikimedia Commons, https://tinyurl.com/4nn3wj3t
Figure 148 credit: Comet Photo AG (Zürich)/CC-BY-SA 4.0 International via Wikimedia Commons (image converted to black and white), https://tinyurl.com/azj8wfu2
Figure 149 credit: SPC 5 James Cavalier, U.S. Military/Public domain via Wikimedia Commons (image converted to black and white), https://tinyurl.com/mwmajjvz
Figure 150 credit: Anefo/Dutch National Archives/Public domain via Wikimedia Commons, https://tinyurl.com/3rzvhtad
Figure 151 credit: Federal Bureau of Investigation/Public domain via Wikimedia Commons, https://tinyurl.com/3ekn965e
Figure 152 credit: Dutch National Archives, The Hague/CC-BY-SA 3.0 via Wikimedia Commons, https://tinyurl.com/3w5dxb4x

Figure 153 credit: Public domain via Wikimedia Commons (image converted to black and white), https://tinyurl.com/4m3zz3xa
Figure 154 credit: Balmore A. Ramos, National Archives and Records Administration/Public domain via Wikimedia Commons (image converted to black and white), https://tinyurl.com/bdnnzb52
Figure 155 credit: Presidential Press and Information Office, Kremlin.ru/ Public domain via Wikimedia Commons (image converted to black and white), https://tinyurl.com/mr3d2rx9
Figure 156 credit: Ethan Doyle White/CC-BY-SA 4.0 International via Wikimedia Commons (image converted to black and white), https://tinyurl.com/2ajdkjjc
Figure 157 credit: Blaues Sofa/CC-BY-SA 2.0 Generic via Wikimedia Commons (image converted to black and white), https://tinyurl.com/yabfsfmc
Figure 158 credit: Peter Curbishley/CC-BY-SA 2.5 Generic via Wikimedia Commons (image converted to black and white), https://tinyurl.com/3nry97u9
Figure 159 credit: Dmitry Aleshkovskiy/CC-BY-SA 2.0 Generic via Wikimedia Commons (image converted to black and white), https://tinyurl.com/47nwmsut
Figure 160 credit: Press Service of the President of the Russian Federation, Kremlin.ru/CC-BY-SA 4.0 International via Wikimedia Commons (image converted to black and white), https://tinyurl.com/4vdpza8e
Figure 161 credit: Norman Einstein/CC-BY-SA 3.0 via Wikimedia Commons (image converted to black and white), https://tinyurl.com/yzuabjtw
Figure 162 credit: Addicted04/CC-BY-SA 3.0 via Wikimedia Commons (image converted to black and white), https://tinyurl.com/7s44kbhy
Figure 163 credit: Jamie Eilat/CC-BY-SA 4.0 International via Wikimedia Commons (image converted to black and white), https://tinyurl.com/y77hwycw
Figure 164 credit: Public domain via Wikimedia Commons, https://tinyurl.com/ye26h9pz
Figure 165 credit: Travelpleb/CC-BY-SA 3.0 via Wikimedia Commons (image converted to black and white), https://tinyurl.com/562sxjky
Figure 166 credit: Avi Ohayon, Government Press Office/CC-BY-SA 3.0 via Wikimedia Commons (image converted to black and white), https://tinyurl.com/4zwdk68e
Figure 167 credit: Mikhail Evstafiev/CC-BY-SA 2.5 Generic via Wikimedia Commons (image converted to black and white), https://tinyurl.com/m83367kr

List of Figure Credits 355

Figure 168 credit: Kremlin.ru/CC-BY-SA 4.0 International via Wikimedia Commons, https://tinyurl.com/4as6k28x
Figure 169 credit: Randam/CC-BY-SA 4.0 International via Wikimedia Commons, https://tinyurl.com/3nwstd4r
Figure 170 credit: President.gov.ua/CC-BY-SA 4.0 International via Wikimedia Commons, https://tinyurl.com/2y73eceu
Figure 171 credit: President.gov.ua/Public domain via Wikimedia Commons, https://tinyurl.com/bdf923wp
Figure 172 credit: Ministry of Internal Affairs of Ukraine, Mvs.gov.ua/CC-BY-SA 4.0 International via Wikimedia Commons, https://tinyurl.com/pwsr4uhh
Figure 173 credit: Ministry of Defence of the Russian Federation, Mil.ru/CC-BY-SA 4.0 International via Wikimedia Commons, https://tinyurl.com/4shhtdze
Figure 174 credit: Government of the Russian Federation/CC-BY-SA 3.0 via Wikimedia Commons (image converted to black and white), https://tinyurl.com/35v6nx3u
Figure 175 credit: Public domain via Wikimedia Commons, https://tinyurl.com/hfxb2rku
Figure 176 credit: Ernmuhl/CC-BY-SA 3.0 via Wikimedia Commons, https://tinyurl.com/2p8vbb8d
Figure 177 credit: Central Intelligence Agency/Public domain via Wikimedia Commons, https://tinyurl.com/5yf9ecr5
Figure 178 credit: Central Intelligence Agency/Central Intelligence Agency/Public domain via Wikimedia Commons (image converted to black and white), https://tinyurl.com/tc368vz2
Figure 179 credit: Hamid Mir/Public domain via Wikimedia Commons (image converted to black and white), https://tinyurl.com/mpn7ruk8
Figure 180 credit: Mass Communication Specialist 2nd Class David Quillen, U.S. Navy/CC-BY-SA 2.0 Generic via Wikimedia Commons (image converted to black and white), https://tinyurl.com/53nw6b38
Figure 181 credit: Tamir Eshel/Defense Update (image converted to black and white), https://tinyurl.com/4tucfahj
Figure 182 credit: Public domain via Wikimedia Commons (image converted to black and white), https://tinyurl.com/vx28d2a3
Figure 183 credit: Public domain via Wikimedia Commons, https://tinyurl.com/y8mfsm83
Figure 184 credit: President.gov.ua/CC-BY-SA 4.0 International via Wikimedia Commons (image converted to black and white), https://tinyurl.com/erf58xmp

356 Appendix F

Color Centerfold Credits

Plate 1 credit: National Archives and Records Administration/Public domain via Wikimedia Commons, https://tinyurl.com/bde9573y
Plate 2 credit: Time, Inc./Public domain via Wikimedia Commons, https://tinyurl.com/6x52zn5f
Plate 3 credit: Archivi Mondadori/CC-BY-SA 4.0 International via Wikimedia Commons, https://tinyurl.com/mr2cj5t9
Plate 4 credit: White House Photographic Collection/Public domain via Wikimedia Commons, https://tinyurl.com/46h58wft
Plate 5 credit: Thierry Noir/CC-BY-SA 3.0 via Wikimedia Commons, https://tinyurl.com/yscm2y9p
Plate 6 credit: White House Photographic Collection/Public domain via Wikimedia Commons, https://tinyurl.com/vf6ffskc
Plate 7 credit: Mary Anne Fackelman, Ronald Reagan Presidential Library/Public domain via Wikimedia Commons, https://tinyurl.com/ypc89493
Plate 8 credit: National Archives and Records Administration/Public domain via Wikimedia Commons, https://tinyurl.com/4c2r3jss
Plate 9 credit: Troublemaker1949/Public domain via Wikimedia Commons, https://tinyurl.com/3b55yude
Plate 10 credit: Voice of America/Public domain via Wikimedia Commons, https://tinyurl.com/3d4na728

Front Cover Collage Credits

Top Left credit: U.S. Signal Corps/Public domain via Wikimedia Commons, https://tinyurl.com/35cc54e2
Top Center credit: Lyxacii Falgen/CC-BY-SA 4.0 International via Wikimedia Commons, https://tinyurl.com/bdes8247
Top Right credit: People's Republic of China Printing Office/Public domain via Wikimedia Commons, https://tinyurl.com/mu5fs2d4
Middle Left credit: Eric Koch for Anefo/Dutch National Archives, The Hague/CC-BY-SA 3.0 via Wikimedia Commons, https://tinyurl.com/2wysbcdt
Middle Center credit: Bert Verhoeff for Anefo/Dutch National Archives, The Hague/Public domain via Wikimedia Commons, https://tinyurl.com/4368t894
Middle Right credit: Public domain via Wikimedia Commons (image converted to black and white), https://tinyurl.com/43f4j6rb

Bottom Left credit: Kremlin.ru/CC-BY-SA 4.0 International via Wikimedia Commons, https://tinyurl.com/2zz9mee5
Bottom Center credit: CC-BY-SA 3.0 via Wikimedia Commons, https://tinyurl.com/mrxnhsfx
Bottom Right credit: China News Service/CC-BY-SA 3.0 via Wikimedia Commons, https://tinyurl.com/3yznkbhe

NOTES

Introduction

1. Karl Marx, *The Communist Manifesto* (Appleton, WI: American Opinion, 1974), 3.
2. Miguel A. Faria, Jr., "Stalin, communists, and fatal statistics," *HaciendaPublishing.com*, January 8, 2012.
3. For two books that most accurately describe, epitomize, and exemplify the evils of totalitarianism and communism, see Aleksandr Solzhenitsyn, *The Gulag Archipelago (1918–1956): An Experiment in Literary Investigation, Parts I-II—The Prison Industry and Perpetual Motion,* trans. Thomas P. Whitney (New York: Harper & Row, 1974); and Aleksandr Solzhenitsyn, *The Gulag Archipelago (1918–1956): An Experiment in Literary Investigation, Parts III-IV—The Destructive Labor Camps and The Soul and Barbed Wire,* trans. Thomas P. Whitney (New York: Harper & Row, 1975).
4. For an excellent book on why and how Vladimir Putin came to power in Russia and his ruthless methods in consolidating power in post-communist Russia, see Alex Goldfarb, and Marina Litvinenko, *Death of a Dissident: The Poisoning of Alexander Litvinenko and the Return of the KGB* (New York: Free Press, 2007).
5. James H. Billington, *Fire in the Minds of Men: Origins of the Revolutionary Faith* (New Brunswick, NJ: Transaction Publishers, 1999).
6. Besides standard textbooks on Russia and China in the 20th and 21st centuries, I recommend a couple of books for the initiate: Orlando Figes, *Revolutionary Russia, 1891–1991: A History* (New York: Henry Holt and Company, 2014); and for Stalin, the reader will encounter several great tomes cited throughout this book. For China and Mao Tse-tung, I recommend for the initiate as well as for scholars: Jung Chang and Jon Halliday*, Mao: The Unknown Story* (New York: Alfred A. Knopf, 2005). For a history of the KGB and the repressive apparatus of the Soviet Union from its inception until just before its collapse, see Christopher Andrew and Oleg Gordievsky, *KGB: The Inside Story of Its Foreign Operations from Lenin to Gorbachev* (New York: Harper Collins, 1990). For the events surrounding the East European Show

Trials orchestrated by Stalin, a period that followed after World War II when Stalin seized a large part of Central and all of Eastern Europe, except notably Albania and Yugoslavia, I recommend: Tony Sharp, *Stalin's American Spy: Noel Field, Allen Dulles and the East European Show Trials* (London: Hurst & Company, 2014), especially because events relating to the East European Show Trials are not covered in the present book.

Part I

Chapter 1

1. Simon Sebag Montefiore, *Young Stalin* (London: Weidenfeld & Nicolson, 2007), 1-11.
2. Miguel A. Faria, Jr., "Stalin, communists, and fatal statistics," *HaciendaPublishing.com*, January 8, 2012.
3. Montefiore, *Young Stalin*, 15-74.
4. While some Tsarist prison conditions could be harsh, exile in Siberia was relatively lenient for exiled revolutionaries. Fyodor Dostoevsky spent four years in a forced-labor, prison camp in Siberia, following his conviction for involvement in the Petrashevsky Circle. Those were very difficult years but, ironically, his subsequent years in exile in Siberia were much better. Therefore, one must not confuse Russia's Tsarist legacy of autocracy and authoritarianism with Soviet-style communism and totalitarianism. In fact, Dostoevsky could not muster approval from the Tsar's censors for some of his passages because his description of life in exile was deemed too comfortable and would invite criminals to commit crimes to get there. Compare that to the much more severe and savage Soviet Gulag system. Imagine the irony when Dostoevsky had to edit his manuscript (magnify his discomfort in exile) in order to pass the censors and get published in Tsarist Russia. See: Fyodor Dostoevsky, *The House of the Dead* (St. Petersburg: Yremya, 1860–62). In several passages in his books, Aleksandr Solzhenitsyn also mentioned the Tsarist prison and exile system and found it to be very lenient and in no way comparable to the brutal communist Gulag, destructive labor camps, see Aleksandr Solzhenitsyn, *The Gulag Archipelago (1918–1956): An Experiment in Literary Investigation, Parts I-II—The Prison Industry and Perpetual Motion*, trans. Thomas P Whitney (New York: Harper & Row, 1974) and Aleksandr Solzhenitsyn, *The Gulag Archipelago (1918–1956): An Experiment in Literary Investigation, Parts III-IV—The Destructive Labor Camps and The Soul and Barbed*

Wire, trans. Thomas P. Whitney (New York: Harper & Row, 1975). For a colorful and autobiographical novel of Solzhenitsyn's description of life and his serious illness while living in Soviet exile after his imprisonment, survival, and release from the Gulag, see Aleksandr Solzhenitsyn, *Cancer Ward,* trans. Nicholas Bethell and David Burg (New York: Bantam Books, 1972).
5. Montefiore, *Young Stalin,* 92n1.
6. Montefiore, *Young Stalin,* 95-96.
7. Montefiore, *Young Stalin,* 98.
8. Robert E. Quirk, *Fidel Castro* (New York: W.W. Norton & Company, 1993), 2-12, 72-75. This book is the most comprehensive biography of the Cuban communist dictator to date; yet it is quite readable. Quirk's scholarship is superlative. No other book about the life of Fidel Castro comes close to matching this objective magnum opus. See also: Miguel A. Faria, Jr., *Cuba in Revolution: Escape From a Lost Paradise* (Macon, GA: Hacienda Publishing, Inc., 2002), 29-37; and Miguel A. Faria, Jr., *Cuba's Eternal Revolution through the Prism of Insurgency, Socialism, and Espionage* (Newcastle upon Tyne, UK: Cambridge Scholars Publishing, 2023). *Cuba's Eternal Revolution* notes the salient points contained in Quirk's book as well as other writers like the psychological analysis of Fidel Castro contained in Brian Latell, *After Fidel: The Inside Story of Castro's Regime and Cuba's Next Leader* (New York: Palgrave Macmillan, 2005), 114-132. The similarities in the personalities of Joseph Stalin and Fidel Castro are striking.
9. The comparison between Joseph Stalin and Fidel Castro is further accentuated as they became older and assumed supreme power, see Miguel A. Faria, Jr., *Cuba's Eternal Revolution through the Prism of Insurgency, Socialism, and Espionage* (Newcastle upon Tyne, UK: Cambridge Scholars Publishing, 2023); and Simon Sebag Montefiore, *Stalin: The Court of the Red Tsar* (New York: Alfred A. Knopf, 2004). Lord Acton's aphorism comes from an observation he made in a letter to Bishop Creighton on April 5, 1887. The letter was published in 1907 as part of a collection of Lord Acton's works, see John Acton, *Historical Essays and Studies,* ed. John Neville Figgis and Reginald Vere Laurence (London: Macmillan and Company, Ltd., 1908).
10. The evolving sour relationship that existed between Joseph Stalin and Leon Trotsky is captured in the narrative of Dmitri Volkogonov, *Stalin: Triumph and Tragedy* (New York: Grove Press, 1991), 44-47, 56-57, 61, 74-75.
11. Vladimir Lenin's state of mind is eloquently analyzed in Aleksandr Solzhenitsyn, *November 1916: The Red Wheel,* trans. H.T. Willets (New

York: Farrar, Straus and Giroux, 1999), which contains Solzhenitsyn's famous psychological-historical "Lenin in Zurich" essay.
12. The possibility that Joseph Stalin may have served as an Okhrana agent at the time he was a bandit revolutionary has not been completely disproved despite Montefiore's view to the contrary. For an alternative theory of Stalin as a possible Okhrana agent and other related items, see Miguel A. Faria, Jr., "The astounding case of Soviet defection deception," *HaciendaPublishing.com*, October 31, 2003.
13. Montefiore, *Young Stalin*, 329.

Chapter 2

1. Dmitri Volkogonov, *Stalin: Triumph and Tragedy* (New York: Grove Press, 1991).
2. Volkogonov, *Stalin: Triumph and Tragedy*, 30n1.
3. Volkogonov, *Stalin: Triumph and Tragedy*, 54-66.
4. Volkogonov, *Stalin: Triumph and Tragedy*, 57-62, 67-75.
5. For the relationship between Joseph Stalin and Leon Trotsky, see Volkogonov, *Stalin: Triumph and Tragedy*, 44-47, 56-57. For Trotsky's assignation of "outstanding mediocrity" to Stalin, see Leon Trotsky, *Stalin: An Appraisal of the Man and His Influence*, trans. Charles Malamuth (New York: Grosset & Dunlap, 1941), 392-393.
6. Volkogonov, *Stalin: Triumph and Tragedy*, 61-144, 275-340.
7. Miguel A. Faria, Jr., "Stalin, communists, and fatal statistics," *HaciendaPublishing.com*, January 8, 2012.
8. Miguel A. Faria, Jr., "Bastille Day and the French Revolution (Part I): The Ancien Régime and the storming of the Bastille," *Newsmax.com*, July 15, 2004. https://haciendapublishing.com/bastille-day-and-the-french-revolution-part-i-the-ancien-regime-and-the-storming-of-the-bastille/.
9. For an engaging and well-organized book for scholars and readers interested in further details on Soviet history and Stalinism, see Robert Conquest, *Stalin, Breaker of Nations* (New York: Penguin Random House, 1991).
10. Conquest, *Stalin, Breaker of Nations*, 76.
11. Conquest, *Stalin, Breaker of Nations*, 172-173.
12. Conquest, *Stalin, Breaker of Nations*, 176-181.
13. Conquest, *Stalin, Breaker of Nations*, 178-221.
14. Joseph Conrad, *Under Western Eyes* (New York: Harper & Brothers, 1911).

15. More will be said about a generic, fictionalized, and introspective Nikolai Bukharin during his last few hours of life when, in chapter 4, we examine the historical novel and literary masterpiece by Arthur Koestler, *Darkness at Noon*, trans. Daphne Hardy (Norwalk, CT: Easton Press, 2000).
16. Conquest, *Stalin, Breaker of Nations*, 96-104. See also: Volkogonov, *Stalin: Triumph and Tragedy*, 67-98.
17. Conquest, *Stalin, Breaker of Nations*, 106-107
18. Jonathan Brent and Vladimir P. Naumov, *Stalin's Last Crime: The Plot Against the Jewish Doctors, 1948-1953* (New York: Harper Collins, 2003).
19. Edvard Radzinsky, *Stalin: The First In-depth Biography Based on Explosive New Documents from Russia's Secret Archives*, trans. H.T. Willets (New York: Anchor Books, 1997). This magnificent and absorbing tome is necessary reading for the initiate student as well as the savvy scholar of Soviet history, Stalinism, and the life of Joseph Stalin.
20. Radzinsky, *Stalin*, xi-xii.
21. David Horowitz, "Socialism by any other name," *National Review*, April 13, 1992, 30-35.
22. Miguel A. Faria, Jr., *Controversies in Medicine and Neuroscience: Through the Prism of History, Neurobiology and Bioethics* (Newcastle upon Tyne, UK: Cambridge Scholars Publishing, 2023), 129-142.
23. Radzinsky, *Stalin*, 517-581.
24. Simon Sebag Montefiore, *Stalin: The Court of the Red Tsar* (New York: Alfred A. Knopf, 2004.)

Chapter 3

1. The total number of Joseph Stalin's victims and the full extent of the massive human devastation he caused may never be fully known, but it is safe to say the toll was enormous—perhaps only surpassed by Mao Tse-tung and the communist Chinese. Some revisionist historians more recently have come up with lower figures attempting to soften the devastation of Stalin's long-term reign of terror; but the sources listed here provide the more conventional statistics gathered by historians in the 20th century and early 21st century and to this author have proved to be the most convincing figures to date. Unless otherwise cited, the information in this chapter, the estimates, and the figures cited were gathered from the following sources: Robert Conquest, *The Great Terror: Stalin's Purge of the Thirties* (New York: The Macmillan Company, 1968); Robert Conquest, *The Great Terror: A Reassessment*

(Oxford: Oxford University Press, 1990); Stéphane Courtois and Mark Kramer, *The Black Book of Communism: Crimes, Terror, Repression* (Cambridge, MA: Harvard University Press, 1999); Roy A. Medvedev, *Let History Judge: The Origins and Consequences of Stalinism* (New York: Alfred A. Knopf; 1972); Simon Sebag Montefiore, *Stalin: The Court of the Red Tsar* (New York: Alfred A. Knopf, 2004); Edvard Radzinsky, *Stalin: The First In-depth Biography Based on Explosive New Documents from Russia's Secret Archives*, trans. H.T. Willets (New York: Anchor Books, 1997); R. J. Rummel, *Death By Government: Genocide and Mass Murder Since 1900* (New Brunswick, NJ: Transaction Publishers, 1994); and Dmitri Volkogonov, *Stalin: Triumph and Tragedy* (New York: Grove Press, 1991).

2. For the quote by Joseph Stalin, see Marc Jansen and Nikita Petrov, *Stalin's Loyal Executioner: People's Commissar Nikolai Ezhov 1895-1940* (Stanford, CA: Hoover Institution Press, 2002), 195.

3. Volkogonov, *Stalin: Triumph and Tragedy*, 61-144, 275-340.

4. John Costello and Oleg Tsarev, *Deadly Illusions: The KGB Orlov Dossier Reveals Stalin's Master Spy* (New York: Crown Publisher's, Inc., 1993), 274; and Volkogonov. *Stalin: Triumph and Tragedy*, 41, 66, 87, 164.

5. S.V. Bezberezhev, "Maria Alexandrovna Spiridonova," *Voprosy istorii*, No. 9, 1990. For the fate of Spiridonova, see *Politicheskii Dnevnik 1964-1970*, Amsterdam, 1972, p. 726, referenced in Harrison E. Salisbury, *Black Night, White Snow: Russia's Revolutions 1905-1917* (Franklin Center, PA: The Franklin Library, 1977), 582n2. See also: Alexander Rabinowitch, "Maria Spiridonova's 'last testament,' " *Russian Review*, Vol. 54, No. 3 (July 1995), 424-446.

6. For details about the methods of assassinations or "wet affairs," and events surrounding the assassination of Leon Trotsky in Mexico City in 1940, revealed by one of the main NKVD protagonists in the drama, see Pavel Sudoplatov, Anatoli Sudoplatov, Jerrold L. Schechter, and Leona P. Schechter, *Special Tasks: Memoirs of an Unwanted Witness a Soviet Spymaster* (Boston: Little, Brown and Company, 1994), 65-83. See also: Christopher Andrew and Oleg Gordievsky, *KGB: The Inside Story of Its Foreign Operations from Lenin to Gorbachev* (New York: Harper Collins, 1990), 167-172; and Christopher Andrew and Vasili Mitrokhin, *The Sword and the Shield: The Mitrokhin Archive and the Secret History of the KGB* (New York: Basic Books, 1999), 76, 86-88.

7. Costello and Tsarev, *Deadly Illusions*, 134-170, 198-212, 237-242, 295-296, 312.

8. Andrew and Gordievsky, *KGB*, 56-67, 79; and Andrew and Mitrokhin, *The Sword and the Shield*, 173-232.
9. Andrew and Gordievsky, *KGB*, 43, 55-65, 78-79, 81, 281; and Andrew and Mitrokhin, *The Sword and the Shield*, 201-204, 212-217, 220-225.
10. Andrew and Gordievsky, *KGB*, 48, 59, 63-67, 78- 83, 91; and Andrew and Mitrokhin, *The Sword and the Shield*, 183,198-201, 213, 217-224, 325.
11. Andrew and Gordievsky, *KGB*, 50-52, 78.
12. Andrew and Gordievsky, *KGB*, 45,50, 80-81; and Andrew and Mitrokhin, *The Sword and the Shield*, 138-140, 148-149, 160-163, 198, 217, 237, 244.
13. For a biography of Stalin's diminutive executioner during the Great Terror (1937–1938), Nikolai Yezhov, and the gruesome accounts of his victims as well as his own execution, see Marc Jansen and Nikita Petrov, *Stalin's Loyal Executioner: People's Commissar Nikolai Ezhov 1895-1940* (Stanford, CA: Hoover Institution Press, 2002), xi, 50, 53-54, 188-189, 210.
14. Andrew and Gordievsky, *KGB*, 26-27; and Andrew and Mitrokhin, *The Sword and the Shield*, 158, 173-175.
15. Volkogonov. *Stalin: Triumph and Tragedy*, 316-329.
16. Andrew and Gordievsky, *KGB*, 49-50, 54, 155, 168; Andrew and Mitrokhin, *The Sword and the Shield*, 40-41; and Radzinsky, *Stalin*, 146-148. See also: Conquest, *The Great Terror*, 29.
17. Andrew and Gordievsky, *KGB*, 44, 63-64.
18. Andrew and Gordievsky, *KGB*, 89, 174, 225; Andrew and Mitrokhin, *The Sword and the Shield*, 26, 53; Harrison E. Salisbury, *Black Night, White Snow: Russia's Revolutions 1905-1917* (Franklin Center, PA: The Franklin Library, 1977), 583n1; and Aleksandr Solzhenitsyn, *The Gulag Archipelago (1918–1956): An Experiment in Literary Investigation, Parts I-II—The Prison Industry and Perpetual Motion,* trans. Thomas P. Whitney (New York: Harper & Row, 1974), 622.
19. Andrew and Gordievsky, *KGB*, 341-343, 382, 416, 420, 443; Andrew and Mitrokhin, *The Sword and the Shield*, 146; and Radzinsky, *Stalin*, 513, 518, 520, 528, 530-531, 551-553.
20. Jonathan Brent and Vladimir P. Naumov, *Stalin's Last Crime: The Plot Against the Jewish Doctors, 1948-1953* (New York: Harper Collins, 2003), 122-145, 310-311.
21. For an idealized but well-written and researched history of the Russian Revolutions of 1905 and 1917, see Salisbury, *Black Night, White Snow,* xx, xxii, 397-405. This book provided a surreal look at what was to come, and made researchers aware of Roy A. Medvedev's work.

22. Salisbury, *Black Night, White Snow*, 544n. See also: Medvedev, *Let History Judge*, 201; and Volkogonov. *Stalin: Triumph and Tragedy*, 345.
23. Salisbury, *Black Night, White Snow*, xxii, 483-484, 541-542.
24. Andrew and Gordievsky, *KGB*, 83-84, 136, 417; Radzinsky, *Stalin*, 349-350; and Volkogonov. *Stalin: Triumph and Tragedy*, 285.
25. Brent and Naumov, *Stalin's Last Crime*, 212-327. See also: Andrew and Gordievsky, *KGB*, 414, 420; Radzinsky, *Stalin*, 495, 504, 529-532; Sudoplatov, *Special Tasks*, 296-297; and Volkogonov. *Stalin: Triumph and Tragedy*, 567.
26. Salisbury, *Black Night, White Snow*, 251-257, 413-415. See also: Montefiore, *Stalin: The Court of the Red Tsar*, 101. As to how the Soviet state attempted to portray Vladimir Mayakovsky, see Chantal Sundaram, *Manufacturing Culture: The Soviet State and the Mayakovsky Legend 1930-1993* (Ottawa, Canada: National Library of Canada: Acquisitions and Bibliographical Services, 2000). For the suffering and travails of members of the intelligentsia who were banned, purged, arrested, and sent to the Gulag, see Anne Applebaum, *Gulag: A History* (New York: Doubleday, 2003); Brent and Naumov, *Stalin's Last Crime*; Montefiore, *Stalin: The Court of the Red Tsar*; Radzinsky, *Stalin*; and Solzhenitsyn, *The Gulag Archipelago (1918-1956): An Experiment in Literary Investigation, Parts I-II—The Prison Industry and Perpetual Motion*; and Aleksandr Solzhenitsyn, *The Gulag Archipelago (1918-1956): An Experiment in Literary Investigation, Parts III-IV—The Destructive Labor Camps and The Soul and Barbed Wire*, trans. Thomas P. Whitney (New York: Harper & Row, 1975). For Polina Molotova's travails, see Montefiore, *Stalin: The Court of the Red Tsar*, 651.
27. Brent and Naumov, *Stalin's Last Crime*, 233-270.
28. Brent and Naumov, *Stalin's Last Crime*, 93-103, 107, 111-112, 159-170. See also: Montefiore, *Stalin: The Court of the Red Tsar*, 610-611.
29. For the magnum opus on this subject that was told in mesmerizing and graphic detail, see Solzhenitsyn, *The Gulag Archipelago (1918-1956): An Experiment in Literary Investigation, Parts I-II—The Prison Industry and Perpetual Motion*; and Solzhenitsyn, *The Gulag Archipelago (1918-1956): An Experiment in Literary Investigation, Parts III-IV—The Destructive Labor Camps and The Soul and Barbed Wire*. See also: Applebaum, *Gulag*; and Robert Conquest, *The Harvest of Sorrow: Soviet Collectivization and the Terror-Famine* (Oxford. Oxford University Press, 1986).

30. Costello and Tsarev, *Deadly Illusions*, 27; Montefiore, *Stalin: The Court of the Red Tsar*, 235; and Radzinsky, *Stalin,* 125, 188, 242, 251-258, 394-395.
31. Montefiore, *Stalin: The Court of the Red Tsar*, 100n; Radzinsky, *Stalin,* 105, 108, 161-162; and Volkogonov. *Stalin: Triumph and Tragedy*, 8-20, 27-32, 42, 46, 65.
32. Radzinsky, *Stalin*, 246-250.
33. Radzinsky, *Stalin*, 211, 227, 237-238, 356.
34. Medvedev, *Let History Judge,* 247; Montefiore, *Stalin: The Court of the Red Tsar*, 169; Salisbury, *Black Night, White Snow,* 583n2; and Volkogonov. *Stalin: Triumph and Tragedy*, 8.
35. Martin van Creveld, *The Encyclopedia of Revolutions and Revolutionaries: From Anarchism to Zhow Enlai* (New York: Facts on File, 1996), 392.
36. Dmitry Solovyov, "Stalin voted third most popular Russian," *Reuters*, December 28, 2008.
https://www.reuters.com/article/us-russia-stalin/stalin-voted-third-most-popular-russian-idUSTRE4BR17620081229.

Chapter 4

1. Marc Jansen and Nikita Petrov, *Stalin's Loyal Executioner: People's Commissar Nikolai Ezhov, 1895-1940* (Stanford, CA: Hoover Institution Press, 2002).
2. From the perspective of those arrested, prisoners, and those sent to the Gulag, see Aleksandr Solzhenitsyn, *The Gulag Archipelago (1918–1956)***:** *An Experiment in Literary Investigation, Parts I-II—The Prison Industry and Perpetual Motion,* trans. Thomas P. Whitney (New York: Harper & Row, 1974); and Aleksandr Solzhenitsyn**,** *The Gulag Archipelago (1918–1956): An Experiment in Literary Investigation, Parts III-IV—The Destructive Labor Camps and The Soul and Barbed Wire,* trans. Thomas P. Whitney (New York: Harper & Row, 1975). For a broad perspective of the Russian Revolution, see Alan Moorehead, *The Russian Revolution* (New York: Bantam Books, 1959), and Leonard Shapiro, *The Russian Revolutions of 1917: The Origin of Modern Communism* (New York, Basic Books, 1984). From the perspective of scholars who studied the later period under Stalin, see Robert Conquest, *The Great Terror: Stalin's Purge of the Thirties* (New York: The Macmillan Company, 1968); Robert Conquest, *The Great Terror: A Reassessment* (Oxford: Oxford University Press, 1990); Simon Sebag Montefiore, *Stalin: The Court of the Red Tsar* (New York: Alfred A.

Knopf, 2004); and Dmitri Volkogonov. *Stalin: Triumph and Tragedy* (New York: Grove Press, 1991).
3. Jansen and Petrov, *Stalin's Loyal Executioner,* 21-51.
4. Jansen and Petrov, *Stalin's Loyal Executioner,* 53-78.
5. Jansen and Petrov, *Stalin's Loyal Executioner,* xi.
6. Jansen and Petrov, *Stalin's Loyal Executioner,* 17-19, 121-124, 171-174.
7. Jansen and Petrov, *Stalin's Loyal Executioner,* x.
8. For an excellent book about espionage and Stalin's purge of the communist leaders in the East European satellite nations during his later years, see Tony Sharp, *Stalin's American Spy: Noel Field, Allen Dulles and the East European Show Trials* (London: Hurst & Company, 2014).
9. Jansen and Petrov, *Stalin's Loyal Executioner*, ix.
10. Jansen and Petrov, *Stalin's Loyal Executioner*, 113.
11. Amy Knight, *Beria. Stalin's First Lieutenant* (Princeton, NJ: Princeton University Press, 1993), 3. For Beria's enforcement of the collectivization policies in Georgia and Transcaucasia, see Knight, *Beria,* 43-46.
12. Jansen and Petrov, *Stalin's Loyal Executioner*, 148-150.
13. Knight, *Beria*, 87-109. See also: Jansen and Petrov, *Stalin's Loyal Executioner*, 159-211.
14. Knight, *Beria*, 110-131.
15. Knight, *Beria*, 132-141, 153.
16. Aleksandr Solzhenitsyn, *The First Circle*, trans. Thomas P. Whitney (New York: Harper & Row, 1968).
17. Knight, *Beria*, 146-175. See also: Jonathan Brent and Vladimir P. Naumov, *Stalin's Last Crime: The Plot Against the Jewish Doctors, 1948 1953* (New York: Harper Collins, 2003).
18. Knight, *Beria*, 176-191.
19. Knight, *Beria*, 191-194.
20. Knight, *Beria*, 194-198.
21. Knight, *Beria*, 198-200.
22. Knight, *Beria*, 200-203.
23. Knight, *Beria*, 203-204.
24. Knight, *Beria*, 204-224.
25. Knight, *Beria*, 218.
26. Knight, *Beria*, 227.
27. Knight, *Beria*, 229.
28. Quote by Jacques Mallet du Pan. https://www.goodreads.com/quotes/8738629-like-saturn-the-revolution-devours-its-children.
29. Aleksandr Solzhenitsyn. *One Day In The Life of Ivan Denisovich*, trans. Max Hayward and Ronald Hingley (New York: Bantam Books, 1970).

30. The Easton Press Great Books of the 20th Century Collector's Notes in Arthur Koestler, *Darkness at Noon*, trans. Daphne Hardy (Norwalk, CT: Easton Press, 2000).
31. "Koestler, Arthur, CBE, 1905-1983 (Hungarian-British author and journalist)," The University of Edinburgh, Archives Online. https://archives.collections.ed.ac.uk/agents/people/4320.
32. Arthur Koestler, "I: Bridge Burning," in *The Invisible Writing: The Second Volume Of An Autobiography, 1932–1940* (New York: MacMillan Publishing Company, 1970).
33. Arthur Koestler, *Darkness at Noon*, trans. Daphne Hardy (Norwalk, CT: Easton Press, 2000), 59.
34. Koestler, *Darkness at Noon*, 60.
35. Koestler, *Darkness at Noon*, iv.
36. Katherine G. Dorsey, "Bukharin's rehabilitation foreshadowed in Darkness at Noon," *The New York Times*, February 29, 1988. https://www.nytimes.com/1988/02/28/opinion/l-bukharin-s-rehabilitation-foreshadowed-in-darkness-at-noon-650088.html.

Chapter 5

1. Dave Roos, "Why so many foreigners volunteered to fight in the Spanish Civil War," *History.com*, A&E Television Networks, March 4, 2022. https://www.history.com/news/spanish-civil-war-foreign-nationals-volunteer.
2. John Costello and Oleg Tsarev, *Deadly Illusions: The KGB Orlov Dossier Reveals Stalin's Master Spy* (New York: Crown Publisher's, Inc., 1993), 164. This book was published during the Russian presidency of Boris Yeltsin when KGB files were briefly made available to scholars following the collapse of the USSR.
3. Edward Gazur, *Alexander Orlov: The FBI's KGB General* (New York: Basic Books, 2001). This book was written by retired FBI agent, Edward Gazur, who debriefed Alexander Orlov and protected Stalin's NKVD general after Orlov defected to the United States following the communist defeat in the Spanish Civil War. However, the book is by no means an authoritative, historic, or literary biography of the elusive KGB general; and should be considered only part of a much larger jigsaw puzzle whose mismatched pieces are still being fully assembled. I would only recommend Gazur's book to knowledgeable scholars who are seeking specific details about the Cold War, the Soviet KGB, and its predecessor agencies, realizing that the details are selected pieces of information that Orlov chose to reveal to his friend and executor, former

FBI agent Edward Gazur, during 1971-1973 in the last few years of his life.
4. Pavel Sudoplatov, Anatoli Sudoplatov, Jerrold L. Schechter, and Leona P. Schechter, *Special Tasks: Memoirs of an Unwanted Witness a Soviet Spymaster* (Boston: Little, Brown and Company, 1994), 30-31.
5. Miguel A. Faria, Jr., *Cuba's Eternal Revolution through the Prism of Insurgency, Socialism, and Espionage* (Newcastle upon Tyne, UK: Cambridge Scholars Publishing, 2023), 96-97.
6. George Orwell, *Homage to Catalonia* (Orlando, FL: Harcourt, 1980). The book is a "lost" classic in literature and the best book written by a prominent literary figure that was also an active participant in the Spanish Civil War. Orwell recounted fascinating events of the war and related the fate of the Trotskyites in Spain in general and the anarchists of Catalonia in particular. Orwell's experiences during the war changed his political philosophy and his life, making possible the writing of his other treasures of literature, namely, *Animal Farm* and *1984*.
7. Costello and Tsarev, *Deadly Illusions*, 305-314. For the blackmail threat to Stalin, see 305-306.
8. "Testimony of Alexander Orlov: Hearings before the United States Senate Committee on the Judiciary, Subcommittee To Investigate the Administration of the Internal Security Act and Other Internal Security Laws, Eighty-Fourth Congress, first session, on Sept. 28, 1955," Berkeley Law. https://lawcat.berkeley.edu/record/305149.
9. Pavel Sudoplatov, *Special Tasks*, 46.
10. Costello and Tsarev, *Deadly Illusions*, 389.
11. Gazur, *Alexander Orlov*, xvii.
12. Sudoplatov, *Special Tasks*, 34n.3.
13. Costello and Tsarev, *Deadly Illusions*, 253-266.
14. Costello and Tsarev, *Deadly Illusions*, 261.
15. Costello and Tsarev, *Deadly Illusions*, 263.
16. Costello and Tsarev, *Deadly Illusions*, 285, 306, 368-369, 411.
17. Simon Sebag Montefiore, *Stalin: The Court of the Red Tsar* (New York: Alfred A. Knopf, 2004), 221-227.
18. Walter Schellenberg, *Walter Schellenberg: The Memoirs of Hitler's Spymaster* (London: André Deutsch, 2006), 46-49.
19. Orwell, *Homage to Catalonia*, 64.
20. Orwell, *Homage to Catalonia*, 170, 177.
21. Orwell, *Homage to Catalonia*, 184-194.
22. Orwell, *Homage to Catalonia*, 195.
23. Costello and Tsarev, *Deadly Illusions*, 285-292.
24. Orwell, *Homage to Catalonia*, 198.

25. Orwell, *Homage to Catalonia*, 223-226.
26. George Orwell, *Animal Farm* (Norwalk, CT: Easton Press, 1992).
27. George Orwell, *1984* (Norwalk, CT: Easton Press, 1992).
28. Orwell, *Homage to Catalonia*, 232.

Chapter 6

1. M. Stanton Evans and Herbert Romerstein, *Stalin's Secret Agents: The Subversion of Roosevelt's Government* (New York: Simon & Schuster, 2012). This book discloses many eye-opening revelations and is essential reading for scholars, researchers, and interested readers, searching the historical record about Soviet spies and agents of influence that worked in the FDR administration and the inimical part they placed in the Cold War story.
2. Evans and Romerstein, *Stalin's Secret Agents*, 8. See also: Whittaker Chambers, *Witness* (Chicago: Regnery Gateway, 1988), 427. For FDR's lack of attention to possible agents of communist influence or spies in his administration, see Christopher Andrew and Vasili Mitrokhin, *The Sword and the Shield: The Mitrokhin Archive and the Secret History of the KGB* (New York: Basic Books, 1999), 107.
3. Evans and Romerstein, *Stalin's Secret Agents*, 19. For Harry Hopkins documentation as an agent of influence associated with the Nathan Silvermaster Soviet espionage network in wartime Washington, D.C., see Allen Weinstein and Alexander Vassiliev, *The Haunted Wood: Soviet Espionage in America—The Stalin Era* (New York: Random House, 1999), 154-160.
4. Robert A. Sherwood, *Roosevelt and Hopkins* (New York: Harper & Brothers, 1948), 749.
5. Evans and Romerstein, *Stalin's Secret Agents*, 20. Quoted in Robert Nisbet, *Roosevelt and Stalin* (Chicago: Regnery Gateway, 1989), 6.
6. Kilzer, Louis C. *Churchill's Deception: The Dark Secret That Destroyed Nazi Germany* (New York: Simon & Schuster, 1994).
7. Evans and Romerstein, *Stalin's Secret Agents*, 19. See also: Winston Churchill, *The Gathering Storm* (New York: Bantam Books, 1962), viii.
8. Evans and Romerstein, *Stalin's Secret Agents*, 117.
9. William Rusher, "Harry Hopkins, Soviet agent," *The Washington Times*, January 4, 2001. https://www.washingtontimes.com/news/2001/jan/4/20010104-020500-7670r. See also: Herbert Romerstein and Eric Breindel, *The Venona Secrets: Exposing Soviet Espionage and America's Traitors* (Washington, DC: Regnery, 2000), 210-219; and Evans and Romerstein, *Stalin's Secret Agents*, 120-121.

10. Christopher Andrew and Oleg Gordievsky, *KGB: The Inside Story of Its Foreign Operations from Lenin to Gorbachev* (New York: Harper Collins, 1990), 287, 349-350.
11. Christopher Andrew and Vasili Mitrokhin, *The Sword and the Shield: The Mitrokhin Archive and the Secret History of the KGB* (New York: Basic Books, 1999), 111-112.
12. Richard C.S. Trahair, *The Encyclopedia of Cold War Espionage, Spies, and Secret Operations* (Westport, CT: Greenwood Press, 2004). For a review of this book, see Miguel A. Faria, Jr., "Spies of the Cold War," *HaciendaPublishing.com*, February 28, 2013. https://haciendapublishing.com/spies-of-the-cold-war/.
13. Evans and Romerstein, *Stalin's Secret Agents*, 199-255. See also: Romerstein and Breindel, *The Venona Secrets*.
14. Evans and Romerstein, *Stalin's Secret Agents*, 2-7.
15. Allen Weinstein and Alexander Vassiliev, *The Haunted Wood: Soviet Espionage in America—The Stalin Era* (New York: Random House, 1999); and John Earl Haynes, Harvey Klehr, and Alexander Vassiliev, *Spies: The Rise and Fall of the KGB in America* (New Haven, CT: Yale University Press, 2009).
16. Christopher Andrew and Vasili Mitrokhin, *The Sword and the Shield: The Mitrokhin Archive and the Secret History of the KGB* (New York: Basic Books, 1999).
17. Herbert Romerstein and Eric Breindel, *The Venona Secrets: Exposing Soviet Espionage and America's Traitors* (Washington, DC: Regnery, 2000).
18. John A. Stormer, *None Dare Call It Treason—25 Years Later* (Florissant, MO: Liberty Bell Press, 1990).
19. For two books that fill a serious gap in historical knowledge about events leading up to World War II, see Evans and Romerstein, *Stalin's Secret Agents*, 90-91; and John Koster, *Operation Snow: How a Soviet Mole in FDR's White House Triggered Pearl Harbor* (Washington, DC: Regnery History, 2012), 32-35, 51, 117.
20. Stuart D. Goldman, "The forgotten Soviet-Japanese war of 1939," *TheDiplomat.com*, August 28, 2012. https://thediplomat.com/2012/08/the-forgotten-soviet-japanese-war-of-1939/.
21. Joseph V. Micallef, "Japan strikes north: how the Battle of Khalkhin Gol transformed WWII," *Military.com*, August 27, 2019. https://www.military.com/daily-news/2019/08/27/japan-strikes-north-how-battle-khalkhin-gol-transformed-wwii.html.
22. Evans and Romerstein, *Stalin's Secret Agents*, 155-175, and for the "rape of Poland," 165-175.

23. Evans and Romerstein, *Stalin's Secret Agents*, 140-154, 199-221. See also: John A. Stormer, *None Dare Call It Treason—25 Years Later* (Florissant, MO: Liberty Bell Press, 1990); and Miguel A. Faria, Jr., "Spies of the Cold War," *HaciendaPublishing.com*, February 28, 2013. https://haciendapublishing.com/spies-of-the-cold-war/.
24. Bob Farquhar, *Duck and Cover: A Pictorial History of Nuclear Weapons* (Self-published, https://www.wagingpeace.org/duck-and-cover-a-pictorial-history-of-nuclear-weapon/, 2012). In a personal communication with Robert Farquhar, I asked: "Could your source be wrong about the figure of 7 atomic bombs at that very critical time (1946) in history? Does this include uranium and plutonium fission material? And what would it have taken for the nuclear physicists to assemble those bombs, time wise?" On July 19, 2011, Mr. Farquhar replied: "I don't see how many sources could all be wrong about the 1946 stockpile. The Federation of American Scientists, Bulletin of Atomic Scientists, and most recently, Jerry Miller in *Stockpile: The Story Behind 10,000 Strategic Nuclear Weapons*, all cite the same general figures in addition to other books, including Pulitzer Prize winner Richard Rhodes *The Making of the Atomic Bomb*: Seven to 9 bombs of the Fat Man implosion type. There were only seven 'Urchin' neutron initiators made from beryllium and polonium-210 which had limited half-lives. Two bombs were used at Crossroads in July 1946, a very provocative action to the Soviets, leaving the stockpile slightly smaller. Even Truman at the time had no idea how many bombs existed. By June 1947, there were 13 nuclear cores and 29 casings, 1951 showed 300. The Little Boy uranium fueled bomb was never mass-produced because of its inherent danger, the amount of fissile material needed (75kg of U-235), and its inefficiency, burning less than 1% of the uranium before tearing itself apart. These are the stockpile figures for all years, https://journals.sagepub.com/doi/full/10.2968/056002019."
25. Pavel Sudoplatov, Anatoli Sudoplatov, Jerrold L. Schechter, and Leona P. Schechter, *Special Tasks: Memoirs of an Unwanted Witness a Soviet Spymaster* (Boston: Little, Brown and Company, 1994), 210-211. In the Foreword to the book, British historian Robert Conquest wrote, "This is the most sensational, the most devastating, and in many ways the most informative autobiography ever to emerge from the Stalinist milieu. It is perhaps the most important single contribution to our knowledge since Khrushchev's Secret Speech…The range of Sudoplatov's activities…is remarkable." Moreover, Sudoplatov provided the following summary of his career in the Prologue: "My name is Pavel Anatolievich Sudoplatov, but I do not expect you to recognize it, because for fifty-eight years it

was one of the best-kept secrets in the Soviet Union…I was responsible for Trotsky's assassination and, during World War II, I was in charge of guerrilla warfare and disinformation in Germany and German-occupied territories. After the war I continued to run illegal networks abroad whose purpose was to sabotage American and NATO installations in the event hostilities broke out. I was also in charge of the Soviet espionage efforts to obtain the secrets of the atomic bomb from America and Great Britain. I set up a network of illegals who convinced Robert Oppenheimer, Enrico Fermi, Leo Szilard, Bruno Pontecorvo, Alan Nunn May, Klaus Fuchs, and other scientists in America and Great Britain to share atomic secrets with us. It is strange to look back fifty years and re-create the mentality that led us to take vengeance on our enemies with cold self-assurance…" *Special Tasks* is an incredible memoir by the man who was also in charge of "special tasks," a euphemism for the department of "wet affairs" (assassinations) and other top secrets of the USSR under Lavrenti Beria and Joseph Stalin from 1939 to 1953.

26. Jonathan Brent and Vladimir P. Naumov, *Stalin's Last Crime: The Plot Against the Jewish Doctors, 1948-1953* (New York: Harper Collins, 2003).

27. Miguel A. Faria, *Cuba's Eternal Revolution through the Prism of Insurgency, Socialism, and Espionage* (Newcastle Upon Tyne, UK: 2023), 61-68. See also: Jerrod L. Schecter and Peter S. Deriabin, *The Spy Who Saved the World: How a Soviet Colonel Changed the Course of the Cold War* (New York: Charles Scribner's Sons, 1992).

Part II

Chapter 7

1. Richard Z. Freemann, Jr., "Operation Barbarossa: how Stalin was blindsided by Berlin," *Warfare History Network*, Spring 2018. https://warfarehistorynetwork.com/article/operation-barbarossa-how-stalin-was-blindsided-by-berlin/. See also: "Operation Barbarossa," *History.com*, November 14, 2022. https://www.history.com/topics/world-war-ii/operation-barbarossa. This article also described the Molotov-Ribbentrop Pact and its ramifications.

2. "Operation Barbarossa and Germany's failure in the Soviet Union," *Imperial War Museums*, https://www.iwm.org.uk/history/operation-barbarossa-and-germanys-failure-in-the-soviet-union.

3. Louis C. Kilzer. *Churchill's Deception: The Dark Secret That Destroyed Nazi Germany* (New York: Simon & Schuster, 1994), 53.

4. "Adolf Hitler: Declaration of War on the Soviet Union, June 22, 1941," Jewish Virtual Library, American-Israeli Cooperative Enterprise (1998–2023), citing *The New York Times*, June 23, 1941. https://www.jewishvirtuallibrary.org/adolf-hitler-declaration-of-war-on-the-soviet-union-june-1941.
5. Louis C. Kilzer. *Hitler's Traitor: Martin Bormann and the Defeat of the Reich* (Presidio Press, Novato, California, 2000), 99-118.
6. Kilzer. *Churchill's Deception*, 81-82.
7. For the material, documenting the German-Japanese strategic alliance, and supporting the Japanese concerns for the Imperial Army not invading Siberia and instead pursuing the Imperial Navy's southern strategy of conquering Indochina, see the excellent History Channel documentaries, *The Samurai and the Swastika* (2000) and *The Last Secrets of the Axis* (2001). Even though the British and Americans could read German and Japanese secret messages during World War II via SIGINT, and the German high command was infiltrated by Western agents in the Black Orchestra as well as Soviet spies in the Red Orchestra and the *funkspiel* radio broadcast, the Germans put up a long and protracted fight against the allies. For their part, the Japanese, instead of invading Siberia and putting a two-front war into effect with the Germans against the Soviets, chose not to cooperate with the German grand strategy. Perhaps too overconfident in their estimate that they could defeat the British and American forces in the Far East by themselves, or at least force them to negotiations, decided to go along with Pearl Harbor and the Navy's plan to invade Indonesia to the south.
8. For two excellent books that disclose in detail and document how the FDR administration was completely subverted by Stalin's secret agents and communist American traitors militating for a foreign policy favorable to Stalin and the USSR and detrimental to Japan and America by pushing Japan into war against the United States, see M. Stanton Evans and Herbert Romerstein. *Stalin's Secret Agents: The Subversion of Roosevelt's Government* (New York: Simon & Schuster, 2012); and John Koster, *Operation Snow: How a Soviet Mole in FDR's White House Triggered Pearl Harbor* (Washington, DC: Regnery History, 2012). In *Operation Snow*, Koster actually discloses the identity of the Soviet agent who handled Harry Dexter White, the man most responsible for the manipulation of the Japanese into war against America and the betrayal of U.S. foreign policy vis-à-vis the Japanese.
9. Manhattan Project National Park Service, "Japan during World War II," *NationalParkService.gov*, April 4, 2023. https://www.nps.gov/articles/000/japan-during-world-war-ii.htm.

10. John Simkin, "Richard Sorge," https://spartacus-educational.com/GERsorge.htm.
11. Christopher Andrew and Oleg Gordievsky, *KGB: The Inside Story of Its Foreign Operations from Lenin to Gorbachev* (New York: Harper Collins, 1990), 261.
12. Evans and Romerstein, *Stalin's Secret Agents*, 90-91; and John Koster, *Operation Snow*, 32-35, 51, 117.
13. Charles A. Willoughby, *The Shanghai Conspiracy: The Sorge Spy Ring* (New York: E.P. Dutton & Company, Inc., 1952). Major General Willoughby served as General Douglas MacArthur's Chief of Intelligence from 1941 to 1951.
14. "Soviet admits Sorge was its spy in wartime Japan," *The New York Times*, September 5, 1964. https://www.nytimes.com/1964/09/05/archives/soviet-admits-sorge-was-its-spy-in-wartime-japan.html.
15. John Swift, "Battle of Moscow," *Britannica*, https://www.britannica.com/event/Battle-of-Moscow. See also: Simon Sebag Montefiore, *Stalin: The Court of the Red Tsar* (New York: Alfred A. Knopf, 2004), 403.
16. John Toland. *Infamy: Pearl Harbor and Its Aftermath* (New York: Doubleday & Company, Inc., 1982).
17. Louis C. Kilzer. *Hitler's Traitor*, 11-14, 91-92. For a short biography of Gestapo Heinrich Müller and what happened to this mysterious Gestapo police chief, and suspected communist who evaded justice, see Charles Whiting, *The Search for Gestapo Müller* (South Yorkshire, England: Pen and Sword Books, Ltd., 2001). For a fascinating memoir, see Walter Schellenberg, *The Memoirs of Hitler's Spymaster* (London: Andre Deutsch, 2006). This book is factual and poignant—after all espionage cuts both ways. Written shortly before Schellenberg's death in Italy in 1952 and published in 1956, the noted historian Alan Bullock wrote that in Schellenberg's memoirs, "It is this lack of self-consciousness, damning as a revelation of character, which makes him all the more valuable as a historical witness."
18. For the secrets of Enigma and Ultra, see Kilzer, *Hitler's Traitor,* 263, 270-273; and Kilzer, *Churchill's Deception,* 219-221. See also: Andrew Sangster, *Blind Obedience and Denial: The Nuremberg Defendants* (Oxford, UK: Casemate, 2022), 25; and "Part II—General Intelligence, The Discovery of Hitler's Wills," Dwight D. Eisenhower Presidential Library,https://www.eisenhowerlibrary.gov/sites/default/files/research/online-documents/holocaust/hitler-will-general-intelligence.pdf.
19. Peter Grose, *Gentleman Spy: The Life of Allen Dulles* (New York: Houghton Mifflin Company, 1994), 185-197, 204-207, 245-252, 266.

20. Grose, *Gentleman Spy,* 171-177, 196-204, 260.
21. Grose, *Gentleman Spy,* 176-188, 193-201, 245. See also: "Hans Gisevius, 68, anti-Nazi, is dead," *The New York Times*, March 27, 1974. https://www.nytimes.com/1974/03/27/archives/hans-gisevius-68-antinazi-is-dead-told-of-plots-to-overthrow-hitler.html.
22. Grose, *Gentleman Spy,* 279, 336-337. See also: "Legacy—History of CIA," Central Intelligence Agency, https://www.cia.gov/legacy/cia-history/.
23. Herbert Romerstein and Eric Breindel, *The Venona Secrets: Exposing Soviet Espionage and America's Traitors* (Washington, DC: Regnery, 2000).
24. Kilzer, *Churchill's Deception*, 20-26, 206.
25. Kilzer, *Churchill's Deception*, 73, 159-203, 269.
26. Kilzer, *Churchill's Deception*, 240-288.
27. Kilzer, *Churchill's Deception*, 28-36, 75-76, 280.
28. Kilzer, *Churchill's Deception*, 268.
29. Kilzer. *Hitler's Traitor*, 84.
30. Kilzer, *Churchill's Deception*, 284-287.
31. For documentation on the extensive espionage carried out by Stalin and his foreign intelligence apparatus against the West, before, during, and after the World War II, see John Earl Haynes, Harvey Klehr, and Alexander Vassiliev, *Spies: The Rise and Fall of the KGB in America* (New Haven: Yale University Press, 2009); Herbert Romerstein and Eric Breindel, *The Venona Secrets: Exposing Soviet Espionage and America's Traitors* (Washington, DC: Regnery Publishing, 2000); and Allen Weinstein and Alexander Vassiliev, *The Haunted Wood: Soviet Espionage in America—The Stalin Era* (New York: Random House, 1999). A lot of historic material exists not only in standard history books but also in excellent books on information gathered from formerly classified intelligence from U.S., German, and Soviet files, such as the books cited above. This treasure trove includes information in the released German files from Enigma deciphered messages in the Venona transcripts, the selectively released KGB files in the early 1990s, and perhaps the most authoritative of all—The Mitrokhin Archive, the nearly complete files from the archives of the KGB's First Chief Directorate up to 1984. As a result of the information contained in the Mitrokhin Archive, hundreds of Soviet spies and traitors were uncovered, and some of them were prosecuted for their treachery many years after it occurred.
32. Kilzer, *Churchill's Deception*, 290.

33. Simon Sebag Montefiore, *Stalin: The Court of the Red Tsar* (New York: Alfred A. Knopf, 2004), 333-334. See also: "Appendix Five: Basis for the Katyn Forest Massacre, Letter from Beria to Stalin, March 5, 1940," in Pavel Sudoplatov, Anatoli Sudoplatov, Jerrold L. Schechter, and Leona P. Schechter, *Special Tasks: Memoirs of an Unwanted Witness a Soviet Spymaster* (Boston: Little, Brown and Company, 1994), 476-478. This translated letter provides documentation that Beria recommended the execution of the Polish officers and the other prisoners. The letter lists by rank or position the number of prisoners being held in the various prisoner-of-war camps or in prisons located in western Ukraine or in Belarus. The appendix also includes a photograph of the first page of Beria's letter showing a bold underlined signature for approval, which Sudoplatov identifies as being the signature of Joseph Stalin.
34. Benjamin B. Fischer, "The Katyn controversy: Stalin's killing field," CIA's Center For the Study of Intelligence, Winter 1999. https://web.archive.org/web/20100324185250/https://www.cia.gov/library/center-for-the-study-of-intelligence/csi-publications/csi-studies/studies/winter99-00/art6.html. See also: "The man who personally executed over 7,000 people in 28 days, one at a time," https://www.youtube.com/watch?v=hhsO5XNDcR8.
35. Montefiore, *Stalin: The Court of the Red Tsar*, 197.
36. Kilzer, *Churchill's Deception*, 160.

Chapter 8

1. Richard Z. Freemann, Jr., "Operation Barbarossa: how Stalin was blindsided by Berlin," *Warfare History Network*, Spring 2018. https://warfarehistorynetwork.com/article/operation-barbarossa-how-stalin-was-blindsided-by-berlin/. See also: "Operation Barbarossa," *History.com*, November 14, 2022. https://www.history.com/topics/world-war-ii/operation-barbarossa. This article also described the Molotov-Ribbentrop Pact and its ramifications.
2. "Operation Barbarossa and Germany's failure in the Soviet Union," *Imperial War Museums*, https://www.iwm.org.uk/history/operation-barbarossa-and-germanys-failure-in-the-soviet-union.
3. Louis C. Kilzer. *Churchill's Deception: The Dark Secret That Destroyed Nazi German* (New York: Simon & Schuster, 1994), 53.
4. John Simkin, "Richard Sorge," https://spartacus-educational.com/GERsorge.htm.
5. Simon Sebag Montefiore, *Stalin: The Court of the Red Tsar* (New York: Alfred A. Knopf, 2004), 349.

6. Kilzer. *Churchill's Deception*, 135.
7. Shane Quinn, "German invasion: Hitler's quest for Russian oil," Global Village Space, June 22, 2021. https://www.globalvillagespace.com/german-invasion-hitlers-quest-for-russian-oil/.
8. Schwendemann, Heinrich. "German-Soviet economic relations at the time of the Hitler-Stalin pact 1939-1941." *Cahiers Du Monde Russe* 36, no. 1/2 (1995): 161–78. http://www.jstor.org/stable/20170949.
9. Charles A. Willoughby, *The Shanghai Conspiracy: The Sorge Spy Ring* (New York: E.P. Dutton & Company, Inc., 1952). Major General Willoughby was General Douglas MacArthur's Chief of Intelligence from 1941-1951.
10. Simon Sebag Montefiore, *Stalin: The Court of the Red Tsar* (New York: Alfred A. Knopf, 2004), 403.
11. For the strategic plans of Germany and Japan against the West and secret weaponry, see the excellent History Channel documentaries, *The Samurai and the Swastika* (2000) and *The Last Secrets of the Axis* (2001).
12. David Glantz. *The Siege of Leningrad 1941–44: 900 Days of Terror* (Osceola, WI: Zenith Press, 2001). See also: Leon Goure, *The Siege of Leningrad* (Palo Alto, CA: Stanford University Press, 1981). The casualty figures are culled from various sources. The two books cited here are good sources for the battles and siege of Leningrad.
13. William L. Shirer, *The Rise and Fall of the Third Reich: A History of Nazi Germany* (New York: Simon & Schuster, 1960).
14. Benjamin R. Simms, "Analysis of the Battle of Kursk," ARMOR, March-April 2003.
15. History.com Editors, "Battle of Kursk," *A&E Television Network*, September 7, 2018. https://www.history.com/topics/world-war-ii/battle-of-kursk.
16. For details of the Battle of Kursk and the espionage assistance given to the Soviets by their spies, see Louis C. Kilzer, *Hitler's Traitor*, 183-206. Kilzer, a Pulitzer Prize-winning journalist, possesses a unique flair for writing history that reads like a novel, but the facts are always well documented. Casualty figures were rounded up and the asset figures for tanks and big assault guns combined for ease of reading. Nevertheless, the material used in this section is based on estimates from various sources, which all showed the Russian advantage in both material and men. Casualties were extremely high; and it is suspected that the Russian soldiers were used as "cannon fodder" to overwhelm the Germans, like in Stalingrad. See also: David M. Glantz and Jonathan M. House, *The*

Battle of Kursk (Lawrence, Kansas: University Press of Kansas, 1999). For the aircraft figures and the air battle, see Christer Bergström, *Kursk: The Air Battle, July 1943* (Midland: Hersham, 2007).
17. Kilzer, *Hitler's Traitor*, 271.
18. Evan Andrews, "5 attacks on U.S. soil during World War II," *History.com*, August 30, 2018. https://www.history.com/news/5-attacks-on-u-s-soil-during-world-war-ii.
19. "Aleutian Islands, World War II: Dutch Harbor bombing, June 1942," *National Park Service*, June 3, 2022. https://www.nps.gov/aleu/learn/historyculture/raid-dutch-harbor.htm.
20. John Bridges, "True history and the lies we were told: Japanese attacked the U.S. mainland," *Discover Hub Pages*, July 23, 2018. https://discover.hubpages.com/politics/True-History-and-the-Lies-We-Were-Told-Japanese-Attacked-the-US-Mainland. This is another succinct article on the Japanese belligerent activities in the West Coast of the United States during World War II.

Part III

Chapter 9

1. Jonathan Brent and Vladimir P. Naumov, *Stalin's Last Crime: The Plot Against the Jewish Doctors, 1948-1953* (New York: Harper Collins, 2003), 105, 151, 169, 179. This book provides an in-depth study in psychological survival in the nightmarish police state—namely Stalin's Russia circa 1948-1953. The untangling of the Gordian knot of conspiracies and plots is the convincing achievement of the authors of this suspenseful, historical drama. Brent and Naumov accomplished an almost inscrutable task—the successful unraveling of Joseph Stalin's byzantine, evil and anti-Semitic plot against the Jewish doctors.
2. United States Holocaust Memorial Museum, "January 27, 1945, Soviet Forces liberate Auschwitz," Holocaust Encyclopedia. https://encyclopedia.ushmm.org/content/en/timeline-event/holocaust/1942-1945/soviet-forces-liberate-auschwitz.
3. Brent and Naumov, *Stalin's Last Crime*, 94-98, 184, 217.
4. Brent and Naumov, *Stalin's Last Crime*, 114-151.
5. Brent and Naumov, *Stalin's Last Crime*, 102-150.
6. Brent and Naumov, *Stalin's Last Crime*, 66-72.
7. Brent and Naumov, *Stalin's Last Crime*, 171.
8. Brent and Naumov, *Stalin's Last Crime*, 190-234.
9. Brent and Naumov, *Stalin's Last Crime*, 11-62.

10. Brent and Naumov, *Stalin's Last Crime*, 71-86. See also: Miguel A. Faria, Jr., *Vandals at the Gates of Medicine: Historic Perspectives on the Battle Over Health Care Reform* (Macon, GA: Hacienda Publishing, Inc., 1994), 242-243.
11. Brent and Naumov, *Stalin's Last Crime*, 20-115.
12. Brent and Naumov, *Stalin's Last Crime*, 192-233.
13. Brent and Naumov, *Stalin's Last Crime*, 151-226.
14. Brent and Naumov, *Stalin's Last Crime*, 93-170.
15. Brent and Naumov, *Stalin's Last Crime*, 120-198.
16. Brent and Naumov, *Stalin's Last Crime*, 139-270.
17. Brent and Naumov, *Stalin's Last Crime*, 104-263.
18. Brent and Naumov, *Stalin's Last Crime*, 216-291, 323-333.
19. Brent and Naumov, *Stalin's Last Crime*, 167-168.
20. Brent and Naumov, *Stalin's Last Crime*, 267-269.
21. Brent and Naumov, *Stalin's Last Crime*, 165-166, 252-253, 273-275.
22. Brent and Naumov, *Stalin's Last Crime*, 128-129, 207-233.
23. Brent and Naumov, *Stalin's Last Crime*, 55-65, 134-276.
24. Brent and Naumov, *Stalin's Last Crime*, 30-160, 186-249.
25. Brent and Naumov, *Stalin's Last Crime*, 235-248.
26. Brent and Naumov, *Stalin's Last Crime*, 249-311.
27. Brent and Naumov, *Stalin's Last Crime*, 283-289.
28. Dmitri Volkogonov, *Stalin: Triumph and Tragedy* (New York: Grove Press, 1991), 571.
29. Brent and Naumov, *Stalin's Last Crime*, 105.
30. Brent and Naumov, *Stalin's Last Crime*, 312-336. See also: Miguel A. Faria, Jr., *Controversies in Medicine and Neuroscience: Through the Prism of History, Neurobiology and Bioethics* (Newcastle upon Tyne, UK: Cambridge Scholars Publishing, 2023), 129-142.
31. Brent and Naumov, *Stalin's Last Crime*, 323-328. See also: Amy Knight, *Beria: Stalin's First Lieutenant* (Princeton, NJ: Princeton University Press, 1993), 176-224.

Chapter 10

1. Daniel J. Mahoney, *The Other Solzhenitsyn: Telling the Truth about a Misunderstood Writer and Thinker* (South Bend, IN: St. Augustine's Press, 2014).
2. Michael Scammell, *Solzhenitsyn: A Biography* (New York: W. W. Norton & Company, 1984), 993.
3. Aleksandr Solzhenitsyn, *One Day In The Life of Ivan Denisovich*, trans. Max Hayward and Ronald Hingley (New York: Bantam Books, 1970).

4. Aleksandr Solzhenitsyn, *The Gulag Archipelago (1918–1956): An Experiment in Literary Investigation*, Parts I-II—The Prison Industry and Perpetual Motion, trans. Thomas P. Whitney (New York: Harper & Row, 1974).
5. Aleksandr Solzhenitsyn, *The Gulag Archipelago (1918–1956): An Experiment in Literary Investigation*, Parts III-IV—The Destructive Labor Camps and The Soul and Barbed Wire, trans. Thomas P. Whitney (New York: Harper & Row, 1975).
6. Scammell, *Solzhenitsyn*, 935-936.
7. Miguel A. Faria, Jr., "Classical liberalism vs modern liberalism (socialism)—a primer," *HaciendaPublishing.com*, May 21, 2012. https://haciendapublishing.com/classical-liberalism-vs-modern-liberalism-socialism–a-primer-by-miguel-a-faria-md/. See also: Miguel A. Faria, Jr., "The Enlightenment — a triumph of classical not modern liberalism!" *HaciendaPublishing.com*, September 29, 2015. https://haciendapublishing.com/the-enlightenment–a-triumph-of-classical-not-modern-liberalism-by-miguel-a-faria-md/.
8. Scammell, *Solzhenitsyn*, 878.
9. Scammell, *Solzhenitsyn*, 642.
10. Scammell, *Solzhenitsyn*, 969.
11. Aleksandr Solzhenitsyn, *The Oak and the Calf: Memoirs of a Literary Life*, trans. H.T. Willets (Franklin Center, PA: Franklin Library, 1980).
12. Brian C. Anderson, "Solzhenitsyn's permanence," *The New Criterion*, February 4th, 2015. https://newcriterion.com/issues/2015/2/solzhenitsyns-permanence.
13. Aleksandr Solzhenitsyn, *March 1917: The Red Wheel / Node III*, trans. Marian Schwartz (Notre Dame, IN: University of Notre Dame Press, 2017).
14. For other notable works, see Aleksandr Solzhenitsyn, *The First Circle*, trans. Thomas P. Whitney (New York: Harper & Row, 1968); Aleksandr Solzhenitsyn, *Cancer Ward*, trans. Nicholas Bethell and David Burg (New York: Bantam Books, 1972); and Aleksandr Solzhenitsyn, *Prussian Nights: A Narrative Poem*, trans. Robert Conquest (London: Collins and Harvill Press, 1977).
15. Aleksandr Solzhenitsyn, *The Gulag Archipelago (1918–1956): An Experiment in Literary Investigation*, Parts I-II—The Prison Industry and Perpetual Motion, trans. Thomas P. Whitney (New York: Harper & Row, 1974), v.
16. Aleksandr Solzhenitsyn, *The Gulag Archipelago (1918–1956): An Experiment in Literary Investigation*, Parts III-IV—The Destructive

Labor Camps and The Soul and Barbed Wire, trans. Thomas P. Whitney (New York: Harper & Row, 1975), 605.
17. Scammell, *Solzhenitsyn,* 136.
18. Scammell, *Solzhenitsyn,* 137.
19. Solzhenitsyn, *The Gulag Archipelago, Part I,* 18.
20. Scammell, *Solzhenitsyn,* 155.
21. Aleksandr Solzhenitsyn, "The Socially Friendly" in *The Gulag Archipelago (1918–1956): An Experiment in Literary Investigation, Parts III-IV—The Destructive Labor Camps and The Soul and Barbed Wire,* trans. Thomas P. Whitney (New York: Harper & Row, 1975), 425-446.
22. Solzhenitsyn, *The Gulag Archipelago, Part III,* 430.
23. Solzhenitsyn, *The Gulag Archipelago, Part I,* 13n5.
24. Solzhenitsyn, *The Gulag Archipelago, Part I,* 4-5.
25. Solzhenitsyn, *The Gulag Archipelago, Part III,* 431.
26. Miguel A. Faria, Jr., *America, Guns and Freedom: A Journey Into Politics and the Public Health & Gun Control Movements* (Herndon, VA: Mascot Books, 2019), 258-262.
27. Solzhenitsyn, *The Gulag Archipelago, Part II,* 48-49, 75-80, 91-92, 99, 138-141, 155, 276, 535, 587. See also: Anne Applebaum, *Gulag: A History* (New York: Doubleday, 2003), 54, 59, 97-98, 257. For Frenkel at the Solovetsky camp, 31-37. For Frenkel at the White Sea Canal, 54, 63.
28. Applebaum, *Gulag,* 32-34.
29. Applebaum, *Gulag,* 31.
30. Applebaum, *Gulag,* 54.
31. Solzhenitsyn, *The Gulag Archipelago, Part II,* 49.
32. Applebaum, *Gulag,* 59, 63, 97-98, 257.
33. Solzhenitsyn, *The Gulag Archipelago, Part II,* 75-80, 91-92, 99, 138-141, 155, 276, 535, 587.
34. Scammell, *Solzhenitsyn,* 838.
35. *Pravada,* 14 February 1974, quoted in Scammell, *Solzhenitsyn,* 840.
36. Scammell, *Solzhenitsyn,* 841.
37. History.com Editors, "Nobel laureate Aleksandr Solzhenitsyn returns to Russia after exile," *A&E Television Network,* May 26, 2020. https://www.history.com/this-day-in-history/solzhenitsyn-returns-to-russia.

Part IV

Chapter 11

1. Jung Chang and Jon Halliday, *Mao: The Unknown Story* (New York: Alfred A. Knopf, 2005), 631. This authoritative biography and history is a powerful exposé on Mao Tse-tung and the People's Republic of China. Illustrated with rare photographs and detailed maps of specific areas discussed in the text, the supportive material includes meticulously compiled notes followed by comprehensive bibliographies of both Chinese and non-Chinese language sources. There is an index and lists of interviewees and archives consulted. The authors should be commended for their herculean task, vivid narration, and encyclopedic scholarship. Additionally, I must mention at this time that most readers left positive reviews for *Mao: The Unknown Story* on Amazon.com. However, it soon became obvious that there was also a shockingly unfair and orchestrated political campaign of vilification taking place, which frankly reminded me of the Active Measures and Disinformation Department of the Soviet KGB. This campaign was not, of course, directed from Moscow but, we must suppose, from Beijing and bolstered by the remaining bastions of Marxism in Western academia.
2. Simon Sebag Montefiore, "History: Mao by Jung Chang and Jon Halliday," *The Times*, May 29, 2005. https://www.thetimes.co.uk/article/history-mao-by-jung-chang-and-jon-halliday-3j99x9pxwzh.
3. Chang and Halliday, *Mao: The Unknown Story*, 630.
4. Chang and Halliday, *Mao: The Unknown Story*, 631.
5. The definitive number of Chinese people who died under the yoke of Mao Tse-tung in communist China will never be known. Many scholars dispute the figures. Some revisionist historians have come up with lower figures, but Chang and Halliday provided the most convincing approximation. The estimate of 40 to 60 million people is a conservative estimate based on the scholarship on the subject. The reader is advised to not only consult Jung Chang and Jon Halliday, *Mao: The Unknown Story*, but also inspect additional sources for an accurate estimate, including Stéphane Courtois and Mark Kramer, *The Black Book of Communism: Crimes, Terror Repression* (Cambridge, MA: Harvard University Press, 1999); and R. J. Rummel, *Death By Government: Genocide and Mass Murder Since 1900* (New Brunswick, NJ: Transaction Publishers, 1994).
6. Chang and Halliday, *Mao: The Unknown Story*, 332.
7. Chang and Halliday, *Mao: The Unknown Story*, 193-292.

8. Chang and Jon Halliday, *Mao: The Unknown Story,* 157-213. See also: Sun Shuyun, *The Long March: The True History of Communist China's Founding Myth* (New York: Doubleday, 2006), 111-160. It should be noted that in Sun Shuyun's book some of the Chinese proper names are spelled differently from the spellings in Chang and Halliday's book. For example, Shuyan writes Mao Zedong (instead of Mao Tse-tung); Chiang Kaishek (instead of Chiang Kai-shek) and Zhang Guotao (instead of Chang Kuo-t'ao).
9. For documentation of the extensive espionage carried out by Stalin and his foreign intelligence apparatus against the West before, during, and after World War II, see John Earl Haynes, Harvey Klehr, and Alexander Vassiliev, *Spies: The Rise and Fall of the KGB in America* (New Haven, CT: Yale University Press, 2009); Herbert Romerstein and Eric Breindel, *The Venona Secrets: Exposing Soviet Espionage and America's Traitors* (Washington, DC: Regnery Publishing, 2000); and Allen Weinstein and Alexander Vassiliev, *The Haunted Wood: Soviet Espionage in America—The Stalin Era*, (New York: Random House, 1999). When relevant, intelligence information was sent from Stalin to Mao Tse-tung and communist China. A few of the agents, such as Owen Lattimore and Lauchlin Currie in the FDR administration, actually favored China more than the Soviet Union. Additional historic material can be found in standard history books and in declassified intelligence files from the U.S., Germany, and the former Soviet Union.
10. Chang and Halliday, *Mao: The Unknown Story,* 281-292. For the American moles in the FDR administration helping Stalin as well as Mao, see John Koster, *Operation Snow: How a Soviet Mole in FDR's White House Triggered Pearl Harbor* (Washington, DC: Regnery History, 2012); and M. Stanton Evans and Herbert Romerstein, *Stalin's Secret Agents: The Subversion of Roosevelt's Government* (New York: Simon & Schuster, 2012).
11. Chang and Halliday, *Mao: The Unknown Story,* 293-300.
12. Chang and Halliday, *Mao: The Unknown Story,* 301-311.
13. Chang and Halliday, *Mao: The Unknown Story,* 210-229. For Peng Dehuai contravening Mao's order, see 237 and subsequently attacked by Mao, see 263.
14. Chang and Halliday, *Mao: The Unknown Story,* 287.
15. Chang and Halliday, *Mao: The Unknown Story,* 77-119.
16. Chang and Halliday, *Mao: The Unknown Story,* 236-292.
17. Chang and Halliday, *Mao: The Unknown Story,* 312-333.
18. Chang and Halliday, *Mao: The Unknown Story,* 503.
19. Chang and Halliday, *Mao: The Unknown Story,* 515.

20. Tom Phillips, "The Cultural Revolution: all you need to know about China's political convulsion," *The Guardian*, May 10, 2016. https://www.theguardian.com/world/2016/may/11/the-cultural-revolution-50-years-on-all-you-need-to-know-about-chinas-political-convulsion.
21. Chang and Halliday, *Mao: The Unknown Story*, 594.
22. Chang and Halliday, *Mao: The Unknown Story*, 592-593.
23. Chang and Halliday, *Mao: The Unknown Story*, 286-287.
24. Chang and Halliday, *Mao: The Unknown Story*, 504.
25. Chang and Halliday, *Mao: The Unknown Story*, 557-561.
26. Chang and Halliday, *Mao: The Unknown Story*, 563.
27. Chang and Halliday, *Mao: The Unknown Story*, 216
28. Chang and Halliday, *Mao: The Unknown Story*, 470.
29. Chang and Halliday, *Mao: The Unknown Story*, 471.
30. Chang and Halliday, *Mao: The Unknown Story*, 528-536.
31. Chang and Halliday, *Mao: The Unknown Story*, 198-199.
32. Chang and Halliday, *Mao: The Unknown Story*, 614.
33. Chang and Halliday, *Mao: The Unknown Story*, 610.
34. Chang and Halliday, *Mao: The Unknown Story*, 159-165.
35. Chang and Halliday, *Mao: The Unknown Story*, 212-213.
36. Chang and Halliday, *Mao: The Unknown Story*, 222.
37. Chang and Halliday, *Mao: The Unknown Story*, 423.
38. Chang and Halliday, *Mao: The Unknown Story*, 625.
39. Chang and Halliday, *Mao: The Unknown Story*, 623.
40. Chang and Halliday, *Mao: The Unknown Story*, 223.
41. Chang and Halliday, *Mao: The Unknown Story*, 363-366.
42. Chang and Halliday, *Mao: The Unknown Story*, 536.

Chapter 12

1. Harrison E. Salisbury, *The Long March: The Untold Story* (Franklin Center, PA, The Franklin Library, 1985). For another hagiographic biography of Mao Tse-tung, see Edgar Snow, *Red Star Over China* (New York: Random House, 1937).
2. Harrison E. Salisbury, *Black Night, White Snow: Russia's Revolution, 1905–1917* (Franklin Center, PA: The Franklin Library, 1977).
3. Salisbury, *The Long March: The Untold Story*, 71.
4. Jung Chang and Jon Halliday, *Mao: The Unknown Story* (New York: Alfred A. Knopf, 2005).
5. Sun Shuyun, *The Long March: The True History of Communist China's Founding Myth* (New York: Doubleday, 2006).

6. Herbert Romerstein and Eric Breindel, *The Venona Secrets: Exposing Soviet Espionage and America's Traitors* (Washington, DC: Regnery, 2000).
7. Shuyun, *The Long March*, 195.
8. History.com Editors, "The Long March," *A&E Television Network*, October 14, 2021. https://www.history.com/this-day-in-history/the-long-march. See also: Chang and Halliday, *Mao: The Unknown Story*, 130-167.
9. Chang and Halliday, *Mao: The Unknown Story*, 139.
10. Chang and Halliday, *Mao: The Unknown Story*, 155.
11. Chang and Halliday, *Mao: The Unknown Story*, 158-159.
12. Chang and Halliday, *Mao: The Unknown Story*, 150.
13. Chang and Halliday, *Mao: The Unknown Story*, 159-165, 180-181. See also: Shuyun, *The Long March*, 219-244. Despite writing, *Mao Tse-tung on Guerrilla Warfare*, originally published in China in 1937, Mao's knowledge was belatedly gained. He did not follow many of his own precepts during the Long March. For example, riding in a litter and protected by bodyguards, he seldom followed the dictum that "the guerrilla must move amongst the people *as fish* swim in the *sea*." However, he did follow the precepts of a Chinese military treatise dating from approximately the 5th century B.C.—namely, Sun Tzu, *The Art of War*. Mao avoided engagement of the enemy until he was sure he could win a battle; not to mention the fact that he frequently used many forms of deception.
14. Shuyun, *The Long March,* 140-148. For the conversation between Shuyun and the Beijing military historian, see 140-141.
15. Chang and Halliday, *Mao: The Unknown Story,* 153-154.
16. Chang and Halliday, *Mao: The Unknown Story,* 175-190. For Stalin's order to the CCP, see 179. For Stalin's message to Mao after the kidnapping of Chiang Kai-shek and Mao's reaction, see 187-189.
17. Shuyun, *The Long March*, 3.
18. Shuyun, *The Long March,* 220-244.
19. Shuyun, *The Long March,* 57-63. For the pain and suffering of the people as a result of Mao's harsh policies during this period, see 47-100. For the quotation about Mao's purge, see 57-58. For Sun Shuyun's introspective quotation, see 62.
20. Shuyun, *The Long March*, 84-85.
21. Shuyun, *The Long March*, 64-69.
22. "Turkey demands China close camps after reports of musician's death," *BBC*, February 10, 2019. https://www.bbc.com/news/world-asia-47187170. The Uighurs are not alone in their persecution in China today.

In the past, they suffered massacres by the Chinese communists, as did other minorities, including the ethnic Chinese. From 1949 to the present, an estimated 40 to 60 million Chinese people—including Uighurs, alleged "class enemies," and religious minorities, such as Christians, Muslims, Tibetan Buddhists, and Kazakhs—have been killed by China's communist authorities. See also: R.J. Rummel, *Death By Government: Genocide and Mass Murder Since 1900* (New Brunswick, NJ: Transaction Publishers, 1994); Stéphane Courtois and Mark Kramer, *The Black Book of Communism: Crimes, Terror, Repression* (Cambridge, MA: Harvard University Press, 1999); Jay Simkin, Alan M. Rice, and Aaron S. Zelman, *Lethal Laws: Gun Control Is the Key to Genocide* (Bellevue, WA: Jews for the Preservation of Firearms Ownership, 1994); and Jung Chang and Jon Halliday, *Mao: The Unknown Story* (New York: Alfred A. Knopf, 2005).

Chapter 13

1. Edward Timperlake and William C. Triplett, II, *Year of the Rat: How Bill Clinton Compromised U.S. Security for Chinese Cash* (Washington, DC: Regnery Publishing, 1998).
2. "Tiananmen Square protest death toll 'was 10,000,' " *BBC*, December 23, 2017. https://www.bbc.com/news/world-asia-china-42465516.
3. Timperlake and Triplett, *Year of the Rat*, 3-78.
4. Timperlake and Triplett, *Year of the Rat*, 212.
5. Timperlake and Triplett, *Year of the Rat,* 83-84, 137, 142, 187-199, 206-207.
6. Timperlake and Triplett, *Year of the Rat*, 76-77, 94, 137-138, 207-213.
7. Timperlake and Triplett, *Year of the Rat,* 190.
8. Timperlake and Triplett, *Year of the Rat*, 178-179.
9. Timperlake and Triplett, *Year of the Rat*, 131-196.
10. Timperlake and Triplett, *Year of the Rat*, 144, 226.
11. Timperlake and Triplett, *Year of the Rat*, 165-166.
12. The Congressional Record, "China's Theft of Nuclear Secrets (Senate - March 15, 1999)." https://irp.fas.org/congress/1999_cr/s990315-prc.htm.
13. Timperlake and Triplett, *Year of the Rat*, 7-50.
14. David Johnston, "Committee told of Beijing cash for Democrats," *The New York Times*, May 12, 1999. https://www.nytimes.com/1999/05/12/us/committee-told-of-beijing-cash-for-democrats.html
15. U.S. Department of Justice, "James Riady pleads guilty, will pay largest fine in campaign finance history for violating federal election law," Press Release, January 11, 2001. https://www.justice.gov/archive/opa/

pr/2001/January/017crm.htm; and Andrew Higgins, "How the disgraced James Riady, barred from travel to the U.S., made it back," *Washington Post*, January 5, 2010. https://www.washingtonpost.com/wpdyn/content/article/2010/01/04/AR2010010403106.html. For the U.S. companies that violated export laws, see Jeff Gerth, "2 companies pay penalties for improving China rockets," *The New York Times*, May 6, 2003. https://www.nytimes.com/2003/03/06/world/2-companies-pay-penalties-for-improving-china-rockets.html.

16. Timperlake and Triplett, *Year of the Rat,* 110.
17. "Taiwan flashpoint—US role," *BBC*, February 28, 2015. https://web.archive.org/web/20150228051216/http://news.bbc.co.uk/2/shared/spl/hi/asia_pac/04/taiwan_flashpoint/html/us_role.stm. See also: Michael J. Green and Bonnie S. Glaser, "What is the U.S. 'one China' policy, and why does it matter?" *Center for Strategic & International Studies*, January 13, 2017. https://www.csis.org/analysis/what-us-one-china-policy-and-why-does-it-matter.
18. Susan V. Lawrence, "President Reagan's Six Assurances to Taiwan," *Congressional Research Service*, June 13, 2023. https://crsreports.congress.gov/product/pdf/IF/IF11665.
19. Michael Callahan, "Biden administration approves potential $440 million arms sales to Taiwan," *CNN.com*, June 20, 2023. https://www.cnn.com/2023/06/30/politics/us-arms-sales-taiwan/index.html.
20. Evelyn Cheng, "Taiwan's trade with China is far bigger than its trade with the U.S.," *CNBC.com*, August 4, 2022. https://www.cnbc.com/2022/08/05/taiwans-trade-with-china-is-far-bigger-than-its-trade-with-the-us.html.
21. Miguel A. Faria, Jr., "Trump, Taiwan, and China—A phone call and a change in direction?" *HaciendaPublishing.com*, December 4, 2016. https://haciendapublishing.com/trump-taiwan-and-china-a-phone-call-and-a-change-in-direction/.
22. Miguel A. Faria, Jr., "Donald Trump president elect—one man's view of the 2016 election coverage," *HaciendaPublishing.com*, November 9, 2016. https://haciendapublishing.com/donald-trump-president-elect–one-mans-view-of-the-2016-election-coverage/.
23. Daniel Politi, "Trump slams China on Twitter amid debate over significance of Taiwan call," *Slate.com*, December 4, 2016. https://slate.com/news-and-politics/2016/12/trump-slams-china-on-twitter-amid-debate-over-significance-of-taiwan-call.html. See also: Nyshka Chandran, "Donald Trump insults China with Taiwan phone call and tweets on trade," *CNBC.com*, December 5, 2016.

https://www.cnbc.com/2016/12/05/donald-trump-insults-china-with-taiwan-phone-call-and-tweets-on-trade-south-china-sea.html.
24. Louis Nelson, "China: Trump team aware of Beijing's 'solemn attitude' on Taiwan," *Politico.com*, December 15, 2016. https://www.politico.com/story/2016/12/trump-taiwan-china-response-232198.
25. The Editors of Encyclopaedia Britannica, "Hu Yaobang: Chinese political leader," *Encyclopedia Britannica*, July 10, 2023. https://www.britannica.com/biography/Hu-Yaobang.
26. "Gen. Yang Baibing dies at 93; led Tiananmen crackdown," *The New York Times*, January 17, 2013. https://www.nytimes.com/2013/01/18/world/asia/gen-yang-baibing-dies-at-93-led-tiananmen-crackdown.html.
27. Man vs. tank in Tiananmen Square, *YouTube.com*, June 5, 1989. https://www.youtube.com/watch?v=YeFzeNAHEhU.
28. Christopher Bodeen, "Prosperity, repression mark China 30 years after Tiananmen," *APNews.com*, June 3, 2019.

Chapter 14

1. David Wise, *Tiger Trap: America's Secret Spy War with China* (Boston: Houghton Mifflin Harcourt, 2011), 10-14. *Tiger Trap* is a critically important book because most Westerners know very little about espionage activities conducted by China in the United States and the West. The book is 292 pages, contains a good index, and is fully annotated and illustrated with an insert of glossy photographs identifying most of the villains, some innocent bystanders, and even a few heroes. The book can be exasperating at times but always thrilling, and in the end, a wakeup call. See also: David Wise, "America's other espionage challenge: China", *The New York Times*, March 5, 2018. https://www.nytimes.com/2018/03/05/opinion/china-espionage.html.
2. David Wise, *Tiger Trap*, 21-201.
3. David Wise, *Tiger Trap*, 71-241. For the SEGO PALM investigation and outcome, see 99-108, 138.
4. David Wise, *Tiger Trap*, 2-92, 144, 149, 167, 205, 238.
5. David Wise, *Tiger Trap*, 202-213.
6. Richard C. S. Trahair, *The Encyclopedia of Cold War Espionage, Spies, and Secret Operations* (Westport, CT: Greenwood Press, 2004), 6-7, 357.

7. Harvey Klehr and Ronald Radosh, *The Amerasia Spy Case: Prelude to McCarthyism* (Chapel Hill, NC: University of North Carolina Press, 1996).
8. M. Stanton Evan and Herbert Romerstein, *Stalin's Secret Agents: The Subversion of Roosevelt's Government* (New York: Simon & Schuster, 2012), 212-223, 231-234.
9. Richard C. S. Trahair, *The Encyclopedia of Cold War Espionage, Spies, and Secret Operations*, 290-292.
10. For the case of John Stewart Service, see Evans and Romerstein, *Stalin's Secret Agents,* 213-246. See also: Herbert Romerstein and Eric Breindel, *The Venona Secrets: Exposing Soviet Espionage and America's Traitors* (Washington, DC: Regnery, 2000), 168-169. Curiously, the photo used in this chapter shows John Stewart Service in an intense conversation with Soong Ching-ling, who was the third wife of Sun Yat-sen. After his death, she travelled to the Soviet Union to meet with Stalin. She was an ardent communist opponent of Chiang Kai-shek whose wife was Soong May-ling, her younger sister. Author Jung Chang in her book, *Big Sister, Little Sister, Red Sister: Three Woman at the Heart of 20th Century China* (New York: Alfred A. Knopf, 2019) referred to Ching-ling as the "Red Sister." She served under Mao Tse-tung's communist regime as a Vice Premier. For the case against Solomon Adler, see Evans and Romerstein, *Stalin's Secret Agents,* 82-85, 102-103, 146-254.
11. Christopher Andrew and Vasili Mitrokhin, *The Sword and the Shield: The Mitrokhin Archive and the Secret History of the KGB* (New York: Basic Books, 1999), 106-107, 129-130, 142-143.
12. Evans and Romerstein, *Stalin's Secret Agents,* 95-98, 212-230. Further evidence of Lattimore's betrayal of China to the communists is furnished in the testimony of Stanley K. Hornbeck, February 15, 1952. U. S. Congress, Senate Committee on the Judiciary, Internal Security Subcommittee, Institute of Pacific Relations, Hearings, 82nd Congress, First Session, Washington, D.C., Government Printing Office, 1951, Part 9, p. 3209-10.
13. For documentation confirming Harry Hopkins as an "agent of influence" associated with the Nathan Silvermaster Soviet espionage network in wartime Washington, D.C., see Evans and Romerstein, *Stalin's Secret Agents*, 19. See also: Allen Weinstein and Alexander Vassiliev, *The Haunted Wood: Soviet Espionage in America—The Stalin Era* (New York: Random House, 1999), 154-160. For Harry Hopkins' closeness to FDR, see Robert A. Sherwood, *Roosevelt and Hopkins* (New York: Harper & Brothers, 1948), 749.

14. History.com Editors, "Joseph McCarthy charges that Owen Lattimore is a Soviet spy," *A&E Television Networks*, March 24, 2021. https://www.history.com/this-day-in-history/mccarthy-charges-that-owen-lattimore-is-a-soviet-spy.
15. William F. Buckley, Jr. and L. Brent Bozell, *McCarthy and His Enemies, The Record And Its Meaning* (Washington, DC: Henry Regnery Company, 1954).
16. Toby Westerman, "The dragon's eyes are on us," *International News Analysis*, June 27, 2013. https://www.traditioninaction.org/HotTopics/i99ht_035_Espionage.html.
17. Daniel F. Runde, "Key decision point coming for the Panama Canal" *Center for Strategic & International Studies*, May 21, 2021. https://www.csis.org/analysis/key-decision-point-coming-panama-canal.
18. "China likely to share SIGINT with Russians," *Robert Lansing Institute for Global Threats and Democracies Studies*, June 27, 2023. https://lansinginstitute.org/2023/06/27/china-likely-to-share-sigint-with-russians/.
19. Chuck DeVore, "What China is doing in Cuba is a big threat to all of us," *Fox News*, June 27, 2023. https://www.foxnews.com/opinion/what-china-doing-cuba-big-threat-all-us.
20. Miguel A. Faria, Jr., *Cuba's Eternal Revolution through the Prism of Insurgency, Socialism, and Espionage* (Newcastle upon Tyne, UK: Cambridge Scholars Publishing, 2023), 139-163.
21. Sam LaGrone, "Report: China hacked two dozen U.S. weapon designs," *United States Naval Institute*, May 28, 2013. https://news.usni.org/2013/05/28/report-china-hacked-two-dozen-u-s-weapon-designs.
22. Ellen Nakashima, "Confidential report lists U.S. weapons system designs compromised by Chinese cyberspies," May 27, 2013. https://www.washingtonpost.com/world/national-security/confidential-report-lists-us-weapons-system-designs-compromised-by-chinese-cyberspies/2013/05/27/a42c3e1c-c2dd-11e2-8c3b-0b5e9247e8ca_story.html.
23. David E. Sanger, David Barboza, and Nicole Perlroth, "Chinese army unit is seen as tied to hacking against U.S.," *The New York Times*, February 18, 2013. https://www.nytimes.com/2013/02/19/technology/chinas-army-is-seen-as-tied-to-hacking-against-us.html.
24. Mikko Hypponen, "Viewpoint: Stuxnet shift the cyber arms race up a gear," *BBC*, July 14, 2012. https://www.bbc.co.uk/news/technology-18825742. See also: " 'Red October' cyber-attack found by Russian

researchers," *BBC*, January 14, 2023. https://www.bbc.com/news/technology-21013087.
25. David Shepardson and Karen Freifeld, "Trump administration hits China's Huawei with one-two punch," *Reuters*, May 15, 2019. https://www.reuters.com/article/us-usa-china-trump-telecommunications/trump-administration-hits-chinas-huawei-with-one-two-punch-idUSKCN1SL2QX.
26. "Huawei: China threatens to retaliate over US sanctions," *BBC*, May 16, 2019. https://www.bbc.com/news/world-us-canada-48299522?ocid=socialflow_twitter.
27. "Huawei role in UK 5G network an unnecessary risk, ex-MI6 chief says," *BBC*, May 16, 2019. https://www.bbc.com/news/uk-48297407.
28. "UK extends deadline to remove Huawei equipment from 5G network core," *Reuters*, October 13, 2022. https://www.reuters.com/business/media-telecom/uk-extends-deadline-remove-huawei-equipment-5g-network-core-2022-10-13/.
29. "Harvard University professor and two Chinese nationals charged in three separate China related cases," U.S. Department of Justice, January 28, 2020. https://www.justice.gov/opa/pr/harvard-university-professor-and-two-chinese-nationals-charged-three-separate-china-related.
30. James I. Ausman and Russell L. Blaylock, *The China Virus: What is the Truth?* Independently published, July 8, 2021.
31. "Harvard University professor convicted of making false statements and tax offenses," United States Attorney's Office, District of Massachusetts, Department of Justice, December 21, 2021. https://www.justice.gov/usao-ma/pr/harvard-university-professor-convicted-making-false-statements-and-tax-offenses.
32. Bernd Debusmann Jr., "Suspected Chinese spy balloon was 200 ft tall—US defense official," *BBC*, February 6, 2023.
33. "2 US Navy sailors charged with spying for China," Newsmax.com, August 4, 2023. https://www.newsmax.com/newsfront/espionage-navy-arrests/2023/08/03/id/1129553/.

Part V

Chapter 15

1. John Barron, *KGB: The Secret Work of Soviet Secret Agents* (New York: Reader's Digest Press, 1974). This book is 462 pages and includes appendices, notes, bibliography, and index. It is fully illustrated with 16 pages of photographs revealing the faces of many of the main

protagonists and antagonists as well as operational methods. The appendices are still useful to scholars as invaluable mines of information for Western intelligence services. For example, Appendix C, "The Practice of Recruiting Americans in the USA and Other Countries" describes how Americans can be duped into spying for a foreign tyranny; and Appendix D, "Soviet Citizens Engaged in Clandestine Operations Abroad" was particularly damaging to the Soviets and revealed the identity of hundreds of their active spies throughout the world.

2. John Barron, *Operation Solo: The FBI's Man in the Kremlin* (Washington, DC: Regnery Publishing, 1996). See also: Brian Latell, *Castro's Secrets: The CIA and Cuba's Intelligence Machine* (New York: Palgrave Macmillan, 2012).
3. Christopher Andrew and Vasili Mitrokhin, *The Sword and the Shield: The Mitrokhin Archive and the Secret History of the KGB* (New York: Basic Books, 1999), 19.
4. Barron, *KGB: The Secret Work of the Soviet Secret Agents*, 271.
5. Barron, *KGB: The Secret Work of the Soviet Secret Agents*, 301.
6. Barron, *KGB: The Secret Work of the Soviet Secret Agents*, 305.
7. Barron, *KGB: The Secret Work of the Soviet Secret Agents*, 141-163.
8. Miguel A. Faria, Jr., *Cuba's Eternal Revolution through the Prism of Insurgency, Socialism, and Espionage* (Newcastle upon Tyne, UK: Cambridge Scholars Publishing, 2023), 140-163.
9. Barron, *KGB: The Secret Work of the Soviet Secret Agents*, 169.
10. Faria, *Cuba's Eternal Revolution through the Prism of Insurgency, Socialism, and Espionage*, ix, 126-128.
11. Barron, *KGB: The Secret Work of the Soviet Secret Agents*, 207.
12. Barron, *KGB: The Secret Work of the Soviet Secret Agents*, 230-257. See also: Jefferson Morley, *Our Man in Mexico: Winston Scott and the Hidden History of the CIA* (Lawrence, KS: University of Kansas Press, 2008).
13. Barron, *KGB: The Secret Work of the Soviet Secret Agents*, 29-62.
14. Christopher Andrew and Oleg Gordievsky, *KGB: The Inside Story of Its Foreign Operations from Lenin to Gorbachev* (New York: Harper Collins, 1990).
15. Andrew and Mitrokhin, *The Sword and the Shield*, 20.
16. Ben Macintyre, *The Spy and the Traitor: The Greatest Espionage Story of the Cold War* (London: Penguin Books, 2019), 227-337.
17. Andrew and Mitrokhin, *The Sword and the Shield*, 1.
18. Andrew and Mitrokhin, *The Sword and the Shield*, 22.

19. Christopher Andrew and Vasili Mitrokhin, *The World Was Going Our Way: The KGB and the Battle for the Third World* (New York: Basic Books, 2005).

Chapter 16

1. David C. Martin, *Wilderness of Mirrors: Intrigue, Deception, and the Secrets that Destroyed Two of the Cold War's Most Important Agents* (Guilford, CT: The Lyon Press, 2003), 108-116.
2. Joseph J. Trento, *The Secret History of the CIA* (New York: Prima Forum, 2010), 232-234. James Jesus Angleton was the primary source for this book, which takes a somewhat sympathetic view of the destructive mole hunt Angleton conducted in the CIA and even goes so far as to reveal the name and identity of the spy who Angleton so avidly searched for—Igor Orlov.
3. Christopher Andrew and Vasili Mitrokhin, *The Sword and the Shield: The Mitrokhin Archive and the Secret History of the KGB* (New York: Basic Books, 1999), 184-186.
4. Ben Macintyre, *A Spy Among Friends: Kim Philby and the Great Betrayal* (Toronto, ON: Signal, McClelland & Stewart, 2015), 241.
5. Trento, *The Secret History of the CIA*, 286-288.
6. Trento, *The Secret History of the CIA*, 33-39.
7. Macintyre, *A Spy Among Friends*, 301.
8. Martin, *Wilderness of Mirrors*, 56.
9. Edward J. Epstein, *Deception: The Invisible War Between the KGB and the CIA* (New York: Simon & Schuster, 1989), 260. Epstein supports Golitsyn and Angleton in their espionage assessment. The book is revealing and may be used by scholars for both espionage and historical research. Some of the conclusions Epstein draws, however, have been found to be incorrect, as newer contrarian information has come to light with the passage of time. See also: Peter Wright, *Spy Catcher: The Candid Autobiography of a Senior Intelligence Officer* (New York: Viking Pinguin, 1987). Wright was an Assistant Director of MI5 and a key figure in the British Secret Service for nearly a quarter of a century. Like Epstein, Wright shared similar views to those of Angleton and Golitsyn.
10. Anatoliy Golitsyn, *New Lies for Old: The Communist Strategy of Deception and Disinformation* (New York: Dodd, Mead & Company, 1984).
11. Epstein, *Deception*, 43-64.
12. Trento, *The Secret History of the CIA*, 285.

13. Jerrold L. Schecter and Peter S. Deriabin, *The Spy Who Saved the World: How a Soviet Colonel Changed the Course of the Cold War* (New York: Charles Scribner's Sons, 1992), 378-380, 390-396.
14. Sandra Grimes and Jeanne Vertefeuille, *Circle of Treason: A CIA Account of Traitor Aldrich Ames and the Men He Betrayed* (Annapolis, MD: Naval Institute Press, 2012), 23.
15. Grimes and Vertefeuille, *Circle of Treason*, 26-54.
16. Ben Macintyre, *The Spy and the Traitor: The Greatest Espionage Story of the Cold War* (London: Penguin Books, 2019), 66-67, 310.
17. Macintyre, *The Spy and the Traitor*, 274-305.
18. Alex Goldfarb, and Marina Litvinenko, *Death of a Dissident: The Poisoning of Alexander Litvinenko and the Return of the KGB* (New York: Free Press, 2007).
19. Anatoliy Golitsyn, *The Perestroika Deception: The Second October Revolution* (London: Edward Harle Ltd., 1995).
20. Joseph Persico, *Casey: The Lives and Secrets of William J. Casey: From the OSS to the CIA* (New York: Viking, 1990), 213.
21. Miguel A. Faria, Jr., "A history of (and tribute to) the CIA and the hunting down and death of Osama bin Laden," *HaciendaPublishing.com*, May 9, 2011. https://haciendapublishing.com/faria-a-history-of-and-tribute-to-the-cia-and-the-hunting-down-and-death-of-osama-bin-laden/. See also: Appendix B, "An Abbreviated History of the CIA to the 2011 Death of Osama bin Laden," in this book for a revised and updated version of the article.
22. Christopher Andrew and Vasili Mitrokhin, *The World Was Going Our Way: The KGB and the Battle for the Third World* (New York: Basic Books, 2005).
23. Andrew and Mitrokhin, *The World Was Going Our Way*, 456.
24. Jihan El Tahri, director. *Cuba: An African Odyssey*, 2007. This is an informative but biased documentary relating to events of the Cold War in Africa from 1961-1999. The documentary synopsis stated: "The Soviet Union wanted to extend its influence into a new continent; the U.S. lusted after Africa's natural resources; former European empires felt their grip on the area weaken; and newly formed African nations fought to defend their recently won independence. When the latter called on Cuban guerillas to aid them in their struggle, Castro and Cuba stepped in to build a new offensive strategy, which would have long-lasting influence on developing countries in their battles against colonialism… *Cuba: An African Odyssey* tells the story of those internationalists who won their battles but ultimately lost the war." To read an updated review of the documentary, see Appendix A in this book. See also: Miguel A.

Faria, Jr., *Cuba's Eternal Revolution through the Prism of Insurgency, Socialism, and Espionage* (Newcastle upon Tyne, UK: Cambridge Scholars Publishing, 2023). In the book, chapter 7 details the misadventures of Ernesto "Che" Guevara in the African Congo.
25. Andrew and Mitrokhin, *The World Was Going Our Way*, 182.
26. Michael Omer-Man, "This Week in History: Ayatollah Khomeini returns to Iran." *Jerusalem Post*, February 4, 2011. https://www.jpost.com/Features/In-Thespotlight/This-Week-in-History-Ayatollah-Khomeini-returns-to-Iran. See also: Reza Kahlili. *A Time to Betray: The Astonishing Double Life of a CIA Agent Inside the Revolutionary Guards of Iran* (New York: Simon & Schuster, 2010); and History.com Editors, "Iran hostage rescue mission ends in disaster," *A&E Television Networks*, May 15, 2020. https://www.history.com/this-day-in-history/hostage-rescue-mission-ends-in-disaster.
27. "The Hostage Crisis in Iran," Jimmy Carter Presidential Library & Museum. https://www.jimmycarterlibrary.gov/research/additional-resorces/hostage-crisis-in-iran.
28. Milt Bearden and James Risen, *The Main Enemy: The Inside Story of the CIA's Showdown with the KGB* (New York: Random House, 2003), 207-296; and Mohammad Yousaf and Mark Adkin, *Afghanistan, The Bear Trap: The Defeat of a Superpower* (Philadelphia, PA: Casemate Publishers, 2008), 25, 142-144, 216-235. Both books relate to the invasion of Afghanistan, the coup d'état, the Soviet occupation and the collaborating communist government, the Mujahadeen and U.S. and Pakistani assistance, and the eventual decline and fall of the communist Soviet occupation and liberation of Afghanistan.
29. Persico, *Casey*, 225-226.
30. Andrew and Mitrokhin, *The Sword and the Shield*, 1.
31. John Barron, *Operation Solo: The FBI's Man in the Kremlin* (Washington, DC: Regnery Publishing, 1996).

Chapter 17

1. Richard C. S. Trahair, *The Encyclopedia of Cold War Espionage, Spies, and Secret Operations* (Westport, Connecticut: Greenwood Press, 2004).
2. Christopher Andrew and Oleg Gordievsky, *KGB: The Inside Story of Its Foreign Operations from Lenin to Gorbachev* (New York: Harper Collins, 1990).

3. Christopher Andrew and Vasili Mitrokhin, *The Sword and the Shield: The Mitrokhin Archive and the Secret History of the KGB* (New York: Basic Books, 1999).
4. Christopher Andrew and Vasili Mitrokhin, *The World Was Going Our Way: The KGB and the Battle for the Third World* (New York: Basic Books, 2005). This book continues to bring forth revelations from the Mitrokhin Archive about the surrogate nations of the Third World involved in the CIA-KGB contests of the Cold War. None of the material in this tome was available for inclusion in Trahair's encyclopedia because this book was not published until the following year.
5. Pete Earley, *Comrade J: The Untold Secrets of Russia's Master Spy in America After the End of the Cold War* (New York: G.P. Putnam's Sons, 2007).
6. Sandra Grimes and Jeanne Vertefeuille, *Circle of Treason: A CIA Account of Traitor Aldrich Ames and the Men He Betrayed* (Annapolis, MD: Naval Institute Press, 2012), 169-170.
7. Elaine Shannon and Ann Blackman, *The Spy Next Door: The Extraordinary Secret Life of Robert Philip Hanssen, the Most Damaging FBI Agent in U.S. History* (New York: Little, Brown, and Company, 2002).
8. David Wise, *Spy: The Inside Story of How the FBI's Robert Hanssen Betrayed America* (New York: Random House, 2002).
9. Sergei Kostin and Eric Raynaud, *Farewell: The Greatest Spy Story of the Twentieth Century*, trans. Catherine Cauvin-Higgins (Las Vegas: AmazonCrossing, 2011).
10. Trahair, *The Encyclopedia of Cold War Espionage, Spies, and Secret Operation,* 89-91.
11. Robert J. Lamphere and Tom Shachtman, *The FBI-KGB War: A Special Agent's Story* (Macon, GA: Mercer University Press, 1986). See also: Trahair, *The Encyclopedia of Cold War Espionage, Spies, and Secret Operation,* 83-84, 104-105.
12. Marcia Mitchell and Thomas Mitchell, *The Spy Who Seduced America: Lies and Betrayal in the Heat of the Cold War—The Judith Coplon Story* (Montpelier, VT: Invisible Cities Press, 2002).
13. Ben Macintyre, *A Spy Among Friends: Kim Philby and the Great Betrayal* (Toronto, ON: Signal, McClelland & Stewart, 2015), 143. See also: "Historic photographs of NSC and its predecessor organization," National Security Agency/Central Security Service. https://www.nsa.gov/Helpful-Links/NSA-FOIA/Declassification-Transparency-Initiatives/Historical-Releases/Arlington-Hall/.

14. Herbert Romerstein and Eric Breindel, *The Venona Secrets: Exposing Soviet Espionage and America's Traitors* (Washington, DC: Regnery Publishing, 2000).
15. Trahair, *The Encyclopedia of Cold War Espionage, Spies, and Secret Operation*, 93-94. For the detailed entry relating to George Blake, see 25-27. See also: "The Berlin Tunnel," Central Intelligence Agency. https://www.cia.gov/legacy/museum/exhibit/the-berlin-tunnel/.
16. Trahair, *The Encyclopedia of Cold War Espionage, Spies, and Secret Operation*, 189-190. For "the irrational fears," see 414-415. For a contrarian view on McCarthyism, see M. Stanton Evans, *Blacklisted by History: The Untold Story of Senator Joe McCarthy and His Fight Against America's Enemies* (New York: Crown Forum, 2007).
17. Trahair, *The Encyclopedia of Cold War Espionage, Spies, and Secret Operation*, 212.
18. Trahair, *The Encyclopedia of Cold War Espionage, Spies, and Secret Operation*, 217.
19. Trahair, *The Encyclopedia of Cold War Espionage, Spies, and Secret Operation*, 269-270. See also: Grimes and Vertefeuille, *Circle of Treason: A CIA Account of Traitor Aldrich Ames and the Men He Betrayed* for a more precise and favorable view of General Dmitri Polyakov.
20. Trahair, *The Encyclopedia of Cold War Espionage, Spies, and Secret Operation*, 41-42, 179-182, 332.
21. Trahair, *The Encyclopedia of Cold War Espionage, Spies, and Secret Operation*, 426.
22. John Barron, *KGB: The Secret Work of Soviet Secret Agents* (New York: Reader's Digest Press, 1974), 271, 301, 305.
23. Trahair, *The Encyclopedia of Cold War Espionage, Spies, and Secret Operation*, 431.
24. Trahair, *The Encyclopedia of Cold War Espionage, Spies, and Secret Operation*, 98-100.
25. Trahair, *The Encyclopedia of Cold War Espionage, Spies, and Secret Operation*, 429.
26. Trahair, *The Encyclopedia of Cold War Espionage, Spies, and Secret Operation*, 127-128.
27. Trahair, *The Encyclopedia of Cold War Espionage, Spies, and Secret Operation*, 138-139, 368, 369.
28. Trahair, *The Encyclopedia of Cold War Espionage, Spies, and Secret Operation*, 102-103.
29. Romerstein and Breindel, *The Venona Secrets*, 168-169, 184.

30. M. Stanton Evans and Herbert Romerstein, *Stalin's Secret Agents: The Subversion of Roosevelt's Government* (New York: Simon & Schuster, 2012), 213-246 relate to the case of John Stewart Service. For the case against Solomon Adler, see 82-85, 102-103, 146-254.

Chapter 18

1. Sergei Kostin and Eric Raynaud, *Farewell: The Greatest Spy Story of the Twentieth Century*, trans. Catherine Cauvin-Higgins (Las Vegas: Amazon Crossing, 2011).
2. "NATO—Declassified: the Pâques affair." https://www.nato.int/cps/en/natohq/declassified_138448.htm.
3. Kostin and Raynaud, *Farewell*, 166.
4. Gus W. Weiss, "The Farewell Dossier," Defense Technical Information Center, Washington, DC, January 1, 1996. https://apps.dtic.mil/sti/citations/ADA527328.
5. Kostin and Raynaud, *Farewell*, 384-385.
6. Kostin and Raynaud, *Farewell*, 387.
7. Kostin and Raynaud, *Farewell*, 180.
8. Kostin and Raynaud, *Farewell*, 358-360.
9. Kostin and Raynaud, *Farewell*, 389. At this point, a few relevant issues should be mentioned pertaining to the authors' alleged psychological profile and asserted possible motivation for Vladimir Vetrov's espionage and calculated, irrational, self-destructive end. Those highly subjective sections—mostly speculation derived from KGB sources, friends, and particularly, the "confessions" of Vetrov's mistress, Ludmila Ochikina, contained in chapters 22, 23 and parts of chapters 24 and 30—should have been omitted. The authors subliminally admit the superfluity of these pages: "In fact, thirteen years after having written these lines, even Sergei Kostin no longer believes it." (p. 319) And yet, this superfluous and erroneous detraction—that is, speculating sinister motives—was not discarded in the English version of the book published in 2011. Nevertheless, this is a magnificent book. The tome has relevant illustrations and helpful notes but no index, which surprisingly is only a minor annoyance because the book, written in colloquial terms, has almost no need for an index anyway. Other than those two detractions, the book is a suspenseful cliffhanger with the most plausible explanation formulated for why the USSR suddenly imploded between 1989-1991, followed by the precipitous collapse of the totalitarian Soviet and Eastern Bloc communist empire.

10. John Barron, *KGB: The Secret Work of Soviet Secret Agents* (New York: Reader's Digest Press, 1974), 29-62.
11. Barron, *KGB: The Secret Work of the Soviet Secret Agents*, 258-305.
12. Martha D. Peterson, *The Widow Spy: My Journey from the Jungles of Laos to Prison in Moscow* (Wilmington, NC: Red Camary Press, 2012).
13. Jerrold L. Schecter and Peter S. Deriabin, *The Spy Who Saved the World: How a Soviet Colonel Changed the Course of the Cold War* (New York: Charles Scribner's Sons, 1992).
14. Sandra Grimes and Jeanne Vertefeuille, *Circle of Treason: A CIA Account of Traitor Aldrich Ames and the Men He Betrayed* (Annapolis, MD: Naval Institute Press, 2012).
15. Ben Macintyre, *The Spy and the Traitor: The Greatest Espionage Story of the Cold War* (London: Penguin Books, 2019).
16. David E. Hoffman, *The Billion Dollar Spy: A True Story of Cold War Espionage and Betrayal* (New York: Doubleday, 2015).
17. *L'affaire Farewell*, directed by Christian Carion, (Pathé, 2009), 113 minutes.

Chapter 19

1. John Barron, *Operation Solo: The FBI's Man in the Kremlin* (Washington, DC: Regnery Publishing, 1996), 4-6. See also: Richard C.S. Trahair, *The Encyclopedia of Cold War Espionage, Spies, and Secret Operations* (Westport, CT: Greenwood Press, 2004), 243-244.
2. Harvey Klehr and John Earl Haynes, "Running SOLO: FBI's case of Morris and Jack Childs, 1952–77," *Studies in Intelligence* Vol. 66, No. 1 (Extracts, March 2022). https://www.cia.gov/static/Article-FBI-Project-Solo.pdf.
3. Trahair, *The Encyclopedia of Cold War Espionage, Spies, and Secret Operations*, 47-48.
4. Barron, *Operation Solo*, 56.
5. Barron, *Operation Solo*, 300.
6. Barron, *Operation Solo*, 236.
7. Barron, *Operation Solo*, 92.
8. Barron, *Operation Solo*, 93.
9. Barron, *Operation Solo*, 94-95.
10. Barron, *Operation Solo*, 123.
11. Barron, *Operation Solo*, 177-189.
12. Barron, *Operation Solo*, 191-207.
13. Barron, *Operation Solo*, 261-314.
14. Barron, *Operation Solo*, 254.

15. Barron, *Operation Solo*, 287.
16. Barron, *Operation Solo*, 315-316.
17. Barron, *Operation Solo*, 318.
18. Ben Macintyre, *The Spy and the Traitor: The Greatest Espionage Story of the Cold War* (London: Penguin Books, 2019), 144-162.
19. Barron, *Operation Solo*, 317.
20. Macintyre, *The Spy and the Traitor*, 178-201.
21. Barron, *Operation Solo*, 326-327.

Part VI

Chapter 20

1. Daniel Sandford, "Moscow coup 1991: with Boris Yeltsin on the tank," *BBC*, August 20, 2011. https://www.bbc.com/news/world-europe-14589691.
2. David Horowitz, "Socialism by any other name," *National Review*, April 13, 1992.
3. John Paull, "War in Ukraine: treaty to treachery," in the Proceedings of Russia-Ukraine War: Consequences for the World, 3rd International Scientific and Practical Internet Conference, March 2-3, 2023, WayScience, Dnipro, Ukraine, 18-20. https://www.academia.edu/98199478/War_in_Ukraine_From_Treaty_to_Treacher.
4. Mariana Budjeryn, "The breach: Ukraine's territorial integrity and the Budapest Memorandum," *WilsonCenter.org*, Issue Brief #3.
5. Peter Dickinson, "The 2008 Russo-Georgian War: Putin's green light," *Atlantic Council*, August 7, 2021. https://www.atlanticcouncil.org/blogs/ukrainealert/the-2008-russo-georgian-war-putins-green-light/.
6. The Editors of Encyclopedia Britannica, "The crisis in Crimea and eastern Ukraine," *Encyclopedia Britannica*, https://www.britannica.com/place/Ukraine/The-Russian-invasion of Ukraine.
7. Michael Ray, "Russia-Ukraine War," *Encyclopedia Britannica*, August 15, 2023. https://www.britannica.com/event/2022-Russian-invasion-of-Ukraine.
8. Anatoliy Golitsyn, *New Lies for Old: The Communist Strategy of Deception and Disinformation* (New York: Dodd, Mead & Company, 1984), and Anatoliy Golitsyn, *The Perestroika Deception: The Second October Revolution* (London: Edward Harle Ltd., 1995).
9. Joseph D. Douglass, Jr., "Organized crime in Russia: Who's taking whom to the cleaners?" U.S. Department of Justice, Office of Justice

Programs, June 1995. https://www.ojp.gov/ncjrs/virtual-library/abstracts/organized-crime-russia-whos-taking-whom-cleaners. See also: Joseph D. Douglass, Jr., *Red Cocaine: The Drugging of America* (Atlanta, GA: Second Opinion Publishing, Inc., 1990).
10. Federation of American Scientists, "Narcotics trafficking, the KGB—and Castro," *Congressional Record*, Senate–April 20, 1994, S4495. https://irp.fas.org/congress/1994_cr/s940420-kgb.htm.
11. Russell L. Blaylock, "Vladimir Putin—a reinvigorated Soviet apparatchik?" *HaciendaPublishing.com*, April 7, 2017. https://haciendapublishing.com/vladimir-putin-a-reinvigorated-and-dangerous-soviet-apparatchik-by-russell-l-blaylock-md/.
12. Yuri Bezmenov, *The Life and Legacy of the Influential KGB Informant Who Defected to the West*, Independently published, 2020.
13. Miguel A. Faria, Jr., *Cuba's Eternal Revolution through the Prism of Insurgency, Socialism, and Espionage* (Newcastle upon Tyne, UK: Cambridge Scholars Publishing, 2023), 80-81.
14. Alice Murphy, "SVR Russia: inside the secret intelligence agency once known as the infamous KGB," *The Independent*, December 28, 2022. https://www.independent.co.uk/news/world/europe/svr-russia-meaning-putin-agency-b2252416.html.
15. Robert W. Pringle, "Federal Security Service," *Encyclopedia Britannica*, June 27, 2023. https://www.britannica.com/topic/intelligence-international-relations.
16. Andrew S. Bowen, "In Focus: Russian cyber units," Congressional Research Service, February 2, 2022. https://crsreports.congress.gov/product/pdf/IF/IF11718.
17. "Russian state-sponsored and criminal cyber threats to critical infrastructure," *Cybersecurity & Infrastructure Security Agency*, May 9, 2022. https://www.cisa.gov/news-events/cybersecurity-advisories/aa22-110a.
18. Edward Jay Epstein, *Dossier: The Secret History of Armand Hammer* (New York: Random House, 1996). In this book, Epstein uncovered information that Armand Hammer thought would remain deeply buried and unrecoverable. From his childhood until his death, every fact about Hammer's life was exposed by Epstein's superb investigative journalism. While carefully building a sterling reputation that was central to his duplicitous life—posing as a capitalist, art connoisseur, philanthropist, American patriot and photographed with every American President—Hammer was a Soviet agent, the Kremlin's man in America.

19. Francis Fukuyama, "The end of history?" *The National Interest* (16):3–18;1989. See also: Francis Fukuyama, *The End of History and the Last Man* (New York: Free Press,1992).
20. Pete Earley, *Comrade J: The Untold Secrets of Russia's Master Spy in America After the End of the Cold War* (New York: G.P. Putnam's Sons, 2007), 2. The cover of this book reads insightfully: "In 1991, the Soviet Union collapsed, the Cold War ended, and a new world order began. We thought everything had changed. But one thing never changed: the spies. Spymaster, defector, and double agent—the remarkable true story of Sergei Tretyakov who ran Russia's post-Cold War spy program in America…" This is an important book that American and Western policymakers need to study along with scholars of international studies, political science, and Russian history.
21. Earley, *Comrade J*, 4.
22. Earley, *Comrade J*, 320.
23. Earley, *Comrade J*, 8.
24. Alex Goldfarb, and Marina Litvinenko, *Death of a Dissident: The Poisoning of Alexander Litvinenko and the Return of the KGB* (New York: Free Press, 2007), 331.
25. Goldfarb, *Death of a Dissident,* 338-342.
26. Goldfarb, *Death of a Dissident,* 312-313.
27. Anna Politkovskaya, *Putin's Russia: Life in a Failing Democracy*, trans. Arch Tait (New York: Metropolitan Books, 2004).
28. Shaun Walker, "The murder that killed free media in Russia," *The Guardian*, October 5, 2016. https://www.theguardian.com/world/2016/oct/05/ten-years-putin-press-kremlin-grip-russia-media-tightens. See also: David Hearst, "Obituary: Anna Politkovskaya," *The Guardian*, October 8, 2006. https://www.theguardian.com/news/2006/oct/09/guardianobituaries.russia.
29. "Sergei Skripal: who is former Russian intelligence officer?" *BBC News*, March 29, 2018. https://www.bbc.com/news/world-europe-43291394. See also: "A hundred grand and hundreds of betrayed agents—what was former GRU Colonel Sergey Skripal's treason against Russia?" *Meduza*, March 6, 2018. https://meduza.io/en/feature/2018/03/06/a-hundred-grand-and-hundreds-of-betrayed-agents.
30. "Russia spy: allies condemn nerve agent attack," *BBC News*, March 15, 2018. https://www.bbc.com/news/world-europe-43415271. See also: Heather Stewart, Peter Walker, and Julian Borger, "Russia threatens retaliation after Britain expels 23 diplomats," *The Guardian,* April 21,

2020. https://www.theguardian.com/uk-news/2018/mar/14/may-expels-23-russian-diplomats-response-spy-poisoning.
31. "Russia billionaire Mikhail Prokhorov to challenge Putin," *BBC*, March 6, 2012. https://www.bbc.com/news/world-europe-16138739.
32. Ted Mann, "Thousands more protest against the Kremlin," December 24, 2011. https://www.theatlantic.com/international/archive/2011/12/thousands-more-protest-against-kremlin/333710/. See also: "Alexei Navalny: Russia's jailed vociferous Putin critic," *BBC*, August 4, 2023. https://www.bbc.com/news/world-europe-16057045.
33. John H. Mathews, "Gennady Andreyevich Zyuganov," *Encyclopedia Britannica*, June 22, 2023. https://www.britannica.com/biography/Gennady-Andreyevich-Zyuganov.
34. DW staff, "Putin edges closer to re-election," *DW.com*, March 14, 2004. https://www.dw.com/en/putin-edges-closer-to-re-election/a-1141466.
35. Chrystia Freeland and Steve Gutterman, "Billionaire Kremlin hopeful says Putin must change," *Reuters*, January 17, 2012. https://www.reuters.com/article/us-russia-prokhorov/billionaire-kremlin-hopeful-says-putin-must-change-idUSTRE80G0ZY20120117
36. Miguel A. Faria, Jr., "The political spectrum (part 1): the totalitarian left from communism to social democracy," *HaciendaPublishing.com*, September 28, 2011. https://haciendapublishing.com/the-political-spectrum-part-i-the-totalitarian-left-from-communism-to-social-democracy/.
37. Aleksandr Solzhenitsyn, *The Gulag Archipelago (1918–1956): An Experiment in Literary Investigation, Parts I-II—The Prison Industry and Perpetual Motion,* trans. Thomas P. Whitney (New York: Harper & Row, 1974); and Aleksandr Solzhenitsyn, *The Gulag Archipelago (1918–1956): An Experiment in Literary Investigation, Parts III-IV—The Destructive Labor Camps and The Soul and Barbed Wire,* trans. Thomas P. Whitney (New York: Harper & Row, 1975).
38. Stéphane Courtois and Mark Kramer, *The Black Book of Communism: Crimes, Terror, Repression* (Cambridge, MA: Harvard University Press, 1999).

Chapter 21

1. History.com Editors, "St. Petersburg founded by Peter the Great," *A&E Television Network*, March 3, 2010. https://www.history.com/this-day-in-history/st-petersburg-founded-by-peter-the-great.
2. Carolyn Harris, "When Catherine the Great invaded the Crimea and put the rest of the world on edge," *Smithsonian Magazine*, March 4, 2014.

https://www.smithsonianmag.com/history/when-catherine-great-invaded-crimea-and-put-rest-world-edge-180949969/.
3. "NATO ups military presence amid Russian threat," *The Morning Journal*, April 16, 2014. https://www.morningjournal.com/2014/04/16/nato-ups-military-presence-amid-russian-threat/.
4. John Paull, "War in Ukraine: treaty to treachery," in the Proceedings of Russia-Ukraine War: Consequences for the World, 3rd International Scientific and Practical Internet Conference, March 2-3, 2023, Dnipro, Ukraine, 18-20.
https://www.academia.edu/98199478/War_in_Ukraine_From_Treaty_to_Treachery.
5. "US military leaders propose sending more forces to Europe to deter Russia," *FoxNews.com*, December 20, 2015. https://www.foxnews.com/politics/us-military-leaders-propose-sending-more-forces-to-europe-to-deter-russia.
6. Robert Conquest, *The Harvest of Sorrow: Soviet Collectivization and the Terror-Famine* (Oxford: Oxford University Press, 1986). The book's overview tells the reader that, "*The Harvest of Sorrow* is the first full history of one of the most horrendous human tragedies of the 20th century. Between 1929 and 1932, the Soviet Communist Party struck a double blow at the Russian peasantry: dekulakization, the dispossession and deportation of millions of peasant families, and collectivization, the abolition of private ownership of land and the concentration of the remaining peasants in party-controlled 'collective' farms. This was followed in 1932-33 by a 'terror-famine,' inflicted by the State on the collectivized peasants of the Ukraine and certain other areas by setting impossibly high grain quotas, removing every other source of food, and preventing help from outside—even from other areas of the Soviet Union—from reaching the starving populace. The death toll resulting from the actions described in Conquest's book was an estimated 14.5 million—more than the total number of deaths for all countries in World War I. Ambitious, meticulously researched, and lucidly written, *The Harvest of Sorrow* is a deeply moving testament to those who died, and it will register in the Western consciousness a sense of the dark side of this century's history."
7. Christopher Andrew and Oleg Gordievsky, *KGB: The Inside Story of Its Foreign Operations from Lenin to Gorbachev* (New York: Harper Collins, 1990), 464-465.
8. Christopher Andrew and Vasili Mitrokhin, *The Sword and the Shield: The Mitrokhin Archives and the Secret History of the KGB* (New York: Basic Books, 1999), 355-393.

9. "Syrian War: US launches missile strike in response to 'chemical attack,' " *BBC,* April 7, 2017. https://www.bbc.com/news/world-us-canada-39523654.
10. "Israel PM says supports strong message sent by US to Syria strike," *The Indian Express*, April 7, 2017. https://indianexpress.com/article/world/israel-pm-says-supports-strong-message-sent-by-us-syria-strike/.
11. "Syrian War: world reaction to US missile attack," *BBC*, April 7, 2017. https://www.bbc.com/news/world-us-canada-39526089.
12. Martin McCauley, *Russia, America and the Cold War, 1949-1991.* (London: Pearson Longman; 2009), 142.
13. "Syria crisis: Russia begins air strikes against Assad foes," *BBC*, September 30, 2015. https://www.bbc.com/news/world-middle-east-34399164.
14. The Editors of Encyclopaedia Britannica, "Quds Force," *Encyclopedia Britannica*, https://www.britannica.com/topic/Quds-Force.
15. "Foreign terrorist organizations: Islamic Revolutionary Guard Corps," National Counterterrorism Center, March 2022. https://www.dni.gov/nctc/ftos/irgc_fto.html.
16. Mark Galeotti, "The three faces of Russian spetsnaz in Syria," *Warontherocks.com*, March 21, 2016. https://warontherocks.com/2016/03/the-three-faces-of-russian-spetsnaz-in-syria/.
17. "Russia's Wagner group fighters sighted in Syria," *RBC Magazine*, August 31, 2016. https://www.rbth.com/economics/defence/2016/08/31/russias-wagner-group-fighters-sighted-in-syria_625551.
18. Roger McDermott, "Putin the 'peacemaker' ends operations in Syria," *Eurasia Daily Monitor* 13, no. 51 (March 2016). https://jamestown.org/program/putin-the-peacemaker-ends-operations-in-syria/.
19. Thomas Gibbons-Neff, "How a 4-hour battle between Russian mercenaries and U.S. commandos unfolded in Syria," *The New York Times*, May 24, 2018. https://www.nytimes.com/2018/05/24/world/middleeast/american-commandos-russian-mercenaries-syria.html. The article is an excellent piece of objective journalism, well researched and written with perceptive details and eloquent narrative.
20. Dexter Filkins, "The war in Syria and the Russian jet," *The New Yorker*, November 24, 2015. https://www.newyorker.com/news/news-desk/the-war-in-syria-and-the-russian-jet.
21. Maria Tsvetkova and Denis Pinchuk, "RPT—the enemy within: Russia faces different Islamist threat with metro bombing," *Reuters*, April 5, 2017. https://www.reuters.com/article/russia-blast-metro-islamists/rpt-

the-enemy-within-russia-faces-different-islamist-threat-with-metro-bombing-idUSL5N1HD0QX.
22. Miguel A. Faria, Jr., "What is happening in Europe that's making the elites of the EU tremble?" *HaciendaPublishing.com*, March 23, 2019. See also: Miguel A. Faria, Jr., "The UN, the EU, and gun control versus the Czech Republic, Poland, and freedom," *GOPUSA.com*, August 6, 2021. https://www.gopusa.com/the-un-the-eu-and-gun-control-versus-the-czech-republic-poland-and-freedom.

Epilogue

1. "Full text: Putin's declaration of war on Ukraine," *The Spectator*, February 24, 2022. https://www.spectator.co.uk/article/full-text-putin-s-declaration-of-war-on-ukraine/. See also: Rachel Treisman, "Putin's claim of fighting against Ukraine 'neo-Nazis' distorts history, scholars say," National Public Radio, March 1, 2022. https://www.npr.org/2022/03/01/1083677765/putin-denazify-ukraine-russia-history.
2. "Ukraine conflict: Russian forces attack from three sides," *BBC*, February 24, 2022. https://www.bbc.com/news/world-europe-60503037.
3. "One year of the Black Sea Initiative: key facts and figures," *The United Nations*, July 10, 2023. https://news.un.org/en/story/2023/07/1138532; and "Black Sea grain deal: Russia refuses to renew and says no guarantees for ships now," *Reuters*, July 17, 2023. https://www.reuters.com/world/europe/russia-halts-participation-black-sea-grain-deal-kremlin-says-2023-07-17/.
4. "Ukraine in maps: tracking the war with Russia," *BBC*, June 23, 2023. https://www.bbc.com/news/world-europe-60506682; and "Poland's leader says Russia's moving tactical nuclear weapons to Belarus, shifting regional security," *Associated Press*, August 22, 2023. https://apnews.com/article/poland-belarus-portugal-nuclear-weapons-russia-ff3ce6cfc7880cf5b6f9b5901b07c2b4.
5. Miguel A. Faria, Jr., "What is happening in Europe that's making the elites of the EU tremble?" *HaciendaPublishing.com*, March 23, 2019. See also: Miguel A. Faria, Jr., "The UN, the EU, and gun control versus the Czech Republic, Poland, and freedom," *GOPUSA.com*, August 6, 2021. https://www.gopusa.com/the-un-the-eu-and-gun-control-versus-the-czech-republic-poland-and-freedom/.
6. Ewan Palmer, "U.S. biological weapons in Ukraine—separating the facts from the fiction," *Newsweek*, March 8, 2022.

https://www.newsweek.com/us-biological-weapons-ukraine-labs-germ-warfare-1685956.
7. "Vladimir Lenin's dictum," quoted in *People's Daily World*, February 25, 1961.
8. Robert Conquest, *The Harvest of Sorrow: Soviet Collectivization and the Terror-Famine* (Oxford: Oxford University Press, 1986).
9. "Hunter Biden, Burisma, and corruption: The impact on U.S. government policy and related concerns," U.S. Senate Committee on Homeland Security and Governmental Affairs, U.S. Senate Committee on Finance Majority Staff Report, September 23, 2020. https://www.finance.senate.gov/imo/media/doc/HSGAC%20-%20Finance%20Joint%20Report%202020.09.23.pdf. See also: Betsy Woodruff Swan, "The Burisma board, a laptop scandal and struggles with addiction: What to know about Hunter Biden's legal troubles," *Politico.com*, June 20, 2023.
10. Judy Woodruff and Dan Sagalyn, "Turkey president Erdoğan on Russia's invasion of Ukraine and the future of NATO," *PBS.org*, September 19, 2020. https://www.pbs.org/newshour/show/turkey-president-erdogan-on-russias-invasion-of-ukraine-and-the-future-of-nato.
11. Yevgeniya Gaber, "One year into the war, it's time for Turkey to reconsider its Ukraine-Russia balancing act," *Atlantic Council.org*, March 1, 2023. https://www.atlanticcouncil.org/blogs/turkeysource/one-year-into-the-war-its-time-for-turkey-to-reconsider-its-ukraine-russia-balancing-act/.
12. Gabby Orr, Sara Murray and Steve Contorno, "Trump defends praise of Putin even as he calls Ukrainian president 'brave,' " *CNN.com*, February 27, 2022. https://www.cnn.com/2022/02/26/politics/trump-cpac-putin-ukraine/index.html.
13. Bellingcat Investigative Team, "Putin chef's kisses of death: Russia's shadow army's state-run structure exposed," *Bellingcat.com*, August 14, 2020. https://www.bellingcat.com/news/uk-and-europe/2020/08/14/pmc-structure-exposed/.
14. "Switzerland imposed sanctions on Wagner group," *European Pravda*, April 20, 2013. https://www.eurointegration.com.ua/eng/news/2023/04/20/7160213/.
15. "Russia's Wagner boss: It's prisoners fighting in Ukraine, or your children," *BBC*, September 16, 2022. https://www.bbc.com/news/world-europe-62922152.

16. "Russia-supporting Wagner group mercenary numbers soar," *BBC*, December 22, 2022. https://www.bbc.com/news/world-europe-64050719.
17. Kevin Shalvey, "Russian rebellion timeline: How the Wagner uprising against Putin unfolded and where Prigozhin is now," *ABC News*, July 10, 2023. https://abcnews.go.com/International/wagner-groups-rebellion-putin-unfolded/story?id=100373557.
18. Mark Osborne and Ivan Pereira, "Wagner group leader Yevgeny Prigozhin presumed dead in plane crash in Russia," *ABC News*, August 23, 2023. https://abcnews.go.com/International/wagner-group-leader-yevgeny-prigozhin-passenger-list-plane/story?id=102497445.
19. Dan Rosenzweig-Ziff, Joyce Sohyun Lee, Andrew Jeong and Mary Ilyushina, "Who was on the crashed Russian plane's passenger list?" *Washington Post*, August 24, 2023. https://www.washingtonpost.com/world/2023/08/24/prigozhin-wagner-plane-crash-list-dmitry-utkin/.
20. Pjotr Sauer and Graham Russell, "Biden points finger at Putin as Prigozhin's reported death seen as a warning to 'elites,'" *The Guardian*, August 24, 2023. https://www.theguardian.com/world/2023/aug/24/wagner-boss-yevgeny-prigozhin-reported-killed-death-russia-biden-suggests-putin.
21. "A decade after death, Solzhenitsyn draws a blank with young Russians," *Agence France-Presse*, February 8, 2018. https://www.france24.com/en/20180802-decade-after-death-solzhenitsyn-draws-blank-with-young-russians.
22. "Russia secretly orders destruction of gulag prisoners' records, media warns," *The Moscow Times*, June 8, 2018. https://www.themoscowtimes.com/2018/06/08/russia-secretly-orders-destruction-gulag-prisoners-records-media-warns-a61724.
23. Michele Klimecki, Facebook communication, March 24, 2023.
24. Miguel A. Faria, Jr., Facebook communication, March 24, 2023.

Appendix A

1. Jihan El Tahri, director. *Cuba: An African Odyssey*, 2007.
2. Miguel A. Faria, Jr., *Cuba's Eternal Revolution through the Prism of Insurgency, Socialism, and Espionage* (Newcastle upon Tyne, UK: Cambridge Scholars Publishing, 2023), 102-106.
3. Faria, *Cuba's Eternal Revolution through the Prism of Insurgency, Socialism, and Espionage*, 72-73, 80-81, 105, 143.

Appendix B

1. "The Office of Strategic Services: America's first intelligence agency," *Central Intelligence Agency*. https://www.cia.gov/legacy/museum/exhibit/the-office-of-strategic-services-n-americas-first-intelligence-agency/.
2. "Mission and vision," *Central Intelligence Agency*. https://www.cia.gov/about/mission-vision/.
3. Brianna Nofil, "The CIA's appalling human experiments with mind control," *History.com*, A&E Television Networks. https://www.history.com/mkultra-operation-midnight-climax-cia-lsd-experiments.
4. Christopher Andrew and Vasili Mitrokhin, *The Sword and the Shield: The Mitrokhin Archive and the Secret History of the KGB* (New York: Basic Books, 1999), 244-245.
5. Miguel A. Faria, Jr., *America, Guns and Freedom: A Journey Into Politics and the Public Health & Gun Control Movements* (Herndon, VA: Mascot Books, 2019), 265, 326; and Miguel A. Faria, Jr., "So you think tyranny can't happen here?" *HaciendaPublishing.com*, May 23, 2020. https://haciendapublishing.com/so-you-think-tyranny-cant-happen-here-by-miguel-a-faria-md/.
6. "Top 10 CIA movies," *Time*, October 9, 2008.
7. Peter Grose, *Gentleman Spy: The Life of Allen Dulles* (New York: Houghton Mifflin Company, 1994), 363-385.
8. Miguel A. Faria, Jr., *Cuba's Eternal Revolution through the Prism of Insurgency, Socialism, and Espionage* (Newcastle upon Tyne, UK: Cambridge Scholars Publishing, 2023), 48-60. See also: Miguel A. Faria, Jr., *Cuba in Revolution: Escape From a Lost Paradise* (Macon, GA: Hacienda Publishing, Inc., 2002), 93-102; and Mario Lazo, *Dagger in the Heart: American Policy Failures in Cuba* (New York: Twin Circle Publishing Company, 1970), 259-302.
9. Faria, *Cuba's Eternal Revolution through the Prism of Insurgency, Socialism, and Espionage*, 28-38; and Lazo, *Dagger in the Heart*, 414.
10. Bayard Stockton, *Flawed Patriot: The Rise and Fall of CIA Legend Bill Harvey* (Dulles, VA: Potomac Books, 2006), 111-189. Bill Harvey's story is told as a thriller even though it is all nonfiction and well documented.
11. Christopher Andrew and Vasili Mitrokhin, *The World Was Going Our Way: The KGB and the Battle for the Third World* (New York: Basic Books, 2005), 423-470. See also: Appendix A.

12. Joseph Persico, *Casey: The Lives and Secrets of William J. Casey: From the OSS to the CIA* (New York: Viking, 1990), 201-206, 341-342, 572-577.
13. Andrew E. Busch, "Ronald Reagan and the defeat of the Soviet empire," *Presidential Studies Quarterly*. Volume 27, No. 3 (Summer 1997), 451-466. https://www.jstor.org/stable/27551762.
14. Pete Earley, *Confessions of a Spy: The Real Story of Aldrich Ames* (New York: G. P. Putnam's Sons, 1997), 143-144.
15. David Wise. *Nightmover: How Aldrich Ames Sold the CIA to the KGB for $4.6 Million* (New York: HarperCollins Publishers, 1995), 254-271.
16. Milt Bearden and James Risen, *The Main Enemy: The Inside Story of the CIA's Final Showdown with the KBG* (New York: Random House, 2003), 525-526.
17. David Wise, *Spy: The Inside Story of How the FBI's Robert Hanssen Betrayed America* (New York: Random House, 2002), 233-250.
18. Elaine Shannon and Ann Blackman, *The Spy Next Door: The Extraordinary Secret Life of Robert Philip Hanssen, the Most Damaging FBI Agent in U.S. History* (New York: Little, Brown, and Company, 2002), 211-230.
19. Christopher Andrew and Oleg Gordievsky, *KGB: The Inside Story of Its Foreign Operations from Lenin to Gorbachev* (New York: Harper Collins, 1990), 620-623, 638.
20. Andrew and Mitrokhin, *The Sword and the Shield*, 378-380.
21. Andrew and Mitrokhin, *The World Was Going Our Way*, 484-493.
22. Randall Mikkelsen, "U.S. government vows not to use 'waterboarding,'" *Reuters*, March 2, 2009.
23. David Folkenflik and Alex Chadwick, "Novak reveals details of CIA identity leak," *NPR.org*, July 12, 2006. https://www.npr.org/templates/story/story.php?storyId=5551690.
24. "Secret details of Bin Laden burial revealed," *Aljazeera*, November 22, 2012. https://www.aljazeera.com/news/2012/11/22/secret-details-of-bin-laden-burial-revealed.
25. Andrew and Mitrokhin, *The World Was Going Our Way*, 483.

Appendix C

1. Christopher Andrew and Vasili Mitrokhin, *The World Was Going Our Way: The KGB and the Battle for the Third World* (New York: Basic Books, 2005), 355-367.
2. Pete Earley, *Confessions of a Spy: The Real Story of Aldrich Ames* (New York: G. P. Putnam's Sons, 1997), 344-347.

3. Milt Bearden and James Risen, *The Main Enemy: The Inside Story of the CIA's Final Showdown with the KBG* (New York: Random House, 2003), 525-536.
4. David Wise, *Nightmover: How Aldrich Ames Sold the CIA to the KGB for $4.6 Million* (New York: HarperCollins Publishers, 1995), 1-5.
5. David Wise, *Spy: The Inside Story of How the FBI's Robert Hanssen Betrayed America* (New York: Random House, 2002), 3-4.
6. Elaine Shannon and Ann Blackman, *The Spy Next Door: The Extraordinary Secret Life of Robert Philip Hanssen, the Most Damaging FBI Agent in U.S. History* (New York: Little, Brown, and Company, 2002), 20-22.
7. "Martyrs Week, Massoud's death anniversary commemorated," *Tolo News*, September 9, 2019. https://tolonews.com/afghanistan/martyrs-week-massoud%E2%80%99s-death-anniversary-commemorated.
8. Declan Walsh, "Whose side is Pakistan's ISI really on? *The Guardian*, May 12, 2011. https://www.theguardian.com/world/2011/may/12/isi-bin-laden-death-pakistan-alqaida.
9. Milt Bearden and James Risen, *The Main Enemy: The Inside Story of the CIA's Final Showdown with the KBG* (New York: Random House, 2003), 531-533. See also: Mohammad Yousaf and Mark Adkin, *Afghanistan, The Bear Trap: The Defeat of a Superpower* (Philadelphia, PA: Casemate Publishers, 2008), 213-219.
10. "TTP release video showing Col Imam dead," *YouTube.com*, February 15, 2011. https://www.youtube.com/watch?v=it2236z0BFc.
11. "Taliban leader Baitullah Masood & 40 Taliban killed in a USA drone attack," *YouTube.com*, 2010.
https://www.youtube.com/watch?v=fgkpGfp8WZI.
12. "Pakistan Taliban chief killed in drone strike," *YouTube.com*, 2013. https://www.youtube.com/watch?v=p9YEYeryXZ0.
13. "Top Pakistan Taliban commander Asmatullah Shaheen 'shot dead,' " *BBC*, February 24, 2014.
https://www.bbc.com/news/world-asia-26323200.

Appendix D

1. Reza Kahlili. *A Time to Betray: The Astonishing Double Life of a CIA Agent Inside the Revolutionary Guards of Iran* (New York: Simon & Schuster, 2010), 1-7, 119-157, 328-338.
2. Miguel A. Faria, Jr., *Cuba in Revolution: Escape From a Lost Paradise* (Macon, GA: Hacienda Publishing, Inc., 2002), 76-82. 177-228.

3. Miguel A. Faria, Jr., *Cuba's Eternal Revolution through the Prism of Insurgency, Socialism, and Espionage* (Newcastle upon Tyne, UK: Cambridge Scholars Publishing, 2023), 108-138.
4. Maureen Dowd, "Pumping up Ahmadinejad," *The New York Times*, September 26, 2007. https://www.nytimes.com/2007/09/26/opinion/26iht-eddowd.1.7643131.html.

Appendix E

1. "Turkey coup attempt: Some 6,000 people detained, says minister," *The Kathmandu Post*, July 17, 2010. https://kathmandupost.com/world/2016/07/17/turkey-coup-attempt-some-6000-people-detained-says-minister.
2. Matina Stevis-Gridneff, "Will Turkey become a member of the EU now? Here's what to know," *The New York Times*, July 11, 2023. https://www.nytimes.com/2023/07/11/world/europe/turkey-eu-membership.html.
3. Claire Sadar, "Who is Fethullah Gulen? And why is the US talking about extraditing him to Turkey?" *Religion News*, January 4, 2019. https://religionnews.com/2019/01/04/who-is-fethullah-gulen-and-why-is-the-us-talking-about-extraditing-him-to-turkey/.
4. "Chomsky hits back at Erdoğan, accusing him of double standards on terrorism," *The Guardian*, January 14, 2016. https://www.theguardian.com/us-news/2016/jan/14/chomsky-hits-back-erdogan-double-standards-terrorism-bomb-istanbul.
5. Matthew d'Ancona, "Putin and Trump could be on the same side in this troubling new world order," *The Guardian*, December 19, 2016. https://www.theguardian.com/world/commentisfree/2016/dec/19/trump-putin-same-side-new-world-order.

SELECTED BIBLIOGRAPHY

Andrew, Christopher, and Oleg Gordievsky. *KGB: The Inside Story of Its Foreign Operations from Lenin to Gorbachev.* New York: Harper Collins, 1990.
Andrew, Christopher, and Vasili Mitrokhin. *The Sword and the Shield: The Mitrokhin Archive and the Secret History of the KGB.* New York: Basic Books, 1999.
Andrew, Christopher, and Vasili Mitrokhin. *The World Was Going Our Way: The KGB and the Battle for the Third World.* New York: Basic Books, 2005.
Applebaum, Anne. *Gulag: A History.* New York: Doubleday, 2003.
Barron, John. *KGB: The Secret Work of Soviet Secret Agents.* New York: Reader's Digest Press, 1974.
Bearden, Milt, and James Risen. *The Main Enemy: The Inside Story of the CIA's Final Showdown with the KGB.* New York: Random House, 2003.
Billington, James H. *Fire in the Minds of Men: Origins of the Revolutionary Faith.* New Brunswick, NJ: Transaction Publishers, 1999.
Brent, Jonathan, and Vladimir P. Naumov. *Stalin's Last Crime: The Plot Against the Jewish Doctors, 1948-1953.* New York: Harper Collins, 2003.
Chang, Jung, and Jon Halliday. *Mao: The Unknown Story.* New York: Alfred A. Knopf, 2005.
Conquest, Robert. *The Great Terror: Stalin's Purge of the Thirties.* Oxford: Oxford University Press, 1968.
Conquest, Robert. *Stalin, Breaker of Nations.* New York: Penguin Random House, 1991.
Costello, John, and Oleg Tsarev. *Deadly Illusions: The KGB Orlov Dossier Reveals Stalin's Master Spy.* New York: Crown Publisher's, Inc., 1993.
Courtois Stéphane, and Mark Kramer. *The Black Book of Communism: Crimes, Terror, Repression.* Cambridge, MA: Harvard University Press, 1999.
Douglass, Jr., Joseph D. *Red Cocaine: The Drugging of America.* Atlanta, GA: Second Opinion Publishing, Inc., 1990.

Earley, Pete. *Comrade J: The Untold Secrets of Russia's Master Spy in America After the End of the Cold War*. New York: G.P. Putnam's Sons, 2007.

Epstein, Edward Jay. *Deception: The Invisible War Between the KGB and the CIA*. New York: Simon & Schuster, 1989.

Evans, M. Stanton, and Herbert Romerstein. *Stalin's Secret Agents: The Subversion of Roosevelt's Government*. New York: Simon & Schuster, 2012.

Faria, Jr., Miguel A. *Controversies in Medicine and Neuroscience: Through the Prism of History, Neurobiology and Bioethics*. Newcastle upon Tyne, UK: Cambridge Scholars Publishing, 2023.

Faria, Jr., Miguel A. *Cuba's Eternal Revolution through the Prism of Insurgency, Socialism, and Espionage*. Newcastle upon Tyne, UK: Cambridge Scholars Publishing, 2023.

Gazur, Edward. *Alexander Orlov: The FBI's KGB General*. New York: Basic Books, 2001.

Goldfarb, Alex, and Marina Litvinenko. *Death of a Dissident: The Poisoning of Alexander Litvinenko and the Return of the KGB*. New York: Free Press, 2007.

Golitsyn, Anatoliy. *New Lies for Old: The Communist Strategy of Deception and Disinformation*. New York: Dodd, Mead & Company, 1984.

Haynes, John Earl, Harvey Klehr, and Alexander Vassiliev. *Spies: The Rise and Fall of the KGB in America*. New Haven, CT: Yale University Press, 2010.

Hoffman, David E. *The Billion Dollar Spy: A True Story of Cold War Espionage and Betrayal*. New York: Doubleday, 2015.

Jansen, Marc, and Nikita Petrov. *Stalin's Loyal Executioner: People's Commissar Nikolai Ezhov, 1895-1940*. Stanford, CA: Hoover Institution Press, 2002.

Kilzer, Louis C. *Churchill's Deception: The Dark Secret That Destroyed Nazi Germany*. New York: Simon & Schuster, 1994.

Kilzer, Louis C. *Hitler's Traitor: Martin Bormann and the Defeat of the Reich*. Novato, CA: Presidio Press, 2000.

Knight, Amy. *Beria: Stalin's First Lieutenant*. Princeton, NJ: Princeton University Press, 1993.

Koestler, Arthur. *Darkness at Noon*. Translated by Daphne Hardy. Norwalk, CT: Easton Press, 2000.

Koster, John. *Operation Snow: How a Soviet Mole in FDR's White House Triggered Pearl Harbor*. Washington, DC: Regnery History, 2012.

Kostin, Sergei, and Eric Raynaud. *Farewell: The Greatest Spy Story of the Twentieth Century*. Translated by Catherine Cauvin-Higgins. Las Vegas: AmazonCrossing, 2011.

Macintyre, Ben. *A Spy among Friends: Kim Philby and the Great Betrayal*. Toronto, ON: Signal, McClelland & Stewart, 2015.

Macintyre, Ben. *The Spy and the Traitor: The Greatest Espionage Story of the Cold War*. London: Penguin Books, 2019.

Mahoney, Daniel J. *The Other Solzhenitsyn: Telling the Truth about a Misunderstood Writer and Thinker*. South Bend, IN: St. Augustine's Press, 2014.

Montefiore, Simon Sebag. *The Romanovs, 1613-1918*. New York: Alfred A. Knopf, 2016.

Montefiore, Simon Sebag. *Stalin: The Court of the Red Tsar*. New York: Alfred A. Knopf, 2004.

Montefiore, Simon Sebag. *Young Stalin*. London: Weidenfeld & Nicolson, 2007.

Moorehead, Alan. *The Russian Revolution*. New York: Bantam Books, 1959.

Morley, Jefferson. *Our Man in Mexico: Winston Scott and the Hidden History of the CIA*. Lawrence, KS: University of Kansas Press, 2008.

Orwell, George. *Animal Farm*. Norwalk, Connecticut: The Easton Press, 1974.

Orwell, George. *Homage to Catalonia*. Orlando, FL: Harcourt, 1980.

Orwell, George. *1984*. Norwalk, Connecticut: The Easton Press, 1977.

Pacepa, Ion Mihai, and Ronald J. Rychlak. *Disinformation: Former Spy Chief Reveals Secret Strategies for Undermining Freedom, Attacking Religion, and Promoting Terrorism*. Independently published, 2013.

Quirk, Robert E. *Fidel Castro*. New York: W.W. Norton and Company, 1993.

Radzinsky, Edvard. *Stalin: The First In-depth Biography Based on Explosive New Documents from Russia's Secret Archives*. Translated by H.T. Willets. New York: Anchor Books, 1997.

Romerstein, Herbert, and Breindel, Eric. *The Venona Secrets: Exposing Soviet Espionage and America's Traitors*. Washington, DC: Regnery, 2000.

Salisbury, Harrison E. *Black Night, White Snow: Russia's Revolution, 1905-1917*. Franklin Center, PA: The Franklin Library, 1977.

Salisbury, Harrison E. *The Long March: The Untold Story*. Franklin Center, PA: The Franklin Library, 1985.

Scammell, Michael. Solzhenitsyn: A Biography. New York: W.W. Norton & Company, 1984.

Schapiro, Leonard. *The Russian Revolutions of 1917: The Origins of Modern Communism.* New York: Basic Books, 1984.

Schecter, Jerrold L., and Peter S. Deriabin. *The Spy Who Saved the World: How a Soviet Colonel Changed the Course of the Cold War.* New York: Charles Scribner's Sons, 1992.

Schellenberg, Walter. *Walter Schellenberg: The Memoirs of Hitler's Spymaster.* London: André Deutsch, 2006.

Sharp, Tony. *Stalin's American Spy: Noel Field, Allen Dulles and the East European Show Trials.* London: Hurst & Company, 2014.

Shuyun, Sun. *The Long March: The True History of Communist China's Founding Myth.* New York: Doubleday, 2006.

Solzhenitsyn, Aleksandr. *Cancer Ward.* Translated by Nicholas Bethell and David Burg. New York: Bantam Books, 1972.

Solzhenitsyn, Aleksandr. *The First Circle.* Translated by Thomas P. Whitney. New York: Harper & Row, 1968.

Solzhenitsyn, Aleksandr. *The Gulag Archipelago (1918–1956): An Experiment in Literary Investigation, Parts I-II—The Prison Industry and Perpetual Motion.* Translated by Thomas P. Whitney. New York: Harper & Row, 1974.

Solzhenitsyn, Aleksandr. *The Gulag Archipelago (1918–1956): An Experiment in Literary Investigation, Parts III-IV—The Destructive Labor Camps and The Soul and Barbed Wire.* Translated by Thomas P. Whitney. New York: Harper & Row, 1975.

Solzhenitsyn, Aleksandr. *August 1914: The Red Wheel / Node I.* Translated by Michael Glenny. New York: Farrar, Straus and Giroux, 1971.

Solzhenitsyn, Aleksandr. *November 1916: The Red Wheel / Node II.* Translated by H.T. Willets. New York: Farrar, Straus and Giroux, 1999.

Solzhenitsyn, Aleksandr. *March 1917: The Red Wheel / Node III.* Translated by Marian Schwartz. Notre Dame, IN: University of Notre Dame Press, 2017.

Solzhenitsyn, Aleksandr. *The Oak and the Calf: Memoirs of a Literary Life.* Translated by H.T. Willets. Franklin Center, PA: Franklin Library, 1980.

Solzhenitsyn, Aleksandr. *One Day In The Life of Ivan Denisovich.* Translated by Max Hayward and Ronald Hingley. New York: Bantam Books, 1970.

Solzhenitsyn, Aleksandr. *Prussian Nights: A Narrative Poem.* Translated by Robert Conquest. London: Collins and Harvill Press, 1977.

Stormer, John A. *None Dare Call It Treason—25 Years Later.* Florissant, MO: Liberty Bell Press, 1990.

Sudoplatov, Pavel, Anatoli Sudoplatov, Jerrold L. Schechter, and Leona P. Schechter. *Special Tasks: Memoirs of an Unwanted Witness a Soviet Spymaster*. Boston: Little, Brown and Company, 1994.

Timperlake, Edward, and William C. Triplett, II. *Year of the Rat: How Bill Clinton Compromised U.S. Security for Chinese Cash*. Washington, DC: Regnery Publishing, 1998.

Trahair, Richard C.S., *The Encyclopedia of Cold War Espionage, Spies, and Secret Operations*. Westport, CT: Greenwood Press, 2004.

Volkogonov, Dmitri. *Stalin: Triumph and Tragedy*. New York: Grove Press, 1991.

Weinstein, Allen, and Vassiliev, Alexander. *The Haunted Wood: Soviet Espionage in America—The Stalin Era*. New York: Random House, 1999.

Wise, David. *Tiger Trap: America's Secret Spy War with China*. Boston: Houghton Mifflin Harcourt, 2011.

INDEX

A
Abakumov, Viktor, 14, 30, 122-130
Abel, Colonel Rudolf (aka, Willie Fisher), 247, 350
Abkhazia (Georgia), 294, 298-299
Abraham Lincoln Brigade, 58
Abwehr (German military intelligence), 99-101
Adler, Solomon, 75, 80, 200, 202, 253
Adriatic Sea, 156
Afghanistan, xii, 219, 237, 256, 302, 314, 329, 335-336
Africa, 227, 243, 279, 320, 321-324, 329
African national liberation movements, 323
Agee, Philip, 252
Agence France-Presse, 318
agents of influence: in FDR administration, 71-72, 75-76, 79-80, 247; inciting Japan, 97; helping China, 170, 200-202, 254
Ahmadinejad, Mahmoud, 340
air strikes, 302, 304, 309
Akhmerov, Iskhak, 75
Akselrod, Moisei, 26
Aleutian Islands, 116
Alexander Orlov: The FBI's KGB General (Gazur), 61, 63
Alexander II, Tsar of Russia, 305
Algeria, 256
Allen, Richard V., 262
al-Qaeda, 282, 331
Amerasia scandal, 200, 253
Amerasia (magazine), 200
American commandos, 304-305
American warplanes, 304

Ames, Aldrich "Rick," 197, 242, 253, 329, 334
Amin, Hafizullah, 302
anarchists (anarcho-tyranny; anarchy), 58, 60, 64, 68, 69, 70, 160
Andrew, Christopher, 16, 201, 219, 225-229, 240, 242, 332
Andropov, Yuri, 134, 240, 266, 271, 272
Angleton, James Jesus, 229-235, 246
Angola, 237, 256, 321, 323-324, 329
Animal Farm (Orwell), 70
Anschluss, 102, 294
anti-Semitism, 48, 121, 130
Antonov-Ovseenko, Vladimir, xi, 23
Applebaum, Anne, 143-144
Arabs, 340
ARDOV (Soviet agent). *See* Mikhail K. Polonik
Armenia, 45, 299
Art of War, The (Sun Tzu), 195, 386
Assad, Bashar al-, 300-303, 305
assassinations, 3, 25, 41, 220, 236, 248, 281, 285
Auschwitz, 121
Ausman, James I., 212
Australia, 142, 204, 205, 298
Austria, 102, 294, 320
atomic bomb, 46, 47, 63, 80-83, 197, 281
atomic espionage, 46, 81
Attlee, Clement, 82
Azerbaijan, 45, 282, 289, 293, 298, 299, 300

B

Baku oil fields (Azerbaijan), 7, 91, 299, 300
Ballistic Missile Defense System, 206
Baltic Sea, 88, 90, 91, 108, 111, 138, 144, 156, 291, 293
Baltic states, 90, 93, 291
Banderas, Stepan, 297
Barcelona, 58, 68, 69
Barron, John, 218-225
Batista, Fulgencio, 7, 338, 339
Bay of Pigs invasion (Cuba), 327, 328
Beck, Ludwig, 99
Beijing: in the Long March, 161, 169, 173, 175; opening of China and Taiwan relations, 188-190; in Tiananmen Square Massacre, 192-194; role in espionage, 195, 198, 199, 208, 214; using Cuba as base, 203, 205
Bejucal (base in Cuba), 205
Belarus, 111, 293, 309, 311, 317
Belgium, 55, 103, 321
Beloborodov, Aleksandr, 38
Bentley, Elizabeth, 246
Beria, Lavrenti, 9; during the Great Purge and the terror, 15, 34, 40, 43, 44-48; Stalin paranoia, 48; Beria in power, 49; fall 50-53; and Orlov, 62; and the atomic project, 81, 82; in Doctors' Plot 124, 131, 132
Beria: Stalin's First Lieutenant (Knight), 44, 47, 49, 51-53
Berle, Adolf, 72, 73
Berlin, 82, 257, 286, 327
Berlin Spy Carousel, 252
Berlin Tunnel, 245
Berlin Wall, xii, 53, 84, 133, 263, 278, 279, 281, 336
Berzin, Jan, 27
Bezmenov, Yuri A., 279
Biden, Joe, 189, 191, 210, 211, 213, 214, 313, 314, 315

bin Laden, Osama, 325, 331, 332, 333
Birkenau (concentration camp), 121
Bissell, Richard, 248
Black Book of Communism: Crimes, Terror, Repression, The (Courtois), 363
Blacklisted by History (Evans), 71
Black Nights, White Snow (Salisbury), 167
Black Orchestra, 99, 100
Black Sea, 88, 108, 113, 127, 291, 292, 293, 294, 298, 299, 307, 311
Black Sea Grain Initiative, 310-311
Blake, George, 244, 245, 252
Blaylock, Russell L., 212, 278
Bletchley Park (secret British facility), 98, 102
Blinken, Anthony, 214
blitzkrieg, 88, 94, 102
Blokhin, Vasily, 105-107
Blunt, Anthony, 26, 62, 249
Blyukher, Vasily, 28
Blyumkin, Yakov, 29
Bokii, Gleb, xi, 30
Bolivia, 279
Bolsheviks: with Lenin, xii, 2, 3, 5, 10, 12, 16, 24, 25, 31, 32, 36, 37, 136, 167, 289, 297; with Stalin 16-18, 24-25, 29-34, 37, 41, 42, 45, 55, 56, 133, 152; the "Brown Bolshevik," 100; Jewish, 108, 121; the "old Bolshevik" 240, 266
Bolshoi Theater (Moscow), 24
bombers (airplanes), 303, 304
Bormann, Martin, 98-101
Boxiong, Guo, 203, 204
Brandt, Willy, 253
Brazil, 279
Breindel, Eric, 75
Brent, Jonathan, 120, 121, 130
Brexit, 342
Brezhnev, Leonid, xii, 50, 84, 134, 240, 241, 260, 261, 266, 269

Brissot, Jacques Pierre, 14
British Broadcasting Corporation (BBC), 70, 179-180, 207, 213-214, 286, 300, 337, 342
Brussels, 293
Budapest Memorandum, 276, 278, 294
Bukharin, Nikolai, xi, 12, 13, 16, 17, 18, 23, 27, 29, 40, 42, 56
Bulganin, Nikolai, 15, 48, 49, 50
Bulgaria, 127, 293, 312
Bureau of Alcohol Tobacco and Firearms (ATF), 326
Burgess, Guy, 26, 62, 249, 250
Burma, 157
Burton, Dan, 185
Bush, George H.W., 258, 336
Bush, George W., 186, 331
Byelorussia, 90

C
Cairncross, John, 26, 249
Cairo Conference (1943), 73, 201
Cambridge Five (British spy ring), 26, 62, 63, 232, 244, 249, 250
Cambodia, 18, 44, 166
Canada, 103, 107, 117, 142, 163, 205, 251, 252, 259, 298
Canaris, Wilhelm, 99-100
Canton, 156
capitalism, 52, 56, 221, 281
Caribbean sea, 216
Carter, Jimmy, 187, 191, 236, 237, 239, 256, 267, 328-329, 396
Casablanca Conference (1943), 73
Casey, William J. "Bill," 239, 262, 265, 271, 272, 329-330
Caspian Sea, 91, 289, 292, 298-299
Castro, Fidel, xi, 7-8, 18, 204, 266, 321-322, 327, 338, 339
Catalonia (Spain), 58, 59, 67-68
Catherine II "the Great," Tsarina of Russia, 291, 305
Catholicism, 320
Caucasus, 45, 90, 91, 103, 112, 289, 292, 298-300

Central America, 204
Central Committee (USSR), 38, 44, 49, 51, 62, 124, 125, 126, 177, 222, 266, 267
Central Europe, 82, 102, 279
Central Intelligence Agency (CIA): with Penkovsky, 84; in Chinese intelligence operations, 182, 199, 200; in Latin America, 223, 224, 227; in counterintelligence, 229- 235; defanged 235-239; resurgent, 239- 246; versus KGB, 239-246, 247-249, 252-253, 259, 262, 264; in Africa, 322; media perception and function, 325-326; history of 102, 327-331; tracking bin Laden, 331-333; in Pakistan and Afghanistan, 334-337; in Iran, 338-340. *See also* double agents
Central Military Commission (China), 203, 210
Chalet, Marcel, 258
Chamberlain, Neville, 93, 94, 294
Chambers, Whittaker, 56, 71, 72
Chang Hsüeh-liang, 174
Chang, Jung, 150-151, 154-155, 169, 171, 172, 174, 176-177
Chang Kuo-t'ao (Zhang Guotao), 154, 163-165, 176, 178
Chaumett, Pierre Gaspard, 14
Chechen War. *See* Second Chechen War
Chechnya (and Chechens), 22, 91, 283, 284, 289
Cheka (and Chekists), xi, xii, 18, 30, 37, 41, 106, 121, 143, 220
Chekalov, Valeriy, 317
Chekhov, Anton, 135
Chemical Weapons Convention (1993), 307
Chernyshevsky, Nikolai, 131, 132
Chiang Kai-shek: calumniated and subjected to communist disinformation, 80, 82, 168, 170, 200-201, 202, 253-254,

390; fighting Mao and the Japanese, 153, 156-158, 161, 163, 164, 165, 171, 176-179; relations with Stalin, 174
Chi Chao-ting, 200, 253
Childs, Eva Lieb, 267, 270
Childs, Jack, 266, 267, 270
Childs, Morris, 240, 266-270, 272
China (People's Republic of China; PRC), 150; as PRC, 160, 161, 164, 166, 168, 169, 175, 176, 187-189, 191, 193, 209, 210, 213; Mao Tse-tung in China history, and communism, 150-156; American traitors working for China 156-157; Chinese infernal tragedy 158-165; Long March, 166-180; China, Taiwan and U.S. relations, 181-191; Tiananmen Square Massacre 192-194
China Ocean Shipping Company (COSCO), 183-184
China Virus: What is the Truth?, The (Ausman and Blaylock), 212
Chinese Civil War, 153-158, 160, 163, 164
Chinese Communist Party (CCP), 150-153, 164, 172, 177-179, 191-197, 209-211
Chinese espionage (intelligence), 182-187, 191, 195-209, 211-216, 247
Chinese Red Army, 150, 153, 157, 163, 164, 170-173, 175-179
Chinese surveillance balloon, 213-214
Chomsky, Noam, 343-344
Chou En-lai, 153, 157, 158-160, 165, 171, 172, 188, 269
Chung, Johnnie, 183, 186
Chungking (city), 200, 253
Church, Frank, 236, 328
Churchill, Winston, 73-75, 97-98, 102-105, 108-109, 111, 155, 201

Churchill's Deception: The Dark Secret that Destroyed Nazi Germany (Kilzer), 102
Church Senate Select Committee, 236, 270
CIA officers (and operatives), 259, 262, 322
Cleveland Jr., William B., 197-198
Clinton, Hillary Rodham, 186, 286
Clinton, William Jefferson, 181-187, 330
Cohen, Lona, 247, 250, 251
Cohen, Morris, 247, 250, 251
Colby, William, 235, 248, 329
Cold War, 63, 71, 82, 104, 187, 200, 201, 218-227, 229, 240-241, 242-254
Colombia, 7, 280
Comintern, 8, 16, 23, 30, 266
Commander of the Order of the British Empire (CBE), 55, 229
communism (and communists), x-xiii, 10-20, 32, 38–85, 362, 368, 374; during World War II, 93, 108; during anti-cosmopolitanism campaign, 121-132; and Solzhenitsyn, 134, 135, 142; in China, 150-216, 390; in KGB-CIA battles during the Cold War 218-271; end of communism and Russian politics, 276-281, 287-292; involving Ukraine and Ukrainian history, 297, 302, 312, 313; in Poland 320; in Africa, 321-324; CIA fights, 327-331; in the Third World, 331, 334, 338, 360, 396
Communist Party Congresses (Soviet Union): 17th Party Congress of 1934 (Congress of Victors), 16-17, 38; 12th Party Congress of 1923, 18; 20th Party Congress of 1956, xii, 132
Communist Party USA (CPUSA), xi, 266-267

Comrade J: The Untold Secrets of Russia's Master Spy in America After the End of the Cold War (Earley), 403
Congo (Democratic Republic of the Congo), 321-323
Conquest, Robert, 16-18, 219, 297
Conrad, Joseph, 17-18,
"conspiracy of the litters," 168
Coplon, Judith, 244, 252
corporativist (China), 191
Cosmopolitanism (Stalin's anti-Jewish campaign), 19
Costello, John, 58-59, 61-62, 65
counterintelligence, 46, 59, 122, 138; in Chinese "sexpionage" 197-198; in Cuba-Chinese operations, 203; in CIA-KGB operations, 218, 229-236, 244, 246, 252, 259, 262, 264, 332; French 258-259; betrayal of CIA, 329, 330
COVID pandemic, 211, 213
Cox Committee Report, 185, 187
Crimea (and Crimean Peninsula), 30, 155, 278, 289, 291-294, 296-297, 302, 307, 309, 312
Crimean War (1853-1856), 307
Cripps, Stafford, 108
Cuba (and Cuban): in Missile Crisis, xii 7, 84-85, 221; supporting Soviets, 8, 18, 84-85; supporting China, 203-206, 216; intelligence services and operations, 223, 237, 252, 256, 266, 279, 280; in Africa 321-324, 329, 395; Bay of Pigs, 327; Revolution similarities to Iran, 338-339
Cuba: An African Odyssey (Jihan El Tahri), 321
Cuba's Eternal Revolution through the Prism of Insurgency, Socialism and Espionage (Faria), 205
Cuban Missile Crisis (October Missile Crisis), xii, 84, 221,

cult of personality: Fidel Castro and Stalin 8; Stalin, 9, 45-46, 134, 241; Mao, 160-161
Cultural Revolution (China), 44, 158-162, 164, 166, 168, 176
Cultural Revolution: A People's History (1962-1976), The (Dikötter), 159
Currie, Lauchlin, 72, 75-76, 155, 201, 202
cyber espionage, 205-208, 280
cyber warfare (cyber wars and cyberattacks), 197, 207, 280
Czechoslovakia (and Czechs), 22, 43, 79, 93, 102, 294, 314

D

Dadu River (China),173
Daladier, Edouard, 94, 294
dangles, 197, 233, 241
Danton, Georges, 14
Darkness at Noon (Koestler), 53-56
Deadly Illusions: The KGB Orlov Dossier Reveals Stalin's Master Spy (Costello and Tsarev), 58, 63
Dearlove, Richard, 209
defector (and defectors), 59, 61, 62, 75, 80, 202, 205, 219, 227, 229-230, 232-235, 240-244, 246, 249, 251, 254, 255, 258, 265, 278-279, 281-282, 326
de Gaulle, Charles, 256, 257
Deir al-Zour (Syria), 304
Delta Force, 304
democracy (and democratic), xii, 12, 53, 74, 151, 182, 192, 281, 286-289, 291
Democratic National Committee (DNC), 183, 184
Democratic Party (and Democrats), 183, 184, 186, 313, 328, 331
Deng Xiaoping, 162, 168, 184, 192, 193
Denikin, Anton, 297
Denmark, 103

denunciation rallies (China), 159, 177
denunciations (Soviet Union), 124-126, 130, 241
Derg (Marxist-Leninist junta, Ethiopia), 237, 238, 324, 329
Desmoulins, Camille, 14
de-Stalinization, 10, 48, 52, 132
détente, xii, 84, 241, 260, 269
Deutsch, Arnold, 26
Dikötter, Frank, 158
Dimitrov, Georgi, 127
Dirección General de Inteligencia (DGI), 222, 280
Direction de la Surveillance du Territoire (DST), 243, 257-259, 263, 264
disinformation, 71; against Stalin, 66, 67, 97; against Chiang, 80, 200, 202, 253, 254; KGB, 219, 220, 222, 235, 240, 241, 326; against Ukraine by Russia, 312
Djugashvili, Ekaterina "Keke" Geladze, 4
Djugashvili, Joseph Vissarionovich. *See* Joseph Stalin
Djugashvili,Vissarion "Beso," 4
Doctors' Plot, 19, 30, 32, 48, 120-132
Donbas (Ukraine), 309, 316
Donetsk (Ukraine), 309, 311
Donovan, William J. "Wild Bill," 325
Dostoevsky, Fyodor, 5, 135
double agents, 241, allegations against Stalin, 10, 67; Soviets and communists *for* the Americans or British, 59, 220, 221-225, 234, 240, 245, 250, 253, 263, 284, 403; Germans for the Americans, 99; Germans for the Soviets, 99; possible dangles, 197; Chinese against America, 197-198; Soviets and communists *against* America, 233, 234, 240, 245, 249-253, 263, 284, 334; Iranian, 338, 341

Douglass, Joseph, 278
Dreke, Victor, 322-323
drugs, 278, 312; drug gangs, 184; drug trade, 278, 280
Duke of Hamilton, 103
Duke of Windsor, 103
Dulles, Allen, 101-102, 231, 327-328
Dungavel House, 103
Dybenko, Pavel, 28
Dzerzhinsky, Felik, xi, 18, 30, 41, 121

E
EAGLE CLAW. *See* Larry Wu-Tai Chin
Eastern Europe, xiii, 79, 82, 94, 102, 121, 156, 266, 279, 292, 312, 330, 344
East Germany (German Democratic Republic, GDR), 48, 49, 252-253
Ecuador, 279
Egypt, 219, 225, 237, 305, 306
Eitingon, Leonid, 25-26
El Salvador, 329
El Tahri, Jihan, 321
Encyclopedia of Cold War Espionage, Spies, and Secret Operations, The (Trahair), 200-201, 242, 246, 252, 254
England, 55, 58, 63, 69-70, 79, 93, 95, 102-105, 175, 231, 281, 284, 305, 307. *See also* Great Britain
Enigma (German codes), 98, 102, 115
Erdoğan, Recep Tayyip, 300, 305-307, 313, 342-344
espionage (and spies), 195-196, 205, 223-225, 230-239, 242-265, 279-285, 330, 338, 341. *See also* double agents
Estonia, 94, 293, 318
Ethiopia, 237, 238, 256, 324, 329
Etinger, Yakov G., 32, 125, 126
European Union (EU), 298, 299, 306, 307, 311, 315, 342, 344

Evans, M. Stanton, 71, 74, 75, 80
executions, 15, 22, 27, 28, 36-38, 105-107, 146, 264, 284, 329, 337

F
famines, 17, 22, 104, 313
Far East, 77, 96, 97, 110, 200, 216
Farewell Dossier, 255, 259, 262, 265
FAREWELL. *See* Vladimir I. Vetrov
Farewell: The Greatest Spy Story of the Twentieth Century (Kostin and Raynaud), 255
Faria, Miguel Angel, Jr. (author), xiii, 324, 333, 337, 341, 344
Farquhar, Bob, 80
Fascism (and fascists), 58, 69, 250, 279, 288
Fauci, Anthony, 211
Federal Bureau of Investigation (FBI), 61-63, 73, 186, 196-200, 208, 210, 211, 218, 221-222, 227, 234, 240-244, 247, 249, 250, 253, 258, 266-272, 282, 326, 329-330, 334. *See also* double agents
Federal Security Service (FSB), 129, 241, 278, 280, 283, 284, 303, 319
FEDORA (FBI agent), 234
Felfe, Heinz, 245
Fermi, Enrico, 373
Ferrant, Patrick, 263-265
Fifth Campaign (Chiang Kai-shek in China), 178-179
Finland, 94, 226, 229, 295, 315
First Chief Directorate (KGB), 218, 227, 229, 230, 240, 242, 250, 261, 280
First Circle, The (Solzhenitsyn), 46
Ford, Gerald, 235-236, 267, 269-270
Foreign Intelligence Service of the Russian Federation (SVR), 227, 278, 280, 281-282, 319

Fouquier-Tinville, Antoine, 15
France, 14, 55, 58, 62, 69, 79, 93-95, 102-103, 255-260, 262-264, 294, 305, 307, 342
Franco, Francisco, 54, 60, 61, 64, 68, 69, 250
freedom (and liberty), 58, 70, 75, 88, 105, 133, 135, 136, 138, 140, 147, 150, 151, 166, 168, 179, 192-193, 207, 221-226, 234, 246, 249, 255, 259, 264, 265, 270, 276-278, 289, 290, 292, 297, 316, 323-326, 333-335, 342
Freeh, Louis, 186
Free Syrian Army (and militias), 303, 304
French Indochina, 97, 256
French Revolution, 14, 15
Frenkel, Naftaly A, 143-145
Fuchs, Klaus, 81, 244, 373
Führer Directive 21, 97
Führer Directive 34, 91
Fukuyama, Francis, 281
funkspiel, 99, 114

G
G7 economic summit, 259
Galkin, Aleksei, 221
Ganetsky, Yakov A., xi, 30
Gang of Four (China), 44, 161, 162, 168
Gardner, Meredith, 102, 243-244
Gates, Robert M., 236-237
Gazur, Edward, 61, 63
Gehlen Organization, 245
genocide, 101, 297, 326
geopolitics (and geopolitical), 289, 291-308
Georgia (country), 2-3, 5, 6, 9, 16, 43-46, 51, 278, 282, 289, 294, 297-300, 302, 312, 315
Gerasimov, Valery, 316
Gerhardt, Dieter F., 243
Germany, xii, 30, 55, 58, 62, 66, 67, 74, 79, 90-97, 100–117, 155, 283, 294, 320, 342

Gestapo, 99
Ginzberg,Yevgeniya, 33
Girondins, 14
Giscard d'Estaing, Valéry, 257, 258
Gisevius, Hans Bernd, 99, 101
glasnost, 11, 192, 193, 241, 276, 278
Goglidze, Sergo A., 46, 127
Goleniewski, Michael, 244-247, 253
Golitsyn, Anatoliy M., 229-235, 240, 246, 257, 278
Goloshchekin, Filipp, 38
Gorbachev, Mikhail, 11, 192, 225, 263, 272-273, 276, 287
Gordievsky, Oleg, 75, 225-228, 234, 240, 242, 265, 271
Gore, Albert, 182, 184, 187
Göring, Hermann, 100, 104
Gorky, Maxim, 32-33, 126
Gouzenko, Igor, 251, 252, 281
Graham, Daniel O., 262
Graham, William, 184
Great Britain (and United Kingdom), 73, 93, 94, 107, 111, 142, 150, 209, 229, 247, 248, 276, 284-285, 294, 300, 307, 315, 342
Great Depression, 75
Great Leap Forward, 158, 162, 168
Great Patriotic War, 47
Great Purge (China). *See* Cultural Revolution
Great Terror (and Purge, Russia), 15, 17, 26, 29-30, 33-34, 40-46
Great Terror: Stalin's Purge of the Thirties, The (Conquest), 362
Green Berets, 304
GRU (Soviet Military Intelligence), 27, 84, 225, 233-234, 242-251, 261-262, 271, 281, 284, 302-303, 315, 317. *See also* double agents
Guantanamo (U.S. base in Cuba), 331
Guatemala, 327, 329
Guderian, Heinz, 90, 92, 111

guerrilla warfare, 59
Guevara, Ernesto "Che," 322-323
Guillaume, Günter, 252-253
Gulag, xi, xii, 6, 17, 22-25, 30-35, 41, 46-48, 137-145, 253, 291, 319-320
Gulag Archipelago, The (Solzhenitsyn), xii, 46, 104, 134-140, 146
Gulen, Fethullah, 342-343
Guzman, Abimael "Gonzalo," 166

H
hackers, 206-207, 280
Halliday, Jon, 150-151, 154-155, 169, 171-172, 174, 176-177
Hall, Theodore, 81, 244
Hammer, Armand, 281
Hanssen, Robert, 197, 242, 253, 330, 334
Harvey, William K. "Bill," 327
Haunted Wood: Soviet Espionage in America—The Stalin Era, The (Weinstein), 370
Havana, 7, 203, 205
Hawaii. *See* Pearl Harbor
Haynes, John Earl, 266
Hébert, René, 14
Helms, Richard, 235-236, 328-329
HERO (U.S. agent). *See* Oleg Penkovsky
Hess, Rudolf, 103-104
Heydrich, Reinhard, 66-67, 93, 99
Hezbollah, 306
Hiss, Alger, 72, 75, 79-80, 247, 249
Hitler, Adolf, 47, 61, 67, 78, 88, 90-105, 108-114, 121, 264, 294, 317
Hitler's Traitor: Martin Bormann and the Defeat of the Reich (Kilzer), 98
Holocaust, 101, 131
Homage to Catalonia (Orwell), 67-68
Honeytrap (KGB operation), 252
Hoover, J. Edgar, 240, 326

Hopkins, Harry, 73-75, 79, 201, 202
Horowitz, David, 344
House of the Dead, The
 (Dostoevsky), 359
Huang, John, 182
Huawei Technologies, 191, 204, 208-210
HUMINT (human intelligence), 205, 216, 337
Hundred Flowers Campaign, 167-168
Hungary (and Hungarians), xii, 43, 54, 143
Hu Yaobang, 192

I

ideological deviationists. *See* "Right deviationists"
Ignatiev, Semyon D., 124, 128, 129, 131
Illegals (agents), 26
Imam, Colonel (Sultan Amir Tarar), 334-337
India, 219, 300, 334
INO (*Inostranny Otdel*), 26
Institute for Pacific Relations (IPR), 75
Intercontinental Ballistic Missile (ICBM), 184-185
International Brigades (Spain), 58, 250
Inter-Services Intelligence (ISI; Pakistan), 335-336
Ipatiev House, 37
Iran, 185, 205, 207, 216, 219, 237-239, 256, 281, 300-306, 327-329, 338-341
Iranian Quds Force, 303
Iron Curtain, 246, 291
ISIS (Islamic State of Iraq and Syria), 300, 307
Islam (religion), 179, 335, 340, 342
Islamic Republic, 339, 340, 344
Islamic Revolution, 238, 340,
Islamic Revolutionary Guard Corps (IRGC), 303

Islamic Revolutionary Guards (Iran),
Islamic State (IS), 302, 304,
Islamic terrorism (and terrorists), 306, 307, 331, 336,
Israel, 120-122, 300-301, 334
Ivan the Terrible, 279

J

Jansen, Marc, 40, 43
Japan, 76-79, 83, 92, 95-98, 102, 110-116, 153-158, 164-166, 174-175, 300, 308
Jewish Anti-Fascist Committee (JAC), 31, 121, 123
Jews, 6, 47, 54, 100-101, 105, 120-122, 128, 131
Jiang Qing "Madame Mao," 158, 161-163
Jiangxi ("Red Jiangxi" base), 172, 177-179
Ji Shengde, 186
John, Otto, 252
Joint Special Operations Command (U.S. in Syria), 304
Jordan, 306

K

Kabila, Laurent, 321
Kadets (Constitutional Democrats), xi, 25
Kaganovich, Lazar, 5, 12, 15, 48, 50, 110, 121
Kamenev, Lev, xi, 12, 13, 16, 17, 18, 23, 42, 56, 121
kangaroo trials, 15, 23, 127, 130, 322
Kang Sheng, 158, 159
Karmal, Babrak, 302
Karpai, Sophia, 125-126
Kasparov, Garry, 287
Katyn Forest Massacre, 105-107
Kazakhstan, 293
Kearns, Alicia, 318
Kennan, George F., 135, 327
Kennedy, John F., 85, 327-328

Kennedy, Robert F., 327
Kerensky, Alexander, xii, 136
Kerry, John, 296, 344
KGB (Committee for State Security), 16, 23, 26, 27, 53, 62-63, 71, 75, 94, 122, 134, 141-143, 218-229, 232-237, 240-255, 258-265, 271, 278-282, 288, 290, 312, 319, 326, 330, 332, 334
KGB: The Inside Story of Its Foreign Operations from Lenin to Gorbachev (Andrew and Gordievsky), 225-226
KGB: The Secret Work of the Soviet Secret Agents (Barron), 218-225
Khalkhin Gol, Battle of, 76-78, 92, 95-96
Khamenei, Ali, 306
Khomeini, Ayatollah, 237, 329, 338-339
Khrushchev, Nikita, 29, 30, 84, 124, 132; during Hungarian Revolution, xii; dismantling Stalin's cult of personality 9, 132, 134, 269; during Stalin's purges, 14, 15; during the time of Yezhov and Beria, 44, 45; intriguing for leadership, 48-52; during CIA-KGB wars, 240-241; during Operation SOLO, 266; repressing kulaks and forced collectivization, 297.
Kiev, 39, 90, 92, 112, 309
Kilzer, Louis C., 98-99, 102-105
Kim Jong-un, 308
Kimmel, Husband E., 98
KINDRED SPIRIT (FBI operation), 198-199
Kissinger, Henry, 187-188, 267-270
Klehr, Harvey, 266
Knight, Amy, 44, 47, 49, 51-53
Koestler, Arthur, 53-57
Kolbe, Fritz, 101
Kolchak, Alexander, 297
Kondratiev, Nikolai, 37-38

Kostin, Sergei, 255
Kravchenko, Victor, 75
Kremlin, 32, 46-49, 53, 75, 120, 124, 128-130, 147, 240, 267-272, 277, 289, 290, 300, 305-306
Krestinsky, Nikolay, 23, 29
Kronstadt rebellion, 18
Kruglov, Sergei, 51
Krupskaya, Nadezhda, 18
Krylenko, Nikolai, 36
kulaks, 33-34, 36, 120, 297
Kuntsevo, 16
Kuomitang Army, 165
Kurdish rebels (Syria), 304
Kursk, Battle of, 101, 113-115
Kuznetsov, A.A., 128

L

labor camps. *See* Gulag
L'affaire Farewell (French film), 265
Lake Tanganyika, 322
Lamphere, Robert, 243-244
Lapseng, Ng, 183
Larry Wu-Tai Chin, 199
Latin America, 204-206, 227, 279
Latsis, Martyn, 30
Lattimore, Owen, 75, 80, 155, 201, 202
Latvia, 94, 293
Lebanon, 219, 281
lebensraum (living space), 95, 102, 108
Lee, Duncan, 75
Lefortovo (prison), 129, 145
"leftist Trotskyites," 23, 42, 60
Left Socialist-Revolutionaries Party (Left SR), 24
Leningrad, 17, 42, 48, 90, 91, 111, 113, 123, 128, 140
Leninism. *See* Marxist-Leninist philosophy
Lenin, Vladimir I., xi, xii, 2, 6, 9, 12, 13, 16-25, 30-41, 55, 95, 131, 135-137, 151-152, 167, 240, 289, 297, 312

Leung, Katrina (PARLOR MAID), 197-198
Levchenko, Stanislav, 75
Lewis, Jr., John F., 196
liberty. *See* freedom
Libya, 219, 305
Lieber, Charles, 211-213
Lin Biao, 158, 160-162, 165
Lippo Group (Indonesia), 182-183, 186
Lithuania, 293
Litvinenko, Alexander "Sasha," 282-283, 285, 318
Litvinov, Maxim, 121
Liu Chaoying, 183, 186
Liu Shao-ch'i, 161-162
Lockhart, Bruce, 24
Lockheed Martin (corporation), 184, 186
Lomov-Oppokov, Georgi, 33
Long March, 153-154, 160-179, 192
Long March: The True History of Communist China's Founding Myth, The (Shuyun), 169, 176
Long March: The Untold Story, The (Salisbury), 167
Lonsdale, Gordon, 247, 248, 250
Los Alamos National Laboratory, 81, 198-199, 247
Lourdes Radio Electronics Center (REC), 205
Loyalists (Spain), 58
Lucy spy ring, 99
Luding Bridge (China), 173
Luftwaffe, 104
Lumumba, Patrice, 321-322
Lysenko, Trofim D., 124

M

MacFarlane, Robert, 262
Maclean, Donald, 26, 62, 244, 249, 250
Mahoney, Daniel J., 133-134, 136
Makarov, Nikolai, 286
Makaryan, Evgeniy, 317
Malyarov, Mikhail P., 145, 146

Maly, Theodore, 26
Manchuria (and Manchurian), 77, 155, 160
Manhattan Project, 244, 247
Mao: The Unknown Story (Chang and Halliday), 150, 169, 174, 176
Mao Tse-tung (Mao Zedong), x, xi, xiii, 10, 18, 44, 80, 82, 135; in Chinese history and Long March, 150-178; 188, 200, 210, 254, 266, 269
Marines. *See* United States Marine Corps
Markov, Georgi, 282
Martin, David, 233
Martov, Yuli, 2
Martynov, Valery, 253
Marxist ideology (Marxism), x, xii, xiii, 20, 56, 58, 68, 269, 276
Marxist-Leninist philosophy, 8
Marx, Karl, xi, xiii
Mas (Muslim tribesmen in China), 176, 180
Massoud, Ahmad Shah, 335, 336
Mayakovsky, Vladimir, 31-32
May, Alan Nunn, 373
May, Teresa, 285
McCarthyism, 201, 246
McCarthy, Joseph, 246
Mediterranean Sea, 292, 293, 300, 301, 303, 305, 306, 307
Medvedev, Dmitry, 147, 284, 286-287
Mehsud, Baitullah, 336, 337
Mehsud, Hakimullah, 336, 337
Mein Kampf (Hitler), 102, 105
Meir, Golda, 121
Memoirs of Hitler's Spymaster, The (Schellenberg), 375
Mensheviks, xii, 2, 3, 25
Mercader, Caridad, 26
Mercader, Ramón, 17, 26
mercenaries. *See* Russian mercenaries
Mexico, 9, 223, 224

Mexico City, 17, 25, 26
Middle East, 219, 224, 227, 300-307, 334, 343, 344
Mihailovich, Draza, 79
Mikhoels, Solomon, 31, 121-123
Mikoyan, Anastas, 15, 48, 50, 124
Milhollin, Gary, 184
Milley, Mark, 295
Mingrelian conspiracy, 48
MI6 (Military Intelligence, Department 6), 209, 225, 226, 231-234, 244, 245, 271, 284. *See also* Secret Intelligence Service (SIS; British)
Mironov, Sergei, 288, 289
missile gap, 84
missile launching technology, 183-184
missiles: in Cuba xii, 84, 221, 233; Japanese, 116; intercontinental, 184-186, 206, 271, 286; Chinese against Taiwan 187, 308; in Syria, 300, 306-307; Ukrainian crisis, 311, 315
Mitrokhin Archive, 16, 72, 75, 201, 219, 226-227, 240-242
Mitrokhin, Vasili, 226-228, 240, 242, 326
Mitterrand, François, 257-260, 263, 265
Mobutu, Joseph (Mobutu Sese Seko), 321
Moldova, 293, 315
Molotova, Polina Zhemchuzhina, 34, 121
Molotov-Ribbentrop Non-Aggression Pact, 93-97, 108-109, 291, 294
Molotov, Vyacheslav, 6, 12, 15, 34, 48-50, 93, 96, 108-109, 121, 123
Mongolia (and Mongolian), 77, 92, 95, 96, 155-156, 161
Montefiore, Simon Sebag, 2, 4-6, 8-10, 20, 21, 67, 105-108, 110, 150

Moore, Paul D., 195-196
Morley, Jefferson, 223
Moscow Center (Yasenevo), 99, 101, 161, 261, 263, 271, 280
Moscow (city), 16, 24, 26, 29, 46, 49, 54, 55, 62, 75, 90-93, 97, 109-111, 129, 141, 145-147, 152, 196, 222, 225-227, 241, 248, 251, 253, 263, 268, 276, 283, 287, 316-318
Moscow (as seat of government), 38, 74, 97, 174, 177, 205, 262, 267, 270, 293, 296, 304
Moscow Thermal-Technical Institute, 37
Moscow Times, The (newspaper), 319
Moscow Trials, 17, 32, 56
Moskalenko, K.S., 50
Moslem. *See* Islamic
Mossad, 334
Mossadegh, Muhammad, 340
Motorin, Sergei, 253
Mozambique, 237, 256, 323, 324, 329
Mujahideen, 302, 335-337
Müller, Heinrich, 99
Munich Agreement (and negotiations), 93-94, 294
Museum of the History of the Gulag, 319
Mussolini, Benito, 94

N
1984 (Orwell), 56, 70
Nagorno-Karabakh (Azerbaijan), 299
Nanchang Uprising, 164
Nart, Raymond, 258
NASA (National Aeronautics and Space Administration), 184
National Institute of Allergy and Infectious Diseases, 211
Nationalists (China), 80, 82, 153, 158, 163, 164, 165, 168, 170, 171, 178, 202, 254

Nationalists (Spain), 60. *See*
  Francisco Franco
National Review (magazine), 135
National Security Agency (NSA),
  198, 243, 244, 322
National Union for the Total
  Independence of Angola. *See*
  UNITA
NATO (North Atlantic Treaty
  Organization), 223, 256-257,
  262, 282, 293-295, 299-300,
  305, 312-315, 342-343
Naumov, Vladimir P., 120-121, 130
Navalny, Alexei, 286-287
Nazism (National Socialists), 66,
  79, 93, 94, 97-106, 109, 111,
  114, 121, 244, 248, 250, 281,
  294, 312, 320, 325
Negrín López, Juan, 68
Netherlands, 103
Nevsky, Alexander, 38
Nevsky, Vladimir I., 33
New World Order (NWO), 307,
  311, 315, 344
Nicaragua, 237, 256, 279, 329
Nicholas I, Tsar of Russia, 305, 307
Nicholas II, Tsar of Russia, 4, 38,
  246,
Nietzsche, Friedrich, 170
Nin, Andreu, 69
Nixon, Richard, xii, 160, 187, 232,
  235, 241, 256, 267-269, 328
NKVD (People's Commissariat of
  Internal Affairs), 13-17, 23-35,
  40-46, 50, 59-69, 97, 105, 107,
  128, 250, 320
Nomonhan Incident, 76, 77
Non-Aggression Pact. *See* Molotov-
  Ribbentrop Non-Aggression Pact
North Korea, 185, 216, 279, 308
Norway, 88, 103
Nosenko, Yuri, 222, 233-234
Novak, Robert, 331
Novichok (nerve agent), 285-286
nuclear missiles, 84, 184-185. *See
  also* missiles

O
Oak and the Calf, The
  (Solzhenitsyn), 136
Obama, Barack H., 186, 295-296,
  331, 344
Ochikina, Ludmilla, 263, 399
Ochoa, Arnaldo, 322
October Revolution (1917), xi, xii,
  6, 23, 34, 41, 65, 136, 167
Office of Director of National
  Intelligence (ODNI), 332
Office of Strategic Services (OSS),
  75
Ogorodnik, Aleksandr D., 265
oil fields, 91, 103, 108, 112, 300, 323
Okhrana, 6, 10, 65, 67, 225
Olsen, Frank, 248
"one China" policy, 187, 189
*One Day in the Life of Ivan
  Denisovich* (Solzhenitsyn), 134
Operation Barbarossa, 67, 88-93,
  95-97, 104-105, 108, 110
Operation Mongoose, 327
Operation RYAN, 271-273
Operation Snow, 77-78
Operation SOLO, 240, 266-270,
  272-273
*Operation Solo: The FBI's Man in
  the Kremlin* (Barron), 218
Operation Storm-333, 302
Oppenheimer, Robert, 373
Orbán, Viktor Mihály, 344
Order of Lenin, 44, 47, 253
Order of the Red Banner, 266, 267,
  270
Ordzhonikidze, Sergo, 16
Orlov, Alexander, 27; blackmail
  threat to Stalin, 61-64; in
  Spanish Civil War, 58-59, 69
Orlov, Igor, 394
Orwell, George, 58, 67-70
Ostrovsky, Alexander, 6
Other Solzhenitsyn, The (Mahoney),
  133, 147
Ottoman Empire (and Turks), 291,
  305, 307

Our Man in Mexico: Winston Scott and the Hidden History of the CIA (Scott), 223

P

Pahlavi, Mohammad Reza, 237, 238, 256, 338, 340
Pakistan, 185, 331-337
Palchinsky, Pyotr A., 33
Panama, 280
Panama Canal, 204, 216
Panzers (German tanks), 28, 91, 95, 103, 114, 294
Pâques, Georges, 256-257
PARLOR MAID (FBI agent), 197-199. *See* Katrina Leung
Partido Obrero de Unificación Marxista (POUM), 67-70
Passov, Zelman, 27
Pasternak, Boris, 135
Paulus, Friedrich, 91, 112
Pearl Harbor, 78, 97, 110-111, 115
Peng Dehuai, 157, 160, 162, 164, 165-166
Penkovsky, Oleg, 84, 233, 234, 248, 265
Pentagon, 206, 295
People's Commissariat of Internal Affairs. *See* NKVD
People's Liberation Army (PLA), 160, 183, 192, 197, 207
People's Movement for the Liberation of Angola (MPLA), 323
People's Republic of China (PRC). *See* China
perestroika, 11, 141, 192, 193, 241, 276, 278
Persico, Joseph, 236
Peru, 166
Peter I "the Great," Tsar of Russia, 279, 291
Petrashevsky Circle, 359
Petrov, Nikita, 40, 43
Philby, Harold "Kim," 26, 62, 63, 231, 232, 244, 249

Plame, Valerie (aka Valerie Wilson), 331
"Plan of the Internal Blow," 129
Platten, Fritz, 30
Plekhanov, Georgi, xii, 2
Pletnev, Dmitri D., 33
plutonium, 81, 82, 372
poisoning; of Alexander Litvinenko, 282-283; of Alexei Navalny, 286-287; of Anna Politkovskaya, 284; cyanide, 26; of Maxim Gorky, 126; of Sergei Skripal, 284-285
Poland (and Poles), 6, 22, 43, during World War II, 79, 93-95, 102, 105-109, 291, 294, 314, 320; as NATO member, 293, 312, 315
Poliakova, Maria, 99
police state, 41, 167, 240, 259
Politburo, 12, 13, 17, 18, 38, 44, 47, 50, 65, 94, 105, 123, 124, 130, 153, 261, 271
Politkovskaya, Anna S., 283-285
Polonik, Mikhail K., 219
polonium (radioactive element), 282-283, 372
Pol Pot, 18, 44, 165
Polyakov, Dimitri, 234, 249, 265
Polytechnologies, 183-184
Ponomarev, Boris, 267
Pontecorvo, Bruno, 373
Pope John Paul II St., 133, 265
Portuguese African colonies, 323
Potemkin, Grigory, 305
Potemkin villages, 223
Presidium (USSR), 50, 146
Prévost, Jacques, 258
Prigozhin, Yevgeny, 315-318
private military contractors. *See* Wagner Group
Prokhorovka (city), 113, 155
Prokhorov, Mikhail, 288-289
propaganda: anti-Soviet, 138; in Soviet Union, 32, 95, 121, 125, 272; in China, 151, 152, 159, 170, 173, 174; by media,

56; left-wing, 265; in Russia, 312, 317
Propustin, Sergey, 317
Protectorate of Bohemia and Moravia, 93
Provisional Government (Russia), xii, 112
proxy wars, 292, 316, 321-323
Prudovsky, Sergei, 319
Puerto Rico, 205
Putin, Vladimir: authoritarianism, xii, xiii, 278-279; as Russian leader, 134, 234; SVR assassinations, 281-285; Russian election 2012, 286-289; perilous future for Russia, 289-290, 320; Russian geopolitics, 291-292, 294-300, 305-308; in Syrian Crisis, 300-302, invasion of Ukraine, 309-318; in relations with Turkey, 342-344

Q
Quanyou, Fu, 204
Quds Force (Iranian), 303
Quebec Conference (1943), 73

R
Radek, Karl, xi, 30-31, 42
Radzinsky, Edvard, 19-20
Rahja, Eino, 30
Rakovsky, Christian, 23, 29
Ramzin, M., 37
Rasmussen, Anders Fogh, 293
raw materials, 76-77, 94, 96, 97, 110
Raynaud, Eric, 255
Reagan, Ronald, 133, 188-189, 226, 237, 239, 258-265, 270-273, 329
Red Cocaine (Douglass), 278
Red Guards (China), 159-161, 166, 176
Red Orchestra, 62, 108, 115
Red Star Over China (Snow), 152-153

Red Terror (Lenin), 30, 131
Red Wheel, The (Solzhenitsyn), 136
Reed, Thomas, 262
Reilly, Sidney, 24
Reno, Janet, 181
Republican Party (U.S.), 213-214, 286
Revolutionary Guards (Iran), 338-340
Rezidentura (Soviet spy stations abroad), 63, 271, 281
Riady, James, 182, 186
Riady, Mochtar, 182, 186
"Right deviationists," 13
"rightist Trotskyite Bloc," 23, 29, 42
Robespierre, Maximilien, 14, 15
Rockefeller, Nelson, 235-236
Roland, Marie-Jeanne (Madame Roland), 14
Romania (Rumanian): in Operation Barbarossa, 88-89, 91; as NATO member, 293, 312, 315
Romerstein, Herbert, 71, 74, 75, 80
Roos, Dave, 58
Roosevelt, Franklin Delano (FDR), 97, 98, 106, 111, 325; American traitors in administration, 71-79, 153-157, 200-203, 247-249, 253; Declaration of War against Japan, 79; at Cairo Conference, 201; at Yalta Conference, 155
Rosenberg, Ethel, 244, 247
Rosenberg, Julius, 244, 247
Rostov-on-Don (city), 316
Rote Kapelle (Red Orchestra), 62, 108, 115
Rubashov, N. S., (fiction character), 55-56
Rusher, William, 74
Russia, xii, xiii, 2, 4, 6, 8, 9-13, 15, 17, 19-52, 64-67, 74-83, 88-115, 120-125, 129-138, 142-147, 151-152, 155-158, 167, 174, 175, 184, 196, 205, 207, 216, 218, 226, 227, 234, 237, 241-252, 257- 269, 276-320; 326,

329, 330, 334, 342. *See also* Soviet Union
Russian Aerospace Forces (VKS), 302, 303
Russian elections, 12; of 2012, 286-289
Russian Imperial family: execution of, 36-38
Russian mercenaries, 304, 305, 316
Russification policy, 45, 48
Russo-Mongolian Army, 156
Rykov, Alexei, 13, 17, 23, 29, 42
Ryumin, Mikhail D., 126-130

S
7th Fleet (U.S.), 187
Sadat, Anwar, 225
Sakharov, Andrei, 46
Sakharov, Vladimir N., 224, 265
Salisbury, Harrison, 135, 136, 167-170, 173-174
Sandinista National Liberation Front (FSLN), 237
Sandinistas, 256
SASHA (Soviet mole), 230, 235
Sasse, Ben, 209
satellite communications, 184, 203
satellite technology, 183-184
Saudi Arabia, 300, 340-341
Saunders, Francis, 248-249
Savimbi, Jonas, 323-324
Scammell, Michael, 133, 136, 137
Scandinavia, 90, 91, 95, 100
Schellenberg, Walter, 66-67, 99
Schwendemann, Heinrich, 110
SDECE (French foreign intelligence service), 258-259
Second Chechen War, 283, 317
Second Chief Directorate (KGB), 218, 230, 259, 280
Secret History of the CIA, The (Trento), 231
Secret Intelligence Service (SIS; British). *See* MI6
SEGO PALM. *See also* KINDRED SPIRIT

Selassie I, Haile, 237, 238, 256, 329
Serov, Ivan, 51
Service, John Stewart, 80, 170, 200, 201, 202, 253
"Sexpionage," 197-198
Shaanxi (China), 171, 172
Shaheen, Asmatullah, 337
Shalamov, Varlam T., 33
Shanghai (China), 162, 207
Sharaf, Sami, 225
sharashka (NKVD research centers), 46
Shchervakov, A. S., 126
Shelepin, Alexander, 240
"Shining Path" (*Sendero Luminoso*), 166
Shoigu, Sergei, 316
Short, Walter C., 98
Shpigelglas, Sergey, 27, 121
Shuyun, Sun, 169-170, 173-179
Siberia (and Siberian), 286, 297; elite Soviet army units, 77, 78, 92, 95-98; exile in, 6, 10; political prisoners in, 139; Trans-Siberian railroad, 110
SIGINT (signals intelligence), 205, 216, 337, 374
Silverman, George, 249
Simmons, Chris, 203, 204, 205
Sino-American Mutual Defense Treaty, 188
Sino-Japanese War, 153, 164, 165
Sino-Soviet split, 232, 235, 241, 268, 269
Sioeng, Ted, 183
Six Assurances (U.S.), 188-189
Skripal, Sergei V., 284-286, 318
Skripal, Yulia, 284, 285
"sleeper agents," 156, 250
Slutsky, Abram, 26-27, 121
SMERSH (Death to Spies), 30, 122-123, 138
Smirnov, Ivan, 23
Smirnov, Yefim, 127
Smith, James J., 197
Snow, Edgar, 152, 168, 173

Social-Democratic Workers' Party
 (SDP), 2, 3
socialism (and socialists), x-xiii, 11-
 13, 18, 32, 49, 53, 56, 58, 69,
 70, 88, 93, 134, 135, 205, 221,
 258, 279, 281, 315, 324, 343
Sokolov, Mikhail,33
Soleimani, Qasem, 303
"solemn representations," 190
Solovetsky Islands, 143-145
Solzhenitsyn: A Biography
 (Scammell), 133, 147
Solzhenitsyn, Aleksandr, xi, 5, 46,
 53, 54, 104, 133-147, 265
Somoza, Anastasio, 237
Sorge, Richard, 97-98, 108, 110
South China Sea (and Islands), 210,
 308
South Ossetia, 289, 294, 298, 299
South Vietnam, 134, 301
Soviet-Afghan War, 301
Soviet bloc, 235, 259, 262
Soviet Criminal Code, 138, 142
Soviet Embassy, 252
Soviet espionage, 16, 26, 71-72,
 218, 220-228, 240-241
Soviet Union (USSR), xii, xiii, 5,
 11, 12, 15-19, 25-28, 29, 33, 36,
 38, 40, 44-47, 50, 53, 59-67, 71,
 73, 76-84, 88, 89-98, 109-113,
 120-123, 130, 133-142, 145,
 146, 152, 161, 163, 167, 174,
 193, 203, 215, 218-221, 228,
 230, 232, 241-245, 250, 255,
 257-302, 312, 319-323, 329,
 330, 334
space launch vehicles, 184
Spain, 26, 27, 58-61, 64, 68, 69
Spanish Civil War, 26, 54, 58-70,
 250
Spanish gold reserves, 61, 64
*Special Tasks: Memoirs of an
 Unwanted Witness a Soviet
 Spymaster* (Sudoplatov), 25
Spetsnaz (Soviet special forces),
 301-303, 317

spies. *See* espionage
Spiridonova, Mariya A, 24-25
spy balloon. *See* Chinese
 surveillance balloon
Stalin, Breaker of Nations
 (Conquest), 16
Stalin: The Court of the Red Tsar
 (Montefiore), 20, 67, 105, 150
Stalingrad: Battle of, 101, 112-114;
 city, 112
Stalin, Joseph (Joseph
 Vissarionovich Djugashvili), xi-
 xiii; Georgian bandit, 2-10;
 Stalin speaking at the 17th Party
 Congress of 1934, "the Congress
 of Victors," 17; biographies of,
 11-21; assassination of Leon
 Trotsky, 17, 25-26; terror victims
 of, 22-40; collectivization of
 farms, 34-36; Nikolai Yezhov as
 NKVD chief, 40-44; Lavrenti
 Beria as NKVD chief, 44-53;
 alleged plot to overthrow, 65-67;
 during Spanish Civil War, 58-65-
 70; espionage by agents of
 influence in America, 71-80;
 atomic bomb espionage, 80-85;
 intelligence from Richard Sorge,
 97-98; Katyn Forest Massacre,
 105-107; Molotov-Ribbentrop
 Non-Aggression Pact, 93-97;
 during World War II, 87-117;
 Doctors' Plot, 120-132; Plan of
 the Internal Blow, 129-130;
 Naftaly Frenkel and the Gulags,
 143-145; in *The Gulag
 Archipelago*, 137-145; relations
 with Mao Tse-tung, 151-158,
 177, 203; and Chiang Kai-shek,
 174-175; legacy of, 289-291,
 297, 299, 313, 319
*Stalin's Last Crime: The Plot
 Against the Jewish Doctors*
 (Brent and Naumov), 120
*Stalin's Loyal Executioner:
 People's Commissar Nikolai*

Ezhov, 1895-1940 (Jansen and Petrov), 40, 44
Stalin's Secret Agents: The Subversion of Roosevelt's Government (Evans and Romerstein), 71, 76, 79
Stasi (East German state security service), 253
Stauffenberg, Claus von, 100, 264
Steklov, Yuri M, 33
Stolypin, Pyotr, 38-39
submarine-launched ballistic missiles (SLBMs), 198-199
submarines. *See* Trident submarines
subversion, 71, 205, 279, 280
Sudetenland, 93, 102, 294
Sudoplatov, Pavel, 25-26, 60, 62, 81-83
suicide, 17, 31, 162, 199, 307
Sun Tzu (or Sunzi), 195
surveillance, 236, 280, 293; used by China, 179, 213-214; used by KGB, 131, 120, 220, 225-226, 259
Suslov, Mikhail, 267, 268
Suvorov, Viktor, 302
Sverdlov, Yakov, 16, 36-37, 121
SVR. *See* Foreign Intelligence Service of the Russian Federation
Sweden, 111, 315
Switzerland, 31, 99, 101, 233, 272, 273, 315
Sword and the Shield: The Mitrokhin Archives and the Secret History of the KGB, The (Andrew and Mitrokhin), 226, 228
Syria, 300-307, 317
Szilard, Leo, 373

T

Taiwan, 163, 185, 187-191, 210, 308
Taiwan Relations Act (TRA), 188, 190, 210

Taliban, 314, 336, 337
Talleyrand, Charles Maurice de, 122
Tambov Rebellion, 24
Tehran, 237, 256, 300, 306, 339
Tehran Conference (1943), 73, 74
telecommunications, 184, 208
Thatcher, Margaret, 133, 252, 265, 271, 272
thieves: "socially-friendly" elements in Gulag, 138-139, 142; United Russia party, 286
Third Reich, 98-101, 110, 294
Third World, 227-228, 279, 310
Thomas, Georg, 99
Thousand Talents Plan (and Program), 211, 213
Tiananmen Square (massacre), 151, 182, 192-194
Tiger Trap: America's Secret Spy War with China (Wise), 389
TIGER TRAP (U.S. intelligence operation), 199
Timashuk, Lidia, 124, 131
Time to Betray: The Astonishing Double Life of a CIA Agent Inside the Revolutionary Guards of Iran (Kahlili), 338
Timperlake, Edward, 181-184
Tito, Marshall, 79
Tolkachev, Adolf G., 253, 266
Tolstoy, Leo, 135
Tomahawk cruise missiles, 300
Tomsky, Mikhail, 13, 17
TOPHAT (U.S. agent). *See* Dmitri Polyakov
totalitarian (and totalitarianism), xiii, 5, 12, 15-18, 31, 41, 55, 69, 70, 93, 108, 146, 167, 192, 216, 263, 277, 279, 288, 289, 297, 330
Trahair, Richard C. S., 242, 243, 246-254
Trans-Siberian railroad, 110
Trento, Joseph, 231, 394
Tretyakov, Sergei, 281-283
Trident submarines, 198-199

Trie, Charlie (Yah Lin), 183
Triplett, II, William C., 181, 183, 184
Trotskyites, 23, 29, 30, 42, 60, 61, 64, 68-70, 120
Trotskyite-Zinovievite-Bukharinite conspiracy, 23, 29, 30, 41, 42
Trotsky, Leon: minimizing Stalin's role, 8-9; assassination of, xi, 17, 25, 26; sanctioned violence, 12; feared by other Bolsheviks, 13-14, 16; crushed the Kronstadt rebellion, 18; "permanent revolution" 41, 95; in Koestler's composite 56; as Jewish Bolshevik, 121; admired revolutionary 167, 171
Truman, Harry S., 82, signed "National Security Act" 102, 325; containment policy, 135, 251, 327; loss of China, 202, 203;
Trump, Donald J.: and China 190-191, 208-209; and Syrian Crisis 300, 307; orders drone attack, 303; Middle East diplomacy, 307, 308; conservative leader, 314, 344
Tsai-Ing-wen, 190
Tsarev, Oleg, 58, 59, 60, 62, 65
Tshombe, Moise, 246
Tukhachevsky, Mikhail, 13, 27-28, 65-67
Tunisia, 256
Tuomi, Kaarlo, 220-222, 250, 265
Turgenev, Ivan, 135
Turkey (and Turks), 48, 85, 179-180, 219, 251, 282, 293, 298-299,
Turner, Stansfield, 236-237, 328-330, 305-307, 310, 313-314, 342-344
tyranny, 6, 135, 168, 220, 340

U
Uighurs, 179-180
Ukraine (and Ukrainians), 45, 48, 49, 282, 320, 343; in World War II, 90-92, 101-103, 109, 111-113; Budapest Memorandum, 277, 278; Russian invasion of, 289, 291-317
Ukrainian War. *See* Ukraine
Ultra (British signals intelligence), 98, 102
UNITA (National Union for the Total Independence of Angola), 323
United Kingdom. *See* Great Britain
United Russia (political party), 286-288,
United States Air Force (USAF), 213-214
United States of America (government; America), 63, 72-75, 78, 80-84, 98, 106, 115-116, 120, 121, 130, 134, 152, 183, 184, 188, 190, 196-199, 202-204, 207, 210, 213-214, 221-222, 225, 231-239, 244, 247, 254, 256, 269-271, 277, 281-282, 306, 307, 312, 321, 323, 325-337, 340, 341, 347
United States Congress, 62, 63, 71, 184-188, 200, 206, 235-236, 270, 295, 327, 329, 369
United States Department of Defense (DOD), 213, 214
United States Department of Energy (DOE), 81, 199
United States Department of Homeland Security, 210, 332
United States Department of Justice (DOJ), 181, 198, 208, 210, 216
United States Department of State (U.S. State Department), 75, 186, 188, 189, 194, 200, 249, 344
United States Department of the Treasury, 75, 77, 78, 79
United States missile shield, 286
United States Naval Institute (USNI), 206-207

United States Navy, 216, 218, 300, 335
United States Navy Seal Team Six, 331
uranium, 81, 82, 372
USSR (Union of Soviet Socialist Republics). *See* Soviet Union
Utkin, Dmitry, 317

V
van Creveld, Martin, 38
VanHerck, Glen, 213-214
Varfolomeyev, Ivan I., 129-130
Vasilyev, Pavel N., 33
Vassiliev, Alexander, 75
Vavilov, Nikolai I., 33
Venezuela, 279
Venona files, 16, 76, 80, 102, 202, 243-247, 254, 370
Venona project, 244
Vergniaud, Pierre, 14, 15
Vetrov, Vladimir I. "Volodia," 243, 255, 258-265, 399
Vietnam War, 134, 235, 256, 269, 301
Villegas, Harry, 322
Vinogradov, Vladimir N., 125, 131
Vladivostok (port), 110
Vlasik, Nikolai S., 48, 128
Volga Canal, 29, 35
Volkogonov, Dmitri, 11-13, 16, 20, 28, 131
Voloshin, Maksimilian A., 33
von Bock, Fedor, 90, 91, 111, 112
von Brauchitsh, Walter, 91
von Kluge, Gunther, 113
von Leeb, Wilhelm Ritter, 90, 111
von Manstein, Erich, 112, 113
von Reichenau,Walter, 112
von Rundstedt, Gerd, 90, 112
von Schulze-Gaevernitz, Gero, 101
von Stauffenberg, Claus, 100, 264
von Weichs, Maximilian, 112
Voronezh (Russian region), 115, 316
Voroshilov, Kliment, 12, 28, 48, 50

Voznesensky, N.A., 128
Vyshinsky, Andrey, 15, 36

W
W-88 warhead, 198-199
Wagner Group, 303, 305, 315-317
Wagner, Richard, 317
Walesa, Lech, 265
Walsh, Declan, 335-337
Wang Jun, 183-184
"War Communism," 16
Warsaw Pact, 330
Washington, D.C., 75, 181, 182, 189, 198, 219, 226, 231, 270
Watergate (scandal), 235, 256, 270, 328
Wehrmacht, 46, 294; in Operation Barbarossa, 88-103, 112-114
Weinberger, Caspar, 262
Weinstein, Allen, 370
WERTHER (Soviet spy). *See* Martin Bormann
Westerman, Toby, 203, 205
Western Europe, xiii, 16, 95, 105, 152, 282, 342, 344
Western Legion of the 4th Army (China), 176-177, 179
West Germany, 252, 253
"wet affairs." *See* assassinations
Whampoa Military Academy, 156-157
White, Harry Dexter, 72, 75-80, 97, 247, 250
White Russians, 30, 102, 129, 297
White Sea, 35, 143
White Sea Canal, 144-145
Winter Palace, xi, 23
Wise, David, 195-199
Witness (Chambers), 71
Wolf's Lair, 100
World War II, 8, 28, 30, 38, 46, 62, 120, 123, 126, 138, 231, 248, 281, 291, 294, 309, 312, 329; spies during, 73-79, 98-102, 243, 245, 251, 252, 281; Operation Barbarossa, 88-96;

Pearl Harbor, 97-98; Churchill's deception, 102-105; Katyn Forest massacre, 105-107; in the Russian front, 108-117; in China, 157, 170
World Was Going Our Way: The KGB and the Battle for the Third World, The (Andrew and Mitrokhin), 227-228
Wrangel, Pyotr, 297, 298
Wuhan (city), 211, 213
Wuhan Institute of Virology, 191, 211, 212
Wuhan University of Technology (WUT), 211, 213

X

Xenophon, 177
Xi Jinping, 191, 205, 210
Xinjiang (region), 179

Y

Yagoda, Genrikh, 14, 27, 28-29, 32, 40, 42-43, 121, 123
Yalta Conference (1945), 73, 74, 155
Yang Baibing, 192
Yang Shangkun, 192
Yanqing Ye, 211
Yasenevo. *See* Moscow Center
Yavlinsky, Grigory, 288-289
Year of the Rat: How Bill Clinton Compromised U.S. Security for Chinese Cash (Timperlake and Triplett), 181, 183
Year of the Spy (1985), 329

Yegorov, Alexander, 28
Yegorov, P., 124, 128
Yekaterinburg (Ural city), 37
Yeltsin, Boris, 11, 20, 265, 276-278, 280, 281, 287
Yenan (China), 153, 154, 159, 161, 163, 165, 178
Yezhov, Nikolai (or Ezhov), 14, 27, 29, 40-46, 61-64, 123
Yezhovshchina, 29, 43, 46
Young Stalin (Montefiore), 2, 9-10, 150
Yuan Li, Peter, 207
Yugoslavia, 79
Yurchenko, Vitaly, 264
Yurovsky, Yakov, 37, 38
Yuzhin, Boris, 253

Z

Zaosong Zheng, 211
Zelenskyy, Volodymyr, 311-313, 318
Zhdanov, Andrei A., 124-127
Zhdanov, Yuri, 124
Zhigur, Ian, 28
Zhirinovsky, Vladimir, 288, 289
Zhu De, 160, 164-165, 172
Zhukov, Georgy, 50, 77, 92, 93, 109, 113, 114
Zia-ul-Haq, Mohammad, 334
Zinoviev, Gregory, xi, 12, 13, 16, 17, 23, 42, 56, 121
Zionist conspiracy, 219
Zunyi conference, 161, 164, 165, 170
Zyuganov, Gennady, 288, 289